The
Heartbeat
of
Wounded Knee

Also by David Treuer

Fiction
Prudence
The Translation of Dr. Apelles: A Love Story
The Hiawatha
Little

Nonfiction
Rez Life: An Indian's Journey Through Reservation Life
Native American Fiction: A User's Manual

The

Heartbeat

of

Wounded Knee

NATIVE AMERICA FROM
1890 TO THE PRESENT

DAVID TREUER

CORSAIR

First published in the United States of America in 2019 by Riverhead Books

First published in Great Britain in 2019 by Corsair

1 3 5 7 9 10 8 6 4 2

Portions of this book originally appeared, in different form,
in *Harper's Magazine*, *The New York Times*, and *Saveur*.

A CIP catalogue record for this book is available from the British Library.

ISBN: 978-1-4721-5493-4

Printed and bound by CPI Group (UK) Ltd, Croydon, CR0 4YY

Papers used by Corsair are from well-managed forests
and other responsible sources.

MIX
Paper from
responsible sources
FSC® C104740

Corsair
An imprint of
Little, Brown Book Group
Carmelite House
50 Victoria Embankment
London EC4Y 0DZ

An Hachette UK Company
www.hachette.co.uk

www.littlebrown.co.uk

In Memory

—

Robert Treuer, Sean Fahrlander, Dan Jones

For Elsina, Noka, and Bine

as always and forever

Contents

The
Heartbeat
of
Wounded Knee

Prologue

This book tells the story of what Indians in the United States have been up to in the 128 years that have elapsed since the 1890 massacre of at least 150 Lakota Sioux at Wounded Knee Creek in South Dakota: what we've done, what's happened to us, what our lives have been like.* It is adamantly, unashamedly, about Indian life rather than Indian death. That we even *have* lives—that Indians have been living in, have been shaped by, and in turn have shaped the modern world—is news to most people. The usual story told about us—or rather, about "the Indian"—is one of diminution and death, beginning in untrammeled freedom and communion with the earth and ending on reservations, which are seen as nothing more than basins of perpetual suffering. Wounded Knee has come to stand in for much of that history. In the American imagination and, as a result, in the written record, the massacre at Wounded Knee almost overnight assumed a significance far beyond the sheer number of lives lost. It became a touchstone of Indian suffering, a benchmark of American brutality, and a symbol of the end of Indian life, the end of the frontier, and the beginning of modern America. Wounded Knee, in other words, stands for an end, and a beginning.

What were the actual circumstances of this event that has taken on so much symbolic weight?

In 1890, the Lakota were trying to make the best of a bad situation.

---

*Throughout this book, I use the word "Indian" to refer to indigenous people within the United States. I also use "indigenous," "Native," and "American Indian." These terms have come in and out of favor over the years, and different tribes, not to mention different people, have different preferences. The Red Lake Nation refers to itself as the "Home of the Red Lake Band of Chippewa Indians," for example. Many Native people prefer to describe themselves in their Native languages: Piikuni for Blackfeet, Ojibwe for Chippewa, and so on. My own choices of usage are governed by a desire for economy, speed, flow, and verisimilitude. A good rule of thumb for outsiders: Ask the Native people you're talking to what they prefer.

Ever since the Battle of the Little Bighorn in 1876, the U.S. government had been trying to solve the "Indian problem" on the Plains with a three-pronged approach: negotiation and starvation in addition to open war. Open war on its own had not been going too well. Led by Red Cloud, Crazy Horse, American Horse, Ten Bears, and Sitting Bull, the Plains Indians had won such decisive victories that they had forced the government to the treaty table, not the other way around. This resulted in the second Treaty of Fort Laramie in 1868 and secured a large homeland for the Lakota in southwestern South Dakota and northern Nebraska.

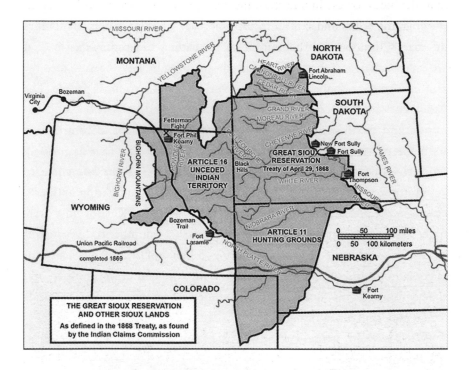

Map of the Great Sioux Reservation, 1868

But the terms of the treaty were violated by the United States shortly thereafter, when gold was discovered in the Black Hills. In response, the Lakota attempted to throw out the gold-seekers and enforce the terms of the treaty. This is what led, directly, to the Battle of the Little Bighorn, where Custer and the Seventh Cavalry were wiped out. During the final hours of the battle, the Lakota and Cheyenne dismounted, put away their guns, and killed the remaining cavalry with their war clubs and tomahawks in a ritual slaughter. Some Dakota women, armed with the jawbones of buffalo, were given the honor of dispatching the soldiers with a sharp blow behind the ear.

After that rout, the U.S. government switched tactics. Instead of confronting the Indians head-on, it encouraged widespread encroachment by settlers (one sees the same tactics in play in the West Bank today), reneged on treaty promises of food and clothing, and funded the wholesale destruction of the once vast buffalo herds of the Plains. The hides and bones were shipped east, the hides for use in industrial machine belts, decoration, blankets, and clothing, the bones and skulls for fertilizer and china. It is estimated that by the late 1870s about five thousand bison were being killed per day.

Buffalo skulls waiting to be ground for use in china and as fertilizer

Without the bison, the Lakota and other Plains tribes could not hope to survive, at least not as they had been surviving. The reservations might have been designed as prisons, but now they became places of refuge.

With the vast buffalo herds no more, and hemmed in by a burgeoning white population of ranchers, hunters, railroad workers, prospectors, homesteaders, and soldiers, the Plains Indians did what many disenfranchised people have done when threatened on all sides: they turned to God. To a government that had long bemoaned the unwillingness of Indians to get with the program and assimilate, this might have been good news. The Indians, however, turned to God in the form of the Ghost Dance.

The Ghost Dance religion initially manifested itself among the Paiute in Nevada, where it was promoted by an Indian named Jack Wilson, who later exclusively used his Paiute name, Wovoka. The dance, the story goes, came to Wilson in a vision during a solar eclipse on January 1, 1889. In his vision he stood near God and looked down on Indian people in the afterlife while they hunted and played. God told Wilson that he had to return home and tell his people to live in harmony with one another, to not drink or steal, to work hard, and to make peace with white people. This was a pretty big leap beyond the divine directives any Indians had claimed to have received in the past. And there was a payoff: if Indians lived lives of peace and worked hard and danced the Ghost Dance, they would find peace on earth, and they would be reunited with the spirits of their ancestors in the afterlife.

As the religion spread from Nevada, it changed. By the time it reached the Lakota, it had taken on a more millennialist flavor: if they did the Ghost Dance the right way and lived by its precepts, the Lakota believed, not only would they find peace in this world and the next but all the white people would be washed away and the New World returned to its Edenic state. If Indians returned to their traditional ways of life and forms of religious observance, the belief went, the world would return to them.

Such a movement greatly alarmed the U.S. government, and it redoubled its ongoing efforts to break up the Great Sioux Reservation into five smaller reservations, so that Indians would have a harder time gathering in large numbers. The government also continued its missionary efforts, pushed through the policy of allotment that sought to impose individual property ownership on the Lakota, and stepped up the removal of Indian children to boarding schools far from the reservation. The Ghost Dance religion was banned, despite the freedom of religion guaranteed by the Constitution (Indians were thirty-four years away from citizenship, in any case), and government troop presence on the Pine Ridge Reservation was increased. A former Indian agent at Pine Ridge, Valentine McGillycuddy, spoke out against the military buildup with rare lucidity: "The coming of the troops has frightened the Indians. If the Seventh-Day Adventists prepare their ascension robes for the second coming of the Savior, the United States Army is not put in motion to prevent them. Why should not the Indians have the same privilege? If the troops remain, trouble is sure to come."

Trouble came. Sitting Bull, the famous Hunkpapa Lakota chief who had led his people to victory against the U.S. military during the Indian Wars and who, with help, wiped out Custer's Seventh Cavalry at the Little Bighorn, had returned to Standing Rock after formally surrendering to government forces in 1881 and touring with Buffalo Bill's Wild West show for most of the next decade. The Indian agent at Standing Rock, James McLaughlin, was afraid that Sitting Bull would use his considerable influence to promote the Ghost Dance, and therefore issued an order for his arrest on December 15, 1890. A scuffle ensued, and one of Sitting Bull's followers shot an Indian police officer, Bull Head, as he was trying to force the chief onto his horse. Bull Head in turn shot Sitting Bull in the chest. Red Tomahawk, another police officer, raised his rifle and shot Sitting Bull through the head.

Afraid for his life and the life of his band, Spotted Elk (also known as Chief Big Foot) left Standing Rock Reservation with 350 followers around December 20, headed for the sanctuary of Pine Ridge at the invitation of Chief Red Cloud. It was thought that Red Cloud, one of the most experienced and able Lakota statesmen, could broker a peace. Before he could get there, on December 28, Spotted Elk and his band were intercepted by a detachment of the Seventh Cavalry under the leadership of Major Samuel M. Whitside and escorted five miles to a camping spot on Wounded Knee Creek. It was bitterly cold. Before dawn the next day, the rest of the Seventh showed up with Colonel James W. Forsyth and set up four rapid-fire Hotchkiss cannons around the band. The soldiers searched the camp and rounded up thirty-eight weapons. When one of the young Lakota men got upset and exhorted his tribemates not to give up their guns so easily, a fight broke out.

What happened next is not clear. Some reported that the Indians opened fire on the government soldiers. Others said that a deaf elder didn't understand the command to give up his rifle, and when a soldier grabbed it to take it away, it went off. Then five young warriors shrugged off their blankets and exposed concealed rifles. They shot at the soldiers. The soldiers opened fire on the entire camp with their rifles and the Hotchkiss guns. The Indian men put up a desperate resistance but were mowed down. The rain of fire from U.S. troops also claimed the lives of many of the soldiers, in one of the deadliest incidents of friendly fire in U.S. military history. The women and children took off running down the frozen creek bed; the soldiers broke formation and, mounted, chased them down and killed them. The fighting lasted an hour, and when it was over, more than 150 Lakota lay dead or dying in the snow. The actual number of dead is still in dispute, with some putting the number at more than three hundred. More than half were women and children. A survivor, the chief American Horse, testified later that "there was a woman with an infant in her arms who was killed as she almost touched the flag of truce. . . . A mother was shot down with her infant; the child not knowing [that] its mother was dead was still nursing. . . . The women as they were fleeing with their babies were killed together, shot right through . . . and after most all of them had been killed a cry was made that all those who were not killed or wounded should come forth and they would be safe. Little boys . . . came out of their places of refuge, and as soon as they came in sight a number of soldiers surrounded them and butchered them there."

General Nelson A. Miles, touring the scene of the carnage after a three-day blizzard that shrouded the dead in snow, was shocked by what he saw. "Helpless children and women with babes in their arms had been chased as far as two miles from the original scene of encounter and cut down without mercy by the troopers. . . . Judging by the slaughter on the battlefield it was suggested that the soldiers simply went berserk. For who could explain such a merciless disregard for life?"

Mass grave at Wounded Knee, South Dakota, January 1891

One of the most poignant stories to come out of Wounded Knee involves a Lakota child named Zintkala Nuni, or Lost Bird. Her mother had been among those shot as she attempted to run with her infant daughter down the frozen creek. It wasn't until four days later that the child was discovered— frostbitten, starving, but alive—in her dead mother's arms. She was passed among the occupying soldiers as a kind of living souvenir of the massacre until, a few weeks after the conflict, a general named Leonard Colby adopted her. Raised partly by his wife, she suffered horribly—she was sent from one isolated boarding school to another, was later impregnated (most likely by Colby), and still later was found working in Wild West shows and in vaudeville, before she died of influenza in 1920, in abject poverty.

THE MASSACRE WAS COVERED by more than twenty newspapers, and the responses it provoked represented the polarized attitudes toward the entire conflict between Indians and government. If white people were determined to take Indians' land, opined a writer named Susette La Flesche in the *Omaha World-Herald* in 1891, "they can go about getting it in some other way than by forcing it from them by starving or provoking them to war and sacrificing the lives of innocent women and children, and through the sufferings of the wives and children of officers and soldiers." General Nelson Miles relieved Colonel James Forsyth of his command and brought action against him in military court for the wanton bloodshed that had occurred under his leadership, provoking immediate opposition from Forsyth and his supporters. (Later in life General Miles would fight for compensation for the Lakota and raise money for survivors of the massacre.)

Some saw Wounded Knee from the opposite angle. "Why," asked a reporter from the Deadwood, South Dakota, *Times*, "should we spare even a semblance of an Indian? Wipe them from the face of the earth." Writing for the Aberdeen, South Dakota, *Saturday Pioneer* after the murder of Sitting Bull, L. Frank Baum—the author of *The Wonderful Wizard of Oz*—said it would be better if all Indians died rather than live as "the miserable wretches they are." Two weeks later, after the massacre, he hit the same note but held it longer: "The *Pioneer* has before declared that our only safety depends upon the total extermination of the Indians. Having wronged them for centuries we had better, in order to protect our civilization, follow it up by one more wrong and wipe these untamed and untamable creatures from the face of the earth."

The moment crystallized something more than sympathy for Indians and Indian causes on the one hand, and bitter and bloody American progress on the other. Rather, both sides joined in seeing the massacre as the end not just of the Indians who had died but of "the Indian," period. There had been an Indian past, and overnight, there lay ahead only an American future.

Frederick Jackson Turner elaborated on this idea in his essay "The Significance of the Frontier in American History," delivered in 1893 at the World's Columbian Exposition in Chicago (itself a celebration of the Indian past and the American future, as if the two eras existed on either side of an unbreachable wall). "The United States lies like a huge page in the history of society," Turner wrote with a self-fulfilling certainty. "Line by line as we read this continental page from West to East we find the record of social evolution. It begins with the Indian and the hunter; it goes on to tell of the disintegration of savagery by the entrance of the trader, the pathfinder of civilization; we read the annals of the pastoral stage in ranch life; the exploitation of the soil by the raising of unrotated crops of corn and wheat in sparsely settled farming communities; the intensive culture of the denser farm settlement; and finally the manufacturing organization with city and factory system." The country begins with Indians but ends with Americans; there is no sense that they can coexist.

Simon Pokagon—a Potawatomi leader who also spoke at the Columbian Exposition—echoed Turner's frontier thesis:

> We shall never be happy here any more; we gaze into the faces of our little ones, for smiles of infancy to please, and into the faces of our young men and maidens, for joys of youth to cheer advancing age, but alas! instead of smiles of joy we find but looks of sadness there. Then we fully realize in the anguish of our souls that their young and tender hearts, in keenest sympathy with ours, have drank [sic] in the sorrows we have felt, and their sad faces reflect it back to us again. No rainbow of promise spans the dark cloud of our afflictions; no cheering hopes are painted on our midnight sky. We only stand with folded arms and watch and wait to see the future deal with us no better than the past. No cheer of sympathy is given us; but in answer to our complaints we are told the triumphal march of the Eastern race westward is by the unalterable decree of nature, termed by them "the survival of the fittest." And so we stand as upon the sea-shore, chained hand and foot, while the incoming tide of the great ocean of civilization rises slowly but surely to overwhelm us.

It is possible that Pokagon was being sarcastic or slyly using the idea of the disappearing Indian politically. But I am not sure.

On his deathbed in 1890, Blackfeet warrior and orator Crowfoot looked back on his life and that of his people and reached much the same

9

conclusion: "What is life?" he mused. "It is the flash of a firefly in the night. It is the breath of a buffalo in the winter time. It is as the little shadow that runs across the grass and loses itself in the sunset." The frontier was closed, Indians were confined to reservations. The clash of civilizations seemed to have wound down. The meaning of America and the myths that informed it had been firmly established. Perhaps this is why the massacre at Wounded Knee became so emblematic. It neatly symbolized the accepted version of reality—of an Indian past and an American present, begun in barbarism but realized as a state of democratic idealism.

This version of history remained largely unquestioned through World War I, the Great Depression, World War II, and the 1950s. But in the 1960s—because of Vietnam and the fight for civil rights; because of an increased focus on the environment and the effects of industrialization and consumerism; because of the newly current idea that "the culture" wasn't the *only* culture, and a counterculture could exist—the story of "the Indian" surfaced with new intensity in the American consciousness. This new awareness, focused on Wounded Knee and the challenge "the Indian" posed to the very idea of America, was epitomized by a highly influential book.

Published in 1970, eighty years after the massacre, *Bury My Heart at Wounded Knee* appeared as scenes of Indian activism were playing out on TV screens across the country, and at a time when many Americans were looking for some other way of being. The book was an enormous success. To date it has sold more than four million copies, and has been published in seventeen languages. It has never gone out of print. The book made big claims about the importance of Indians, in and of ourselves and to the rest of America. The "greatest concentration of recorded experience and observation" of Indian lives and history, wrote Dee Brown in the opening pages, "came out of the thirty-year span between 1860 and 1890. . . . It was an incredible era of violence, greed, audacity, sentimentality, undirected exuberance, and an almost reverential attitude toward the ideal of personal freedom for those who already had it. During that time the culture and civilization of the American Indian was destroyed." Beneath the effort to point a finger back east, to speak truth to power, however, Brown's narrative relied on—and revived—the same old sad story of the "dead Indian." Our history (and our continued existence) came down to a list of the tragedies we had somehow outlived without really living: without civilization, without culture, without a set of selves. As for present-day Native life, Brown wrote only: "If the readers of this book should ever chance to see the poverty, the hopelessness, and the squalor of a modern Indian reservation, they may find it possible to truly understand the reasons why."

I remember, vividly, reading that passage while in college in 1991, and I was doubly dismayed by Brown's telling. I was far from home, on a distant coast. I was homesick—for the northwoods, for my reservation, for the only place on earth I truly loved. I was only just beginning to understand what it was I was missing, and it wasn't squalor and hopelessness and poverty. This book is, in part, an attempt to communicate what it was that I loved. I was also dismayed because I felt so insignificant in the face of the authority and power with which Brown explained us Indians to the world. He had hundreds of years of history behind him, the most powerful and lucid cultural myths of America as evidence, and a command of English I could only dream of. All I had was the small hot point of hope that I mattered, that where I was from mattered, and that someday I would be able to explain—to myself and to others—why.

This book is a counternarrative to the story that has been told about us, but it is something more as well: it is an attempt to confront the ways we Indians ourselves understand our place in the world. Our self-regard—the vision and versions we hold of who we are and what we mean—matters greatly. We carry within us stories of our origins, and ideas about what our families, clans, and communities mean. Sadly, these narratives do not always, or even mostly, stand in opposition to the ways in which we are read by outsiders. We often, too often, agree with accounts of our own demise: for many years—too many years—I understood my reservation, Leech Lake Reservation in northern Minnesota, only as a place of abject suffering, a "nowhere place" where nothing happened and good ideas went to die. I saw it as *in* America but not *of* America. I saw myself and my tribe as a ruined people whose greatness lay behind us.

The evidence seemed to be all around me. A brilliant uncle (*the smartest man I ever knew,* said my mother) was perpetually stoned, and eventually died of an overdose. Another uncle was shot twice in the chest after firing an arrow through the open window of a police cruiser. A cousin was hit by an RV, and another cousin was so thoroughly shot up by the cops that his body leaked and sighed through the unstopped holes when I was asked to shift it in the coffin at his funeral. The first Indian elected to the state legislature was charged with theft and fraud, and convicted. All this misbehavior, all this loss, all this drama was refracted by the attitudes I heard expressed around me. On a field trip to the state capitol during a protest, my high school band teacher muttered to the class that all Indians were on welfare and we should go back to Canada where we came from. A high school friend told me that her parents, who owned property in a nearby town, wouldn't rent to Indians because we were dirty and dangerous. I protested weakly that *I* wasn't dirty, *I* wasn't dangerous. *Oh, well, you're not* really *Indian,* she said. To be "really" Indian, evidently, was to be those things. My best friend's mother told him that the only reason I'd gotten into Princeton and he hadn't was that I was Indian. And when I was young and desperate to matter, desperate at least to be related to someone who mattered, I asked my mother if there was anyone famous in our family. *Infamous, maybe,* she said. *But famous?* She laughed. *We've got bootleggers and safecrackers and convicts in our family, but no one famous for anything good.*

By the time I graduated from high school I was ready to leave the reservation and never come back. In my mind, nothing good came from or of my Indian life, and I was exhausted by all its drama and trauma. I was tired of the poverty and the dusty roads that no one saw fit to pave. I was sick of the late-night calls and the trips to the hospital to witness the damage we were doing to ourselves. I looked ahead to the green, leafy excellence of Princeton, to a future as a composer and Olympic fencer. Nothing was clearer to me than the conviction that my past lay behind me, on the reservation, and the future awaited me beyond our borders, in America. So I left.

As soon as I was gone, I missed it. I missed what I hadn't known was my Indian life, our collective Indian life. I missed the Mississippi, which flows through my reservation as a tiny thing, little more than a stream I could walk across. I missed the ways the pine scratched the window screens at night. I missed my uncle Davey's antics, and I missed his love and I missed how he loved me: completely, without judgment, without measure, without censure. I missed the Memorial Day gatherings at the Bena cemetery with my aunt and uncles and cousins, the sandwiches of canned ham mixed with Miracle Whip and relish on white dinner rolls. The yearning for home was rooted in nostalgia, but I was also trying to grow beyond it, toward a place approaching true knowledge.

As kids do when they leave home, I began to see my parents more clearly. I saw how my mother, born into the meanest of circumstances, had gone to nursing school and then to law school and then—quietly, without self-promotion—had returned to the reservation to practice law a block from the high school that had not thought much of the wiry Indian girl she had been. She represented all sorts of Indians for all sorts of reasons: divorce, DUI, theft. Indians had been appearing in court for centuries, but for most of my mother's clients it was the first time they had shown up in court with an Indian lawyer by their side, arguing for dignity, for fairness, for justice.

I saw, too, how my father—who was Jewish and had just barely survived the Holocaust—had adopted the reservation as his home and had adopted our causes as his own. I asked him about that. I asked him how he had come to feel so comfortable on the reservation. *I was a refugee, I was an outsider. I was told throughout my life I wasn't enough, I wasn't good enough, I didn't belong. When I came here I felt at home. I felt like people understood me.* He taught high school on the reservation and then worked for the tribe, and when I was in high school he worked at Red Lake Reservation, where he had helped get the high school bonded and built in a way that made the tribe proud of their own accomplishments. I learned about my parents from unlikely sources. One summer, when I picked up a woman I was dating from her aunt's house on the reservation, she told me her aunt wanted me to say hi to my father for her. Evidently, on Saturday afternoons back in the 1950s, my father would drive to the small village where she lived and pick up all the Indian kids hanging out there and drop them off in Bemidji, where there was more for them to do, then pick them up later when he was done in town and drive them home. *He was the only white man who even thought about us, and went out of his way to give us something to do, something to look forward to,* the aunt said.

I also started—in my own haphazard way—to think about our collective Indian past and present, and how the story of it was told. I decided on anthropology as my undergraduate major, a choice complicated by the way the discipline had created itself partly in relation to, and often at the expense of, indigenous people around the world. In the 1980s and 1990s, anthropology was reckoning with its colonial past, interrogating itself and its past practices, and that reflexive and self-appraising turn felt right to me. Anthropology was also a great place to have arguments, and for better or worse, I loved having arguments. (One of my professors noted that in America you have arguments with other people but in Britain you could make an argument by yourself; I quipped that in anthropology you could do both.)

Around that time, I launched my life as a fiction writer. In that, too, I was oppositional: I abhorred the publishing industry's pressure to make multicultural fiction engage in cultural show-and-tell. As a result, I wrote novels where the characters never, ever talked about their spirituality or culture; where nary a feather was to be found. Instead I tried (and often failed) to create complex, fully realized characters. Characters who, in Philip Larkin's phrase, had been pushed "to the side of their own lives" and had decided to push back. I went on to get my PhD in anthropology and to publish a few novels and, eventually, to write a nonfiction book about reservation life, a hybrid like me: part history, part reportage, part memoir.

Through it all, I came to see, we Indians often get ourselves wrong. My lack of regard for my own origins and those of my community began to trouble me, and troubles me still. If I could not see myself and my homelands differently from how many non-Indians do—more expansively, more intimately, more deeply—then how could I hope that the future of my people, in the broadest sense, would be any different from the story we kept being told, and kept telling ourselves? One of the mantras of the women's liberation movement in the 1970s was "The personal is political." This is undoubtedly true. But the political is also personal. Many of us have lived bitter and difficult lives, and we have brought the ghost of our modern afterlife inside ourselves, where it sits judging us, shaping us, putting its fingers over our eyes so that all we can see, all we can feel, is that we were once great people but are great no more, and that we are no longer capable of greatness. We may feel that Dee Brown was right: what we have now is not a civilization, not a culture, not even real selves, but rather a collection of conditions—poverty, squalor, hopelessness—and that these are the conditions in which we live, and the state of our spirit.

This, too, is a narrative that must be laid to rest. I came to conceive of a book that would dismantle the tale of our demise by way of a new story. This book would focus on the untold story of the past 128 years, making visible the broader and deeper currents of Indian life that have too long been obscured. It would explore the opposite thesis of *Bury My Heart at Wounded Knee*: The year 1890 was not the end of us, our cultures, our civilizations. It was a cruel, low, painful point, yes—maybe even the lowest point since Europeans arrived in the New World—but a low point from which much of modern Indian and American life has emerged.

To tell that story, I embarked on three journeys. I traveled back into the written record—back into our prehistory and up through the early days of colonial enterprise in North America and beyond, retracing and aiming to set straight the paths made crooked by Dee Brown and Simon Pokagon and L. Frank Baum and others, and also bringing in the efforts of other diligent, lesser-known chroniclers. I also spent the better part of four years traveling the country—Montana, Washington state, New Mexico, Arizona, California, New York, Florida, and everywhere in between. And as I traveled to Indian homelands across the country, researching and writing about our long history, I listened to Indian people telling me what they and their people had experienced, what they had done, what their lives meant to them. I did my best to pair their beautiful lives and beautiful struggles with the recorded past, to link them to the chain of cause and effect, action and response, thought and deed, that is our collective living history. Last, I also continued my inward journey, and included it here. I could not in good conscience ask other Indian people to expose themselves in service to my project, to *trust* me, if I didn't take the same risks. I can't shake the knowledge—and this is perhaps the only place where my anthropological training and my culture actually meet and agree—that it is impossible to separate the teller from the telling: that whatever I say about Indian lives is a way of saying something about myself, and therefore that both I and the project would be best served if I looked back and in, even if I didn't like what I saw.

This book is a result of those journeys. As such, it is not a catalog of broken treaties and massacres and names and dates, of moments when things might have turned out differently. There are, of course, treaties and battles and names and dates; this book is a history, after all. But facts assume a different place in this narrative from that in previous histories, because the project of this book is to do more than bend the broad lines of narrative true. It also tries to trace the stories of ordinary Indian people whose lives remind us of the richness and diversity of Indian life today and whose words show us the complexity with which we Indians understand our own past, present, and future. So this book is a work of history, but it also includes journalism and reportage, and the deeply personal and deeply felt stories of Indians across the country, mine among them.

In the telling, I have done my best to bring Indian life into contact with the larger themes and trends in American life. It is impossible to understand the removal of Indians from the American Southeast in the early nineteenth century without seeing it in the context of the shifting balance of power between the federal government and the states, for example. The federal policy of termination and relocation does not come into focus unless it is understood in relation to the African American Great Migration and how the American city and suburb supplanted the farm in the mid–twentieth century. Similarly, American Indian activism took place against a backdrop of larger activisms that were blooming around the country at the same time. Throughout—in the history, in the reportage, and in my own stories and those of my family—I have tried to show the ways in which Indian fates have been tied to that of the country in which we find ourselves, and the ways that the fate of America has been and forever will be tied to ours.

THIS BOOK IS WRITTEN out of the simple, fierce conviction that our cultures are not dead and our civilizations have not been destroyed. It is written with the understanding that our present tense is evolving as rapidly and creatively as everyone else's. In a sense, it is a selfish project. I want—I need—to see Indian life as more than a legacy of loss and pain, because I want to pass on to my beautiful children a rich heritage and an embracing vision of who we were and who we are. But I have not allowed myself to conjure alternative (hopeful but false) realities out of the desire to make up for a traumatic past or to imagine a better future. Looking at what actually was and is, beyond the blinders that the "dead Indian" narrative has imposed, means reckoning with relentless attacks on our sovereignty and the suffering it has created. But it also brings into view the ingenious and resourceful counterattacks we have mounted over the decades, in resistance to the lives the state would have us live. It has allowed me to trace the many varied paths Indians have forged where old ones have been closed off or obscured.

As Karl Marx wrote at the beginning of *The Eighteenth Brumaire of Louis Bonaparte*: "Men make their own history, but they do not make it as they please; they do not make it under self-selected circumstances, but under circumstances existing already, given and transmitted from the past. The tradition of all dead generations weighs like a nightmare on the brains of the living." This book is about the history we've made and the tools with which we've made it. Indians are not little ghosts in living color, stippling the landscape of the past and popping up in the present only to admonish contemporary Americans to behave.

To treat the lives lost on that cold South Dakota day in 1890 as merely symbolic is to disrespect those lives. It is also to disrespect the more than two hundred Lakota who survived Wounded Knee and lived on—to experience the pain of loss, yes, but much else as well. They survived to live and grow, to get married and have babies. They survived to hold on to their Lakota ways or to convert to Christianity and let those ways recede. They survived to settle on the reservation and, later, to move to cities. They survived to go to school and to college and to work. They survived to make mistakes and recover from them. They survived to make history, to make meaning, to make *life*. This book is about them. And it is about the Indians of other communities and tribes around the country, who survived their own holocausts and went on to make their own lives and their own histories, and in so doing, to make and remake the story of the country itself.

PART 1

Narrating the Apocalypse:
10,000 BCE–1890

Meetings and Beginnings

There is a tendency to view the European settlement of North America, and the corresponding decimation of many tribes and cultures, as sudden and inevitable. It was neither. How, then, did Indians go from being the lords of the continent—controlling all its shores, all the interior, having mastered its climates and terrain and even the inevitable conflict with other tribes—to the scattered remnants present in 1891?

Although the northern Atlantic littoral had been reached and lightly explored by Leif Eriksson (Eriksson the Lucky) in the eleventh century, it wasn't until Christopher Columbus landed in the Bahamas on October 12, 1492, that the age of exploration (and eventually settlement) of the New World truly began. And that is where the story of America usually begins. Like many origin myths, the idea that everything began *in 1492 when Columbus sailed the ocean blue* is a fiction. So, too, are the received notions about why he came: his journey wasn't motivated by ideology or by the desire to prove that the earth was round. Columbus's journey to North America was a mission that would resemble the worst kind of marriage: he came for money and ended up in court.

In many ways, his journey began with the Ottomans and with the rise of a mercantile class—early monopolists, if you will. Prior to 1453, the Silk Road that led from Europe through the Middle East and the subcontinent to China was protected, known, and stable enough to facilitate a robust trade in silk and spices between Asia and Europe. Since at least 3000 BCE, spices had been traded from east to west via coastal routes, and, later, by sea routes. Cinnamon, nutmeg, ebony, silk, obsidian, and all manner of goods moved from east to west, while gold, silver, and gems moved from west to east. A host of other things followed along those routes:

religions, populations, knowledge, philosophy, genes, and disease. The relationships that evolved, from antiquity through the Middle Ages, while not necessarily equitable and certainly not always peaceful, weren't only, or even primarily, exploitative. When the Ottoman Turks conquered Constantinople in 1453, however, the ensuing regime change dismantled that network. The powers in Venice, Genoa, Barcelona, and Lisbon needed new ways to get the goods to which they were accustomed into Europe. Specifically, they needed a cheaper way than traveling through the politically unstable Mediterranean waters and the increasingly risky overland routes across the Arabian Peninsula. Political unrest was widespread, as were piracy and violence.

Making matters worse were Iberian civil wars and a kind of economic headlock imposed on European royal power by feudal mercantilism. Spain wasn't exactly Spain until the end of the fifteenth century; it was a collection of competing states including Portugal, Castile, Granada, and Navarre, united through conquest and the marriage of Isabella and Ferdinand. The Spanish crown in particular had depleted its resources in punitive wars against other Iberian countries and against the Moors, who were finally expelled from Spain in the late 1400s. Though driven from Spain, the Moors were still a force in the Mediterranean, and they effectively choked off trade to Spain's courts. (The effects were dramatic; for example, by 1503 pepper traded through the Mediterranean cost 80 percent more than pepper that came from the New World). Merchants, long denied standing and opportunity in their home countries in favor of royal companies, had in the meantime developed their own foreign trade networks, and they became rich, in some cases richer than the crown. Then, as now, power followed money; European monarchies were losing their grip. What the Portuguese and Spanish (and later the English) crowns needed were royal charters and royal commerce: a way to create central banks as a means of consolidating power, and state-sponsored businesses to fill royal coffers. And although it had long been thought possible, it wasn't until the mid–fifteenth century that it became practical and necessary to try to sail west in order to reach the East. Columbus was a hired gun. The Spanish crown needed someone to advance its interests. Like a gun, Columbus, as a representative of power, quickly became an agent of violence.

Michele da Cuneo, a lifelong friend of Columbus's who came along on the second voyage, is indicative of the scope of violence the expedition entailed:

> While I was in the boat, I captured a very beautiful Carib woman, whom the said Lord Admiral gave to me. When I had taken her to my cabin she was naked—as was their custom. I was filled with a desire to take my pleasure with her and attempted to satisfy my desire. She was unwilling, and so treated me with her nails that I wished I had never begun. But—to cut a long story short—I then took a piece of rope and whipped her soundly, and she let forth such incredible screams that you would not have believed your ears. Eventually we came to such terms, I assure you, that you would have thought that she had been brought up in a school for whores.

In 1495, Columbus shipped 550 Indians in four ships back to Spain for sale. More than two hundred died en route, and their bodies were cast into the sea. By 1499, Columbus was regularly shipping Indians back to Spain, where they were sold in Andalusian markets. While he was funneling Native families into slavery and breaking them apart, his own brothers—Bartholomew and Diego (Giacomo)—joined him in his exploits in the New World. Ferdinand and Isabella were reluctant to allow him to continue slaving, even though slavery was alive and well and widespread in Spain at the time. Muslims who remained after 1492 were sold, as were any "'enemies of the Catholic church and of the crown' who had been taken in a 'good' or 'just' war." Isabella and Ferdinand needed to know if Indian captives met these definitions (although slavers and profiteers and functionaries almost always found a way to make most of their captives fit administratively). The monarchs told Columbus to stop slaving until they figured out what to do. They appointed a committee of lawyers and religious leaders to help them. It took five years for them to reach a decision, during which time Columbus kept slaving and exploring. He was so insistent and pressured the crown so relentlessly while it deliberated that Isabella, exasperated, exclaimed, "Who is this Columbus who dares give out my vassals as slaves?" But eventually he realized it would be more profitable to keep Indians in the New World in slavery than to send them back to Spanish markets. Columbus wrote that he "would have sent many Indians to Castile, and they would have been sold, and they would have become instructed in our Holy Faith and our customs, and then they would have returned to their lands to teach the others," but the Indians stayed in the Caribbean because "the Indians of Española were and are *the greatest wealth of the island*, because they are the ones who dig, and harvest, and collect the bread and other supplies, and gather the gold from the mines, and do all the work of men and beasts alike." In short, while Columbus found gold and silver and other natural resources, the indigenous lives and bodies were the greatest natural resource he came upon.

Schisms emerged. When Columbus returned on his third voyage in 1498, he was greeted by an insurrection at Hispaniola. The colonists claimed he had misled them about the opportunities to be found there. Columbus had some of them hanged for insubordination. Others returned to Spain, where they brought a case against him in the Spanish court. Columbus also ran afoul of the Church for his reluctance to baptize many Native peoples because he preferred to leave them, according to church doctrine, "soulless," which meant that they were free to be enslaved. In 1500 he was removed as governor of Hispaniola and brought to Spain in chains to face charges of cruelty and mismanagement. Not until 2006 did documents surface in Spain that detailed the extent of Columbus's tyranny and depravity. The governor who replaced him, Francisco de Bobadilla, tasked by the crown with fact-finding on the Columbus brothers' rule, deposed twenty-three people, some supporters, some enemies. All had the same tale to tell: the brothers had used torture and mutilation as a means of control. A man convicted of stealing corn had his ears and nose cut off and was sold into slavery; a woman who suggested Columbus was of low birth was paraded naked through the streets and later had her tongue cut out; Natives who rose up against the brutalities of colonial rule were dismembered alive and had their torsos paraded through the streets.

Columbus was somewhat rehabilitated in the eyes of the crown, and he was allowed to return to the Caribbean on a fourth voyage in 1502 with strict instructions not to stop at Hispaniola. But he was ever the same. Things were so bad during his fourth voyage that Columbus was stranded on Jamaica for the better part of a year after sustaining damage in a storm; Nicolás de Ovando y Cáceres, the governor of Hispaniola, who detested Columbus, refused to help him. When aid from Spain finally arrived in June 1504, Columbus returned there for good, never having set foot on the mainland of North America.

STARTING IN THE 1490s and over the next twenty years, John Cabot would reach Atlantic Canada, João Fernandes (Lavrador) would map Labrador, and the Corte-Real brothers would explore the region as well. Juan Ponce de León would found Caparra on what is now Puerto Rico, and Hernán Cortés would conquer Mexico with the help of the Tlaxcalans, as more than forty thousand renegade Inca subjects would aid Francisco Pizarro with his efforts farther south. And through the end of the century, a wave of exploration and many attempts at colonization would follow. The Spanish fought for a foothold in North America, attempting settlements in the area that is now South Carolina in 1526 and again in 1566. Norman, Breton, and Portuguese fishermen were settling Newfoundland by 1527, Huguenots tried Saint Kitts in 1538, the Spanish Pensacola in 1559, and the French Fort Caroline near present-day Jacksonville in 1564 and Chesapeake Bay in 1570. The English settled Roanoke Island in 1585 and Sable Island in 1598. These early attempts failed for a number of reasons: disease, starvation, attack by indigenous tribes, attacks from other colonial powers (Spain was a particularly unapologetic underminer of other colonial efforts). During this period the colonial powers shifted their focus from exploitative colonization (small enclaves of people sent far from their homeland in order to extract resources to be sent back to Europe) to exploitive settlement (permanent communities established to extract and improve upon resources for profit). Many of the early settlements failed because they were looking for a quick buck (gold, slaves); others succeeded when they went for the slow buck: cotton, tobacco, timber, furs, slave-worked gold and silver mines, and gems. How different parts of North America were colonized depended to a great extent on which Europeans were setting up shop. The Spanish attempted Catholic missions in Mexico, Florida, and New Mexico that burned pagan shrines and killed Native worshippers, but they were met with so much resistance that the missionaries gradually incorporated Indian rituals and iconography into the Church. (To this day, in many Pueblos in New Mexico infants are baptized in the Church and, immediately after, taken to a ceremony where the baptism is wiped away.) But in New England, the Puritans attempted little to no integration of what few Indians they had converted into their churches.

There is a tendency to treat Columbus's arrival in the Caribbean and the subsequent colonization of mainland North America as of a piece. Certainly, the narrative still included in many textbooks is that Columbus sailed west to see if the earth was round and "found" Indians; then Europeans who loved freedom and were fleeing tyranny came over, bringing the Old World and the New into a long, friendly handshake. There is another, more recent version, that the colonists arrived intent on genocide and were largely successful at it. Neither account is true. Columbus sailed west for money. The colonists came for money and they stayed for money. Indigenous peoples, for their part, resisted, helped, hindered, played, and constantly negotiated the changes brought by colonization and dispossession. Still, it is true that by the beginning of the seventeenth century, the four dominant European colonizing powers had roughly divided the continent: The Spanish had been relegated to Mexico and parts of what is today the American South. The English controlled the main section of the Eastern Seaboard. The Dutch were clinging to parts of New York and New Jersey. And the French had secured much of what is now eastern Canada.

How did we get from this thin, if relatively secure, European foothold to continental dominance in three centuries? How did we get from Jamestown to Wounded Knee? As we will see, all the colonial powers used violence, strategic dependency, intermarriage, and religious conversion to create and maintain control. And in this process, language would be no less powerful a weapon: a rhetoric of rightful possession coupled with a narrative of Indian aggression, laziness, transgression, and paganism.

Early Tribes and Homelands

When Columbus arrived in the Bahamas in 1492, and when Giovanni Caboto (John Cabot in English) landed on the mainland of North America in 1497, they arrived in a vast land, but also in an equally vast and varied cultural landscape that had been evolving for ten millennia.

The earliest verified archaeological evidence of the settlement of North America comes from two distinct sites, one in Pennsylvania and one in Chile. Meadowcroft Rockshelter, a thirty-five-mile drive southwest of Pittsburgh, was used continuously for centuries but was abandoned by Indians around the time of the Revolutionary War. An amateur archaeologist, Albert Miller, first discovered artifacts in a groundhog burrow there in the 1950s, but it wasn't until the 1970s that the site was properly excavated by a team from the University of Pittsburgh. What they found was an unbroken record of human habitation that may stretch back nineteen thousand years. Tools, bones, campsites, and personal effects were recovered. The presence of 149 species of animals was established, along with evidence of early farming of squash, corn, and beans.

The Monte Verde site in Chile, also excavated in the 1970s, is a rare find: a relatively complete village that was inundated by rising water in a peat bog shortly after it was inhabited and therefore was held in a kind of anaerobic amber. Like the Meadowcroft site, Monte Verde has been dated to as many as nineteen thousand years ago. Together the sites are important and do more than help us understand how and when North America was settled; they also show that there were people in North America well before the Bering land bridge formed about ten thousand years ago, throwing into dispute the theory that North America was settled primarily by Asiatic wanderers over the bridge. Indian stories about our own origins almost all claim we came into being in our native lands. The questions archaeology is struggling to explain—When and how was North America settled? Did the first people come across the land bridge ten thousand years ago? Or on earlier land bridges formed thirty thousand years ago before sea levels rose once again? From Asia by boat earlier? From northern Europe? All of the above? Were there in fact multiple origins of the human species?—are rapidly being answered by ongoing genetic research. This research suggests that prehistoric Indians share a lot of DNA with Asian populations and, surprisingly, with European populations as well. It is quite likely that Europeans migrated into far eastern Asia and mingled with the populations there and that their descendants crossed over to the New World between thirty thousand and twenty thousand years ago. But this is all the science of migration, not the history of peoples.

Most Indians do not see themselves as merely the first in a long series of arrivals to North America; they see themselves as indigenous. And the belief in tribal indigeneity is crucial to understanding modern Indian realities. The rhetorical stance that Indians are merely one group of travelers with no greater stake than any other clashes with Indians' cultural understanding that we have always been here and that our control over our place in this world—not to mention our control over the narrative and history of that place—has been deeply and unjustly eroded.

The Kiowa, for example, believe that they came into the world, one by one, through a hollow log and that a pregnant woman tried to get through, got stuck, and that's why the Kiowa are a small tribe. The Diné, or Navajo, believe they traveled from the center of the earth through a series of worlds until they reached this one, arriving in the Diné homeland, which was bounded, then as now, by four sacred mountains. Many tribes have stories about emerging from the earth—they are bottom-up tribes. Others, like mine, are more top-down: we believe the Creator made the heavens and earth and then placed or draped various handiworks across it. Last of all, after the animals, we people were set down, like a very small final piece being placed in a very large diorama. (And it bears mentioning that in our cosmology we are the most immature of all creation, having been made last, and that as such we have the least tenure upon the land.) Despite the variety of tribal belief (or perhaps in part because of it), North America is uniformly seen as an Indian homeland that has shaped and been shaped by the Indians living there then and living there now. Over these homelands various empires and nation-states—Spanish, British, French, Dutch, and, later, American—have crawled, mapping and claiming as they went. But neither these maps nor the conquests enabled by them have eradicated or obscured the fact that immigrants made their homes and villages and towns and cities *on top of* Indian homelands. Any history that persists in using the old model of New World history as something made by white people and done to Indian people, therefore, is not a real history of this place. Rather, as the historian Colin Calloway has suggested, history didn't come to the New World with Cabot or Columbus; they—and those who followed—brought European history to the unfolding histories already here.

Science tells us only that the humans of the New World arrived a long time ago, and likely in many different ways. Culture and history tell us something more profound: that New World tribal people emerged here, as cultures and as people. No one else can make that claim. Columbus and Cabot and the rest didn't discover the New World or new peoples. They met Indian people with distinct histories, homelands and technologies, and deep—and deeply considered—concepts of themselves and their place in the world.

The Southeast

When Europeans first arrived on the Atlantic coast, they landed on a richly settled and incredibly fecund homeland to hundreds of tribes. When prehistoric first Indians emerged in what is now the eastern United States, the water levels were considerably lower than they are now, because much of the world's water was trapped in glaciers that spread across a large part of the Northern Hemisphere. Because of this, coastal archaeology has uncovered only a very fractured record of habitation. Even so, five-thousand-year-old shell middens in Florida and North Carolina suggest vibrant coastal cultures in this region. In Virginia alone there are thousands of known prehistoric village sites. How these early tribes were organized or how they understood themselves is hard to know. What made for a relatively easy life—abundant rivers, streams, and springs, plentiful fuel, fairly constant aquatic and terrestrial food sources, and a relatively mild climate—makes for bad archaeology. It seems that, in this early period, coastal Indians lived in small villages of about 150 people and that they were fairly mobile, spending part of the year on the coast, part farther inland, and getting most of their calories from fish and game and opportunistic harvests of nuts and berries. Populations seem to have risen and shrunk like the tide, depending on the availability of calories. Archaeological evidence suggests that between 2500 and 2000 BCE, tribal groups began making clay pots, which indicate a more sedentary lifestyle, the need for storage (which in turn suggests that there were food surpluses), and a greater reliance on plants for sustenance. A bit later eastern coastal and woodland Indians were planting or cultivating sunflowers, lamb's-quarter, gourds, goosefoot, knotweed, and Jerusalem artichokes. But this was not the Garden of Eden. Some villages seem to have been fortified by wooden palisades. Tribes did fight and kill one another and, as groups do, sought for themselves what others had.

When Ponce de León arrived in Florida in 1513, with explicit permission from the Spanish crown to explore and settle the region, Indians had been living there for at least twelve thousand years. Because of the lower water levels, during prehistoric times Florida's land mass was double what it is today, so much of the archaeological evidence is under the sea. It was also much drier and supported all sorts of megafauna such as bison and mastodon. As megafauna died out (climate change, hunting), the fruits of the sea in turn supported very large Archaic and Paleolithic societies. Agriculture was late in coming to Florida, appearing only around 700 BCE, and some noncoastal Florida tribes still had no forms of agriculture at the time of Spanish conquest. Presumably the rich fresh and brackish water ecosystems were more than enough to support a lot of different peoples. What the Spanish encountered beginning in 1513 was a vast, heterogeneous collection of tribes, among them the Ais, Alafay, Amacano, Apalachee, Bomto, Calusa, Chatot, Chine, Guale, Jororo, Luca, Mayaca, Mayaimi, Mocoso, Pacara, Pensacola, Pohoy, Surruque, Tequesta, Timicua, and Viscayno, to name but a few. Within a matter of years, all of these tribes, having evolved over many centuries, would decline, and in a hurry.

Spanish colonization was a schizophrenic enterprise, driven first by the search for treasure, then in a quest for slaves, and later taking on a missionary cast. The desire to find a more direct route to the Orient was constant, but to it was added the need to hold territory as a buffer against British and French interests. The Indian response to the Spanish was determined to a great extent by three constants of first contact: the spread of disease, attempts at slavery, and the spread of information.

In all likelihood Ponce de León was not the first Spaniard to reach La Florida (the land of flowers), because the Indians he met on his first voyage already knew some Spanish words and were already deeply distrustful of Spaniards; likely, Spanish from the Caribbean had been there first. Other explorers followed. Pedro de Salazar traveled the Atlantic coast, capturing upward of five hundred slaves and sowing smallpox and measles wherever he went. So it was no wonder that almost every attempt at exploration and colonization—Pedro de Quejo and Francisco Gordillo in 1521, Pánfilo de Narváez in 1527, Hernando de Soto in 1539—was harassed and attacked and impeded by the tribes it encountered. After the Spanish finally succeeded in establishing missions in Florida and Georgia in the sixteenth century, Indians were conscripted and enslaved and forced to live in deplorable conditions in service to the crown and the cross, which only hastened the work of disease. And when the Spanish were attacked from the north by British forces, the enslaved Indians were even more vulnerable than their well-fed and well-rested overlords.

What transpired in Florida would be repeated (with variations) over much of the Indian homeland of North America: disease, slavery, starvation, and disruption. Previously distinct cultures and peoples were mixed together; remnants of once vast tribes banded together and formed new tribal identities. This happened in what would become the states of Florida, Georgia, South and North Carolina, Kentucky, and Tennessee, in Spanish and British territory. By the time the British and Spanish lost out to the newly minted Americans, what had once been the homeland of hundreds of distinct tribes was now in the control of a few amalgamated (polymerized, in the words of historian Jack Page) tribes such as the Seminole, Creek, Muscogee, Chickasaw, and Cherokee.

The colonization of North America is often seen as a binary struggle, a series of conflicts between Indians and settlers. But in the face of disease, starvation, and displacement, conflict occurred along multiple vectors. Tribes allied with other tribes against yet other tribes; colonial powers made alliances with certain tribes against other tribes and against other colonial powers. Later, elements of the federal government (John Marshall's Supreme Court) allied with tribes against states (like Georgia), and other parts of the government (Andrew Jackson's executive branch) allied with states against tribes. Some tribes committed genocide against their neighbors. But while the conflict or conflicts in the Southeast weren't necessarily linear and certainly weren't binary, the trajectory was more or less clear: tribes were diminished through disease and warfare. Two moments stand out in the sordid history of the American Southeast—removal and the Seminole Wars.

In place of the Hatteras, Koroa, Chiaha, Biloxi, and countless others, a few polymerized "supertribes" had arisen in the Southeast: the Chickasaw, Choctaw, Muscogee, Creek, Cherokee, Yamasee, Catawba, Miccosukee, and Seminole. Thomas Jefferson saw the remaining southeastern tribes as impediments to the cultivation of the American nation and American character. He wrote that it was important "to encourage them to abandon hunting, to apply to the raising [of] stock, to agriculture and domestic manufactures, and thereby prove to themselves that less land and labor will maintain them in this, better than in their former mode of living." The problem was that the Indians were already doing just that. By the beginning of the eighteenth century, eastern tribes were all predominantly agricultural anyway: they grew yams, beans, corn, and squash, and more intensively so after the trade in buckskin brought the white-tail deer to near extinction east of the Mississippi. Many of them had had small villages and settlements where they farmed intensively, and effectively. They had seats of government and centers of power. After the colonists arrived they began cultivating cotton and other export crops as well in the eighteenth century, which they farmed plantation style. Many Cherokee and other tribal people bought and kept black slaves, as did Jefferson himself. Jefferson, while in France as a foreign minister, thought much about the state of the new republic and mused: "I think our governments will remain virtuous for many centuries; as long as they are chiefly agricultural; and this will be as long as there shall be vacant lands in any part of America." Of course, there was no "vacant" land for America to settle, and this was nowhere more obvious than in the Southeast. In a series of secret memos to William Henry Harrison written in 1803, Jefferson sketched out a plan by which Indian tribes in the Southeast could be disappeared:

To promote this disposition to exchange lands which they have to spare and we want for necessaries, which we have to spare and they want, we shall push our trading houses, and be glad to see the good and influential individuals among them run in debt, because we observe that when these debts get beyond what the individuals can pay, they become willing to lop them off by a cession of lands. . . . In this way our settlements will gradually circumscribe and approach the Indians, and they will in time either incorporate with us as citizens of the United States, or remove beyond the Missisipi [sic]. The former is certainly the termination of their history most happy for themselves. But in the whole course of this, it is essential to cultivate their love. As to their fear, we presume that our strength and their weakness is now so visible that they must see we have only to shut our hand to crush them, and that all our liberalities to them proceed from motives of pure humanity only. Should any tribe be foolhardy enough to take up the hatchet at any time, the seizing of the whole country of that tribe, and driving them across the Missisipi as the only condition of peace, would be an example to others, and a furtherance of our final consolidation.

Debt, dependency, threats, and force, in that order, was the thinking of the day. These secret memos were written while Jefferson served as president of the United States.

Jefferson wasn't able to achieve any of these outcomes during his tenure; the republic would have to wait until Andrew Jackson took office in 1829. By this point, the eastern Cherokee had consolidated power and launched a new governmental structure based on a balance of power and a judiciary. They published a bilingual newspaper and formally declared New Echota (near what is today Calhoun, Georgia) as the capital of the Cherokee Nation. But Jackson had spent his military years fighting Indians and the British, as well as speculating in real estate (often out of the spoils of war), and he regarded such claims as ridiculous. Earlier, in 1802, Georgia had agreed to give up claims to land in what would become Alabama and Mississippi if the federal government would remove or reduce the Indians in Georgia. Basically, Georgia would give up land outside the state in order to secure more land within its borders. After Jackson assumed the presidency, he was happy to oblige. He offered the tribes two choices: move west of the Mississippi or allow themselves to become subjects of the states in which their tribal homelands existed. In the case of the Cherokee, this meant that they would be citizens of the United States and residents of the state of Georgia, whose laws included a provision that Creek Indians could legally be hunted "wheresoever they may be found within the limits of this state." Invoking not only the tribes' long control over their land but also the treaties, alliances, and decrees that had been written into the Constitution, which also stipulated that only the federal government had the ability to negotiate and treat with tribes, Cherokee chief John Ross brought his people's case to the Supreme Court. In a series of rulings known as the Marshall Trilogy, the court affirmed the rights of the Cherokee and ruled the removal of Indians unlawful. Andrew Jackson did it anyway. Between 1830 and 1850 more than 125,000 Indians of the Southeast were forcibly removed to territory west of the Mississippi, mostly on foot and in wintertime. At least 3,500 Creek and 5,000 Cherokee and many from other tribes died along the way. Many more died of starvation when they reached their new lands.

So it wasn't merely "germs and steel" that spelled the end of the "red race." The Cherokee, Choctaw, Creek, Chickasaw, and many others had weathered disease and rebounded. Moreover, they had done almost everything "right" by the standards of the new republic. They had fought for the government (including under Jackson at the Battle of Horseshoe Bend). They had devoted themselves to farming and trade, developed court and legislative systems—they had proved themselves socially and culturally adaptive. And this had done nothing to assuage the determination of the colonists and settlers to seize their land and resources. "Neither superior technology nor an overwhelming number of settlers made up the mainspring of the birth of the United States or the spread of its power over the entire world," writes historian Roxanne Dunbar-Ortiz. "Rather, the chief cause was the colonialist settler-state's willingness to eliminate whole civilizations of people in order to possess their land."

The Seminole Wars

The Seminole were also, in part, subject to removal, but they charted a very different course for themselves in relation to the American government. An amalgam of other tribes, notably Creek but also some Choctaw, who had fled south from Georgia and Alabama during the eighteenth century and settled in northern Florida, the Seminole worked with the Spanish to displace other tribes (who were moved to Cuba, presumably as slaves or plantation workers). For a time, their numbers grew and life improved somewhat. They learned how to draw sustenance from Florida's swamps and lowlands, and they traded deer hides for weapons, metal, and other goods. After the Red Stick Rebellion (otherwise known as the Creek War), in which traditionalist Creeks sought to rise up against the government and against their own, more assimilationist tribal members, the surviving rebels fled to Florida and joined the Seminole, making the Seminole a large tribe indeed, numbering about six thousand around the time of the War of 1812.

At the behest of the British (and perhaps following their own inclinations), the Seminole began raiding across the border into Georgia—attacking unsympathetic Creek and Georgian settlers alike. In 1818, Andrew Jackson (not yet president) mounted a campaign to put down the Seminole, recover runaway slaves in Florida, and shake the Spanish out of Florida in the same stroke. This was the First Seminole War. When it concluded, the United States secured all of northern Florida, some twenty-eight million acres, and under the Treaty of Moultrie Creek, signed in 1823, moved the Seminoles into a four-million-acre reservation on poor land in central Florida. Another fraudulent treaty, the Treaty of Payne's Landing, in 1832, signed by a few nonrepresentative "chiefs," promised the Seminole land west of the Mississippi. In 1835 the government moved in to enforce it. This time they were met with resistance in the form of Chief Osceola. Osceola, a young warrior of fierce opinions, allegedly had this to say of the government attempts to direct the destiny of his tribe: "Am I a negro, a slave? I am an Indian. The white man shall not make me black. I will make the white man red with blood, and then blacken him in the sun and rain, where the wolf shall smell his bones and the vulture live upon his flesh." Such language was a far cry from Chief John Ross's measured appeals to the U.S. Supreme Court.

On December 28, 1835, an American army column moved into Seminole territory near Fort Brooke, but the Seminole, led by the irascible Osceola, were waiting for them. The Seminole rose from the tall grass on either side of the trail and opened fire. After the first volley, half the soldiers lay dead or dying. They got their artillery going, but then the artillerymen were killed and the rest of the soldiers fell, more than one hundred in total. As was typical, American losses were framed as a massacre and the battle became known as the Dade Massacre. In the ensuing months, the Seminole attacked twenty-one plantations and burned them down, along with army forts and even the Cape Florida lighthouse. Major Ethan Allen Hitchcock felt that the U.S. government was to blame. "The government is in the wrong, and this is the chief cause of the persevering opposition of the Indians, who have nobly defended their country against our attempt to enforce a fraudulent treaty. The natives used every means to avoid a war, but were forced into it by the tyranny of our government." Despite the tyranny, the government was a long time in bringing the war to a close, and only then by luring Osceola into a parley under a flag of truce and then arresting him. Still the war waged on. The Seminole attacked and melted away, attacked again, and fled into the swamps once more. The army, heavily provisioned and often mounted, could not fight effectively in the Florida swamps. But attrition finally had its way, and the wars wound down in 1842 at a cost of nearly $60 million for the second war alone. The total cost to fight the Seminole was much higher. The captured Seminoles were moved west to Indian Territory, but many remained. The end of the war was marked not by treaty or agreement but by exhaustion.

And yet, in the 1850s, the remaining Seminole once again attacked settlers moving onto their land. This was the Third Seminole War. Again, violence swept the state. Again, attrition and exhaustion decided the matter, and many of the combatants were removed west in 1858. The war was declared over (by the United States) on May 8, 1858. But the Seminole made no such pronouncement. The remaining Seminole, numbering fewer than a thousand, resumed life in the backcountry and swamps of Florida, and there they remained, never having surrendered and never having been defeated.

So one wonders: Which was the better path, that of Chief John Ross or that of Osceola? Both men are remembered as having fought for their people, though in radically different ways. Both won Pyrrhic victories. Many of both tribes took up residence in what is now Oklahoma, but many refused to leave their homelands. Despite the best efforts of the government and the millions of dollars it spent, the Southeast was never entirely freed of Indians, and it likely never will be. They lived on in the swamps of Florida, the hills of southern Appalachia, the bayous of Alabama and Louisiana.

The Northeast

The prehistoric tribes of the American Northeast—stretching from Virginia all the way up to the Saint Lawrence—were as diverse as their homeland. From the Atlantic littoral to the Appalachians, the tribes seem to have kept close to the shores, so much of the record of their history was lost to rising water. Life seems to have been particularly good for them from about 3000 BCE to 700 BCE. According to Alice Kehoe, "After around 3000 BCE, sea level stabilized at its historical global level," and the ocean provided seals and swordfish and cod. The innumerable rivers and streams ran with smelt, alewife, salmon, and herring every spring. The warming of the climate helped create vast beds of shellfish from Manhattan Island north to Maine. One archaeological site in southern Maine dated to 3000 BCE included the remains of deer, moose, seal, walrus, beaver, mink, sea mink, river otter, fisher, bear, swordfish, cod, sturgeon, sculpin, mallards, black ducks, loons, eagles, and shellfish. With the increasing availability of dependable calories came a population boom, which in turn facilitated cultural growth. Villages grew in size. Funerary rites and burials became more elaborate. By about 1000 BCE, pottery became prevalent.

Within a few hundred years the climate cooled again, calories became scarce (hickory nuts were particularly hard to find), and tribes fractured into smaller groups that seem to have relied more on inland hunting. Moose replaced deer, and foraging included wild grapes, hickory nuts, and acorns. Elaborate burial practices disappeared. During this time maize had begun its slow crawl as a domesticated food source from Mexico. It reached the Northeast and was in robust production by 1200 CE. Ever the companion of culture, corn caused populations to grow again. Internecine wars became common. By the time of contact with European fishing fleets in the early sixteenth century, there was a distinct division between what had become the tribes of the Iroquois Confederacy inland and the polymorphous collection of Algonquian tribes scattered along the Atlantic coast. The perils and opportunities this division created played out very differently for the respective groups.

The Algonquian-speaking tribes included the Powhatan, Nanticoke, Pennacook, Massachuset, Mohegan, Delaware, Mahican, Abenake, Mi'kmaq, Pequot, Wampanoag, and scores of other small tribes. Opportunities for seasonal fishing, foraging, and hunting large game farther from shore encouraged the growth of numerous small seasonal villages of no more than a few hundred, organized by clan. The tribes spent the summer netting birds (loons, ducks, geese, and cormorants) and harvesting berries and nuts near the sea. In the fall they moved to other temporary villages better situated to net spawning fish. In the winter they congregated in larger villages and lived in multifamily longhouses to conserve heat, water, and material for shelter. They grew corn, beans, and squash but favored slash-and-burn methods that dictated moving to new planting grounds every few years. This is one reason early European explorers and colonists found cathedral-like old-growth forests and rich, open country ready for planting. The "virgin land" they described was hardly virgin at all, having been shaped by the tribes of the region for millennia.

The border region between the eastern Great Lakes and the Appalachian Mountains that was home to the five original tribes of the Iroquois Confederacy required a different kind of organization. By the end of the Woodland period (around 1100 CE) the separate Iroquoian tribes of the area—Cayuga, Oneida, Seneca, Onondaga, and Mohawk—though to a degree united culturally and linguistically, had fought one another often for hunting and fishing grounds. But corn, when it arrived from Mexico, required intensive cultivation and a kind of seasonal stability not possible with constant, even if low-grade, conflict. The best way to organize in this region, compared to the resource-rich coast, seemed to be to create protected villages surrounded by cornfields and acres of squash and beans. As the Iroquois telling has it, members of three different tribes—two men, Dekanawida and Hiawatha, and one woman, Jigonhsasee, known as the

Mother of Nations—met at Jigonhsasee's home to discuss creating bonds of mutual protection that would enable them all to make the most of the gift of corn. They sought out men from two other tribes—Dekanawida and Tadadaho—to cement their union, which they referred to as the Great League of Peace. Each of the tribes had ownership and control of its own territory and its own political and spiritual functions.

By the time of European contact, the Onondaga, Mohawk, Seneca, Oneida, and Cayuga were living in this way, their palisaded villages sometimes exceeding a few acres in size, surrounded by fields, with webs of tribal relations that extended over a wide territory beyond. (The Tuscarora would later join as well, when they arrived as refugees from wars in the Carolinas in the early eighteenth century.) In addition, the inland tribes, in an effort to increase the range of the American bison, burned large areas of Ohio, Pennsylvania, and New York. Bison were habituated as far east as central New York, which is why Buffalo, New York, bears that name; bison frequented the town site, where natural salt licks encouraged them to stay, though the name is lightly disputed to have come from a Seneca man named De-gi-yah-goh, which means "buffalo" in the Seneca language. Much has been said about the "warlike" aspects of the confederacy. But it wasn't any more warlike than other nations or alliances of nations, though it did consolidate its power and expand its territory through armed conflict with neighboring tribes.

It is tempting to think of first contact in the Northeast as the binary story of Pilgrims arriving in New England in the early seventeenth century while the Wampanoag stood by and watched the English sails gradually grow nearer. In reality, contact was varied, complex, and gradual. One must imagine that many tribes—with intricate social networks that followed well-established trade routes and waterways—had heard of Europeans long before they encountered them: the first import to the New World was surely rumor. As it was, English fishing fleets—largely frozen out of the Icelandic cod fishery by Denmark and the northern European Hanseatic League—began plying Newfoundland waters beginning in the early 1500s. They sailed out of Bristol for twenty days until they reached the rich waters off the coast, fished the short summer months, and made the twenty-day journey back. During the weeks that they fished, they landed to replenish their fresh water, to pack fish, and to trade with northern tribes. Breton and Basque fishermen joined the fray, trading knives, cooking vessels, and other goods for food, fresh water, and animal hides. However much reciprocal trade there was in those early years, theft followed closely behind.

Portuguese explorer Gaspar Corte-Real, upon landing in Maine in 1501, captured fifty-seven Mi'kmaq and brought them back to Portugal, where they were sold into slavery. In 1580 an English crew who had landed in Maine found three hundred moose hides in an empty lodge and simply took them. French explorers brought Indians back to France, and in England, three Indians were put on public display, along with hawks and an eagle. In 1614, Thomas Hunt (on the same expedition as John Smith) captured twenty-six Wampanoag and brought them to Spain, where they were sold as slaves. John Smith, of Pocahontas fame, back after the failed Jamestown experiment, was involved in slave raids into New England, where his crew captured a number of Algonquian Indians, all of whom were sold into slavery. Although the English weren't nearly as bad as the Spanish (at least as regards Indian slavery), the actions of northern European explorers and colonists—theft, massacres, slavery—should be remembered.

Still more disastrously, European diseases often arrived well in advance of Europeans and decimated Indian populations even more ruthlessly, especially when paired with slavery. In 1592, well before the Seneca had direct and prolonged contact with Europeans, a measles epidemic spread among the tribe, killing many thousands of the population within a decade. The Pequot and Wampanoag and other New England tribes were laid low by an epidemic of leptospirosis. Between 1616 and 1619, as much as 90 percent of the population of the New England tribes was wiped out. Rather than welcoming Europeans with open arms when the *Mayflower* landed at Plymouth in mid-November 1620, precious few Indians remained alive on the Eastern Seaboard to lift their arms at all. Those who had survived were in turmoil, their homelands shifted and their old alliances and webs of trade arrangements—their very cultures—in tatters. Other tribes, untouched by disease, filled power vacuums. Some tribes ceased to exist at all.

As the Pilgrims and subsequent settlers flooded into New England, the tribes (and some of the settlers) tried to forge alliances and understandings that would benefit them all. But these efforts failed. In the 1630s, when Indian populations had rebounded to some extent, the Pequot launched an all-out war. It was crushed by the Pilgrims, and the remaining Pequot were sold into slavery. John Mason, after attacking a stockade filled with Pequot women and children and setting it on fire, wrote that God "laughed his Enemies and the Enemies of his People to scorn making [the Pequot] as a fiery Oven. . . . Thus did the Lord judge among the Heathen, filling [Fort Mystic] with dead Bodies." The Pequot were exterminated not only from the land but from memory: uttering the tribe's very name was forbidden. By 1890, all Indian lands in coastal New England had long since been expropriated, and most remaining Indians had been assimilated into other tribes, relocated, or exterminated. Most, but not all. Wampanoag, Mashantucket, Mi'kmaq, Abenake, and others made peace and endured. As in the Southeast, total war had not yielded total extermination. Indians remained.

The Great Lakes and Ohio River Valley

The Great Lakes region—including the Ohio River valley, the area around the lakes themselves, and the Mississippi basin up to the edge of the Great Plains—was home to some of the bloodiest fighting and also some of the most aggressive and effective Indian resistance to colonization on the entire continent.

Our present mapmaking turns the lakes into a border between the United States and Canada, an upper limit, rather than the crossroads that they were. Moving from south to north, the Mississippi River and its twin tributaries—the Missouri and the Ohio, draining the west and east, respectively—point like a trident at the belly of the lakes. The lakes themselves draw water from as far west as northern Minnesota and bring it all the way to the ocean. To the north of the lakes, great rivers like the Rainy, Hayes, Severn, and Albany feed north into Hudson Bay and beyond into the Arctic. Seen this way, the Great Lakes and the land that rises on their northern and southern flanks are the confluence of a vast network of waterways. For Indians as far back as the Paleolithic they were the hub of the New World.

Migrating waterfowl, fish, and game have followed these waterways since the end of the last North American ice age twelve thousand years ago. The earliest Native peoples, who lived alongside the game on which they depended, used these waterways, too. By the beginning of the Woodland period in 500 BCE there was a vast cultural and technological network that followed the water, spreading knowledge along with the cultures that carried it. The use of the bow and arrow, pottery, plant domestication, architecture, and burial practices flowed from the Gulf of Mexico all the way up to north of Lake Ontario and back again. In the various climates found in this vast and fecund area native plants, including gourds, sumpweed, goosefoot, sunflower, knotweed, little barley, and maygrass, were cultivated long before the arrival of corn and beans. In the Middle Woodland period, what is known as the Hopewell culture (also called the Hopewell complex or Hopewell exchange network) arose. The Hopewell cultures typically made their homes in or near oxbows and floodplains that seasonally replenished rich planting grounds, aquatic food sources, and waterfowl. The villages could reach significant size and were surrounded by mounds of all shapes and sizes that were one of the hallmarks of the culture. The Hopewell Ceremonial Earthworks near Chillicothe, Ohio, for example, measures 1,254 feet long and connects thirty-eight mounds within an earthen rectangle measuring more than one hundred acres.

Most, but not all, mounds contained burials of staggering richness. (The purpose of many effigy mounds—like the Great Serpent Mound, southeast of Chillicothe, Ohio, the largest effigy mound in the world— remains unknown or, at the least, hotly debated among archaeologists.) The mounds themselves were constructed using large poles that supported a thatched roof. The deceased were placed inside the shelter and buried with an abundance of trade goods. In Ohio some mounds were found to contain thousands of freshwater pearls, mica, tortoise shells, Knife River flint (from North Dakota), and conch (from Mexico). The finds indicate that these communities were both well-off and well-connected. Around the burial structure, heaps of animal bones suggest that the dead were feasted in fine fashion by their relatives. After the feasting, the gathered goods were burned down and covered over with earth. Along with larger villages and greater economic and caloric security came an explosion in artistic expression. Hopewell Indians were expert carvers. One burial mound at the Mound City site in Ross County, Ohio, contained more than two hundred intricately carved smoking pipes.

But around 500 CE, the Hopewell exchange network, along with the large villages and the mound building, disappeared. So did the artwork. Populations seem to have gone into decline. No one knows why, exactly. Trade and commerce brought goods from all over the continent, but they might also have brought war: some villages from the end of the period were bounded by moats and wooden palisades. The climate grew colder, which may have made game grow scarce. Likewise, improvements in hunting technology may have caused a collapse in animal populations. Agriculture itself may have been a culprit: as of 900 CE, maize and beans were well established throughout the region, and the rise of agriculture could have generated a shift in social organization. Much later, the Mississippian period, from 1100 to 1541 CE, saw the advent of the bow, small projectile points, pottery, and a shift from gathering to intensive agriculture. Large villages replaced small seasonal camps. The largest Mississippian village was surely Cahokia, which was at its peak around 1050–1250 CE, situated at the confluence of the Mississippi and Missouri Rivers near present-day St. Louis, spreading over five square miles and with a population estimated to reach thirty thousand. One burial site there contained twenty thousand shell beads, another eight hundred arrowheads. That, too, went into decline and was abandoned. Whatever the cause, by the time Europeans arrived in the region in the mid–

seventeenth century, Cahokia and similar settlements had been long abandoned.

While tribes in the Southeast, Southwest, and Northeast were involved in countless local struggles (and not a few large ones) with the Spanish, English, Dutch, and French, Indians west of the Appalachians had at first only fleeting contact with the newcomers. But as happened elsewhere, harbingers arrived first, in the form of trade goods and disease. Some of this arrived with waves of tribal newcomers as refugees from the coastal groups headed inland, sparking territorial conflicts well west of the Atlantic even before Europeans set foot in the contested territories. The political disruptions caused by masses of refugees were compounded by disruptions to seasonal hunting and gathering cycles brought on by disease. The time and energy it took to weave nets, knap spear and arrow points, set traps, spear fish, and weave material was lost to war, illness, and death. Native technologies had already evolved that were well suited to the worlds of the Indians who invented them, yet what was wanting were specialists to make and use that technology. European knives were no better at cutting. European axes were no better at felling. In the chaos of the times, it became expedient to trade for them rather than to make them. The increased reliance on European trade goods in turn caused more geopolitical conflict.

In times of upheaval as in times of strife and instability, the region was defined by its prehistoric routes and cultures. Jacques Cartier, exploring the Gulf of Saint Lawrence in the 1530s and early 1540s, did ship-side trading with Natives there, exchanging knives and kettles and the like for fur used in trim—unaware of the wealth waiting to be extracted from the Pays d'en Haut (Upper Country) in the form of beaver pelts. According to Cartier, the Indians he met "made frequent signs to us to come on shore, holding up to us some furs on sticks. . . . They bartered all they had to such an extent that all went back naked without anything on them; and they made signs to us that they would return on the morrow with more furs." Basque fishermen—present since the 1490s—became deeply enmeshed in the beaver trade. Seasonal fishermen, operating on the Grand Banks as early as

1512, traded metal items for beaver furs, which would be sewn into robes to keep the sailors warm during their endeavors and then be sold back in France. It wasn't long before beaver fur's unique felting qualities dramatically increased European demand for it (the barbed strands clung to one another with extraordinary strength). This led to an increased focus on exploration into the Gulf of Saint Lawrence, and the returning reports of a vast continent loaded with furs and Indians eager to trade drove Europeans deeper still into the interior, with a predictable increase in conflict.

The Iroquois Confederacy maintained a stranglehold on travel into the interior via the Great Lakes waterways, which meant, in the middle to late sixteenth century, control over all the trade in the region. Unlike the loosely affiliated Algonquian tribes and nonaffiliated Iroquoian tribes such as the Huron, they had access to trade goods: metal traps, kettles, axes, blankets, guns, shot, powder, and knives. Such items conferred a decided military advantage, and between the end of the sixteenth century and the full blossoming of the fur trade, the Iroquois were engaged in endless wars of advantage with their tribal neighbors to the east. They also managed to negotiate punitive trade deals with the French along the Saint Lawrence and the English down the Hudson.

The tribes to the west of the Iroquois were numerous and powerful but spread out over a vast territory. They included the Shawnee, Odawa, Potawatomi, Ojibwe, Sac, Fox, Menominee, Ho-Chunk (Winnebago), Osage, Miami, Dakota, Cree, Mandan, Arikara, Hidatsa, and Huron (to name but a few). With the exception of the Huron, who lived in large agricultural settlements on the north side of Lake Ontario and later near Georgian Bay and whose population numbered 20,000 to 40,000 or more, western Great Lakes tribes were broken into small mobile villages of around 150 to 300 people, organized by kinship ties. These were the Indians of storybook legend: plying the vast woodlands in birchbark canoes and treading the hushed forests in moccasins. They were primarily hunter-gatherers, though they, too, grew corn, beans, and squash. More westerly tribes such as the Ojibwe had also begun harvesting and cultivating naturally occurring wild rice—a swampy aquatic plant in the oat family that provided a very stable and nutrient-rich food source.

In 1608, Samuel de Champlain (the "father of New France") pushed deeper into the Saint Lawrence and landed at the site that would become Quebec. As historian Michael McDonnell notes, Quebec was less a colony of settlement than the site of a warehouse and trading factory. Trading posts or factories—which in no way resembled factories as we know them—were combination free-trade zones, consulates, military garrisons, and settlements. European and American goods would be brought there, while Indian trade goods (usually furs and buckskin) were brought from the interior. The factory would be run by a "factor," essentially a trader, and staffed with other traders who worked under him, along with crafts-men with needed skills, such as blacksmiths and tanners.

The hope at Quebec was to catch furs coming out of the northland and thereby bypass the British to the east and the Spanish creeping up the Mis-sissippi from the south. The French mode of settlement was for Indians in many ways preferable to that of the British and the Spanish. Instead of following a pattern of conquest, subjugation, settlement, and displace-ment, the French, preferring to trade rather than to settle, were much more inclined to adapt to the new country and its inhabitants. The new outpost was deep in Indian country, and to survive it needed the help of its neighbors. The French began trading with the Huron: metal goods and guns in exchange for stores of surplus corn. The Huron maintained good trade relations with their Algonquian neighbors, the Odawa and Ojibwe, so that, while they themselves did not have access to furs, they had access to and good relations with those who did. A year after Champlain landed at Quebec, the Huron were trading with the French vigorously, then trad-ing with the Odawa and Ojibwe in turn. It wasn't long, however, before Champlain recognized that in order to get premium northern furs (and at a better price), he had to deal directly with the Odawa and Ojibwe.

As they say: Location, location, location. At this time the Odawa and Ojibwe (Anishinaabe) were located around Michilimackinac, which sat at the straits that separated Lake Michigan from Lake Huron, a day's paddle from the outlet of Lake Superior and perhaps the most strategically im-portant location in North America at that time. Control the straits and you controlled travel and trade for the majority of the continent. The location also suited the cultural prerogatives of kinship unique to the Algonquians of the region: they were principally exogamous and had a very well developed clan system. Children took the clan of their fathers and typically married out of their village into nearby villages and even other tribes. The son would move out of his family's home and into that of his wife, bringing with him his clan and sense of relatedness. As a result, "family" became a large thing indeed and pulled populations of mobile and separate tribes into incredibly durable and mutually beneficial relationships over great distances. This well-woven network was an incredible boon in times of war and matters of trade. Moreover, Michilimackinac offered access to reliable food sources. The lakes in all directions mitigated the effects of latitude with a microclimate that allowed for corn production well north of its usual limit and supported an incredible diversity of plants and trees. Ash, oak, maple, elm, spruce, cedar, and white pine grew in profusion. The fall spawn of whitefish was said to be so intense that one could walk across the straits on the backs of the spawning fish. Villages tended to be seasonal and small—groups of usually no more than 150 relatives who lived in largely single-family wigwams, made from saplings driven into the ground and bent and tied together into a dome shape, then covered with woven reeds, cedar bark, birchbark shingles, or elm bark. These populations shifted between winter hunting grounds, spring fishing sites, sugar bush, and summer berrying locations. In summer, when insects were at their worst, villages shifted to high bluffs or rocky promontories to catch the breeze. In winter, when temperatures dropped below zero, as in the Northeast, families often consolidated into larger oblong wigwams or lodges to conserve resources and heat.

In this way the Great Lakes Indians made the most of their homelands in the heart of the heartland. They also had the benefit of timing: they were there at the beginning of the seventeenth century, when the fur trade blossomed into the first—and for centuries the most important—global industry. Their strong position allowed the allied Anishinaabe tribes (Odawa, Ojibwe, Potawatomi) to pressure the French to supply more than trade goods if they were going to be suffered to stay in the Pays d'en Haut. In 1609, they coerced the French into joining them in war parties against the Iroquois Confederacy, who were a constant threat on the southeastern flank of the Great Lakes. And so began a well-regulated pattern of trade.

By the late seventeenth century the Anishinaabe allowed the French to build forts and trading posts as far north and west as Michilimackinac itself, sustaining a seasonal cycle of trade in Indian lands. The French followed Ojibwe and Odawa trade terms and their cultural protocols for feasting and gift-giving. When they failed to comply or tried to dictate new terms, the Anishinaabe would court the British and trade with them until the French fell back in line. With such leverage, the fate of the Great Lakes Indians came to differ radically from that of Indians in tribal homelands everywhere else in North America. Even during the French and British conquest of the Great Lakes, and disease notwithstanding, the population of Algonquian tribes such as the Odawa, Ojibwe, and Potawatomi boomed, quadrupling between 1600 and 1800. The land base of the northern Algonquians expanded by a factor of twenty. Material culture, arts, and religion flourished. The strategic alliances and balance of power that inspired this "golden age" were nowhere more in evidence than in the attack at Pickawillany in 1752.

The French, after early successes in the seventeenth century, had been losing (globally and in North America) to the British. Piankashaw chief Memeskia, having grown dissatisfied with French trade goods and the French themselves, formed an intertribal coalition and began attacking the French. Many disaffected bands and individuals joined him. They formed a village at Pickawillany (at present-day Piqua, Ohio). They welcomed the British and allowed them to build a garrison and trading post nearby. Memeskia was becoming formidable, and his pan-Indian alliances threatened the balance among European powers so crucial to continued Indian control of the Great Lakes. If the British and French were kept wrong-footed, neither could consolidate their power and expand. With that in mind, the Anishinaabe played to their strengths and engaged in some furious diplomacy with their allies and their enemies. They warned the British that they were going to attack them in a general war. And they traveled from Michilimackinac by canoe to meet with the Onondaga Iroquois far to the east. The Iroquois Confederacy claimed the land in Ohio as their own, but they were in a tough place: they were allied with the British, and the British were trading and working with Memeskia. They gave the Algonquians their tacit blessing to remove Memeskia and his people, saying that they would "not permit any Nation to establish posts there; the Master of Life has placed us on that territory, and we alone ought to enjoy it, without anybody having the power to trouble us there." In other words, they would not clear out the offenders, but they gave the Algonquians leave to do so.

In the winter of 1751–1752, Charles Langlade, a young mixed-race Odawa-French leader, began assembling a war party of Odawa, Potawatomi, and Ojibwe warriors who traveled by canoe south to Detroit and then upriver and over land to Pickawillany. They attacked the village in mid-morning on June 21, 1752, when the women were in the fields, and killed thirteen Miami men and captured five English traders. The survivors of the first assault fled back to a rough stockade, where Langlade and the Anishinaabe warriors fired on them for the better part of the day. Eventually the Miami, down to twenty or so warriors and low on water, tried to negotiate terms of surrender. Langlade said he wanted submission, not defeat, and said the survivors could leave if they promised to return home and if they handed over the English. The Miami failed, however, to honor the agreement, sending out only three of the five Englishmen. When they reached Langlade's lines his men set on one of them, "stabbed him to death, scalped him, and ripped his heart out. They ate it in front of the defenders." Then they seized Memeskia himself. They ordered the remaining defenders to stand and watch as they "killed, boiled, and ate Memeskia in front of his family and kinsmen." Afterward, they released the Miami women they had captured and left for Detroit with the four captured Englishmen and more than $300,000 (in today's money) of trade goods. This frontier victory against the English set off the First Anglo-Indian War, helped to ignite the French and Indian War, and was one of the sparks that began the worldwide conflagration known as the Seven Years' War.

Whatever balance had been reestablished between the French and British in this region was lost during the Seven Years' War, after which, for all intents and purposes, the French ceased to be a force in the New World. This left the British, who could be played off against the colonists only until the Revolutionary War, after which the Americans remained the sole colonial force in the Great Lakes region. This was the worst possible outcome for the Indians there. With the fur trade drawing to a close (by the mid-1800s the beaver was extinct east of the Mississippi), the Americans were free to force Great Lakes tribes into punitive treaties that reduced their territories, confined many to reservations, relocated others to Indian Territory (in what is now Oklahoma), and further eroded Indian influence. But while it lasted, the power of the Great Lakes tribes was immense, if under-acknowledged. In part this is because these tribes, while they killed many French and English, didn't engage in outright war with the new Americans. The cultural habit of negotiation (even from positions of relative powerlessness) persisted through the treaty period of 1830–1865. For this reason, as of 1891, Odawa, Potawatomi, Ho-Chunk, Oneida, Meskwaki, and Ojibwe tribes remained in their homelands around the Great Lakes in the same geographical range they had at the height of their power.

The Southwest

It is tempting to think of the Southwest of a piece—generically hot, arid, and rocky (if blessed with some stunning views). In reality the area between western Texas and eastern California, bounded by the Rio Grande to the south and the Cimarron River in the north (comprising the land from present-day Needles, California, east through Arizona, New Mexico, southern Nevada and Utah, to far-west Texas and Oklahoma, and including southern Colorado and southwest Kansas) is not an environment as much as a collection of radically different landscapes that supported four major prehistoric cultures and are the homelands, still, of a radical diversity of modern tribal people.

Around 2,300 years ago a small band of wanderers traveled north through the Sonoran Desert and settled on the Gila River, about thirty miles from modern-day Phoenix. They built small single-family dwellings of branches and mud and promptly began digging canals that siphoned off the river a few miles upstream. They planted the seeds they had most likely brought with them. The canals they dug would be in use for more than a thousand years. These were people who knew what they were doing. This first village is known as Snaketown because of the preponderance of those creatures and their images in the artifacts found there. The village grew (some estimates suggest its population swelled to as much as two thousand), and other satellite villages grew up near it, connecting their own canals with Snaketown's until, within a couple hundred years, the entire flatlands between the Gila and Salt Rivers were laced with them, providing irrigation to upward of a hundred thousand acres, on which they grew corn, cotton, tepary, sieva, jack beans, warty squash, and agave. The Hohokam, as the people were called, were master cultivators and seem to be the first not to simply harvest agave but to cultivate it on unirrigated ground to supplement their wetter crops. Contrary to the myth of the desert as more or less "the great empty," it was a homeland that supported an incredible number of species, including sixty mammal species (mule deer, bears, jaguars, jackrabbits, cottontails, ground squirrels, wolves, gray fox, and javelina among them), three hundred fifty bird species, twenty different amphibians, more than a hundred reptile species, thirty native fish, at least two thousand plant species, and, rather shockingly, a thousand different species of bees. By 750 CE the Hohokam peoples had evolved cultures that created incredibly ornate pottery, ever more complex ceremonies, and ball courts half the size of football fields next to their ever higher ceremonial structures, which were indeed not unlike the football stadiums and churches that would rise up in the American heartland some twelve hundred years later. But just as quickly as it arose, the Hohokam culture fell. Around 1450 CE, Snaketown was possibly burned and then abandoned, and other major Hohokam sites were abandoned as well. It is unclear why—warfare? drought? disease?—but the Hohokam scattered into small bands and found new lands and new ways of life. According to oral tradition, they became the Tohono O'odham (People of the Desert) and the Akimel O'odham (People of the River) in the region that is now Arizona. The O'odham were variously at odds with the Apache and other regional tribes but suffered the most under Spanish rule, beginning in the sixteenth century.

The prehistoric Mogollon culture of southern Arizona and New Mexico and much of northern Mexico was another ancient society that emerged from the desert, as foragers and hunters transformed into agrarians. The earliest Mogollon villages were small hamlets clustered in the mountainous region on what is now the Arizona–New Mexico border. At first they comprised a handful of pit houses—dwellings dug into the ground and roofed at ground level with beams, branches, and earth. With the region's much greater precipitation than the Sonoran Desert, less energy needed to be expended on irrigation. As food security increased through agriculture, so did the material and architectural culture of the Mogollon. Some evidence suggests that this borderland between deserts became a kind of multicultural zone, with early Indians arriving in traveling bands from the east, south, and west. After half a millennium, the pit houses gave way to freestanding structures of earth and adobe and, later, complex fortified cliff dwellings like those found at Cueva de las Ventanas. A subset of the Mogollon culture, known as Mimbres, seems to have evolved vibrant ceremonial traditions, as evidenced by the remains of a unique (and arguably the most beautiful) pottery tradition, typified by striking black-on-white geometric and animal shapes, including hummingbirds, fish, snakes, and other flora and fauna of southeastern Arizona and southwestern New Mexico. But around 1400 CE, like the Hohokam, the Mogollon culture vanished, although the people certainly did not. Villages were burned or abandoned. Cliff dwellings were no longer occupied. The western Pueblo (Zuni and Acoma) as well as the Hopi trace their ancestry to the Mogollon.

The most dramatic of the prehistoric southwestern "supercultures" was probably that of the Anasazi, whose homeland was the Four Corners area of Arizona, New Mexico, Colorado, and Utah, a rocky, canyon-scoured landscape of indescribable beauty. "Anasazi" is a Diné (Navajo) word meaning "Enemies of the Old Ones," though apart from the fact that the word is anglicized and should more properly be spelled and pronounced "Násaazí" and given a more nuanced translation, as a name it makes no sense: the Diné came on the scene only after the fall of the Anasazi. The Hopi name for the Anasazi, Hisatsinom, means "Ancestors," and the Diné name makes greater sense as a reflection of the long-standing friction between the two groups.

The Násaazí started out much like the Hohokam and Mogollon, as hunter-gatherers who, probably because they ate up all the available game and were introduced to domesticated crops from the south, began farming intensively. By 300 CE the advent of pottery meant better food and seed storage and this in turn fueled an agricultural revolution. In typical immigrant fashion, modest dwellings (pit houses) gave way to what can be seen as a prehistoric middle-class way of life, with complex adobe structures of interconnected rooms accessed by ladders dropped down from roofs. At Chaco Canyon, Mesa Verde, and Bandelier, the Násaazí began work on what would become known as the "stone palaces," great houses that could hold more than five thousand people (though they probably never held more than two thousand at any one time except during large gatherings, most of the rooms being given over to food storage). These rooms were carved out of the rock under overhanging cliffs that offered protection from the weather and from enemies. These multistory palaces, still solid to this day, were also incredibly advanced in terms of ecological engineering. A set of multistory dwellings in Chaco Canyon, Pueblo Bonito, has been deemed "one of the cleverest bits of passive solar architecture anywhere," with efficiency unsurpassed by modern methods. From Chaco Canyon, raised roads of rock thirty feet wide extended hundreds of miles in fanatically straight lines, linking remote villages and agricultural sites. Yet by 1400 CE or so, these beautiful and sophisticated dwellings were abandoned as well. Chaco was abandoned first, in the wake of an extreme drought that struck around 1100; it was followed by Mesa Verde and Bandelier and Pecos Pueblo near Santa Fe. The Násaazí people took what they could carry and migrated along the rivers, settling closer to what water remained and forming the basis for present-day Pueblo peoples including the Hopi, Cochiti, Zia, Santa Ana, San Felipe, Santo Domingo, and Taos.

Around 1200 CE, a wave of Athabascan newcomers arrived in the region who would change the Southwest forever. While the southwestern "supercultures" (Hohokam, Mogollon, and Násaazí) were in full swing, small groups of Athabascan-speaking hunters and gatherers began migrating south from what is now Alaska and British Columbia. They were subarctic peoples, and it is likely that at first they stuck to the ways they knew by hewing to similar climates in the Rocky Mountains while in search of game. As they traveled south over the course of a few centuries, they picked up various skills—pottery making, basket weaving, the use of the bow and arrow—that certainly eased their way. By the time of their arrival in the Southwest between 1300 and 1500 CE, the great culture groups of the region had disbanded and scattered, and the new hunter-gatherers found ample room for settlement, though legend has it that the newly minted Apache (one set of these arrived northerners) fought the Pima (derived from the Hohokam) fiercely and lost. The northerners, having grown and divided and divided again as they moved south, divided themselves still further by settling in different parts of the Southwest. In doing so they came into being as distinct peoples. Those who would become known as the Diné (Navajo) fetched up in the Four Corners area. The future Western Apache (Tonto, Chiricahua, White Mountain) set up on the western side of the Rio Grande, whereas the Mescalero Apache settled between the Rio Grande and the southwestern edge of the Llano Estacado, which straddles northwestern Texas and eastern New Mexico. The Jicarilla Apache settled into northern New Mexico northeast of the Rio Grande. Other Athabascans swung farther east and adapted to the Plains. They would become the Kiowa and Lipan people.

In 1540, when the Spanish first ventured into New Mexico looking for Cibola (one of the fabled Seven Cities of Gold), they found a well-populated, well-demarcated Indian homeland that had been settled for millennia by constantly evolving tribal groups, among them the Diné, Pueblo (who themselves included the Zuni, Acoma, Cochiti, Taos, and more), Pima, O'odham, and Apache. It should be emphasized again that wherever the groups came from or whomever they descended from, they were defined more by their spiritual and cultural genesis in the lands that sustained them than by their wanderings. This sense of identity is reflected, for instance, in the way the Diné speak of themselves as traveling through three worlds only to emerge into this one, the fourth. Their creation story, like all Indian creation stories, is significant not just as folklore, and not just for Native people. Such stories explain how Indian peoples and Indian homelands came to define each other. The Diné recognize that they come from someplace else just as Americans recognize they come from someplace else and likewise became who they are through struggle and loss and hardship. Just as we might recognize that Americans were once French and English or Dutch or Italian, their origins don't invalidate their claim to the country or alter the fact that Indians of all kinds were here before any colonial power, and remain here. It also explains why the Spanish, when they did come, were met by Indians ready to protect their homelands.

Of all the colonial powers that came to America, the Spanish have the worst reputation, and it appears to be earned. When Hernando de Soto staged his entrada into Florida, in addition to soldiers and clergy, he brought attack dogs and blacksmiths to forge chains to control Indian slaves. During his exploits in the Southeast, he demanded that Indians in a town in South Carolina feed his army. The chief, a woman, said they could not because they had lost so many people to disease that they could barely attend to the harvest. She gave him as much food as she could spare and some freshwater pearls. In return, he used his chains on her and many other villagers and hauled them, manacled, west. Later, in 1542, de Soto fell ill on the west bank of the Mississippi. He demanded that Indians on the other side help him cross because he was the "Son of the Sun." Their chief said that if that were true, he could very well just dry up the river and cross that way. De Soto died shortly thereafter.

It was Francisco de Coronado who led the first entrada into New Mexico in 1540, largely on the basis of false reports of gold and riches made by a black former slave named Esteban. Esteban had survived the disastrous Narváez expedition, most of whose members had perished in Florida, and escaped with others by boat, washing up in Galveston Bay. He and the others lived in captivity to coastal Indians in Texas for six years before they escaped and made their way over time, incredibly, to Mexico City. There Esteban and the other survivors told fabulous tales of cities and gold and riches ripe for the plucking. Ever a glutton for punishment, Esteban found a berth in the 1540 Coronado expedition as a guide. On a recon mission to scout the way for Coronado's thrust, he and a band of Mexican Indians arrived at a Zuni village named Hawikuh. The Zuni seem to have been waiting for them, having drawn a line of cornmeal on the ground. Esteban stepped over it and demanded food, turquoise, and women. The Zuni withdrew to consider this. After three days they emerged and promptly killed Esteban. The others escaped to inform Coronado, who arrived at Hawikuh the following year. He, too, was greeted by a line of cornmeal on the ground, with more than two hundred warriors on the other side of it and a warning not to cross.

Coronado had been ordered to explore and take possession of land in the north but not to harm Indians—after four decades in the New World even the Spanish recognized that their prior treatment of Indians had been horrific. Nonetheless, he charged. The Zuni fought but lost and scattered to the mountains to rejoin their families. Coronado stayed in Hawikuh for five months, during which time his army ate all the Zunis' corn and other vegetables and their domesticated turkeys. The Zuni, anxious to be rid of Coronado, told him the Hopi had more wealth than they did. And so the story repeated itself throughout the Southwest as Coronado "explored" his way east and up the Rio Grande past Santa Fe, with a detachment going as far north as Taos, a region over time almost continuously inhabited by Pueblo people settled in their neat villages, surrounded by lush fields and cottonwoods. Informed by his Native guide that there was gold to the east, Coronado made it as far as the Plains and saw the then-limitless herds of bison. But no gold. He executed his guide and returned to New Mexico. In 1580, Spanish explorers reached the Diné near Mount Taylor. The Diné asked that some of their people, stolen by the Hopi and in turn by the Spanish, be returned. The Spanish refused. A battle ensued.

Although there were no Seven Cities of Gold to be found, the Spanish persisted. In 1600 the first real attempts at settlement took place. At Acoma Pueblo in 1598, Juan de Zaldívar, nephew of the Spanish expeditionary leader Juan de Oñate, demanded food. The Indians refused. The Spanish attacked. Twelve of the Spaniards were killed. Two escaped. The Spanish returned in force and killed more than eight hundred Acoma Pueblo Indians and enslaved the rest. Every man over the age of twenty-five had his right foot cut off.

Spanish settlers moved into land bordering the Pueblos, but when they could not make it fertile—it was bare and dry, with hardly enough forage for sheep and horses—they began encroaching on Pueblo land. The Franciscans who were there to convert Indians didn't behave much better. They conscripted Indian labor and forced the Indians to build the missions while at the same time whipping Indian spiritual leaders, smashing idols and ceremonial objects, and banning dances and ceremonies as devil worship. This was the face of Spanish settlement: slavery, subjugation, and extermination.

Over the 150 years after first contact, the Pueblo, Pima, Diné, Apache, and (later) Tohono O'odham were buffeted by settlers, the Church, and the Spanish military—and increasingly by one another. The introduction of horses and sheep had a profound effect on intertribal relations. By the late seventeenth century, smaller tribes were being raided regularly by mounted Apache and Diné. Pueblo people in turn raided the Diné. Diné took Hopi slaves. The Hopi took their own. For the first time wealth—in the form of cattle and sheep—could be captured and kept.

In 1675, the Spanish military, along with the Franciscans there, publicly whipped forty-seven Pueblo ceremonial leaders. Four of them died and the rest were imprisoned temporarily. The atrocity brought home to the Pueblo people, forcefully and finally, that the Spanish colonial presence in the Southwest was an assault on their way of life. Although there had been small, sporadic revolts in the 150 years that the Spanish had been raping Indian homelands and Indians themselves, this event precipitated the largest and most successful resistance to Spanish rule yet seen. Within days of their release, one of the leaders—Popé from San Juan Pueblo—returned home and began plotting in concert with other Pueblo leaders. This entailed uniting dozens of communities with vast cultural differences (exogamous, endogamous; matrilineal, patrilineal; all corn-centered, but with radically different methods of agriculture and rituals). Popé met with other leaders in secret, often under cover of chaotic feast days and other celebrations. They carefully weeded out potential snitches, including Popé's own son-in-law. On August 12, 1680, they struck.

Sweeping down from the north, they attacked haciendas and settlements, killing men, women, and children. They attacked the hateful Franciscans as well, destroying churches and altars and sometimes smearing feces on religious icons. The Spanish settlers fled from all directions and gathered in the walled plaza adjacent to the governor's mansion in Santa Fe. For the next few days, Pueblo Indians continued to attack the plaza, loosing arrows and throwing rocks. They diverted the Santa Fe River away from the plaza, thereby depriving the colonists of water. The Spanish sallied out in a "heroic" attempt to break free. They killed some Pueblo Indians, captured some water, and retreated to the plaza. After a week or so the situation was once again desperate. This time their exodus met with no resistance. The Pueblo watched them go, having accomplished what they wanted: the departure of the Spanish.

The few Spanish survivors traveled down to what is now Juárez to regroup. They wouldn't return for twelve years. When they did, they would never again assume their superiority over the Indian people of the Southwest. It should be noted that today Indian artisans from all over the Southwest gather on the weekends to sell their work under the portico of the plaza: the Indians are still there. And while their descendants remain, the Spanish crown and government do not.

Meanwhile, over to the west, in Arizona, the Jesuits rather than the Franciscans made contact with and settled in among the Tohono O'odham and Pima. The Jesuits employed an entirely different method of colonization through conversion than did the Franciscans. They did not, as a rule, conscript Indians to build missions or cut off their feet or whip them publicly. Instead, they brought livestock and seed. They learned the Indian languages of the region and even seemed to enjoy the company of the people they were intent on converting. A kinder, gentler sort of assault, but an assault nonetheless. The Spanish remained in the Southwest, though they never expanded farther north and west than Santa Fe and Tucson. The northern tribes—Hopi, Diné, and Apache—were too strong. The Spanish had to content themselves with pushing west to California.

Over the next 150 years, although the Spanish exerted less (and more cautious) influence, other forces they had set in motion came into play. The horse, which they had loosed upon the Plains and in the Southwest, changed life in those regions forever. Formerly scattered and relatively small bands of Apache, Comanche, and Ute became mobile, richer, and, as a result, larger. No longer was the struggle in the Southwest merely binary—with the Indians, collectively, on one side and the invaders on the other. Now the region was formed by shifting alliances of some Pueblo people with the Spanish to hold off the Comanche, and the Tohono O'odham and Pima acting as buffers between the Apache and the Spanish. The Diné and Hopi, despite fighting on and off with each other, effectively kept the Spanish at bay.

In the mid-1800s the annexation of Texas and the outcome of the Mexican-American War—culminating in the Gadsden Purchase in 1853—ended Spanish and Mexican control of what we now think of as the Southwest. The centuries-old mix of Native and Spanish cultures that had evolved in Texas, New Mexico, and Arizona came under American rule even if the cultures of the region were not then and are not now what we think of when we say "American culture." And with the Americans came new land grabs and cultural assaults. Still, contrary to the familiar narrative of erasure, wherein tribes (lumped together) were gradually reduced to nothingness by successive waves of first European and then American power, this history tells a more complicated and accurate story: tribes charted different courses and in the process embraced different fates.

The Pueblos of the Rio Grande and the Hopi, for example, allied themselves with the United States against northern raiders, principally the Apache and Comanche. And in 1848 the United States recognized Spanish land grants and included those made to the Pueblos by the Spanish. As such the Pueblo weren't coded (or treated politically) as Indians. This meant that much of the Pueblo homelands remained intact. So, too, did their governmental and ceremonial structures, a combination of

chiefhood, representative democracy, and clan systems. Not that this ensured that Pueblo ways of life were respected by the United States government. The government built a boarding school to educate Hopi children
in 1887, but most of the Hopi wanted to have nothing to do with it: they
could see that it meant being severed from their children and allowing
their children to be severed from Hopi life. Nevertheless, the U.S. government prevailed, by arresting the parents and holding them hostage until
the children were sent to the school.

The Diné suffered horribly. By the time the Americans began administering the Southwest in 1848, the Diné and Apache were well horsed and
numerous. They killed the village-bound Pueblo and mestizo New Mexicans regularly. For their part, the Pueblo and New Mexicans raided and
killed the Diné and stole women and children to sell into slavery. The trade
on which the Athabascans had come to rely had largely dried up, and in the
context of the Spanish-inflicted amputations and conscriptions, this was
not an extraordinary escalation of patterns of conflict that had long existed. When the Americans arrived, they began grazing their horses and
livestock on the homelands of the Apache and Diné, tried to force the Diné
into punitive treaty arrangements, and in countless ways attempted to impose their will on an already fraught cultural and political landscape. Attempts to negotiate with the Diné were also complicated by the lack (or at
least the apparent lack) of a centralized government. Different clans and
bands of Diné took their own counsel, and there was no single government,
much less a spokesperson, for the thousands of Diné living within the borders of their four sacred mountains. In 1846 and again in 1849 the U.S.
government sent military detachments into Dinétah to sign treaties. The
treaties were signed both times, but they were not recognized by the bands
and leaders not present at the signings. To make matters worse, Narbona,
a prominent Diné leader intent on establishing peace between the Diné and
the Americans, was killed en route to one of the signings, and further
bloodshed resulted. The Diné resisted. The Americans pushed back by
building forts in the Diné homelands. The forts were attacked and burned.

In 1863 the military launched a series of campaigns against the Diné
meant to bring them into the embrace of the United States by force. Led

and masterminded by Kit Carson, the military eschewed direct conflict or battles (this would become a signature of U.S. military action in the Southwest and, later, on the Plains). Instead, they systematically destroyed flocks and crops wherever they were encountered. The Diné called this "the fearing time." They could perhaps flee and hide, but their corn, orchards, and sheep could not. Many Diné surrendered until only some holdouts were left, who made Canyon de Chelly their "last stand." There they persisted for weeks while Carson and his militia destroyed century-old peach trees and orchards in the canyon—a wound that, for the Diné, has not yet healed. Once these last fighters were captured, all the Diné were marched to Bosque Redondo, three hundred miles away in eastern New Mexico, for resettlement. Bosque Redondo had sustenance for only half the number of Indians who arrived. It was scant on wood for fuel and shelter and watered by an alkaline river that caused intestinal disease. And it was peopled by Mescalero Apache, longtime enemies of the Diné. It was, in short, a hell. Smallpox arrived, taking even more lives. The relocation was, even according to the government, a failure. After five hard years, the Diné were able to return to a portion of their homelands to live a version of the lives they had lived before they were marched to "the suffering place."

By 1891, just after the massacre at Wounded Knee, life was hard in the Southwest. But there was life. Village structure (as well as ceremonial and political structures) persisted for the Pueblos. The Diné were back in their homelands, much the poorer but still in possession of the land within the four sacred mountains. The Apaches were largely where they had first made their homelands in Arizona and New Mexico, though their territory had shrunk drastically. The Tohono and Akimel O'odham, having passed between the warring Spanish on one side and the northern raiders on the other, remained in Arizona. Elsewhere in the United States tribes had largely been displaced or decimated, or had persisted only as islands in the stream of settlement. But in the Southwest tribes did much more than that. With every wave of immigration—Spanish, Mexican, American— they shaped the culture and fabric of the place, so much so that to be in the Southwest is to feel the continued lived presence of Native America to a degree not found in most other homelands in the United States.

California

Nearby, in California, a wholly different history unfolded. Among the most brutal and bloody treatment of any people anywhere on the globe played out in one of the most beautiful landscapes and Indian homelands ever to greet the eye.

Spanish explorer Juan Cabrillo left from Navidad, Mexico, in 1542, determined to round the Baja cape and explore what we now know is the west coast of North America. He, like other Spanish explorers before and after, was spurred to find "cities of gold," a passage to the Indies, and the Northwest Passage.

Cabrillo had served under Cortés in Mexico and had become one of the richest conquistadors in service when he discovered and mined gold in Honduras and Guatemala. He was also one of the cruelest and most bloodthirsty. While there he broke up Indian families, sending the men to work in the gold mines or to harvest timber for shipbuilding, and selling the children and women, or giving them to his soldiers for their pleasure.

Cabrillo rounded Baja and landed in what is now San Diego Bay on September 28. He continued on to Catalina Island and then to Santa Monica Bay. In each place he stopped he was greeted by Indians. He noted that there was little material wealth among them—no large cities, not even any form of agriculture. He traveled the coast and engaged in an orgy of naming. San Miguel. San Salvador. Baya de los Fumos. Cabo de Pinos. His expedition made it to far northern California before turning back because of storms. Cabrillo decided to overwinter on Catalina Island (San Salvador). Around Christmas, while under attack by Tongva Indians, he slipped and fell, breaking his leg. The leg became infected, and gangrene set in. He died without really recognizing California for the paradise it was.

At the time of contact, it is estimated, more Indians lived in California than in the rest of the United States combined. There were more than five hundred distinct tribes, who spoke three hundred dialects of one hundred different languages. From San Diego Bay inland to the Mohave and Colorado deserts, north through the Central Valley, the Sierras, and the timbered, rocky lands of northern California, the region was more densely settled than any area north of southern Mexico—more densely settled than most places in Europe at the time, for that matter. Indian people had called the place home for more than seventeen thousand years. Tribes themselves were small, rarely consisting of more than a hundred members. They made the most of the abundant aquatic food supply, evidenced by shell middens many meters deep on Catalina Island. Further inland, game was plentiful—elk, grizzly bear, deer, and bison. Food was so plentiful that once a tribe had carved out its own small territory it rarely left. Yet contrary to what Cabrillo and subsequent explorers noted, the Indians of California did practice agriculture by encouraging low-intensity fires, which in turn facilitated the loose rotation of crops such as nuts, berries, and yucca: a form of permaculture that suited the now unimaginable resources of the region. Basketry and canoe making were both high art and utilitarian endeavors.

Change came, but not quickly: California was at the farthest point in North America from Spain. No sources of easily identifiable or exploitable wealth were discovered during the contact period. The eastern topography of California effectively isolated it from the rest of North America. Named after a mythical island in a Spanish novel said to be populated by beautiful black women who kept griffins as pets and fed any men who ventured there to them, California effectively was an island in terms of contact, utility, and exploration. It was a place apart until the late sixteenth century.

By 1565 the Spanish had engaged in a lucrative trade with China. Spanish ships would sail from China loaded with spices and silk, stop over in the Philippines, and then aim east for northern California. Once there, they used coastal wind and water currents to move south down the coast until they reached Mexico. Reliance on this trade route introduced

European invasive plant species, cattle, and pigs to the rich but fragile Mediterranean climate of California.

It wasn't until the late eighteenth century that the Spanish began trying to colonize and settle California in earnest—both by sailing around Baja and trekking overland from present-day Arizona. These early attempts were disastrous: the Portolá and Anza expeditions between 1769 and 1776 were chronically short of food. Many of the would-be colonists died at sea or along the trail. The survivors reached California only to suffer starvation and disease. Scurvy, in particular, hit them hard. The explorers and the expeditions they led did not, or could not, find a way to work with the Indian food cultures of the region, which did not have at their base intensive agriculture or reliance on staple crops. By comparison, expeditions in the Northeast, Southeast, and Southwest were able to buy, trade, or steal enough food to eat, usually in the form of corn. But the California climate did not support corn despite the availability of the seed from Mexico. Subsequent expeditions, which included Jesuit priests, remedied earlier errors by driving large herds of goats, cows, and sheep with them. This saved their lives but ruined California.

European livestock quickly overgrazed the grasslands. Invasive species took root and displaced native plants. A million acres of land were seized for each mission; they were constructed, along with forts or "presidios," within a day's ride of one another along the Camino Real. Soon, Indians began flocking to them. They came not because they had heard the word of God or recognized the superiority of European ways, but because the ecological disaster that was settlement quickly became a cultural disaster for them. The missions, forts, and stolen land of the invaders became places of refuge from famine.

The missions quickly put this circumstance to use. They forced conversions, conscripted labor, and evolved a system of patronage and control. The Jesuits, with their relatively gentler ways, were recalled to Spain and banned from mission work in the New World. They were replaced with Dominicans and Franciscans, who unleashed the same punitive policies they practiced in the Southwest. When California passed to Mexico as a possession in 1822, it disbanded and secularized the missions but essentially kept the mission system intact, administering it even more poorly than the Spanish had. For the Indians at the missions—now called "ranchos"—there was no other place to go. Often the missions and ranchos covered and controlled all of the Indians' former homelands. Colonial neglect of colonial subjects made conditions even worse for the Indians, who were at the bottom of the social structure. Their working conditions were so poor and disease so rampant that deaths far exceeded births. It is estimated that in 1770 nearly 133,000 Californian Indians lived in and around the missions. In 1832 the number was 14,000. In response to this decline, the religious orders sent out militia to capture new labor, principally women.

Some Indians did try to escape into the interior, away from the coast and away from the missions. But such escapes were the exception: with no food, no support network, no clothing or shelter, escape was most often found in death. Things only got worse after California passed into American control in 1847, and after gold was discovered at Sutter's Mill on January 24, 1848.

When the Gold Rush started, there were about nine thousand non-Indian people in California: six thousand Spanish/Mexican settlers and three thousand Americans, most of whom were settled in the south, not in "Alta California," as the northern portion of the state was known. In 1849 alone, ninety thousand new settlers arrived. The argonauts—as those who came in search of gold were known—came from all over the globe: Argentina, China, the United States, and Europe. Ships, having arrived in San Francisco, were abandoned there as entire crews headed inland. People dragged the ships onto mud flats and used them for saloons, brothels, warehouses, and homes. The Alta was filled with businessmen, prospectors, prostitutes, farmers, and gamblers. In order to support the new population, food was shipped in from Chile, Peru, Hawaii, and Mexico. But it wasn't enough.

The first wave of mining used a technique called "placer mining." Water was sluiced away from streambeds, and these were dug up and sifted in order to catch the loose gold flake and nuggets that had been pried free from ore over eons of erosion. More than 370 tons of gold was mined this way in California in the first five years of the rush. With gold harder and harder to find via placer mining, "hydraulicking," or hydraulic mining, came into play. After that, dredging became the preferred method. The land, already stressed by overgrazing and overpopulation, was damaged further. High-pressure water cannons gouged streambeds and canyons. Streams, rivers, and lakes were stirred into a soup of mud, sediment, and sand. The paradise became a wasteland, and the Indians suffered for it most of all.

In order to open up more land for mining, tribes in the interior were systematically and brutally exterminated. The state of California appropriated funds between 1850 and 1860 to hire militia to hunt down and kill Indians. The militia were reimbursed for the ammunition they used in this pursuit, and the state, in turn, was partially reimbursed by the federal government. The very first governor of California, Peter Burnett, speaking of the genocidal policies of the newest member of the Union, said that it "must be expected" that "a war of extermination will continue to be waged between the two races until the Indian race becomes extinct."

The degree of violence in the "Golden State" can't be overemphasized. An instance: In 1847, near present-day Clear Lake, California, two Anglo settlers, Andrew Kelsey and Charles Stone, had purchased cattle and grazing rights from one Salvador Vallejo. They captured and conscripted almost an entire band of Pomo Indians to work as cowboys on their ranch, forcing them to build their own shelter and promising rations in "compensation." The rations amounted to four cups of wheat per family per day. When one man asked for more wheat to feed his sick mother, Kelsey killed him. In 1849, Kelsey conscripted fifty of the Pomo to accompany him to the placer fields to mine for gold. Kelsey got sick during the expedition and sold all the food to other miners. Of the fifty Pomo who accompanied him, only three made it back to the ranch. Once there Kelsey resumed his rule of terror. Pomo women and girls were brought to the ranch house and raped regularly. When they resisted they were whipped, many of them dying from the punishment.

Facing starvation and systematic rape, torture, and enslavement, the Pomo revolted. One night the women poured water on Kelsey and Stone's gunpowder, rendering it useless. The men attacked at dawn, killing Kelsey with an arrow. Stone ran for the woods, where he was chased down and killed with a rock. The surviving Pomo melted into the forests. A regiment of the U.S. Cavalry under the command of Nathaniel Lyon was sent out to bring the Pomo to "justice." Instead of finding the offenders, the cavalry came upon an entirely different band of Pomo at Clear Lake on May 15, 1850. The men were off hunting. The cavalry attacked, killing more than a hundred Pomo women and children. A six-year-old girl survived by submerging herself in the lake and breathing through a reed for the duration of the massacre. The soldiers killed seventy-five more Pomo along the Russian River in the following weeks. This was only one of many such massacres.

The violence that marked the Indian experience in California, from Spanish conquest on through the mission system, Mexican rule, and into the modern age of statehood, had an even more disastrous effect on the Indians of the region than it might have because of the size of most tribes. Unlike, for example, the Diné, whose numbers were such that they could survive even a brutal relocation and repatriation, in addition to the usual assaults and raids, many of the Californian tribes were too small to make it. Of the many hundreds of tribes extant in California at contact, as of the 1890 census fewer than fifty were counted. This number undoubtedly underrepresented the actual number of bands, reservations, mission groups, communities, and tribes. But it was a far cry from the densely settled multiethnic patchwork that had been the Indian paradise of the region upon discovery.

The Pacific Northwest and Columbian Plateau

S teep folded hills and mountain valleys dropping sharply into the sea. Rivers emptying the plateau and inlands in rapids after rapids, pooling and dropping into the North Pacific surf. Stands of fir, cedar, and, farther inland, oak and cottonwood, rising on every flat and incline. Nearly constant rain encourages rampant growth. The Pacific Northwest is a primeval landscape—fecund and raw, old and ever changing. It is also one of the richest ecosystems in the world, supplying abundant material for food and shelter.

As in other wet places, the prehistory of the region is hard to trace. It is clear that prehistoric Indian people lived along the coast and the western side of the Rockies. The most ancient evidence of coastal settlement dates from around 8000 BCE. Farther inland, evidence is emerging from the Paisley Caves in Oregon that suggests robust settlement as early as 14,500 BCE. But the region was undoubtedly inhabited much earlier.

Evidence of pit houses from 1500 BCE has been found in British Columbia. Stone adzes suggest that wooden structures were also built—the tools remain but the houses have long since vanished. And prehistoric fishing weirs are abundant. Tools made from stone quarried far inland have been found on the coast, which suggests a thriving trade between coastal and highland Indians. Middens and trash pits from this era contain remains of salmon, shellfish, halibut, herring, seal, otter, and beaver and the bones of large inland mammals such as moose, sheep, goat, deer, and bear. As elsewhere, rich food sources led to increased population, which in turn led to war. Skeletal remains of (mostly) young men killed by heavy blows to the upper body suggest warfare with clubs; also in evidence is slat armor made of wood and hide, like that found in the Shang Dynasty in China.

By 500 CE, the cultures of the Northwest Coast were in full swing. The tribes of the region evolved crafts unmatched in beauty and expressiveness. Even the most utilitarian objects—bentwood baskets, boxes, and household items, hand tools, houses, and canoes—were works of art. Implements of war—more and more in number after 500 CE—were ornately carved of stone and whalebone. Villages were carefully constructed with an eye to defense. Perhaps, as with the Europeans who would be arriving shortly, for the tribes of the Northwest there was a direct correlation between art and violence.

Northwest Coast wooden club (Tlingit)

The Europeans came late and were greeted by tribal cultures unlike any others on the continent. In 1500, there was little to no agriculture in the Northwest; all the tribes were primarily hunter-gatherers. But unlike the true hunter-gatherers of the Great Basin, whose climate didn't support or encourage agriculture, the tribes of the Northwest were almost completely sedentary. They lived in large villages with fantastically well-developed architectural traditions—cedar bark–covered longhouses, ornate carvings (including the misnamed "totem poles")—and very well developed hierarchical societies. Kwakiutl culture, for instance, was organized around "houses." These were led by chiefs who claimed descent from mythical personages. Lineages were recounted or sung in the manner of Norse sagas. The chiefs and their moieties owned large houses and also owned the right to use certain songs and display certain ceremonial objects. They also owned the rights to local resources such as fishing, berrying, and hunting grounds, a circumstance that directly contradicts the popular belief that Indians didn't understand private ownership. As we will see, the rhetoric of ownership (*Who can own the land? Who can own the air?*) was meant to question the assumed rights of the invaders rather than the inherent rights of the dispossessed.

Sir Francis Drake was the first European to reach the far Northwest, landing somewhere between northern California and Washington in 1579 and rashly naming the place New Albion before continuing his circumnavigation of the world. Juan de Fuca came next, in 1592, though it is not clear he actually discovered the strait that now bears his name. The major problem that confronted European missions of exploration (and subsequently colonization and settlement) was distance. The Pacific Northwest was just beyond the most attenuated range of ships. Supply and resupply were pretty much insurmountable problems until the late eighteenth century. The Russians, however, may have reached as far south as the Russian River in northern California by the mid-1700s. Russian settlements and trading posts followed but never in great numbers. In the 1780s and early 1790s the Spanish and English—aided by better technology and closer ports—made inroads in the region, often running into each other in sheltered bays. One such meeting, between Esteban José Martinez and British captains near Nootka Sound in 1789, led to the "Nootka Crisis." Both powers were keen to claim the area for themselves, and fierce negotiations took place back in Europe. These seemed to be going nowhere, and both sides were gearing up for war when a series of agreements were reached. The "Nootka Conventions" resolved the dispute, and afterward the Spanish were largely content to remain in the sphere of influence on the southern areas of the coast.

This was a victory for the British. The Spanish were confined mainly to California, while the British had a secure hold on the Northwest from Oregon up to Alaska (as the region was known by Aleuts and, later, by Russian explorers; the word means "object to which the action of the sea is directed"). Shortly thereafter, from 1792 to 1794, George Vancouver traveled and mapped much of the area, from Puget Sound up through the Strait of Georgia and along the coast of what is now British Columbia. The tribes he would have met at the time were numerous, densely packed, and heterogeneous. Along the coast there were the Tlingit, Misga'a, Haida, Gitxsan, Tsimshian, Nuxalk, Heiltsuk, Wuikinuxv, Nuu-chah-nulth, Kwakwaka'wakw, Makah, Coast Salish, Quileute, Willapa, Tillamook, and Chinook, among others. The tribes of the Northwest Plateau, enjoying a different climate and topography, were as numerous: the Kathlamet, Clackamas, Clatsop, Multnomah, Wasco-Wishram, Watlata, Flathead, Nespelem, Okanagan, Coeur d'Alene, Wenatchi, Nez Perce, Umatilla, Yakama, Klickitat, Cayuse, Kootenai, Nisqually, Kalapuya, and Modoc, among others. The tribes of the plateau were less reliant on marine life, though the salmon runs were as important to them as to coastal people. When the horse spread across the Plains in the seventeenth century, tribes like the Nez Perce and Flathead adapted quickly and rode far after bison, elk, and deer.

It would be another seventy-five years after Vancouver's expedition of 1791–1795 for the region to be settled in an aggressive manner. In the meantime the British were keen to buy furs and trade with coastal tribes. In exchange they offloaded smallpox and measles and other diseases. Diseases for which the tribes had no immunity spread quickly in the communal longhouses and through the densely settled villages. By the time Meriwether Lewis and William Clark's Corps of Discovery reached the coast and set up shop near the Tillamook and other tribes around Tillamook Bay, their numbers were greatly reduced. The Corps of Discovery introduced a host of new diseases, including chlamydia and syphilis (though these may already have been present—an example of unintended Russian, British, and American epidemiological potluck). Coastal populations that were around two hundred thousand in 1774 had been reduced to fewer than forty thousand a century later.

With the arrival of the Americans came a new struggle for power between the United States and England. During the War of 1812, the English occupied Fort Astoria at the mouth of the Columbia River when it was clear the Americans wouldn't be able to reinforce it. After the war, the Americans sold their holdings to the English-owned Northwest Company, but after 1818 the two countries agreed to administer the region jointly. In 1853 the first plans were drawn up for the city of Seattle, at the expense of the Duwamish, who lived there. And, as happened in the Upper Midwest and Great Lakes regions, after the furs played out, the timber industry rose in its place. Tribal control of land was further eroded, yet never fully extinguished, by the orgy of treaty making that occurred between 1840 and 1870.

In 1836 two American missionaries—Marcus and Narcissa Whitman—set up shop near present-day Walla Walla. They established a mission, built a gristmill and a school, and introduced the concept of irrigation—all of this for the benefit of the Cayuse people, who had had no need for Jesus, grain cultivation, American-style education, or water. In 1842, Marcus traveled east in order to obtain funding from the American Board of

Commissioners for Foreign Missions. They agreed to help fund and staff the mission, and he returned in 1843 with more than a thousand settlers and prospectors. The settlers roamed freely over Cayuse territory, plowed up the ground, and harvested the food (salmon, game, and berries) on which the Cayuse depended. The Cayuse were stunned that anyone could think the settlers had the right to use their land. Tensions rose. In 1847 a measles epidemic unleashed by the settlers killed more than half the Cayuse. Some sources claim that the disease was attributed by the Cayuse to the "dark magic" of Marcus and Narcissa's god. That's unlikely. The Cayuse blamed Marcus personally for treating settlers (some of whom were also sick) but not the Indians. After hundreds of years of disease and epidemic, everyone (especially those who understood the rhythms of the natural world so well) knew that disease spread by physical contact.

Already upset by encroachment, theft, and settlement, the Cayuse sought to eradicate the source of the plague. They attacked the mission, destroying it and killing the Whitmans and some dozen other settlers. This sparked a war that raged for seven years in the region between the Cascades and the Rocky Mountains. The Oregon Territory raised a number of militias (since no colonial power had control over the region) and did battle with the Cayuse from 1847 to 1850, with neither the militia nor the Cayuse able to get the upper hand. At last, disease, exhaustion, and starvation did the work the militia could not. In order to reach a settlement the Cayuse gave up five of their number to stand trial for the murder of the Whitmans. They were tried by a military commission, found guilty, and hanged. But it was dirty work. One of the men, Kimasumpkin, protested his innocence at length before the trapdoor opened below him, claiming that he had not been present for the attack and had only been told by his chief to come tell what he knew about it. His testimony is painful and sincere: "I was not present at the murder, nor was I any way concerned in it. I am innocent. It hurts me to talk about dying for nothing. . . . The priest says I must die to-morrow. . . . This is the last time that I may speak."

The hasty hanging might have mollified Oregon Territory, but it did nothing to help the Cayuse or their cause. And so the war dragged on for another five years, by which time the Cayuse were all but done in. They agreed to a punitive treaty in 1855, creating the Confederated Tribes of the Umatilla Indian Reservation. The Cayuse War had created new paths, however, even as it erased others. Among other things, it forced the government to realize it could not afford to make war with tribes across the West; it was cheaper to make paper in the form of treaties and let the tide of settlers settle the rest by force of numbers.

In Washington Territory to the north, another war dovetailed with the Cayuse War. Beginning in 1855, Isaac Stevens, governor of Washington Territory, entered into a series of treaties with tribes there, principally the Yakama, guaranteeing them half of the fish in the territory in perpetuity, a large tract of land closed to white settlement, money, and supplies. In exchange the tribes gave up access to and control over the majority of the territory. But treaties could (and can) be ratified only by the U.S. Senate. While the treaty worked its way through Congress, gold was discovered in Yakama territory, and prospectors flooded into the region. Already distressed at this encroachment, Yakama men killed two prospectors after they discovered the men had raped a Yakama woman. Hostilities erupted all over the territory. The agent from the Office of Indian Affairs, Andrew Bolon, was assassinated. All-out war ensued. The Nisqually chief Leschi, who had been forced to sign the treaty in the first place (if, in fact, it was signed at all—the matter is in dispute), now saw that even its disgraceful terms were not to be honored. He was further humiliated and disempowered when the territorial militia tried to arrest him in Olympia, where he had traveled to protest the treaty. He remained at large for a year, fighting the colonists, until he was captured in 1856. His half brother Quiemuth turned himself in shortly thereafter but was found murdered by unknown assailants in Governor Stevens's office while awaiting transport. Leschi was tried twice and convicted of the murder of a colonel, although he denied having done it. He was hanged in hastily erected gallows near Lake Steilacoom, a site that is now a housing development, the travesty of his life marked only by a small plaque next to a strip mall in Lakewood, Washington. The Yakama War eventually ground to a halt in 1858 when Colonel George Wright inflicted a serious defeat on the remaining Indians near Latah Creek, resulting in a "peace" treaty that moved the remaining Indians to reservations scattered throughout the territory.

The Great Basin

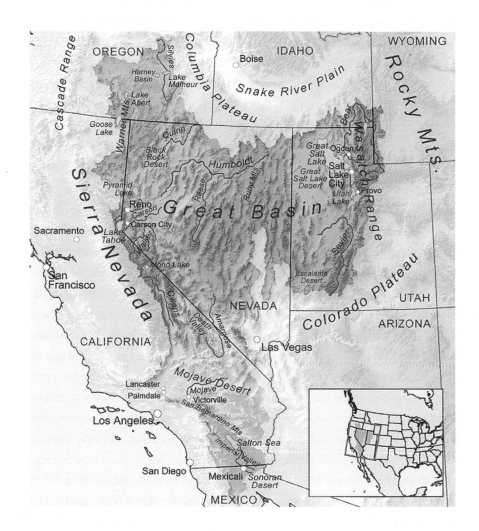

Map of the Great Basin region

The Great Basin—the area stretching from the Wasatch Range in the east, to the Colorado Plateau in the south, to the eastern edge of the Sierras in the west, and to the Columbia Plateau in the north, encompassing most of Nevada and parts of Utah, Oregon, Idaho, and California—is one of the largest endorheic watersheds (flowing nowhere, with no outlet) in the world, and certainly one of the most rugged, beautiful, and strange. From the creosote and Joshua tree–dotted hot deserts to the south and the high, cold deserts of Oregon to the north, from the arid depths of Death Valley to the juniper-clad slopes of the Wasatch near Salt Lake (and including the Great Salt Lake itself), the Great Basin is varied and gorgeous. Pronghorn, mountain lions, and mule deer traverse its range, and it is home to jackrabbits and cottontails as well as rattlesnakes, gopher snakes, lizards, curlews, pelicans, ravens, crows, and a host of other birds and animals.

Humans, too, have made this land their home for about ten thousand years. Paleo-Indians of the basin seem to have come from the south and spoke languages of the Uto-Aztecan language family. These early inhabitants clustered around waterways and lakes, where they killed camels (the last of the North American camels died out around this time), horses, mammoths, and bison along with migrating waterfowl. The Indians made nets for land and water and even constructed decoys to draw the birds closer. They also used digging sticks to unearth tubers and seem to have relied heavily on grass seed, which they collected, roasted, and crushed into a meal using metates. They were highly nomadic people and didn't develop large systems, settlements, or structures like the protocultures of the Southwest. They adopted the bow and arrow around 500 BCE, began living in pit houses (but never year-round), and in some places cultivated maize, which came up from Mexico. As they colonized the region, they split and split again, becoming the Shoshone, Ute, Mono, and Northern Paiute tribes we know today. Some of these offshoots traveled east over the Rockies, changing along the way into the Comanche and other Plains tribes.

Just as the basin was endorheic, so, too, was the culture: it flowed nowhere. More interestingly, this is the one region in North America for which it is hard to find evidence of a violent past: the Paleo-Indians of the basin seemed not to have fought one another. They had such a large range, they were so few, and food was so scarce that there must have been too few to fight over too little. One Shoshone creation legend has it (in the reverse of most tribal mythology) that all animals were once men, and after a series of misdeeds—having mostly to do with stealing pine nuts—they were turned into animals.

Those who stayed in the basin stayed close to their roots: when Europeans came through in the early nineteenth century, the Indians of the basin were living much as their ancestors had for millennia. Jedediah Smith was the first American to cross the Great Basin. He did it twice—from east to west, and then again in 1827 from west to east. He was followed by Peter Ogden and later by Benjamin Bonneville in 1832. A series of treaties first with Spain, then Britain and Mexico, brought the entire region under American control by 1848. It was around this time that the first permanent settlement was created at Salt Lake. But it was the Mormons (rather than the American government) who would settle the area with force and with consequence.

The Mormons had their beginnings in New York under the guidance of Joseph Smith, who claimed to have dug up the golden tablets of the Book of Mormon and translated them for his people. In 1831 the Church followed the word it was spreading west and fetched up in Kirtland, Ohio. But they were met with strong anti-Mormon sentiment. They were expelled and wandered in the desert of goodwill from place to place until they made it to Far West, Missouri. When tensions between the Mormons and the Missouri settlers erupted into the Mormon War, they were ejected from Missouri and headed back east to Illinois. Trouble seemed to follow the religion wherever it went, however. There was another anti-Mormon uprising in 1844, and Joseph Smith and his brother Hyrum were killed by a mob in Carthage, Illinois. Brigham Young won the war of succession for the Mormon throne and led his flock farther west into Utah. There, far away from the society that had treated them so poorly they set about creating a kingdom in a wilderness.

But Utah wasn't far enough away to insulate the Mormons from the control of the United States, which was deeply concerned about the theocracy growing in the Great Basin and by its now open policy of polygamy. James Buchanan sent an army to Utah to bring the Mormons to heel in 1857. At the same time a wagon train left from Arkansas headed to

California. The Baker-Fancher party, as it was known, contained around two hundred fairly well-off settlers. They made it to Salt Lake in early 1857 but they were turned away without being allowed to purchase provisions or resupply; Brigham Young was concerned that the wagon train was in some way connected or related to Buchanan's troops. The Baker-Fancher party rolled away from Salt Lake and spent the better part of the summer trying to get up strength, feed its cattle, and attend to itself in order to cross the mountains into California. However, spurred on by rumor and paranoia, the Mormons decided not to let them go.

On September 7, 1857, Mormon militiamen dressed as Indians attacked them at Mountain Meadows. The settlers literally circled the wagons and dug shallow fortifications. They were besieged. The initial attack resulted in the deaths of seven or so settlers, with fourteen wounded. The siege wore on for days, with the settlers running low on water and ammunition and food. The attacking Mormons became afraid that the settlers had recognized them through their thin disguises. Surely word of the attack would get out. On September 11, members of the militia approached the battle lines waving white flags. They were accompanied by the Indian agent and militiaman John Lee. The settlers were told that the attacking Paiute had agreed to let the settlers go in the care of the Mormons as long as they left all their cattle and supplies. The exhausted settlers agreed. The adult men were separated from the women and children and left under militia escort. Once they were a safe way away, all of the men were murdered by the Mormons. The women and children were then ambushed by more Mormon militia hiding in the brush and ravines. They were killed as well—120 men, women, and children in all. Children deemed too young to remember the incident were "adopted" into Mormon families. The Mormons took all the cattle and supplies. These were sold and auctioned off in Salt Lake City and Cedar City. It was agreed that the whole incident would be blamed on the Paiute.

Brigham Young himself led an investigation into the massacre, which concluded in a report sent to the commissioner of Indian affairs that the attack had been perpetrated by Indians. The government, not quite believing Young's tale, sent its own investigators. But the Civil War intervened, and it wasn't until 1877 that John Lee was charged and convicted and shot for the crimes of the massacre. But not before the Mormons were more deeply embedded, ticklike, in Paiute land. Despite the fact that the Mormon colony had perpetrated a horrible crime, it was the Paiute who had to pay and who continue to pay by way of dispossession.

In the 1860s and 1870s the Shoshone and Ute and Paiute engaged in a series of wars—the Bannock, Snake, and Sheepeater Wars—with similar results to those obtained elsewhere: exhaustion and defeat and confinement to reservations. Yet they, like Indians of other tribes and regions, held on.

The Southern Great Plains:
Texas and Oklahoma

The Great Plains region—the region of short-grass prairie, steppe, and grassland between the tall-grass prairie of the Mississippi basin and the barrier of the Rocky Mountains—has captured the American imagination and entered the mythology of the country like no other landscape. Covering more than 1.3 million square miles, roughly five hundred miles wide and two thousand miles long, the Great Plains stretch over ten states (or rather, ten states were laid over the range): Wyoming, Texas, South Dakota, North Dakota, Kansas, Nebraska, Montana, Colorado, eastern New Mexico, and Oklahoma. It is a massive landscape, mostly flat but varied, with a climate that ranges from the humid subtropical zone of Oklahoma and parts of Texas to the cold steppe of North Dakota. What holds it all together (in reality and the mind) is grass, buffalo, and Indians.

Buffalo grass, blue grama, and big bluestem grass dominated the landscape since the last ice age and encouraged a dizzying variety and density of life. Antelope, mule deer, white-tail deer, moose, coyotes, wolves, bears, bobcats, mountain lions, and jaguars flourished there, along with rabbits, gophers, squirrels, lizards, snakes, and thousands of species of birds. But bison were the species that defined the place. Before 1800, it is estimated, more than 60 million bison roamed the Plains. By 1900 only 541 existed on the earth. The change and loss and yet the life—of grasslands, bison, and homelands—can be seen nowhere better than in the contrast between the fate of Indians in Texas and the fate of those in Oklahoma.

In prehistoric times, the Texas area was, like the Southwest, home to three prototribal groups: the Mound Builders in the east, Mesoamerican cultures in central-south Texas, and proto-Pueblan peoples, the Násaazí, of the western Rio Grande. As we have seen, these cultures ebbed and flowed, breaking apart and coming back together as the tribes grappled with both the changing environment and the social systems they had wrought. By 1500 CE, as elsewhere, these prehistoric cultures had—at least in the east, west, and south—become agriculturalists more than hunter-gatherers. To the east, the Caddo and Wichita (descended from the Mound Builders) lived in sedentary villages, having been pushed to the westernmost part of their range by Siouan people like the Kaw, Osage, and Ponca, who in turn had fled from Iroquois lands in the Ohio River valley. The Caddo grew corn, sunflowers, and pumpkins, domesticated wild turkeys, and hunted large game in the river lowlands. To the northeast of the Rio Grande, the Pueblo people lived much as their counterparts did in New Mexico. Only in central and southern Texas were Indian tribes like the Tonkawa and Coahuiltecan truly hunter-gatherers. They lived in highly amorphous small tribal groups, each probably some version of an extended family. They plied the lowlands of south and central Texas and harvested mesquite beans, maguey root, prickly pear, pecans, and acorns.

The first Europeans to travel through Texas in the sixteenth century were, of course, the Spanish. Alonso Álvarez de Pineda mapped the Gulf Coast in 1519. Almost a decade later, Álvar Núñez Cabeza de Vaca washed up there after he was shipwrecked and promptly began exploring the interior of Texas. He described how the Indians used fire to manipulate the range and behavior of bison. He also noted that half the natives he met soon died from stomach ailments, probably influenza. Two tribes he mentioned in particular—the Teya and the Querecho—are described as nomadic enemies of each other, traveling about attacking bison herds and moving their belongings on travois lashed to the backs of dogs. Who their tribal descendants might be is something of a guess, but most researchers agree that they probably were Athabascan-speaking proto-Apaches. The Spanish wouldn't come back to Texas in force until the late seventeenth century. But by then, as always, new winds were sweeping the Plains.

After the Pueblo Revolt in 1680, horses were unleashed on the Plains. Until then they had been more or less exclusively controlled by the Spanish. They thus became both a kind of currency on the Plains and a prime shaper of its landscape. Rather suddenly, the tribes bordering on or living in the Plains—the Diné, Apache, Shoshone, Kiowa, and Pawnee—were horsed and could fight and hunt in ways never before imaginable. All tribes took horses, but perhaps no other tribe took to them like the Comanche.

The Comanche began as Shoshonean people along the North Platte River in Wyoming, having (to judge from their language) migrated up from Mexico over many hundreds of years. When they started acquiring horses in the late seventeenth century, they began pushing east and south in search of bison. Gone, overnight, were the days when the whole tribe had to lure herds into artificial or natural pens or stampede them off cliffs. Now they could pace the bison on horses and shoot arrows with deadly accuracy into their flanks. They could also run roughshod over any other Indians in their way. By 1700, the Comanche had pushed into Oklahoma, New Mexico, and as far south as central Texas. The eastern Apache were directly in their line of travel and expansion and were caught up in devastating wars with the Comanche, ending after a grueling nine-day battle at the Wichita River in 1723. Soon the Comanche had everything: easy access to food, the ability to attack and defend, and a steady influx of captured enemies (including Spanish and New Mexican settlers as well as other tribal people). Their numbers swelled. By the end of the eighteenth century there were about two million wild horses in the "Comancheria" (the new Comanche homelands that included all of West Texas, eastern New Mexico, western Oklahoma, and southwestern Kansas) alone. The Comanche were so skilled at breaking horses that they had in excess of one hundred thousand of them at their disposal at any given time. By the early nineteenth century, the tribe itself numbered forty thousand. Like other tribes, they lacked a central authority or governing body, however; they were split into as many as thirty distinct bands, each with their own hierarchy and leaders.

As heterogeneous as they were, they were universally feared. Texas—first as part of New Spain, then Mexico, then as an independent republic, and finally as a state in the Union—could not protect, or even define, its western border against them. The Comanche raided the Spanish, Mexicans, and Americans with relative impunity. They raided and fought all their tribal neighbors as well. The whole of Comancheria as well as surrounding areas was a battleground for the better part of two centuries. (Perhaps it is an axiom of war that where there is enough land and resources for everyone, groups fight the most fiercely to deprive others of that bounty.) Especially during the Civil War, the Comanche, Apache, and others (sometimes in alliance and sometimes acting singly) pushed back the "civilized" frontier hundreds of miles, burning homesteads and seizing cattle and horses and captives. While the story of colonial and subsequently American expansion is largely one of "Westward ho!," the historical reality shows us (in the Hudson valley, along the Ohio, in New Mexico, and in Texas) that many tribes successfully pushed settlers out and back, and sometimes resettlement took decades, if it happened at all. And who knows? Without these spasms of war, the fates of tribes might have been very different. Many (like the Comanche) were eventually defeated by disease and by the systematic extermination of the buffalo on which they depended. But perhaps the Comanche bought themselves time (as did the Iroquois and Ojibwe and Pueblo people) to prepare themselves for resettlement and the eventual Anglo onslaught, learning ways and means to protect themselves with the time they had bought with blood. The Comanche empire, however, did come to an end when Quanah Parker, leader of one of the larger Comanche bands, capitulated in 1875. By that time their population had dropped from around forty thousand in the mid–nineteenth century to around three thousand in 1874. The Comanche retired to reservations in Oklahoma.

Oklahoma was (and is) a strange exception to the very concept of Indian homelands. Originally (that is, before the 1830s) it had been home to Caddo, Lipan Apache, Kiowa, and Osage, among others. They were mainly agriculturalists to the east and hunter-gatherers to the west, but all of that was upended after the Louisiana Purchase and the creation of "Indian Territory" shortly thereafter. As intended by Thomas Jefferson, "Indian Territory" was a place to relocate all the eastern Indians where they would be out of the way of Jefferson's imagined army of yeoman farmers. The original territory was vast, but when Indians began to be removed there after the passage of the Indian Removal Act of 1830, it was reduced in size almost immediately. Iowa, Wisconsin, Minnesota, Dakota, Nebraska, and Kansas territories were quickly excluded. Much reduced, Indian Territory began to resemble present-day Oklahoma in size and shape. Indians were moved there anyway. By 1888 more than thirty tribes from all over the country were resettled in Oklahoma, including Cherokee, Choctaw, Chickasaw, Seminole, Seneca, Delaware, Sac, Fox, Ho-Chunk, Creek, Ottawa, Potawatomi, Ponca, Cheyenne, Arapaho, and Pawnee. Crowded together, enemies became neighbors, and relocated tribes were forced on those indigenous to the region.

It was a chaotic mess, but it was a homeland of sorts and seemed, at first, more secure than the ones many tribes left behind. It didn't last. As the cattle industry got under way in Texas in the 1870s and 1880s, Texas ranchers needed a way to get their beef to rail lines in Kansas. Indian Territory was in the way. The cattle drives took place anyway. The passage of the 1889 Indian Appropriations Act sought to undo tribal landownership and replace it with individual ownership of 160-acre parcels. "Surplus" land (which is what the government called the land left over after allotment) did not go back to tribes but was essentially given away to homesteaders. As though the sudden disappearance of Indian land from under their feet wasn't bad enough, "Sooners" didn't wait for the official release of the land but rather snuck out onto the prairie and took the best land first. Some tribes, like the Osage, found ways to resist. They originated in the Ohio River valley but were pushed out during the Iroquois Wars in the seventeenth and eighteenth centuries and made a new homeland in what is now Kansas, Missouri, Arkansas, and northeastern Oklahoma. There they became a force to be reckoned with. George Catlin, who traveled among them and painted them in the nineteenth century, said they were "the tallest race of men in North America, either red or white skins; there being . . . many of them six and a half [tall], and others seven feet." They lost a lot of land in the years leading up to the Civil War, and during the war they variously sided with both the Union and the Confederates. After the war many Osage served as scouts with George Armstrong Custer's Seventh Cavalry in wars with the Cheyenne and Arapaho and at the massacre at the Washita River in 1868. Facing removal and reduction, the Osage were forced to sell their reservation lands in Kansas. With the proceeds they bought themselves a new reservation in Oklahoma. This makes them unique among the many Indian tribes facing the growing power of the American republic because they could negotiate from a position of relative strength. One of the conditions of the purchase of new land was that the Osage retained headrights to mineral and underground wealth in the area under their reservation. When oil was discovered there in the late nineteenth century, the Osage stood to profit. In other negotiations, rather than have their treaty annuities and supplies paid to traders who then paid them out to the Indians, the Osage demanded their payments come to them directly. Clearly the Osage were not only militarily and physically strong; they were fierce and effective negotiators as well. And they remain.

The Northern Plains

Perhaps no other homeland—or the tribes that claimed it as such— has come to stand in for the collective history and fate of Indians in North America as the northern Great Plains. Why? In part, it is because the Indians of the northern Plains—Mandan, Arikara, Hidatsa, Lakota, Dakota, Crow, Cheyenne, Arapaho, Blackfeet, Assiniboine, Cree, Saulteaux, and Plains Ojibwe—lived in one of the last regions of North America to be settled by Europeans. Much of the High Plains was too cold for too much of the year to be desirable agricultural land, at least at first. Major settlement occurred after 1850, and most of that after the Civil War. Also, the drama on the Plains between 1850 and 1890 threw the question of the young republic into stark relief: Was America a democratic country that respected the rights of individuals, or was it just another greedy power in disguise? The Plains Wars raised the question because for the first time Anglo-Indian conflict was staged for all to see. European settlement also came late enough to connect with emergent print and photographic journalism: as with the Vietnam War, the Plains War was there to see in magazines and newspapers and illustrated weeklies. And finally, the Plains tribes were unusually resistant to the colonizers. Resistance, as we have seen, took many shapes across the United States: canny acculturation, armed resistance, negotiation, retreat, alliance, trade, raiding. But rarely was Indian resistance so widespread, successful, and brutal. Something else also marked it as different: the coming together of two very powerful forces that changed struggle in America more generally—horses and firearms.

Paleo-Indians had been hunting and gathering the northern Great Plains since the last glaciation: killing mammoth, musk oxen, horses, and camels. When the megafauna died off—perhaps because of overhunting, perhaps because of climate change—and an ice sheet crept down from the north, Paleo-Indians traveled its margins and hunted its oases. When the ice sheet retreated some ten to fifteen thousand years ago, they turned their attention to new species—elk, deer, antelope, and bison—and followed the newly emerging waterways that would become the Red, Missouri, Yellowstone, Milk, and Powder Rivers.

There isn't a lot of archaeological evidence of how the people of the northern Plains lived, because very little record has been left behind and Plains tribes changed so much after the advent of the horse. What we do know from studying Native languages is that tribal offshoots from Mexico, Canada, and the Rocky Mountains trickled out into the vast grasslands and made their lives there. There were no huge settlements or concentrations of population—as today, "flyover country" didn't support the same density of habitation that could be found elsewhere on the continent. The tribes that emerged from these Paleo-Indians—Crow, Cheyenne, Arapaho—lived in small family-centric bands. They were highly mobile, lived in skin-covered teepees, and used travois to haul their belongings from place to place, following the bison. Everything revolved around the bison.

By the fifteenth century there were tribes along the southeastern edge of the Plains who engaged in relatively intensive farming, among them the Caddoan-speaking Wichita, Caddo, and Pawnee. To the west, tribes that might at one point have been agriculturalists bowed to the climate and gave up farming in favor of hunting and gathering. There is evidence of migration even way back then. In their stories, the Algonquian-speaking Cheyenne recount how they lived at one time in a country surrounded by water but followed the vision of one of their tribe and devoted their lives to hunting buffalo, so becoming the Cheyenne of the western Plains. They looked to the Black Hills (and the buffalo that surrounded them) as their birthplace, spiritual home, and spiritual center. The Blackfeet were, similarly, Algonquian-speaking migrants who made a home against the spine of the Rockies. In the early seventeenth century, other migrants began to arrive from the east, refugees from the bloody struggles of the Iroquois and the Great Lakes.

As the Ojibwe and Odawa consolidated their control of the fur trade and of the Great Lakes, they continued to push west and south. Popular history has it that white settlement on the Eastern Seaboard displaced those tribes, and they in turn displaced their westerly neighbors, and so on, a ripple effect from east to west that ended when woodland Indians like the Mandan, Hidatsa, Arikara, and Dakota were forced out onto the Plains. This is only partly true. There was a kind of ripple effect. But some of the biggest tribes and confederations of tribes—those in the Iroquois Confederacy, the Shawnee of the Ohio River valley, the tens of thousands of Huron, and the majority of the Ojibwe—did no such thing. The Iroquois sheltered in place. The Huron were wiped out and assimilated into other tribes. The Shawnee immolated themselves in conflict with the colonial powers and scattered—some even winding up in Texas. By comparison, the Iroquois Confederacy and confederated Great Lakes Algonquians (Potawatomi,

Ojibwe, Odawa), made rich by the fur trade and armed with guns and numbers, expanded their territory and squeezed everyone else out.

In the seventeenth and eighteenth centuries, Green Bay, Wisconsin, became something like a refugee camp filled with a polyglot collection of tribes fleeing the violence. Sac, Fox, Ho-Chunk, Oneida, and even Potawatomi and Menominee lived, farmed, and hunted in the region. But the Ojibwe onslaught was relentless. By the mid–seventeenth century the Ojibwe had pushed into Minnesota. The Ojibwe war chief Waabojiig (White Fisher) allegedly killed more than fifty Dakota warriors in the Saint Croix River valley in one summer war in the late eighteenth century. Around the same time there was a large Dakota village on the shores of Mde Wakan, Spirit Lake (later renamed Mizizaaga'igan by the conquering Ojibwe, and still later known as Mille Lacs). The Ojibwe attacked in 1750 by throwing bags of gunpowder down the smoke holes of the Dakota lodges and killing the residents as they ran out. The Mandan, Hidatsa, and Arikara—who along with the Dakota and Lakota had made the woodlands of Wisconsin and Minnesota their home—were overcome and fled out onto the Plains to make a way of life there. The enmity between the Lakota and Ojibwe remained for many years. Cree and Assiniboine were similarly ejected from the boreal forests and waterways of northwestern Ontario.

It wasn't long, however, before the former woodland people took to the horse, and the Blackfeet followed suit. Around the same time, the French had been making inroads north of the Great Lakes through Canada in their ever-expanding quest for furs. And while the British were loath to arm Indians, the French had no such qualms. Guns were prevalent by the beginning of the eighteenth century and only became more so. Within a few decades of journeying to the Plains, the Blackfeet, Crow, Arikara, Mandan, Cheyenne, Lakota, Dakota, Nakota, Cree, and Assiniboine were armed and horsed. As such they were, for a while, indomitable.

As of the beginning of the eighteenth century, there were more than thirty distinct tribes on the northern Plains, and within them many sub-bands with their own histories and identities. Bucking the trend of large macrocultures (Hopewell, Násaazí, Hohokam) breaking into smaller ones, the horse and the gun bonded together small roving bands into the horse cultures of the Plains. Now, with easy mobility and access to food (no longer would they need to pull their travois with dogs or lie in wait for passing bison), populations swelled. People were better clothed and better fed. Infant mortality went down, life spans increased, birth rates went up. These were boom times. As James Wilson notes, "There is something deeply ironic—though somehow strangely fitting [about Plains ascendancy]. To begin with, far from predating contact, the Plains Indian culture of the nineteenth century was a relatively recent phenomenon which depended, in part, on innovations introduced by Europeans. It would be difficult to find a native group which better exemplified cultural change and adaptation, or one that gave a less accurate image of pre-Columbian America."

It should also be noted that contrary to popular misconception, tribes didn't wither in the face of superior European technology, thinking, religion, and culture or merely succumb to European diseases. Rather, in the Plains in particular, tribes showed supreme adaptability, resourcefulness, and creative syncretization. They took what Europeans brought and made it wholly their own. What would have happened, one wonders, if Plains tribes had encountered Europeans on foot, in small groups, without any kind of critical cultural or martial mass? Despite their later losses, the Plains tribes are, quite likely, around today only because they fought— armed with guns and mounted on horses—in the eighteenth and nineteenth centuries.

By the early nineteenth century, the Plains tribes were the people we recognize today. They lived on horseback and hunted buffalo. Their ceremonial lives were governed by the sacred pipe (given in a vision to them by White Buffalo Calf Woman) and organized into "societies," each with a different function. While much older ceremonial ways remained, even some from their woodland days centuries earlier, the Siouan and Algonquian tribes of the northern Plains were given new ceremonies that meshed with their new lives, among them the Sun Dance. The horse was the key to this renaissance in Plains cultures. It made everything possible— new art forms, new religions, new societies, and new thinking. It was a time of plenty.

But origins are origins: horses were introduced by the Spanish as weapons of war, and weapons of war they remained. The Lakota introduced a reign of terror on the High Plains, attacking and reducing their Arikara neighbors relentlessly. The Arikara, Mandan, and Hidatsa never shook their woodland roots: they still lived in earthen villages, farmed the river valleys, and were, as a result, relatively sedentary. This was not such a viable way of life when surrounded by mobile, horsed nomadic hunters. The Lakota also fought their Crow and Pawnee neighbors to the west and south. The Blackfeet quarreled with the Crow as well as the Gros Ventre and Cree. It should be noted that Plains tribes were not described as (or experienced as) unduly warlike by the Spanish when they were first encountered in the seventeenth century. But when the Americans began showing up in force in the early and middle nineteenth century, they were greeted with armies the likes of which had not been seen before on the continent.

It all began well enough. At first all the territory west of the Mississippi (but excluding the Northwest and California and portions of the Southwest) was owned by France. The land passed to the United States as a result of the Louisiana Purchase in 1803. President Thomas Jefferson lost no time in trying to get the lay of this vast, relatively unknown land by dispatching the Corps of Discovery under the command of Lewis and Clark in 1804. Their expedition was tasked with mapping and exploring the land, finding a way to the Pacific Ocean, and staking a claim to the territory before the Spanish or British could. Their expedition—now part of legend—lasted from the spring of 1804 through September 1806. They covered thousands of miles of territory, traversed mountains, battled weather and starvation and uncertainty, and, rather startlingly, engaged in no bloodshed or strife with the dozens of tribes they met along the way. Nor did the tribes seem keen on fighting the corps. They wanted to bring the Americans into their spheres of knowledge, too, because in one way or another they knew the Americans were a future with which they would most certainly have to contend.

In 1817 a St. Louis entrepreneur opened a fur trading post called Fort Pierre in South Dakota, among the first of a wave of posts and traders who began moving into the area, squeezing the last furs out of an industry that, after two hundred years, was in its death throes. But this kind of relatively peaceful coexistence and mutually beneficial arrangement (furs for guns and axes and knives and kettles and blankets) didn't last.

Settlers bound for California had been trekking across the Great Plains in steady if not extravagant numbers from the 1820s through 1850, but the California Gold Rush changed all that: beginning in 1849, the northern Plains would see traffic in the tens and eventually hundreds of thousands as the great migration to the gold fields began. Whatever the stance of the northern tribes had been toward the Americans, the Gold Rush made them apprehensive. Wagon trains tore up the ground and disrupted the buffalo. With each new wave of travelers came another wave of disease. The travelers had nothing to offer the tribes. Tribes began attacking them. Even this was a primarily economic rather than militaristic action: raiding had long been a cultural norm for the tribes, a way to redistribute wealth. Intertribal raiding generally left a low body count and was seen by many Plains tribes as a quasi-spiritual activity wherein boys grew into men: raiding was, for some, ceremonial activity vested in masculinity and coming-of-age. So by attacking wagon trains and stealing horses, flour, iron, gunpowder, lead, and other hard-to-obtain items, the Plains tribes were simply responding to unwelcome pressure and continuing a way of life that was fairly stable.

The government, however, didn't see the practice that way and wanted an end to it: violence on the trail was bad for American business. But the government lacked the strength to take on the tens of thousands of efficient and mounted warriors on the Plains. The U.S. Army would certainly lose. Instead they resorted to treaty making. In 1851 the Cheyenne, Lakota, Arapaho, Assiniboine, Crow, Mandan, Gros Ventre, Shoshone, Arikara, and Hidatsa signed the first Treaty of Fort Laramie. The provisions were, on paper, good for both sides. The United States was assured settlers would be able to pass through the Indian homelands unmolested, and they would be able to build forts and supply depots to provision and re-provision the travelers. In return, the tribes' title to the land itself was affirmed and they were guaranteed $50,000 in annuities per year for the right of way.

Farther west, the Blackfoot Confederacy (a loose alliance of three major Blackfeet bands) had come to dominate the region. Before the horse, they had been a confederation of small bands of hunter-gatherers. So, too, were the Shoshone, who pushed the Blackfeet around and back and took over much of present-day Montana before 1730. But then the Blackfeet got the horse and all hell broke loose. They consolidated power and began warring with neighboring tribes. They attacked and raided the Shoshone, Lakota, Cree, Assiniboine, and their archenemies the Crow regularly and effectively. They expanded their stock of horses and, with greater access to buffalo, controlled a vast portion of Montana, Wyoming, and Idaho. Between 1790 and 1850 the Blackfeet were the absolutely dominant force in the northwestern Plains. They brooked no encroachment by other tribes or the tribe of white explorers and trappers who were showing up in their country in increasing numbers.

In 1808, John Colter, a member of the Corps of Discovery, returned to the region to trap furs by canoe. He and his trapping partner were surrounded by hundreds of Blackfeet warriors. His partner refused to surrender and was killed. Colter saw the wisdom in submission. But the Blackfeet stripped him of all his gear and clothes and told him to run away naked; they would give him a head start. He ran, with the Blackfeet in disdainful pursuit, for five miles before hiding in a river under some driftwood. He hid there all night and the next day began a 250-mile journey to "civilization," naked and afraid. And yet the Blackfeet welcomed traders who could help them by tying them into trading networks that provided them with the goods that would allow them to maintain their way of life. And it was this openness that ultimately did them in. In 1837 a packet operated by the American Fur Company in the Blackfeet homeland knowingly sent a smaller boat with traders who had smallpox deep into Blackfeet country. Between ten thousand and fifteen thousand Blackfeet died of the disease, thereby ending their dominance. At that time a vaccine for smallpox had been readily available for at least forty years, but the trading companies didn't require their employees to be vaccinated.

Nor was it made available to Indians. So it was not merely the Indians' lack of immunity that allowed disease to decimate them.

In any event, neither vaccines nor treaties stopped the white settlement of the Plains. Travelers continued to cross the Plains, and settlers began to move in, especially with the Gold Rush and regardless of the Treaties of Fort Laramie or the Treaties of Fort Benton or the many others signed in good faith by Plains tribes but violated immediately by the government and the citizens of the United States. The result: war.

Beginning in 1850 but escalating in the 1860s and 1870s, the Plains Indian Wars drew in almost every single Plains tribe and involved settlers, militia, and the U.S. Army. It is estimated that at least twenty thousand Indians and eight thousand Anglo settlers and soldiers died in twenty-five years of warfare, although the figure for Indian deaths, based on U.S. Army records, should almost certainly be higher. Most of the fighting began in the east, in what is now Minnesota, where in 1862 the Dakota who had remained behind after most of their tribe was pushed out onto the Plains by the Ojibwe rose up in protest over their treatment by the U.S. government and its representatives in the Minnesota River valley. The lands there had been largely set aside for the eastern Dakota by treaty, but the tribe watched (as Indians all over the Plains watched) as settlers moved in, broke the soil, and began farming. Adding injury to injury, the annuity payments and food promised by treaty and on which the Dakota depended were rarely delivered, or were late and of substandard quality. The government's policy had also been to deliver the annuity payments to traders in the territory rather than directly to the Dakota. The traders would skim, falsify records, and otherwise garnish the annuities until there was nothing left.

The Dakota asked the government to pay the agent directly and then have the agent pay them. The government refused. Sensing weakness— with the federal government in the midst of fighting the Confederacy, many troops had been pulled back east—the Dakota (and some Ojibwe allies to the north) rose up. They attacked and burned farms and killed settlers, driving the rest into Fort Snelling in a panic. The whole territory was thick with smoke. Hundreds of settlers and soldiers were killed.

Eventually, the tide turned against the Dakota and their allies. Most of the Dakota warriors surrendered in late September 1862. A few hundred were charged with murder, but President Lincoln reviewed the cases and whittled the number down to thirty-eight. These were tried, and although the charges were not explained, and the accused did not have representation, they were convicted and executed on December 26, 1862, in what is still the largest mass hanging in U.S. history—of members of a sovereign nation who had risen up to expel foreign invaders from their homeland. The corpses were buried in a mass grave in Mankato, Minnesota, after the execution, and many of the bodies were dug up and used to practice autopsies. William Mayo (one of the founders of the Mayo Clinic) acquired the body of Mahpiya Akan Nažin (Stands on Clouds), dissected it before an audience, boiled and cleaned the bones, shellacked them, and kept them on display in his office for many years afterward.

The violence in Minnesota—on both sides—rippled westward from there. Driven by distrust and fear, militia in Colorado began shooting Indians on sight. Indians retaliated. Many of the bands and tribes were able to reach a peace with the U.S. and territorial authorities. The violence seemed to be dying down. But in November 1864, Colonel John Chivington and members of the Colorado and New Mexico militia attacked a peaceful encampment of Cheyenne and Arapaho in southeastern Colorado. These bands had taken no part in any of the hostilities of the preceding years. Chivington's men attacked when most of the Native men were gone from the village hunting, even though an American flag and a white flag of truce were flying over the village at Sand Creek. Women, children, and elders were mowed down.

A kind of blood lust took over Chivington's men, well documented by the media at the time. One eyewitness said he "saw one squaw lying on the bank, whose leg had been broken. A soldier came up to her with a drawn sabre. She raised her arm to protect herself; he struck, breaking her arm. She rolled over, and raised her other arm; he struck, breaking that, and then left her without killing her. I saw one squaw cut open, with an unborn child lying by her side." Major Scott Anthony, who was present at the massacre, remembered "one little child, probably three years old, just big enough to walk through the sand. The Indians had gone ahead, and this little child was behind, following after them. The little fellow was perfectly naked, travelling in the sand. I saw one man get off his horse at a distance of about seventy-five yards and draw up his rifle and fire. He missed the child. Another man came up and said, 'Let me try the son of a b—. I can hit him.' He got down off his horse, kneeled down, and fired at the little child, but he missed him. A third man came up, and made a similar remark, and fired, and the little fellow dropped."

Peaceful Blackfeet were massacred, probably numbering in the hundreds, on the Marais River in 1870. Every time the Indians fought back against clear violations of the treaties they had signed in good faith, a reign of terror was unleashed upon them. America did not conquer the West through superior technology, nor did it demonstrate the advantages of democracy. America "won" the West by blood, brutality, and terror.

Red Cloud, an Oglala Lakota war chief, achieved a lot of success against the United States from 1866 and beyond in southeastern Montana and northeastern Wyoming. In a series of brilliantly staged attacks and battles, he pushed the U.S. Army back hundreds of miles, forcing them to abandon forts, trading posts, and supply lines. The defeats Red Cloud heaped on the U.S. Army forced it to abandon all of its forts in the region and to sign the second Treaty of Fort Laramie, which created the Great Sioux Reservation, in 1868.

The Lakota were also guaranteed the right to hunt in the unceded territory as far as the Sandhills of Nebraska. But the arrangement was too good to last. Trespass continued unabated and only increased after gold was discovered in the Black Hills in 1874. Miners and prospectors, encouraged by the U.S. government, which wanted gold more than it wanted peace with Indians, flooded in. Harassment and murder of Indians continued unabated, and so did Anglo predation of bison herds the Lakota considered theirs. Lieutenant Colonel Custer—he was ranked a general only temporarily during the Civil War—led punitive winter campaigns against the Lakota. Outmaneuvered on the battlefield, Custer began attacking and destroying Indian villages in the winters of 1874 and 1875.

Lakota and other tribal leaders saw that they would have to deliver a resounding defeat to the army before it gave up its present course. So they sent runners, reforged old alliances, strengthened friendships, and plotted. They even went so far as to send messengers to the Dakota and Ojibwe of Minnesota asking for their help. They were refused. The Blackfeet refused them, too. Nonetheless, they built a formidable army of Lakota, northern Cheyenne, and Arapaho and cemented their plans during the annual Sun Dance at Rosebud Agency in June 1876. "Agency" Indians from all over the Great Sioux Reservation had been slipping away already, arming and horsing themselves, and more joined them after the dance. Meanwhile the U.S. Army was conducting a summer campaign to round up any and all Indians who had so far refused to settle on the Great Sioux Reservation.

At dawn on June 25, Custer and his men spotted a large encampment of Indians near the Little Bighorn River. He thought it was perhaps a band or two, not the thousands of warriors it really was, all ready for battle. He determined to take them on, ignoring the advice of their scouts. Custer attacked that day and was quickly surrounded by attacking Lakota, Cheyenne, and Arapaho, as planned by Sitting Bull and the other chiefs. After two days of fighting, Custer's entire command was wiped out. The Indian fighting force disintegrated into small bands. They spent the Fourth of July—America's hundredth birthday—feasting and sharing stories of their victory before heading back to their summer camps and agencies.

Seven weeks later, the military mounted retaliatory attacks, but other tactics proved more decisive. The U.S. government refused to send provisions and payments that obtained from the 1868 Treaty of Fort Laramie to the Lakota until they ceded the Black Hills to the Americans. Soon after, hundreds of buffalo hunters descended on the High Plains and began the systematic slaughter of the great bison herds of North America. Without their traditional food source and deprived of annuities and provisions guaranteed by treaty, the Lakota and their allies were starved into submission, and the reservation period began for these unhappy few as well.

1890

A nd so by the end of 1890 it must have seemed that everything was over. In four hundred years, Indians had lost control of 100 percent of the United States and remained only in small clusters scattered like freckles over the face of the country. By the 1870s, the federal government had stopped making treaties with Indian nations. By 1890, the frontier was officially closed. The ways of life that tribes from Florida to Washington and Maine to the Mohave had evolved over thousands of years were gone. So were the buffalo. Tribal government had been replaced by the dismal and crushing paternalism of the Office of Indian Affairs. The European colonial powers and later the American government had shown themselves to be feckless, cruel, shortsighted, hypocritical, and shameful in their dealings with the original owners of the country. Indians were gone from the East Coast, and on the other side of the country, they lived as tattered remnants around former mission communities in California. The entire United States had been "settled," and Indians had been broken, removed, and safely "settled," too, on reservations where they were expected to either die or become Americans.

And yet: Indians remained. The Seminole still called the swamps and bayous of Florida home and emerged to join the burgeoning ranching trade in the Panhandle. On Martha's Vineyard and elsewhere in New England Indian settlements—Christian but still tribal—were growing. Niagara Falls, Rochester, and Syracuse, New York, sprang up around Iroquois settlements that remained after hundreds of years. Some Iroquois went to church. Many still went to the longhouse. In the Southwest, cultures arose that were a blend of Anglo, Mexican, and Indian. The kivas were still in use, and so were Tewa, Diné, and Apache languages. The buffalo were gone, and that spelled the end to a certain way of life. But the Plains tribes, ever adaptable, adapted to a land without buffalo. The Indians of the Great Lakes, unlike their western neighbors, could still do what they had always done: trap, harvest wild rice, hunt, and ply the waters much as they had done for centuries. The small coastal tribes of the Pacific Northwest traveled and traded and became loggers and fishermen.

In 1890, the U.S. Census Bureau tabulated that there were fewer than two hundred thousand Indians left alive, of populations that had likely numbered over twenty million. Gone were the times when you could not travel anywhere in the United States without knowing that you were trespassing on Indian land and being reminded of your lack of tenure in that place. But Indians remained in all the corners and original places of the land. Some had held on to their homelands, others had been removed and relocated and made new homelands.

In 1891, the Indians who remained everywhere poked their heads aboveground and surveyed the desolation of their homelands and asked the question Indians had been asking since the beginning: What can we do next to survive?

PART 2

Purgatory:
1891–1934

Kevin Washburn slips off his cowboy boots (he has two pairs in his office) and puts on his running shoes before we engage in a "walk and talk" around the golf course at the University of New Mexico, where he is a professor of law. I wanted to talk to Washburn because he served as the assistant secretary of the interior for Indian affairs. And because, as a Chickasaw, he was one of very few Indians to serve Indians and the government in that capacity. I also wanted to talk to him because I'm curious about him.

Kevin has a quick smile and is about the friendliest (former) government official you could hope to meet. He is cheerful and kind and enthusiastically helpful, although under all that cheer is something deep and fierce. Washburn grew up in the Chickasaw Nation and earned his BA in economics with honors from the University of Oklahoma in 1989. "My mom was the key when I was young. I had a powerful, strong-willed mom. She was a single mother for much of my childhood. There were boyfriends and stepdads in the picture now and then, but she was the anchor. I inherited her work ethic. And I had a little bit of a chip on my shoulder. I was raised by a single mom; my mom was 'the divorcée' in a small town in Oklahoma. And I was Indian and had all the baggage that went along with that, too. So I had a chip on my shoulder." That chip and that mother drove Kevin forward. Somehow his mother made ends meet. "My mom, well, my mom's a Republican." He laughs. "She was the first woman to be Chamber of Commerce president in the small town where we lived. At that time she had a children's clothing store because she thought, 'Well, if I own a clothing store at least my kids will be clothed well.'" After the divorce from Kevin's father, she started seeing a man who did not treat her well. She ended the relationship, went to the Small Business

101

Administration, and got a loan to buy a restaurant in a town three and a half hours away. "That was her way of escaping, thinking once again, 'If I buy a restaurant at least my kids will eat.'" If it hadn't been for that government program through the SBA, he points out, "my mother wouldn't have had a way to escape. She made the most of it. I got my drive and work ethic from her."

He got into Vanderbilt but neither he nor his family could afford it, so he went to the University of Oklahoma as a commuter student: he lived at home with his mother. After college, Washburn attended Yale Law School. "Growing up I was never one of those people who wanted to get the hell out." But when he left Oklahoma, he thought, "Oh my gosh! There's a world out there! I've not moved back. It's not for me. It's a very red state." Yet even as he graduated from clerkship to trial attorney for the Department of Justice to assistant U.S. attorney for New Mexico to dean of a law school, his tribe, the Chickasaw Nation, and by extension Indian people across the country, have always been on his mind.

"You know," he says, "the Cherokee suffered terribly on the Trail of Tears, in some ways because they didn't choose the moment of their departure. They were rounded up at gunpoint and forced to march in the winter. It was horrible. But for the Chickasaw it wasn't nearly as bad. We had more time to prepare for removal because we were further west. And so in some ways being victimized has not been as much a part of our tribal identity. We feel that we chose our own destiny. Even today, our tribal seal includes the words 'Unconquered and Unconquerable.'" An example? "The governor of my tribe has been governor since I was a kid. Bill Anoatubby. He had this saying, 'If it's going to be, it's up to me.' It really stuck with me. Basically he meant if you want something done you've got to do it yourself. He took our tribe to self-determination and self-governance." One of Washburn's siblings had asthma, and the family spent a lot of time at the Indian Health Service hospital. They frequently had to wait to be seen, he remembers, often for hours—and their mother took all three of the children to the hospital "because we never knew when we'd be done." Anoatubby proposed that the tribe should take over the operation of the hospital; this met with a great deal of tribal opposition. Washburn remembers that his aunts and uncles were against it. "Who does he think he is? Our tribe can't run a hospital better than the federal government. That's just crazy!" But the governor prevailed. "It was a huge political risk because everyone expected him to fail and he would have been voted out of office in the next election if it turned into a disaster. But within three to six months everybody was saying, 'Dang, this is running a lot better now.'" His mother reported that when appointments were running late, the hospital called her in advance and told her to come in later. "It was a little thing, just that little thing, but she didn't have to be sitting waiting there for two hours. It was like they were saying, '*We care about you. We respect you. We respect your time.*' It's really about accountability. Federal officials are never going to be accountable for the things they do, but a tribal leader may get unelected if people aren't served well. Perhaps there's too much accountability within Indian tribes! They sometimes hold leaders accountable for things they shouldn't. But federal officials have to commit a felony before they lose their jobs. It's not like poorly serving Indian people will get federal employees fired! So that's why I became a believer in tribal self-determination and self-governance very early in my life."

This belief—in the intelligence and capability of Indian people—was on ample display between 2012 and 2015, when Washburn served as an assistant secretary of the interior, a position that put him in charge of the Bureau of Indian Affairs, among other agencies. "Some people say it's the hardest job in government," he says. He adds, in that self-effacing Indian way, "That's not true, but it *is* one of the harder ones. You know—being the dean of the law school was perfect training for being assistant secretary. You have all these constituencies, everyone wants something different, no one is happy, and it's really hard to make everyone happy." In the end, he says, "we got a lot done. We kept cranking things out. But a lot of the things we accomplished are at risk of being overturned by Congress or by courts." He saw to it that federal acknowledgment regulations for extending federal recognition to Indian tribes were updated and reformed, and he recognized the Pamunkey tribe of Virginia, which was the tribe of Pocahontas. And he defeated a House effort to deprive this work of funding. He improved the Indian Child Welfare Act, which had been law since

1978 but is still being resisted in courts around the country. That law is meant to ensure that Indian children put up for adoption go to Indian families, so they aren't deprived of their culture at the same time they are severed from their Indian families. "But when you change anything, anything at all, it gives people standing to complain," he says ruefully.

The End of the Treaty Era
and the Rise of the Bureau

As early as 1775, during the deliberations of the Second Continental Congress, the revolutionary government created two, then three agencies to treat and trade with Indian tribes. These agencies were meant to be the major points of contact for negotiations between the federal government and Indian nations: a structure for working out agreements, settlements, annuities, and the like, more like embassies than anything else. In terms of realpolitik, the colonists were concerned that Indians— who vastly outnumbered them—would side with the British during the Revolutionary War. The declaration read: "In case any agent of the ministry shall induce the Indian tribes, or any of them, to commit actual hostilities against these colonies, or to enter into an offensive alliance with the British troops, thereupon the colonies ought to avail themselves of an alliance with such Indian nations as will enter into the same, to oppose such British troops and their Indian allies." The agencies corresponded with the loose organization of colonies: northern, central, and southern.

Many tribes, notably most of the Iroquois Confederacy, sided with the British anyway; they seemed a stronger force than the colonists. In response, in 1779, George Washington ordered an offensive against the Iroquois, to be mounted under the command of Major General John Sullivan:

> I would recommend that some post in the center of the Indian Country should be occupied with all expedition, with a sufficient quantity of provision, whence parties should be detached to lay waste all the

settlements around with instructions to do it in the most effectual manner, that the country may not be merely overrun but destroyed. . . .

But you will not by any means listen to [any] overture of peace before the total ruin of their settlements is effected. . . . Our future security will be in their inability to injure us . . . and in the terror with which the severity of the chastisement they receive will inspire [them]."

The Sullivan expedition engaged in a scorched-earth policy that destroyed more than forty villages, driving most of the confederacy from the Finger Lakes region north to Buffalo, Rochester, and Syracuse. Among the Iroquois, Washington was already known as Hanodaganears, or "Devourer of Towns." The Oneida, despite being a member of the Iroquois Confederacy, sided with the Americans and fought alongside the colonists at the battles of Oriskany and Saratoga, among others. During the winter of 1777–1778, when Washington and his troops were starving at Valley Forge, the Oneida marched down and provided much needed supplies and support. Polly Cooper, an Oneida woman with the entourage, showed the soldiers how to prepare Indian corn, thereby staving off the encroaching famine. After the war Congress signed a treaty with the Oneida in recognition of their contributions to American victory. It read, in part: "The United States acknowledges the lands reserved to the Oneida . . . to be their property; and the United States will never claim the same, nor their Indian friends residing thereon and united with them, in the free use and enjoyment thereof." A mere thirty years later when General Lafayette returned to America, he was welcomed as a hero in Utica where Revolutionary War veterans met him on a street bearing his name. He wondered to his hosts where the Oneida were, because it was they who had saved the revolutionaries at Oriskany. The whole region had been Oneida territory, and Washington and Schuyler and others had promised it would remain so. No one knew what he was talking about. The Oneida contributions to American victory and the promises that had been made to them, as well as their homelands, had faded away.

After the war, the American government's concerns about and relations with eastern tribes shifted from military to economic ones. It created an Office of Indian Trade within the newly established War Department. The office was charged with regulating trade with tribes, working along the lines of existing trade networks, which were built much like the factory system that had been in use since colonial times. In addition to piggybacking on the factories to maintain political stability—factories often functioned as (and resembled) forts, with garrisons or other capacities to host military detachments as needed—the system was further institutionalized via a series of Indian Intercourse Acts beginning in 1790. On the face of it, these laws were meant to protect Indians from unscrupulous traders or unauthorized and invalid exchanges of land; some Indians did find protection—in trade and in person—under the factory system. But they were designed primarily to extend American trade (and hence influence) into territories the government either controlled or would like to control, at the expense of Indians.

The factory system remained in effect until 1822, by which point the fur trade had waned and the Louisiana Purchase and the War of 1812 had established more or less agreed-upon borders to the country. In 1824, the government constituted the Office of Indian Affairs (the name was changed to the Bureau of Indian Affairs in 1947). Its relationships with tribes weren't merely military or transactional anymore. Scores of treaties had been signed in the intervening years, most of which, in addition to defining Indians' rights and the borders of their homelands, included provisions for annuities in the form of cash, seed, iron, trade goods, and blankets. Thus the government, long an overbearing trading partner and military threat to the tribes, had added yet another role: trustee of money and goods promised to them by treaty. In 1832, Congress created the position of commissioner of Indian affairs, and in 1849 the Office of Indian Affairs was moved from the War Department to the Department of the Interior. Washburn jokes, "This was a bad choice for the BIA. It was better off in the War Department. Today the Department of the Interior's annual appropriation from Congress is $13 billion. The annual appropriation for the Department of Defense is around six hundred billion!" The office's origins in trade and war, however, continued to define its role.

During the Civil War, some tribes, especially in the South, had sided with the Confederates. In 1865, Dennis Cooley, then commissioner of Indian affairs, was charged with finding an apt punishment. Cooley forced a series of treaties on the factions of the Five Civilized Tribes in Indian Territory that had taken the Confederate side. In addition to abolishing slavery among the tribes and granting tribal citizenship to the new freedmen and their descendants, the treaties also forced the tribes to make radically unfair land cessions. "The President is willing to grant them peace," Cooley said, "but wants land for other Indians, and a civil government for the whole Territory." The commission also forced the Seminoles to sell their entire reservation at fifteen cents per acre and then buy a new reservation next door to the Creeks for fifty cents an acre.

The schizophrenic nature of the Office of Indian Affairs was nowhere more clear than in Cooley's report to Congress in 1866:

It does not seem a great task to attend to the business of directing the management of about three hundred thousand Indians; but when it is considered that those Indians are scattered over a continent, and divided into more than two hundred tribes, in charge of fourteen superintendents and some seventy agents, whose frequent reports and quarterly accounts are to be examined and adjusted; that no general rules can be adopted for the guidance of those officers, for the reason that the people under their charge are so different in habits, customs, manners, and organization . . . and that this office is called upon to protect the Indian . . . from abuse by unscrupulous whites, while at the same time it must concede every reasonable privilege to the spirit of enterprise and adventure which is pouring its hardy population into the western country; when these things are considered, the task assigned this bureau will not seem so light as it is sometimes thought.

In 1869, Ely Parker became the first Indian to be placed in charge of the Office of Indian Affairs. Parker was something of a nineteenth-century Indian all-star. A Seneca, he was born and raised on the Tonawanda Reservation in upstate New York, the fourth of seven children. His father, William Parker, was a miller and Baptist minister, and Ely had been brought up in the faith although he, like many others, also participated in Seneca longhouse ceremonies and had a Seneca name: Hasanoanda. When he came of age his parents sent him to a missionary boarding school, where he learned English; his bilingualism would later help his band negotiate a number of treaties regarding land claims upstate. Browsing in an Albany bookstore at sixteen, he struck up a conversation with an important-looking white man who turned out to be Lewis Henry Morgan. Morgan was enthralled by Indians, particularly Indians of the Iroquois Confederacy, and along with friends had formed the Grand Order of the Iroquois, which, besides playing Indian and emulating the fraternalism of the Masonic order, espoused the "virtues and values" of the Iroquois who had until so recently controlled the region. Still, Morgan reasoned, "'to sound the war whoop and seize the youth might have been dangerous,' so he instead chose to speak to the young man." They began a friendship, and Parker invited Morgan to visit him at Tonawanda. The Parker home became a meeting place for people like Morgan (who later made detailed studies of the Iroquois that culminated in a number of books, including *Systems of Consanguinity and Affinity of the Human Family*, *League of the Ho-dé-no-sau-hee or Iroquois*, and *Ancient Society*), Henry Rowe Schoolcraft (likewise an early writer about things Native, and an Indian agent and explorer who "discovered" the headwaters of the Mississippi), and John Wesley Powell (mapper of the Grand Canyon, explorer, and writer). Morgan formed such a strong connection with the young Parker that he dedicated *League of the Ho-dé-no-sau-hee* to him and, more important, helped him gain entrance to Rensselaer Polytechnic Institute to study engineering.

In his mid-twenties, Parker was appointed to an important political and ceremonial position within the Seneca Longhouse, which he used, along with his connections with Morgan and Schoolcraft, to fight federal, state, and private interests (most notably the land-hungry Ogden Lumber Company) that sought to gobble up Tonawanda land and relocate his band out west. The fight against removal and encroachment had been dragging on for two decades until finally, in 1857, the Tonawanda signed a new treaty with the government that preserved a large portion of their original reservation. Other Seneca communities—such as the reservation at

Buffalo Creek—disappeared. After graduating from RPI, Parker worked as an engineer, helping to improve the Erie Canal. In Illinois he befriended Ulysses S. Grant, who had returned there to work after his military service in the Mexican-American War. When the Civil War broke out, Parker tried to muster a company of Iroquois soldiers, but the governor of New York denied them the opportunity because they weren't Americans. (Most American Indians wouldn't be considered citizens until 1924, although there were sometimes paths to citizenship in treaties or negotiations.) Parker then tried to enlist on his own, noting that there was a shortage of engineers in the Union Army, but again he was turned down. In desperation he wrote to Grant, who vouched for him, allowing Parker to be commissioned as a captain in May 1863. Later, Grant had Parker transferred to the Military Division of the Mississippi, then under his command, and he eventually served as Grant's adjutant and secretary, in which capacity he was present at General Lee's surrender at Appomattox in April 1865. Indeed, it was Parker who helped draft and produce the final copy of the articles of surrender that ended the Civil War. Known as a good fighter and thinker, Parker also, according to contemporaries, had wonderfully beautiful handwriting. When it was time to sign, General Lee looked around, bewildered, and then set his eyes on Parker. He extended his hand and said, "I am glad to see one real American here." Parker, by his own account, shook Lee's hand and said, "We are all Americans." The anecdote is more a testament to Parker's attitude than to fact, as he still was not an American citizen.

After the ill-fated administration of Andrew Johnson, Grant ascended to the presidency in 1869. While his tenure was marred by corruption and graft, it represented a welcome change in the ways the federal government worked with Indian tribes. One of his first moves was to appoint Parker as commissioner of Indian affairs. At Parker's urging, Grant began to steer the federal government away from a policy of war with the tribes and toward one of peace. Together they constituted a Board of Indian Commissioners, charged with addressing "what should be the legal status of the Indians; a definition of their rights and obligations under the laws of the United States, of the States and territories and treaty stipulations;

whether any more treaties shall be stipulated with the Indians, and if not, what legislation is necessary for those with whom there are existing stipulations, and what for those with whom no such stipulations exist; should Indians be placed upon reservation and what is the best method to accomplish this." The findings of the board should have been encouraging to Indians across the country. They determined that "the first aggressions have been made by the white man, and the assertion is supported by every civilian of reputation who has studied the subject. In addition to the class of robbers and outlaws who find impunity in their nefarious pursuits upon the frontiers, there is a large class of professedly reputable men who use every means in their power to bring on Indian wars, for the sake of profit to be realized from the presence of troops and the expenditure of government funds in their midst."

Despite his affection for Parker or his apparent concern for Indians and Indian interests, Grant arrived at a disastrous solution to the problem the board had described. If the Indian service was rife with opportunists and ne'er-do-wells and warmongers, he would find a new source of administrators. In his second annual message to Congress, in December 1870, Grant unveiled his plan. Indian affairs would come under the control of a handful of religious orders. The effect of Parker's own Baptist upbringing can be felt in this decision, which would have dire ramifications for every aspect of Indians' daily life, especially, after Wounded Knee, in perhaps the most destructive aspect of Indian policy to come: Indian boarding schools.

In 1871, Ely Parker resigned, calling it a "thankless position." The end of his service was the end of an era: on March 3, 1871, Congress passed the Indian Appropriations Act, a bookend act closing down the "treaty period" opened twenty years before with the Indian Appropriations Act of 1851. This was a small piece of legislation meant to appropriate around $1,500 for the relief of the Lakota, who were experiencing serious hardship at the time. However, a rider was attached that radically changed the government's policy toward Indians by ending the treaty period. It read, in part: "No Indian nation or tribe within the territory of the United States shall be acknowledged or recognized as an independent nation, tribe, or power with whom the United States may contract by treaty; but no obligation of any treaty lawfully made and ratified with any such Indian nation or tribe prior to March 3, 1871, shall be hereby invalidated or impaired." In plain language this meant that the treaty process—the means by which the federal government and the Indian tribes had interacted and defined their relationships with one another—was officially terminated. In its place (as provided by the act), the government would administer Indians not as foreign nations (as they had been) or as citizens (which, by and large, they had yet to become) but as wards of the state, for whom the government assumed the roles of guardian, banker, and protector. In principle this might have been a good thing, but it flew in the face of obvious realities, namely that, where Indians were concerned, the government itself often acted as the aggressor and treated with tribes unfairly and in bad faith. How, then, should Indians, when seeking redress, rely on American courts and American politicians and American people to see to their interests? Juries and governmental committees seldom included any Indians, let alone a majority. No elected officials were Indians. And yet the bureau would assume radical new importance as the sole conduit for all claims and adjudications and assessments.

With the end of the Plains Indian Wars in the 1880s and the closing of the frontier in 1890, the Office of Indian Affairs became even more important. By that time the Indians of the Southwest—including the vast number of Diné, Californian Indians, and all the other Indians in territories not yet states—lived under the American umbrella. The Office of Indian Affairs' payroll grew from 108 employees in 1852 to almost 2,000 by 1888. These employees, organized into agencies, each run by an Indian agent, were clumped into larger regions administered by superintendents, who in turn reported up to the board of commissioners, and from there to the commissioner himself. Each agent was expected to administer to the Indians within his agency, to see that they received treaty rations, to dispense annuities, to hire and train police (often drawn from Indians of the tribes within the reach of the agency), to redress wrongs, to keep the peace, to supervise the missions and religious orders empowered by the government to "civilize" the Indians, to make sure traders and store

111

owners both served Indians and were paid by them, and to file quarterly reports to their superintendent, who would file reports on his region with the office in Washington, D.C. On the ground, the agent was most Indians' point of contact with the government. By 1900, indeed, "the Indian agent had, in effect, become the tribal government." So what did that government look like?

A civilian visiting the agency in Anadarko, in Indian Territory, observed, "There are bluffs and bunches of timber around Anadarko, but the prairie stretches towards the west, and on it is the pen from which cattle are issued. The tepees and camp-fires sprang up over night, and . . . more Indians were driving in every minute, with the family in the wagon and the dogs under it. . . . The men galloped off to the cattle-pen, and the women gathered in a long line in front of the agent's store to wait their turn for their rations. It was a curious line, with very young girls in it, very proud of the babies in beaded knapsacks on their backs—dirty, bright-eyed babies . . . and wrinkled, bent old squaws . . . with coarse white hair, and hands worn [almost] out of shape with work. Each of these had a tag . . . on which was printed the number in each family, and the amount of grain, flour, baking-powder, and soap to which the family was entitled." An Indian agent assigned to the Blackfeet in northwestern Montana reported that the Indians there were in terrible condition: "Their supplies had been limited and many of them were gradually dying of starvation. I visited a large number of their tents and cabins the second day after they had received their weekly rations. . . . All bore marks of suffering from lack of food but the little children seemed to have suffered most. . . . It did not seem possible for them to live long . . . so great was their destitution that the Indians stripped bark from the saplings that grow along the creeks and ate the inner portions to appease their gnawing hunger." Whereas the Blackfeet had, fifty years earlier, the millions-strong bison herd to feed them, now they had the bark of trees. And even in order to hunt they needed the permission of the Indian agent.

Washburn ruefully summed it up this way: "Back in the tail end of the nineteenth century, Indians lived in organized communities, but many of them were living, literally, against the walls of federal forts. It was a real low point for tribes. There was a BIA superintendent for each agency"—the new term for what before 1909 had been referred to as an "Indian agent"—"who was viewed as a god. They were in charge of everything. The superintendent had an amazing amount of authority. Consequently, when people talk about the BIA today there is still a lot of resentment. Back then 'BIA' really did stand for 'Bossing Indians Around.'"

A whole new bureaucracy grew up to support the work of the Indian agent: clerks, stenographers, millers, farmers, carpenters, mechanics, sawyers, stockmen, laborers, freighters, and cops. The mission was, according to Henry L. Dawes, the chief architect of this new phase in federal Indian policy, to turn Indians into Americans through private ownership, religion, and education. Thomas Morgan, the commissioner of Indian affairs in 1890, was clear: "It has become the settled policy of the Government to break up reservations, destroy tribal relations, settle Indians upon their own homesteads, incorporate them into the national life, and deal with them not as nations or tribes or bands, but as individual citizens." Or as Dawes put it more colloquially: What America wanted, at a time when it was drunk on its own power and sense of the rightness of its ways, was for Indians to "wear civilized clothes . . . cultivate the ground, live in houses, ride in Studebaker wagons, send children to school, drink whiskey [and] own property." The Indian agent, together with the bureau he represented, was the administrative tool to achieve this end. His two greatest weapons were schools and land. The attempted control of tribal lives (and the attempt to turn tribes into individuals) through the theft of land and children was guided by greed, ideology, religion, and, of course, good intentions.

The rider to the 1871 Indian Appropriations Act that had brought the treaty period to an end—though barely recognized by most people—was one such instance of good intentions with profound, largely unintended consequences. Grant and Ely Parker hoped to end the patronage system by moving the Office of Indian Affairs from the Interior back to the War Department and by putting religious orders in positions of power. But by legislating the end of the treaty process, the act took all the power of the executive branch to negotiate with the tribes and gave it to Congress. It also prevented Grant from moving the Indian service back to the War Department, as he'd hoped. Now, both houses of Congress (rather than just the Senate and the executive branch) would legislate Indian policy, ensuring that Indian affairs would forever be wrapped up in partisan politics and subject to the local whims of states' rights. This new phase of federal Indian policy was known as assimilation, and as bad as the years of warfare and treaty making had been, assimilation would be immeasurably worse. How Indian policy evolved, and how it was experienced on the ground, is a story that includes the resistance and eventual capitulation of the Nez Perce, the protest of a band of Ponca, the educational reforms of Richard Henry Pratt, Helen Hunt Jackson, the Friends of the Indian, and the resulting Lake Mohonk Conference.

Chief Joseph and Chief Standing Bear

In January 1870, U.S. troops killed 173 Blackfeet Indians (mostly women and children) after being directed to the wrong camp by a soldier who wanted to protect his Indian wife and children. In 1871, four settlers killed thirty Yahi Indians in the Ishi Wilderness near Wild Horse Corral; the entire remnant of the tribe numbered fifteen or so. On December 28, 1872, U.S. troops killed seventy-six Yavapai Indians in the Skeleton Cave Massacre in Arizona. U.S. troops attacked a Nez Perce village in 1877 in Big Hole, Montana, killing as many as ninety before they were driven away by the survivors. After escaping confinement at Nebraska's Fort Robinson in 1879, Northern Cheyenne chief Dull Knife and his band were hunted down and slaughtered, though the chief didn't die until 1883. As many as seventy perished. Regional coverage of these atrocities by papers like the *Portland Standard* and *The Lewiston Teller* was quickly picked up out east.

The struggles of the Nez Perce under Chief Joseph received especially widespread coverage. The tribe had been promised by treaty a reservation in their ancestral lands in Oregon's Wallowa Valley. In 1877, however, they were forcibly removed to a poorer, smaller, and unfamiliar reservation near Lapwai, Idaho. Chief Joseph and his band decided they could not live in this new land, far from the bones of their ancestors, and so they fled, embarking on a twelve-hundred-mile fighting retreat across Idaho, Wyoming, and Montana, on their way to join Sitting Bull's Lakota across the border in Canada. Starving and exhausted, Joseph and his band surrendered to General Nelson A. Miles on October 5, 1877, just forty miles from the Canadian border. John Andrew Rea covered the entire battle over the spring and into the winter for the *Chicago Tribune* and *The New York Herald*. Two years after his surrender, Chief Joseph gave a speech in Washington, D.C., to the government and the public. It is worth reading in full. Few other documents capture both the anguish and the hopes of Indians at that time or provide such a concise account of a tribe's relationship with the United States from the moment of first contact:

My friends, I have been asked to show you my heart. I am glad to have a chance to do so. I want the white people to understand my people. Some of you think an Indian is like a wild animal. This is a great mistake. I will tell you all about our people, and then you can judge whether an Indian is a man or not. I believe much trouble and blood would be saved if we opened our hearts more. I will tell you in my way how the Indian sees things. The white man has more words to tell you how they look to him, but it does not require many words to speak the truth. What I have to say will come from my heart, and I will speak with a straight tongue. Ah-cum-kin-i-ma-me-hut (the Great Spirit) is looking at me, and will hear me.

My name is In-mut-too-yah-lat-lat (Thunder traveling over the Mountains). I am chief of the Wal-lam-wat-kin band of Chute-pa-lu, or Nez Perces (nose-pierced Indians). I was born in eastern Oregon, thirty-eight winters ago. My father was chief before me. When a young man, he was called Joseph by Mr. Spaulding, a missionary. He died a few years ago. There was no stain on his hands of the blood of a white man. He left a good name on the earth. He advised me well for my people.

Our fathers gave us many laws, which they had learned from their fathers. These laws were good. They told us to treat all men as they treated us; that we should never be the first to break a bargain; that it was a disgrace to tell a lie; that we should speak only the truth; that it was a shame for one man to take from another his wife, or his property without paying for it. We were taught to believe that the Great Spirit sees and hears everything, and that he never forgets; that hereafter he will give every man a spirit-home according to his deserts: if he has been a good man, he will have a good home; if he has been a bad man, he will have a bad home. This I believe, and all my people believe the same.

We did not know there were other people besides the Indian until about one hundred winters ago, when some men with white faces came to our country. They brought many things with them to trade for furs and skins. They brought tobacco, which was new to us. They brought guns with flint stones on them, which frightened our women and children. Our people could not talk with these white-faced men, but they used signs which all people understand. These men were Frenchmen, and they called our people "Nez Perces," because they wore rings in their noses for ornaments. Although very few of our people wear them now, we are still called by the same name. These French trappers said a great many things to our fathers, which have been planted in our hearts. Some were good for us, but some were bad. Our people were divided in opinion about these men. Some thought they taught more bad than good. An Indian respects a brave man, but he despises a coward. He loves a straight tongue, but he hates a forked tongue. The French trappers told us some truths and some lies.

The first white men of your people who came to our country were named Lewis and Clark. They also brought many things that our people had never seen. They talked straight, and our people gave them a great feast, as a proof that their hearts were friendly. These men were very kind. They made presents to our chiefs and our people made presents to them. We had a great many horses, of which we gave them what they needed, and they gave us guns and tobacco in return. All the Nez Perces made friends with Lewis and Clark, and agreed to let them pass through their country, and never to make war on white men. This promise the Nez Perces have never broken. No white man can accuse them of bad faith, and speak with a straight tongue. It has always been the pride of the Nez Perces that they were the friends of the white men. When my father was a young man there came to our country a white man (Rev. Mr. Spaulding) who talked spirit law. He won the affections of our people because he spoke good things to them. At first he did not say anything about white men wanting to settle on our lands. Nothing was said about that until about twenty winters ago, when a number of white people came into our country and built houses and made farms. At first our people made no complaint. They thought there was room enough for all to live in peace, and they were learning many things from the white men that seemed to be good. But we soon found that the white men were growing rich very fast, and were greedy to possess everything the Indian had. My father was the first to see through the schemes of the white men, and he warned his tribe to be careful about trading with them. He had suspicion of men who seemed so anxious to make money. I was a boy then, but I remember well my father's caution. He had sharper eyes than the rest of our people.

Next there came a white officer (Governor Stevens), who invited all the Nez Perces to a treaty council. After the council was opened he made known his heart. He said there were a great many white people in the country, and many more would come; that he wanted the land marked out so that the Indians and white men could be separated. If they were to live in peace it was necessary, he said, that the Indians should have a country set apart for them, and in that country they must stay. My father, who represented his band, refused to have anything to do with the council, because he wished to be a free man. He claimed that no man owned any part of the earth, and a man could not sell what he did not own.

Mr. Spaulding took hold of my father's arm and said, "Come and sign the treaty." My father pushed him away, and said: "Why do you ask me to sign away my country? It is your business to talk to us about spirit matters, and not to talk to us about parting with our land." Governor Stevens urged my father to sign his treaty, but he refused. "I will not sign your paper," he said; "you go where you please, so do I; you are not a child, I am no child; I can think for myself. No man can think for me. I have no other home than this. I will not give it up to any man. My people would have no home. Take away your paper. I will not touch it with my hand."

My father left the council. Some of the chiefs of the other bands of the Nez Percés signed the treaty, and then Governor Stevens gave them presents of blankets. My father cautioned his people to take no presents, for "after a while," he said, "they will claim that you have accepted pay for your country." Since that time four bands of the Nez Percés have received annuities from the United States. My father was invited to many councils, and they tried hard to make him sign the treaty, but he was firm as the rock, and would not sign away his home. His refusal caused a difference among the Nez Percés.

Eight years later (1863) was the next treaty council. A chief called Lawyer, because he was a great talker, took the lead in this council, and sold nearly all the Nez Percés country. My father was not there. He said to me: "When you go into council with the white man, always remember your country. Do not give it away. The white man will cheat you out of your home. I have taken no pay from the United States. I have never sold our land." In this treaty Lawyer acted without authority from our band. He had no right to sell the Wallowa (winding water) country. That had always belonged to my father's own people, and the other bands had never disputed our right to it. No other Indians ever claimed Wallowa.

In order to have all people understand how much land we owned, my father planted poles around it and said: "Inside is the home of my people—the white man may take the land outside. Inside this boundary all our people were born. It circles around the graves of our fathers, and we will never give up these graves to any man."

The United States claimed they had bought all the Nez Percés country outside of Lapwai Reservation, from Lawyer and other chiefs, but we continued to live on this land in peace until eight years ago, when white men began to come inside the bounds my father had set. We warned them against this great wrong, but they would not leave our land, and some bad blood was raised.

The white men represented that we were going upon the war-path. They reported many things that were false.

The United States Government again asked for a treaty council.

My father had become blind and feeble. He could no longer speak for his people. It was then that I took my father's place as chief. In this council I made my first speech to white men. I said to the agent who held the council: "I did not want to come to this council, but I came hoping that we could save blood. The white man has no right to come here and take our country. We have never accepted any presents from the Government. Neither Lawyer nor any other chief had authority to sell this land. It has always belonged to my people. It came unclouded to them from our fathers, and we will defend this land as long as a drop of Indian blood warms the hearts of our men."

The agent said he had orders, from the Great White Chief at Washington, for us to go upon the Lapwai Reservation, and that if we obeyed he would help us in many ways. "You must move to the agency," he said. I answered him: "I will not. I do not need your help; we have plenty, and we are contented and happy if the white man will let us alone. The reservation is too small for so many people with all their stock. You can keep your presents; we can go to your towns and pay for all we need; we have plenty of horses and cattle to sell, and we won't have any help from you; we are free now; we can go where we please. Our fathers were born here. Here they lived, here they died, here are their graves. We will never leave them." The agent went away, and we had peace for a little while.

Soon after this my father sent for me. I saw he was dying. I took his hand in mine. He said: "My son, my body is returning to my mother earth, and my spirit is going very soon to see the Great Spirit Chief. When I am gone, think of your country. You are the chief of these people. They look to you to guide them. Always remember that your father never sold his country. You must stop your ears whenever you are asked to sign a treaty selling your home. A few years more, and white men will be all around you. They have their eyes on this land. My son, never forget my dying words. This country holds your father's body. Never sell the bones of your father and your mother." I pressed my father's hand and told him I would protect his grave with my life. My father smiled and passed away to the spirit-land.

I buried him in that beautiful valley of winding waters. I love that land more than all the rest of the world. A man who would not love his father's grave is worse than a wild animal.

For a short time we lived quietly. But this could not last. White men had found gold in the mountains around the land of winding water. They stole a great many horses from us, and we could not get them back because we were Indians. The white men told lies for each other. They drove off a great many of our cattle. Some white men branded our young cattle so they could claim them. We had no friend who would plead our cause before the law councils. It seemed to me that some of the white men in Wallowa were doing these things on purpose to get up a war. They knew that we were not strong enough to fight them. I labored hard to avoid trouble and bloodshed. We gave up some of our country to the white men, thinking that then we could have peace. We were mistaken. The white man would not let us alone. We could have avenged our wrongs many times, but we did not. Whenever the Government has asked us to help them against other Indians, we have never refused. When the white men were few and we were strong we could have killed them all off, but the Nez Perces wished to live at peace.

If we have not done so, we have not been to blame. I believe that the old treaty has never been correctly reported. If we ever owned the land we own it still, for we never sold it. In the treaty councils the commissioners have claimed that our country had been sold to the Government. Suppose a white man should come to me and say, "Joseph, I like your horses, and I want to buy them." I say to him, "No, my horses suit me, I will not sell them." Then he goes to my neighbor, and says to him: "Joseph has some good horses. I want to buy them, but he refuses to sell." My neighbor answers, "Pay me the money, and I will sell you Joseph's horses." The white man returns to me, and says, "Joseph, I have bought your horses, and you must let me have them." If we sold our lands to the Government, this is the way they were bought.

On account of the treaty made by the other bands of the Nez Perces, the white men claimed my lands. We were troubled greatly by white men crowding over the line. Some of these were good men, and we lived on peaceful terms with them, but they were not all good.

Nearly every year the agent came over from Lapwai and ordered us on to the reservation. We always replied that we were satisfied to live in Wallowa. We were careful to refuse the presents or annuities which he offered.

Through all the years since the white men came to Wallowa we have been threatened and taunted by them and the treaty Nez Perces. They have given us no rest. We have had a few good friends among white men, and they have always advised my people to bear these taunts without fighting. Our young men were quick-tempered, and I have had great trouble in keeping them from doing rash things. I have carried a heavy load on my back ever since I was a boy. I learned then that we were but few, while the white men were many, and that we could not hold our own with them. We were like deer. They were like grizzly bears. We had a small country. Their country was large. We were contented to let things remain as the Great Spirit Chief made them. They were not; and would change the rivers and mountains if they did not suit them. . . .

I only ask of the Government to be treated as all other men are treated. If I can not go to my own home, let me have a home in some country where my people will not die so fast. I would like to go to Bitter Root Valley. There my people would be healthy; where they are now they are dying. Three have died since I left my camp to come to Washington.

When I think of our condition my heart is heavy. I see men of my race treated as outlaws and driven from country to country, or shot down like animals.

I know that my race must change. We can not hold our own with the white men as we are. We only ask an even chance to live as other men live. We ask to be recognized as men. We ask that the same law shall work alike on all men. If the Indian breaks the law, punish him by the law. If the white man breaks the law, punish him also.

Let me be a free man—free to travel, free to stop, free to work, free to trade where I choose, free to choose my own teachers, free to follow the religion of my fathers, free to think and talk and act for myself—and I will obey every law, or submit to the penalty.

Whenever the white man treats the Indian as they treat each other, then we will have no more wars. We shall all be alike—brothers of one father and one mother, with one sky above us and one country around us, and one government for all. Then the Great Spirit Chief who rules above will smile upon this land, and send rain to wash out the bloody spots made by brothers' hands from the face of the earth. For this time the Indian race are waiting and praying. I hope that no more groans of wounded men and women will ever go to the ear of the Great Spirit Chief above, and that all people may be one people.

In-mut-too-yah-lat-lat has spoken for his people.

The speech was covered in its entirety by the *North American Review* and generated an incredible amount of sympathy for the Nez Perce specifically, and for Indians more generally.

Meanwhile, another tragic tale was unfolding out west. The Ponca tribe, under Chief Standing Bear, after a series of misfortunes that defy the imagination, had decided to walk from their pitiful home in Indian Territory back to their ancestral lands along the Niobrara River near present-day Ponca, Nebraska, on the South Dakota border. The Ponca, never a terribly big tribe, had numbered around a thousand at first contact, but by the time Lewis and Clark passed through in 1807, their numbers had been reduced to around two hundred by a smallpox epidemic. Nonetheless, the Ponca slowly recovered, growing corn and squash and planting fruit trees near their villages and moved out on the plains seasonally to hunt bison. The hunting put them in conflict with the more numerous Oglala Brulé Lakota, however, and by the mid-1800s they had more or less retreated to their villages to guard against the Lakotas' punitive raids.

But white settlers had begun to flood the area in the 1850s, and this life, too, proved untenable for the Ponca. Cut off from the bison by the Lakota and from their own range by the settlers, in 1858 they signed a treaty that ceded much of their land, reserving for the tribe a small area near their old home on the Niobrara. As part of the treaty, the government promised feed, grain, schools, and protection from other tribes. None of this was forthcoming, however, and the tribe slowly began to starve to death on their pitiful plot of land. In 1865 they signed a new treaty that seemed to cement a better future: in a reverse of the usual narrative, the new treaty gave them more land and more freedoms in most of their old range. Shortly thereafter, however, the Lakota chief Red Cloud so thoroughly defeated U.S. troops that the American frontier was forced back to Fort Laramie, and the Americans themselves were forced to the treaty table on very unfavorable terms. Unwilling to again anger the Lakota, the United States ceded the Poncas' land to the Lakota and then moved the Ponca to Indian Territory in 1877. This land proved unsuitable for farming, and in any event the Ponca were moved too late in the year to plant crops. They were moved yet again that summer, 150 miles west to the Salt Fork of the Arkansas River. There they wintered over without supplies and without succor. By spring, a third of the tribe had died of starvation.

Among the dead was Chief Standing Bear's eldest son, Bear Shield. Standing Bear had promised his son before his death that he would bury him in their ancestral homelands on the Niobrara River. He and a few dozen followers began heading north on foot with the body. En route, desperate for food, they were welcomed warmly by the Omaha in what is now Nebraska. But while they ate and rested, the U.S. government learned of their odyssey, and General George Crook, a notorious Indian fighter, was dispatched to arrest them. The Ponca were imprisoned at Fort Omaha. Then a curious thing happened. Crook, a decorated Civil War veteran who had fought the Paiute in the Snake War, the Yavapai and Apache in the Tonto War, and numerous Lakota during the Great Sioux War, had a change of heart. A lifetime of fighting seems to have helped him to see the true cost of war and the terrible treatment of the Indian combatants. Instead of returning the Ponca to Oklahoma, he let them stay at Fort Omaha and rest. In the meantime, he contacted Thomas Tibbles.

Born in Ohio in 1840, Tibbles was an idealist from an early age. At sixteen, he traveled to Kansas, where he joined John Brown's band of militant abolitionists. He was captured and sentenced to be hanged but escaped. Later he became a Methodist minister and traveled with (and even fought alongside) the Omaha against the Lakota. (Later still, he would be at Wounded Knee in the days following the massacre.) By the time the Ponca landed in Omaha country, Tibbles had become a journalist and an assistant editor at the *Omaha Daily Herald*. When Crook asked Tibbles to make some noise on the Poncas' behalf, Tibbles was happy to comply. One scathing full-page editorial followed another. Soon two local attorneys, John Webster and Andrew Poppleton, offered to represent Standing Bear in court. They filed a writ of habeas corpus in U.S. district court in Omaha, Nebraska. Under the law of habeas corpus, an imprisoned person can sue jailers or captors for unlawful imprisonment. Since Crook was, in fact, in charge of Standing Bear, and the immediate cause of his imprisonment, the case was called *United States ex rel. Standing Bear v. Crook*. It was an unusual case. Standing Bear's lawyers argued for two days. Closing arguments lasted nine hours. On the closing day of the trial, Standing Bear was allowed to address the judge, Elmer Scipio Dundy. This was one of the very first times an Indian had the opportunity to address wrongs against him in open court. Thomas Tibbles recorded both the scene and the entirety of Standing Bear's speech, as delivered by an Omaha translator:

It was late in the afternoon when the trial drew to a close. The excitement had been increasing, but it reached a height not before attained when Judge Dundy announced that Chief Standing Bear would be allowed to make a speech in his own behalf. Not one in the audience besides the army officers and Mr. Tibbles had ever heard an oration by an Indian. All of them had read of the eloquence of Red Jacket and Logan, and they sat there wondering if the mild-looking old man, with the lines of suffering and sorrow on his brow and cheek, dressed in the full robes of an Indian chief, could make a speech at all. It happened that there was a good interpreter present—one who was used to "chief talk."

Standing Bear arose. Half facing the audience, he held out his right hand, and stood motionless so long that the stillness of death which had settled down on the audience, became almost unbearable. At last, looking up at the judge, he said:

"That hand is not the color of yours, but if I prick it, the blood will flow, and I shall feel pain. The blood is of the same color as yours. God made me, and I am a man. I never committed any crime. If I had, I would not stand here to make a defense. I would suffer the punishment and make no complaint."

Still standing half facing the audience, he looked past the judge, out of the window, as if gazing upon something far in the distance, and continued:

"I seem to be standing on a high bank of a great river, with my wife and little girl at my side. I cannot cross the river, and impassable cliffs arise behind me. I hear the noise of great waters; I look, and see a flood coming. The waters rise to our feet, and then to our knees. My little girl stretches her hands toward me and says, 'Save me.' I stand where no member of my race ever stood before. There is no tradition to guide me. The chiefs who preceded me knew nothing of the circumstances that surround me. I hear only my little girl say, 'Save me.' In despair I look toward the cliffs behind me, and I seem to see a dim trail that may lead to a way of life. But no Indian ever passed over that trail. It looks to be impassable. I make the attempt.

"I take my child by the hand, and my wife follows after me. Our hands and our feet are torn by the sharp rocks, and our trail is marked by our blood. At last I see a rift in the rocks. A little way beyond there are green prairies. The swift-running water, the Niobrara, pours down between the green hills. There are the graves of my fathers. There again we will pitch our teepee and build our fires. I see the light of the world and of liberty just ahead."

The old chief became silent again, and, after an appreciable pause, he turned toward the judge with such a look of pathos and suffering on his face that none who saw it will forget it, and said:

"But in the center of the path there stands a man. Behind him I see soldiers in number like the leaves of the trees. If that man gives me the permission, I may pass on to life and liberty. If he refuses, I must go back and sink beneath the flood."

Then, in a lower tone, "You are that man."

There was silence in the court as the old chief sat down. Tears ran down over the judge's face. General Crook leaned forward and covered his face with his hands. Some of the ladies sobbed.

All at once that audience, by one common impulse, rose to its feet, and such a shout went up as was never heard in a Nebraska court room. No one heard Judge Dundy say, "Court is dismissed." There was a rush for Standing Bear. The first to reach him was General Crook. I was second. The ladies flocked around him, and for an hour Standing Bear had a reception.

There is a good chance that Tibbles, like other advocates for Indian rights and journalists who covered such struggles, added his own poetic flair to Standing Bear's words, powerful though they must have been. Not included in Tibbles's account—but part of the court record—are the words Standing Bear spoke to the judge on the first day of the trial: "I wanted to go on my own land, land that I had never sold. That's where I wanted to go. My son asked me when he was dying to take him back and bury him there, and I have his bones in a box with me now. I want to live there the rest of my life and be buried there."

On May 12, 1879, Judge Dundy came back with a verdict. His decision ran to eleven pages and is notable for both its thoroughness and its passion. "During the fifteen years in which I have been engaged in administering the laws of my country," it began, "I have never been called upon to hear or decide a case that appealed so strongly to my sympathy as the one now under consideration." Dundy continued:

On the one side, we have a few of the remnants of a once numerous and powerful, but now weak, insignificant, unlettered, and generally despised race; on the other, we have the representative of one of the most powerful, most enlightened, and most Christianized nations of modern times. On the one side, we have the representatives of this wasted race coming into this national tribunal of ours, asking for justice and liberty to enable them to adopt our boasted civilization, and to pursue the arts of peace, which have made us great and happy as a nation; on the other side, we have this magnificent, if not magnanimous, government, resisting this application with the determination of sending these people back to the country which is to them less desirable than perpetual imprisonment in their own native land. But I think it is creditable to the heart and mind of the brave and distinguished officer who is made respondent herein to say that he has no sort of sympathy in the business in which he is forced by his position to bear a part so conspicuous; and, so far as I am individually concerned, I think it not improper to say that, if the strongest possible sympathy could give the relators title to freedom, they would have been restored to liberty the moment the arguments in their behalf were closed. No examination or further thought would then have been necessary or expedient. But in a country where liberty is regulated by law, something more satisfactory and enduring than mere sympathy must furnish and constitute the rule and basis of judicial action. It follows that this case must be examined and decided on principles of law.

Dundy then went on to detail with great care how and why the Ponca had come to appear before him. He noted that they were not combatants. Nor had they violated the terms of the treaties that established a home for them in Oklahoma. Moreover, since the treaty period was now considered over (as stipulated by the Indian Appropriations Act) and with it, tribal sovereignty, there was even more reason now to consider Indians as people with the rights of citizens. Dundy's reasoning was methodical and clearly intended to stand as a wide and widely applied precedent:

Every "person" who comes within our jurisdiction, whether he be European, Asiatic, African, or "native to the manor born," must obey the laws of the United States. Every one who violates them incurs the penalty provided thereby. When a "person" is charged, in a proper way, with the commission of crime, we do not inquire upon the trial in what country the accused was born, nor to what sovereign or government allegiance is due, nor to what race he belongs. The questions of guilt and innocence only form the subjects of inquiry. An Indian, then, especially off from his reservation, is amenable to the criminal laws of the United States, the same as all other persons. They being subject to arrest for the violation of our criminal laws, and being "persons" such as the law contemplates and includes in the description of parties who may sue out the writ, it would indeed be a sad commentary on the justice and impartiality of our laws to hold that Indians, though natives of our own country, cannot test the validity of an alleged illegal imprisonment in this manner, as well as a subject of a foreign government who may happen to be sojourning in this country, but owing it no sort of allegiance.

At the end of his opinion, Dundy set out his ruling carefully:

1. That an Indian is a "person" within the meaning of the laws of the United States, and has, therefore, the right to sue out a writ of habeas corpus in a federal court, or before a federal judge, in all cases where he may be confined or in custody under color of authority of the United States, or where he is restrained of liberty in violation of the constitution or laws of the United States.

2. That General George Crook, the respondent, being commander of the military department of the Platte, has the custody of the relators, under color of authority of the United States, and in violation of the laws thereof.

3. That no rightful authority exists for removing by force any of the relators to the Indian Territory, as the respondent has been directed to do.

4. That the Indians possess the inherent right of expatriation, as well as the more fortunate white race, and have the inalienable right to "life, liberty, and the pursuit of happiness," so long as they obey the laws and do not trespass on forbidden ground. And,

5. Being restrained of liberty under color of authority of the United States, and in violation of the laws thereof, the relators must be discharged from custody, and it is so ordered.

Standing Bear and his followers were released by Crook and were allowed (and even helped) to continue their journey. He brought the box containing his son's bones back to their village site on the Niobrara River, and he and his people were allowed to resettle there and live out their days. In the years immediately following the court case he, the interpreter (now married to Tibbles), her brother, and Tibbles himself embarked on a speaking tour up and down the East Coast, where Standing Bear was greeted enthusiastically by liberals and former abolitionists, many of whom had turned their attention to the "Indian problem" once the issue of slavery had been (in their minds) laid to rest.

Standing Bear's eloquent assertion of his equal claim to personhood had profound and lasting rhetorical resonance, echoed in legal terms by Dundy's recognition that an Indian, as a person, deserved the same liberties and protections as other people. Yet even as people, they were not considered Americans: the Fourteenth Amendment, added to the U.S. Constitution in 1868, had made all people born in the United States American citizens *except* for Indians. Nevertheless, the struggles of Chief Joseph and Standing Bear and their tribes, the attendant publicity, the abolition of slavery as an institution in the wake of the Civil War, and the rise of an eastern protest class (along with a protest literature) forced a recognition, by the 1880s, that the reservation system by which the government had treated and administered to Indians was a moral and administrative failure. And with that recognition, an Indian rights movement began to grow. As such, it was in part the result of the direct, sustained, brave, and thoughtful actions of Indian leaders like Chief Joseph and Standing Bear along with those of journalists, military leaders, lawyers, translators, and judges. Standing Bear also had a profound impact on a woman named Helen Hunt Jackson.

Born to a liberal family in Amherst, Massachusetts, Helen Hunt Jackson was moved to throw her weight behind Indian causes after hearing Standing Bear speak at a gathering in Boston in 1879 where he detailed the suffering and mistreatment of the Ponca. Two years later, she published *A Century of Dishonor*, a scathing history of U.S. federal policy that ended with strong (and strongly worded) suggestions about how

Indian affairs should be administered in the future. Not content with having written the book, she sent a copy to every member of Congress. Stamped on the cover was a quotation from Benjamin Franklin: "Look Upon Your Hands! They are stained with the blood of your relations!" The book was a massive success. Struck by the influence that Harriet Beecher Stowe's *Uncle Tom's Cabin* had had on public opinion about slavery (in the North at least), Jackson determined to try fiction next. "If I could write a story that would do for the Indian one-hundredth part what *Uncle Tom's Cabin* did for the Negro, I would be thankful the rest of my life." *Ramona* was a romance about a half-Indian half-Scots girl who suffers discrimination and is kept from the love of her life because of her ancestry. It may not have been a good book, but it was hugely popular. It sold more than six hundred thousand copies in the first few years after its publication in 1884, and was subsequently reprinted more than three hundred times and adapted for stage and, later, film. Jackson's two books became founding documents of the emergent Indian rights movement in the late nineteenth century.

The Beginnings of the Indian Rights Movement

In 1882, two reformers—moved by their experience in the Indian service, the public lectures of Chief Joseph and Standing Bear, and Helen Hunt Jackson's fiction and nonfiction—gathered a group in Philadelphia and formed the Indian Rights Association. Within two years they opened offices in Washington, D.C., and Boston as well. Many former members of the Indian service began to write books and essays about what they felt was the criminal treatment of American Indians by the United States. Beginning in 1883, these "Friends of the Indian" met annually at the estate and hotel of reformer Albert Smiley at Lake Mohonk, near Poughkeepsie, New York. To say that there was overlap between the growing cohort of "friends" and government officials within and tied to the Office of Indian Affairs would be putting it mildly. Clinton B. Fisk, the Union officer and abolitionist who endowed Fisk University and was appointed by Grant to the Bureau of Indian Commissioners in 1874, chaired the Mohonk conference for the first years of its existence. Fisk was clear about the relationship among slavery, Indians, and reform: "We could not fit the negro for freedom till we made him free. We shall never fit the Indian for citizenship till we make him a citizen." Citizenship was the watchword for the Friends. So was free-labor ideology. Fisk had written that "every man is born into the world with the right to his own life, to personal liberty, and to inherit, earn, own, and hold property. These rights are given to him by the great God: not because he is a white man, a red man, or a black man, but because he is a MAN."

That Indians themselves might have a different view of their personhood and what constituted their humanity doesn't seem to have crossed the minds of their friends, but the Indian Rights Association (IRA), the Women's National Indian Association (WNIA), and the Lake Mohonk Conference were united in railing against the reservation system, the government service and Indian agents who regularly defrauded Indians, the lack of access to education and courts, and the whole treaty-based set of relationships: "The reservation shuts off the Indians from civilization, and rations distributed unearned tend to pauperize them," wrote one conference regular. The reservation system, wrote a strident member of the WNIA, "keeps the Indian more dependent upon the Government and less able to help himself." It was "fatal to the Indian." Another observed: "Treating the black man as chattel created a 'caste,' a social separation. . . . Treating the Indian as an Indian and not as a person is as false as slavery; it has created a separation, by way of the reservation system." The problems the system created seemed clear to the reformers, as did the solutions: civilization through citizenship, free enterprise, and private ownership of land. As passionate as the Friends of the Indian were, they did not consider what Indians thought and what Indians themselves wanted. They may have wanted to destroy old systems that they felt hurt Indian people, but they wanted to, and did, hang on to the heedless paternalism of the prior age. As such, their reforms were bound to go astray. The friends

131

positioned themselves as guardians of Indian interests and assumed an unofficial capacity as auditors of the Office of Indian Affairs—overseeing the work of agents in the field and writing reports to the Bureau of Indian Commissioners and to Congress. What they lacked, at first, was a method. It was one thing to say that Indians were people and needed citizenship. How would they become "ready" for the rights and responsibilities of citizenship and communion with the body of the country? The reformers soon hit upon paths to this end.

The Indian Boarding Schools

Richard Henry Pratt had a lot of experience with Indians. Born in 1840 in Rushford, New York, he grew up hard. His father moved the family to Logansport, Indiana, in 1846 and then left with the Gold Rush three years later when Pratt was nine. In California he was robbed and murdered, leaving Pratt to take care of his mother and younger brothers. When the Civil War broke out, Pratt signed up immediately and served as a private in the Ninth Regiment, Indiana Infantry. As soon as his first tour was over, he reenlisted and was promoted to sergeant. At the end of the war, he mustered out at the rank of captain and returned to Logansport to run a hardware store. But two years later he rejoined the army, serving as a second lieutenant in the Tenth United States Cavalry in Fort Sill, Oklahoma. The Tenth was a regiment of black freedmen and freed slaves used as shock troops in the escalating violence of the Plains Indian Wars. Pratt served for eight years on the Plains, fighting Indians in the Washita campaign and the Red River War. At the end of the war in 1875, he was assigned the task of interviewing Indian combatants in order to ascertain how they should be charged. Somehow his sympathies were engaged, and he tried to clear as many of them as possible.

Grant's attorney general, Amos T. Akerman, felt that the United States could not afford to be at war with its "wards" but that neither could it repatriate the combatants to their tribes and homelands. The resulting rule (not adjudicated in court) was that the combatants would be imprisoned for life far from their homelands on the Plains. Given his experience, Pratt was tasked with escorting the Indians to Fort Marion, Florida. While stationed at Fort Marion, Pratt, under only vague orders, began experiments in education. He reasoned that if wild turkeys could be domesticated, then surely Indians could be civilized. To that end he hired teachers to begin instructing the prisoners in English, art, and mechanical studies. He elevated some of them to guard duty. He was so impressed by the Indians' aptitude for "civilization" that, after their release, he expanded his mission by placing some of the prisoners in the Hampton Normal and Agricultural Institute, until then reserved for the education of black freedmen. They seemed to thrive there, and Pratt lobbied Congress for funding for a school dedicated to the civilization of American Indians.

In 1879, Pratt opened the Carlisle Indian Industrial School in an abandoned army barracks in Carlisle, Pennsylvania. Its first class numbered eighty-two, most of them the children of Plains Indian leaders, including the children of Oglala leaders American Horse (the war chief), Blue Horse, and Red Shirt. Buoyed by the "support" of tribal leaders out west and the "progress" of students at the school, Pratt waxed philosophical about his mission:

A great general has said that the only good Indian is a dead one, and that high sanction of his destruction has been an enormous factor in promoting Indian massacres. In a sense, I agree with the sentiment, but only in this: that all the Indian there is in the race should be dead. Kill the Indian in him, and save the man. . . . Theorizing citizenship into people is a slow operation. What a farce it would be to attempt teaching American citizenship to the negroes in Africa. They could not understand it; and, if they did, in the midst of such contrary influences, they could never use it. Neither can the Indians understand or use American citizenship theoretically taught to them on Indian reservations. They must get into the swim of American citizenship. They must feel the touch of it day after day, until they become saturated with the spirit of it, and thus become equal to it. Then we cease to teach the

Indian that he is less than a man; when we recognize fully that he is capable in all respects as we are, and that he only needs the opportunities and privileges which we possess to enable him to assert his humanity and manhood; when we act consistently towards him in accordance with that recognition; when we cease to fetter him to conditions which keep him in bondage, surrounded by retrogressive influences; when we allow him the freedom of association and the developing influences of social contact—then the Indian will quickly demonstrate that he can be truly civilized, and he himself will solve the question of what to do with the Indian.

Kill the Indian they did. Or tried to. Students were forbidden to speak their native languages, and Pratt condoned corporal punishment to that end. Upon arrival, students were photographed in their traditional garb and then stripped, stuffed into uniforms, and barbered to within an inch of their lives. Luther Standing Bear, son of Chief George Standing Bear, arrived at Carlisle among the first group of students. Told to point to a name, any name, and not knowing a word of English, he pointed at a figure on a print or picture and thereafter was known as Luther. While Luther Standing Bear came to be fond of Carlisle and of Pratt himself, he remembered a traumatic transition:

"The 'civilizing' process" at Carlisle, he recalled, started "with clothes. Never, no matter what our philosophy or spiritual quality, could we be civilized while wearing the moccasin and blanket. The task before us was not only that of accepting new ideas and adopting new manners, but actual physical changes and discomfort had to be borne uncomplainingly until the body adjusted itself to new tastes and habits. Our accustomed dress was taken and replaced with clothing that felt cumbersome and awkward. Against trousers and handkerchiefs we had a distinct feeling—they were unsanitary, and the trousers kept us from breathing well. High collars, stiff-bosomed shirts, and suspenders fully three inches in width were uncomfortable, while leather boots caused actual suffering. We longed to go barefoot, but were told that the dew on the grass would give us colds. That was a new warning for us, for our mothers had never told us to beware of colds, and I remember as a child coming into the tipi with moccasins full of snow. Unconcernedly I would take them off my feet, pour out the snow, and put them on my feet again without any thought of sickness, for in that time colds, catarrh, bronchitis and *la grippe* were unknown. But we were soon to know them. Then, red flannel undergarments were given us for winter wear and for me, at least, discomfort grew into actual torture. I used to endure it as long as possible, then run upstairs and quickly take off the flannel garments and hide them. When inspection time came, I ran and put them on again, for I knew that if I were found disobeying the orders of the school I should be punished. My niece once asked me what it was that I disliked the most during those first bewildering days, and I said, 'Red flannel.' Not knowing what I meant, she laughed, but I still remember those horrid, sticky garments which we had to wear next to the skin and I still squirm and itch when I think of them. Of course, our hair was cut, and then there was much disapproval. But that was part of the transformation process and in some mysterious way long hair stood in the path of our development. For all the grumbling among the bigger boys, we soon had our head shaven. How strange I felt!" For the Lakota, moreover, to cut one's hair was a sign of mourning, so when the barber commenced there was loud ritual (and heartfelt) wailing.

Pratt, being a military man, organized the school along military lines. Students were woken at dawn and marched in regiments and companies out to the yard for morning roll call. The days were split in half and so was the student body, with half devoting the morning to academic subjects and the afternoon to tradecraft—printing, carpentry, sewing—and the other half on the reverse schedule. There was a military-style court, run by the students themselves, who determined what punishments to dole out for infractions.

Many Indian leaders seemed to support the schools; they had come to recognize that assimilation was the only hope for the survival of their children. And many Indian children educated there seemed to like the experience and to look back on it fondly. I say "seemed" because it is sometimes hard to look behind the rhetoric of "progress" to recognize the acute pain felt by those who had to say goodbye to their children—or parents—for years. Even as Carlisle was a stab at equality, it was also a knife in the heart of the Indian family. With the help of an interpreter, the daughter of American Horse wrote this letter home to her father shortly after her arrival at Carlisle:

I want to tell you something, and it makes me feel very glad. You tell me that my brother is married and that makes me feel very glad. My cousins, and brothers, and I are all very well, at this Carlisle School. We would like to see you again. I am always happy here, but lately I sometimes feel bad, because you tell me that my grandfather is getting very old. Tell me how my brothers are. I would like to see my brother's wife's picture. Tell my brother Two-Dogs to write to me again. Miss Hyde's father died two weeks ago, and I am very sorry. I remember all of my friends. If you don't answer my letter soon, I'll feel bad. I don't always answer your letter soon, but it is because I can not write. As soon as I get so that I can write myself, I will write as often as I can. Tell Brave Bull that Dora (Her Pipe) has been a little sick, but is most well now. Tell if my grandfather is well. If he gets sick tell me. You wrote to my cousin Robert and told him that you had a house to live in, and lots of pigs and cows and such things, and I was very glad. You've got a white man's house to live in now and I am anxious to learn all that I can, so that I can come home by and by and live with you. I hear that they have a big school out there and it makes me very glad. If you can, come again, and tell me if you can come again, when. I want to tell you that some more girls and boys came here. Twenty-five. Fifteen of them are girls. There are a great many of us here now, and Capt. Pratt is very kind to us. That is all I want to say now. Give my love to all of my friends.

Your daughter,
Maggie Stands-Looking

Within a decade there were almost twenty boarding schools run by the Office of Indian Affairs, dozens of "agency schools" on or near Indian agencies around the country, and dozens more boarding schools run by religious orders (the majority by the Catholics), as empowered by Grant. The government had been running "Indian schools" since the first decade of the nineteenth century but now they were plentiful, and attendance became coercive. Federal expenditures on Indian education rose from $75,000 to about $2 million by 1894.

Many students later testified that they had good experiences at Carlisle. Perhaps that school—under Pratt's supervision and congressional scrutiny, constantly held up as the model for Indian education—was better staffed and better run than others around the country, which seem hellish in comparison. At Haskell, in Kansas, many different tribes were grouped. It was natural for Indians from a given tribe to stick together, but the school superintendent found this counterproductive. "It was deemed necessary to establish during the year a stricter system of discipline than heretofore prevailed," he testified. "A cadet battalion organization of five companies broke up the tribal associations." Discipline was instilled by force. Students regularly complained of being beaten, cursed, and made to perform hard physical labor as punishment for speaking their tribal tongues, routine disobedience, or failure to comply with school rules.

There wasn't a hard set of rules about when and how often students were allowed to return home, but in many if not most cases, students had to have money deposited into their personal accounts at the school to pay for their transportation back to their families during the summer. Most tribal communities were so poor as to make this impossible. My grandmother was sent to Tomah Indian Industrial School in Tomah, Wisconsin, in 1930 at age four and did not return home until she was ten. One concerned school official at Flandreau Indian School in South Dakota wrote to the parents of a very young girl at the school in the 1920s: "[Grace] was at the office yesterday and complains that she is very homesick for her mother and father and asked me to write you if you could send her enough money so she can go home for the summer vacation. These children have not been home for two years and this is their second summer here, naturally they would get lonesome." A concerned father wrote to Flandreau around the same time: "I understand you will let me know when Angeline is seriously sick but that might be a little too late then as she has been ailing for a long time. There must be something wrong with her as she spends most of her time in the hospital. . . . She should be examined by the doctor very good. I don't want to take her out of school before the end of the year but if she's ailing all the time she might just as well be home. As she wrote to me herself she wasn't feeling any too good to go to school. We might wait a little too long and then it will be too late."

Conditions "back home" were often worse, and some parents begged the schools to take their children because they couldn't afford to feed them. The majority of Indian parents, however, didn't want to be separated from their children and resisted putting them in the system. The Office of Indian Affairs and its agents in the field did not hesitate to coerce them. One method employed by the government was to disempower Indians in their own communities by stripping them of privileges and position. John Ward, the Indian agent in Mission, California, complained that "the parents of these Indian children are ignorant, and know nothing of the value of education, and there are no elevating circumstances in the home circle to arouse the ambition of the children. Parental authority is hardly known or exercised among the Indians in this agency." He suggested that he "should be endowed with some kind of authority to enforce attendance. The agent here has found that a threat to depose a captain if he does not make the children attend school has had a good effect." In the Dakotas not all the Indians shared the Oglala leadership's enthusiasm for boarding schools, and many kept their children back. John Williamson at the Dakota Agency mused, "Compulsion through the police is often necessary, and should this be required during the coming year, it will be heroically resorted to, regardless of results. The treaty with the Indians gives the children to the Government, for school purposes, nine months in the year, but the punishment therein provided in case they fail to comply is hardly humane or just. If taking ration tickets only meted out merited punishment to the heads of families, who are alone guilty, it would be a wise provision, but the children have to go hungry and suffer the disobedience of the parents. It is better, in my opinion, to compel attendance through the police than taking up ration tickets for non-attendance."

At Carlisle, the punishments of choice were having one's mouth washed out with lye soap (for speaking their native languages), daily beatings, and being locked in an old guardhouse with only bread and water for rations. One former student testified to the intimidations: "We would cower from the abusive disciplinary practices of some superiors, such as the one who yanked my cousin's ear hard enough to tear it. After a nine-year-old girl was raped in her dormitory bed during the night, we girls would be so scared that we would jump into each other's bed as soon as the lights went out. The sustained terror in our hearts further tested our endurance, as it was better to suffer with a full bladder and be safe than to walk through the dark, seemingly endless hallway to the bathroom. When we were older, we girls anguished each time we entered the classroom of a certain male teacher who stalked and molested girls."

So much for personhood. Or rather, the institution of the boarding schools was evidence of what the government understood personhood to mean. To be culturally Indian and live in one's Indian community was to be a savage. In Canada, where the boarding school system was in place until the 1970s (the last school didn't close until 1996) and affected many more aboriginal children, Sir John Macdonald, the first Canadian prime minister, put it this way: "When the school is on the reserve the child lives with its parents, who are savages, he is surrounded by savages, and though he may learn to read and write, his habits and training mode of thought are Indian. He is simply a savage who can read and write. It has been strongly impressed upon myself, as the head of the Department, that the Indian children should be withdrawn as much as possible from the parental influence, and the only way to do that would be to put them in central training industrial schools where they will acquire the habits and modes of thought of white men." To be a person was to be a certain *kind* of person: an American (or Canadian) who owned property and was culturally white. Indian kids went to school to be not-Indian.

They also went there to die. Perhaps no other aspect of Indian education during the sixty years of the boarding school era is more tragic than the fact that the school grounds at Carlisle and Haskell and all the other schools included graveyards. At Haskell, a forlorn cemetery is tucked behind the power plant and marked by more than a hundred small white tombstones. Many of the children who died there didn't even get a marker. At Carlisle, hundreds of students were buried. The names on the graves at Flandreau are a poignant roll call of a whole generation of Indians from across the country who never made it back to their tribal homes and never saw their parents again. Annie Dickson—Arapaho, age nineteen. Josephine Choate—Assiniboine, age twenty-one. Eugene Barber—Caddo, age eight. Harry White Wolf—Cheyenne, age six months. Joseph Rosseau—Chippewa, age sixteen. May Mohajah—Kaw, age seven. Nelson Swamp—Oneida, age three. Andrew Big Snake—Ponca, age sixteen. The list of the fallen children who died far from the arms of their parents and grandparents, far from the laughter of their siblings and cousins, far from the homelands their ancestors had fought so hard to protect and had hoped would always protect them, goes on and on. According to the Meriam Report, Indian children were six times as likely to die in childhood while at boarding schools than the rest of the children in America. Despite the good intentions of progressives (and because of those intentions) significant portions of three entire generations of Indians died in the boarding schools, and countless more were damaged by them.

The full effect of the boarding school system wouldn't be understood until decades after the agenda of "civilizing the savage" ground down. Even during the years the schools were in full swing it was hard for Indian families back in their homelands to know exactly how bad they were. Many couldn't read or write English and so couldn't communicate at all with school officials and teachers. Often children began to forget their own languages, or lost the habit of speaking in them, and so could not speak easily of what had happened to them. And shame played a role, as did a kind of grim realism. It was what it was, and for most it was the only option, so it didn't bear talking about.

In 1928 the government decided to conduct its own investigation of

Indian administration, health, and education. The Meriam Report was nothing if not thorough. It ran to more than eight hundred pages and included detailed statistical analysis. The section on Indian education was particularly alarming. It noted that the boarding schools hired unqualified and underqualified staff and paid them poorly. Turnover was high. In one classroom ten teachers had passed through in the course of a single semester. Most schools ran largely on Indian child labor. Students milked the cows and killed the chickens and split the wood and mowed the fields and whitewashed the walls and cooked the food in the kitchens. The report cautioned that "if the labor of the boarding school is to be done by the pupils, it is essential that the pupils be old enough and strong enough to do institutional work." It also noted that while official policy was to discourage the enrollment of young children, "there are numbers of young children, and in the reservation boarding schools the children are conspicuously small. At Leupp, for instance, one hundred of the 191 girls are 11 years of age or under. The result is that the institutional work, instead of being done wholly by able-bodied youths of 15 to 20 nominally enrolled in the early grades, has to be done, in part at least, by very small children—children, moreover, who, according to competent medical opinion, are malnourished." It went on. The time that children spent on such tasks "is in no sense educational, since the operations are large-scale and bear little relation to either home or industrial life outside; and it is admittedly unsatisfactory even from the point of view of getting the work done."

The report was equally scathing about the schools' teaching and teacher training methods, curriculum, and sensitivity to the individual academic, practical, and emotional needs of Indian children. This disregard for the children as individuals extended even to the uniforms they were forced to wear. In one sad footnote the writers observed that "there is no individuality in clothes in most schools, and suits are apparently passed on interminably, necessitating repeated repair." A single pair of trousers had been worn, for example, by twelve boys successively.

But the report saved most of its indignation for the health conditions at the schools. In a survey of more than seventy schools, the authors noted insufficient ventilation, rampant overcrowding, frequently nonoperational toilets and sinks, and an almost complete absence of "modern" laundry facilities. In one school very small children were discovered working behind piles of laundry that dwarfed them because the superintendent found they folded more when confronted by big piles. At another, the children were too malnourished to play. Even where they had the energy, they were often required to "maintain a pathetic degree of quietness." Some authorities did not allow them to speak at all. Most schools at the time of the survey included a sort of jail used to discipline children. School buildings in general were decrepit, often to the point of being fire risks, dorms were crowded, sanitation was substandard, and boilers and machinery were out-of-date and sometimes unsafe. Medical personnel were insufficiently trained, and the children themselves were offered nothing in the way of health education. Nor were they given sufficient milk, and almost nothing in the way of fresh fruits and vegetables (hence the malnutrition). The school day was unusually long, cutting into sleep, and a lack of recreational opportunities provided children with little exercise. The report concluded, "The generally routinized nature of the institutional life with its formalism in classrooms, its marching and dress parades, its annihilation of initiative, its lack of beauty, its almost complete negation of normal family life, all of which have disastrous effects upon mental health and the development of wholesome personality: These are some of the conditions that make even the best classroom teaching of health ineffective."

Such were the ways in which the U.S. government tried to "kill the Indian" to "save the man." From 1879 to the late 1930s, when the last compulsory boarding school programs were suspended (though some schools continue to this day), tens of thousands of Indian children were torn away from their families, forced to abandon their cultures and religions, and indoctrinated in federally funded religious schools. The effects of this attempt to break a people—and the aim of the boarding schools, albeit guided by "progressive" ideology, was unquestionably that—are still being felt today.

Meanwhile, back in Indian homelands, even worse conditions prevailed as the most crushing form of oppression in America was instituted and expanded across Indian country.

Allotment

According to the passionate progressives in the Indian Rights Association and the Friends of the Indian, education was only one part of the Indian problem. The other issue was the reservation system, which they saw as holding "the Indian" back.

Herbert Welsh, one of the founding members of the Indian Rights Association, had traveled extensively in the Dakotas, Nebraska, and the Southwest in the early 1880s and expressed his dismay at the squalid conditions, poverty, and lack of industry that he felt the reservation system encouraged. He was equally dismayed by the greed and mismanagement rampant among agents in the Indian service. The only solution, he felt, was doing away with the need for an Indian service by doing away with reservations themselves. His group had the ear of the government, which was similarly inclined. The commissioner of Indian affairs, in his annual report of 1886, complained:

> At present the rich Indians who cultivate tribal lands pay no rent to the poorer and more unfortunate of their race, although they are equal owners of the soil. . . . The proprietor grows annually richer, while the laborers, his own race, joint owners of the soil, even of the lands that he claims and individually appropriates, grow annually and daily poorer and less able to assert their equal ownership and tribal claim and, shall I say, constitutional privilege and treaty rights.

Power is power, and like their more "civilized" white counterparts Indians could and often tried to consolidate as much of it as possible for themselves.

Congress and the Executive of the United States are the supreme guardians of these mere wards, and can administer their affairs as any other guardian can. Of course it must be done in a just and enlightened way. It must be done in a spirit of protection and not of oppression and robbery. Congress can sell their surplus lands and distribute the proceeds equally among the owners for the purposes of civilization and the education of their children, and the protection of the infirm, and the establishment of the poor upon homesteads with stock and implements of husbandry. Congress cannot consistently or justly or honestly take their lands from them and give or sell them to others except as above referred to, and for those objects alone. The sentiment is rapidly growing among these five nations that all existing forms of Indian government which have produced an unsatisfactory and dangerous condition of things, menacing the peace of the Indians and irritating their white neighbors, should be replaced by a regularly organized Territorial form of government, the territory thus constituted to be admitted at some future time as a State into the Union on an equal footing with other States, thereby securing all the protection, sympathy, and guarantees of this great and beneficent nation. The sooner this sentiment becomes universal the better for all concerned. . . . The vast surplusage of land in the Indian Territory, much of it, too, not surpassed anywhere for fertility and versatility of production, which can never be utilized by the Indians now within its borders nor by their descendants (for it is not probable that there will be any material increase in numbers of Indian population), must sooner or later be disposed of by Congress some way or other.

Two years later, John Oberly, then commissioner of Indian affairs, echoed the 1886 report in a report of his own, in which he concluded that the Indian "must be imbued with the exalting egotism of American civilization so that he will say 'I' instead of 'We,' and 'This is mine' instead of 'This is ours.'" And in 1896, Merrill Gates, who would later head the Board of Indian Commissioners, stated: "We must make the Indian more intelligently selfish. . . . By acquiring property, man puts forth his personality and lays hold of matter by his own thought and will."

Senator Henry Dawes, a regular attendee of the Lake Mohonk conferences and a member of the Friends of the Indian, with the help of paid lobbyists in Washington, helped push forward the General Allotment Act, otherwise known as the Indian Severalty Act, otherwise known as the Dawes Act. Passed in 1887, it transformed the landscape of America and forever altered the ways in which most tribes lived on their homelands. Its key provision read:

> Be it enacted by the Senate and House of Representatives of the United States of America in Congress assembled, That in all cases where any tribe or band of Indians has been, or shall hereafter be, located upon any reservation created for their use, either by treaty stipulation or by virtue of an act of Congress or executive order setting apart the same for their use, the President of the United States be, and he hereby is, authorized, whenever in his opinion any reservation or any part thereof of such Indians is advantageous for agricultural and grazing purposes, to cause said reservation, or any part thereof, to be surveyed, or resurveyed if necessary, and to allot the lands in said reservation in severalty to any Indian located thereon in quantities as follows:
>
> To each head of a family, one-quarter of a section;
>
> To each single person over eighteen years of age, one-eighth of a section;
>
> To each orphan child under eighteen years of age, one-eighth of a section; and
>
> To each other single person under eighteen years now living, or who may be born prior to the date of the order of the President directing an allotment of the lands embraced in any reservation, one-sixteenth of a section.

The bill was drafted and passed the Senate without consent or even input from Indian tribes or Indian leaders. To the reformers of the Friends of the Indian and the Indian Rights Association, its strengths were that it promised to break up the tribe as a social unit, encourage private enterprise and farming, reduce the cost of Indian administration, fund the emerging boarding school system (with the sale of "surplus land"), and provide a land base for white settlement. If we look back at the period now, it is impossible not to feel a kind of sickness at the thought that the government stole Indian land in order to fund the theft of Indian children.

By the time of the Wounded Knee Massacre in 1890, allotment was in full swing. Indian agents were busy hiring surveyors, recording deeds, and registering heads of household. Armies of surveyors platted Indian homelands and marked them off. Clerks worked nonstop copying and recording deeds (although even under this new system, Indians could not buy or sell land—the allotments "owned" by Indians were in fact owned by the government in trust). Censuses were taken on reservations across the country.

Along with allotment, another program arose: enrollment. Until this point, there had been no official method of determining tribal membership, much less recording it. Tribes recognized their members in a variety of ways, including residence, descent, marriage, language, and who fought for, and with, whom; they determined for themselves who belonged in the tribe. Indian agents had, here and there, made lists of people they considered Indians for the purpose of distributing annuities and rations. But now there was pressure to come up with some system to determine tribal enrollment. It wouldn't do to distribute land—a pretty big gift in American thinking—without making sure the recipient deserved it.

The method the government arrived at was as flawed as the policy it was meant to facilitate. In most cases, the government used "blood quantum" as the way to figure out who was Indian and who was not, and therefore whom to include and (more often) exclude from receiving allotments. Blood quantum was simply a measure of how much Indian blood (full blood, half, quarter, eighth) a person had. It was often wildly inaccurate, culturally incongruous, and socially divisive. It is still used to determine who can be an enrolled member of some federally recognized tribes, and it is just as divisive now as it was then.

Compounding the problem, censuses and subsequent enrollment were conducted by white federal employees on the basis of European kinship terms that might have no analog in the cultures in question; the rolls were compiled by outsiders and kept by them; Indians were not in any way in charge of determining who was in their own tribe or not. And from the outset the process was marked by graft, greed, nepotism, favoritism, and fraud. Indian agents consolidated power by giving good allotments to Indians who supported their policies and even, in some cases, made sure that especially good allotments were excluded from the process so that white people (often business interests who had agents in their pockets) ended up owning vast tracts of the very best land within the boundaries of the reservation. It is no accident that non-Natives own the majority of the lakeshore on all the best lakes in Minnesota, or the richest farmland with access to water in Nebraska, Montana, and South Dakota.

In many contexts, the sheer size of the allotments didn't make much sense. It is one thing to have 160 acres (a quarter section) to farm in the Red River valley or along the Arkansas River. It's another to have 160 acres in the semiarid grasslands and scrub of South Dakota where no crops will grow at all. On much of the land where cultivation of crops was impossible, even grazing would require numerous acres per animal because the land was so poor. And control over the allotments themselves—whether and how they could be transferred between people, even family members—was always subject to the whims of the government as represented by the Indian agent, yet another way for the government to force Indians to do what they wanted. Allotment was as cruel a kind of coercion as the withholding of rations. Sometimes the two were used together—rations for Indians who were reluctant to adopt the allotment system were delivered late, were of even poorer quality, and were sometimes withheld altogether until the requisite signatures were put to paper. Starvation is a powerful motivator.

While the first wave of allotments was crashing on Indian shores in the 1890s, the General Allotment Act was amended and supplemented by further acts of Congress. The Nelson Act, affecting only tribes in Minnesota, went a step further than the General Allotment Act: rather than allot land within the boundaries of existing reservations, it sought to "disappear" all the existing reservations in Minnesota and remove all the Ojibwe Indians there and in parts of North Dakota to the newly established White Earth Reservation in west-central Minnesota, thereby freeing up a fortune in timber found in the northern part of the state. Many Ojibwe managed to hang on to their reservations, but so deep was the disgust and distrust at the government's maneuver that it spurred some Ojibwe to burn down the old-growth pine on their homelands. When asked what they were doing, the men responded by saying they were simply doing to the whites what the whites had done to them: destroying what they loved the most.

The Curtis Act, passed in 1898, brought the provisions of allotment to the so-called Five Civilized Tribes in Indian Territory (they had been excluded from the Dawes Act by the substance of their treaties). The act was officially and unironically titled "An act for the Protection of the People of the Indian Territory, and for other purposes." The sad truth behind it is that Charles Curtis, the legislator from Kansas who authored the bill, was Indian on his mother's side (Kaw, Osage, and Potawatomi) and had been raised for much of his childhood by his grandparents on the Kaw reservation near Garden Grove, Kansas. Once, when he was a child, a Cheyenne war party had attacked the Kaw, who had donned war paint and armed themselves and advanced to confront the Cheyenne. The Cheyenne literally rode circles around the Kaw, and they exchanged bow and arrow shot for the better part of the day while one of the Kaw rode hard for sixty miles to summon help. Charles Curtis, at eight, was along for that mission. His mother left him land upon her death; the Kaw are matrilineal. That didn't stop his non-Indian father from trying to steal it. As an adult, Curtis understood himself as both American and Indian, and the double strands of his cultural identity informed the reasoning behind the Curtis Act. He wanted to create legislation for the tribes of his homeland that respected their tribal ways but further encouraged the process of becoming American. But by the time the bill got through the Senate and the House it had been rewritten and amended five times and bore little resemblance to what Curtis had originally proposed. In its final form, the Curtis Act abolished tribal government, treaty lands, and communal landholdings. It brought allotment to the Five Civilized Tribes with the provision that lots could be held in "fee simple"—actually owned by Indians rather than held in trust by the government. It allowed for public schools and for the incorporation of towns. These provisions have forever marked the Indian communities in Oklahoma as different. Most Oklahoma Indians live in settlements, incorporated towns; they were able to levy taxes and establish public services like fire departments and hospitals; they have held public office at municipal and state levels for more than a century; the whole fabric of Oklahoma is marked by the Indian presence there. Whether this strategy was better for Indian communities than fixing the more traditional reservation system is open to debate. There was much to be gained and much to be lost no matter the course a tribe chose. As for Curtis, he regretted the legislation for the rest of his life even though his own trajectory was meteoric: he was chosen as Herbert Hoover's running mate in 1928 and served as vice president of the United States from 1929 to 1933. He remains the only Indian to date elected to serve in the executive branch of the U.S. government.

Meanwhile, allotment rolled on. In 1906, the Dawes Act was further amended by the Burke Act, an attempt to simplify the process of ownership by introducing fee-simple patents into the allotment process that would, as in Oklahoma, allow "competent" Indians to own their land outright. The fee-simple patent also, however, meant that taxes began accruing on the owned properties immediately. There were no programs in place to educate Indians on what taxes were, much less how to deal with them. Without small businesses, much steady employment, or the reasonable expectation that their allotment would magically begin turning a profit (assuming that crops, much less cash crops, could be grown there in the first place, and that there was transportation to markets and access to those markets), thousands of Indians owed back taxes almost immediately. Local and state governments (as usual directed by the heavy hand of the Indian agent) could collect by foreclosing on the land. It did not help that the allotment of so many Indian lands occurred shortly before the Great Depression and the ecological disaster of the Dust Bowl, when so many small farms and farmers were ruined. It was estimated that within a couple of decades, as much as 95 percent of allotted Indian land would pass into white ownership. The agent at Pine Ridge nevertheless insisted that allotment was a kind of governmental tough love: "It is still the conviction of this office that the issue of a patent in fee for a portion of an

Indian's land who is judged as being competent or near-competent, is the proper procedure in dealing with the land question among the Indians. . . . Even if the proceeds derived from the dispossession of the land are squandered he still has plenty of land left and he may have learned a few lessons that will prove of value in the future."

And then there was the matter of assessing competence. How to measure the competence of people who had never owned land, at least not in that specific way? As landowners? As citizens? As racial "others"? Policy was that Indians who possessed European blood had enough competence (based on the degree of "whiteness") to buy and sell and pay taxes on land. For the purposes of determining who had European blood, teams of phrenologists were sent to Indian country. Using the theory and practice of craniometry developed by Samuel George Morton (which determined "scientifically" that Caucasians had the largest brain capacity—1,426 cubic centimeters versus a paltry 1,344 for American Indians and 1,278 for blacks), the phrenologists set about measuring skulls, and on this basis thousands of Indians were, surprisingly, deemed competent to own land: the better to steal it from them.

AT THE END of the allotment period—which stretched from 1887 to 1934—Indian landholdings had dropped from 138 million to 48 million acres. Without strong Indian governments in place and lacking conscientious advocacy within the American government, and with the passing of law after law in the absence of input from the constituencies (who had no standing as citizens in any event), Indian homelands had been reduced by two-thirds in about thirty years. What the great process of "civilization" had brought to Indian country was poverty, disenfranchisement, and the breakdown of Indian families. It had ground most of them down. One Ojibwe father wrote to the superintendent of the Flandreau boarding school: "I have lost my wife and left me with six children. . . . I would like to ask you to send these little folks over to you two or three years so I can get along. It is hard for me [to] stay here alone home because children not used to home alone when mother gone. When I am going working out it hard for them."

Without steady employment, often homeless on their own reservations, chronically malnourished, Indians across the country were vulnerable to disease. At Grand Portage Reservation in far northern Minnesota, tuberculosis struck more than 30 percent of the population. Poverty took the children, and it also took the parents. Boarding schools gradually filled with orphans. A six-year-old boy from White Earth Reservation "was first sent away to boarding school when his widowed mother was not able to care for him or his five siblings, aged three to seventeen." He spent his entire childhood in boarding schools and then joined the army. He was thrilled to be stationed at Fort Snelling and wrote enthusiastic letters back to the school, which he referred to as his "Shangri-La." For some families boarding schools were the sole option, because to keep their children with them was to starve them to death. But the assault wasn't only on land and family. There were other challenges in store for Indians during these days.

Indian Offenses

In 1878, legislation was passed empowering Indian agents to hire police to keep "law and order" on reservations around the country. That there was an absence of it should come as no surprise. Traditional warrior societies, such as the Dog Soldiers among the Lakota and the Bear Clan among the Ojibwe, which enforced tribal law and kept the peace, were in shambles or underground or suppressed. Many tribes who had been traditional enemies were now clustered cheek by jowl on reservations that were entirely too small to contain them. There were shortages of food, clothing, blankets, and shelter. And the very structure of many reservations was a cancer on a people's sense of self. Who are we, a tribe might ask, when we can no longer hunt or fish or gather or travel? As the living conditions on reservations grew worse, the rhetoric of reformers rose to a higher pitch. In 1877, Episcopal bishop William Hobart Hare wrote:

> Civilization has loosened, in some places broken, the bonds which regulate and hold together Indian society in its wild state and has failed to give people law and officers of justice in their place. This evil continues unabated. Women are beaten and outraged; men are murdered in cold blood; the Indians who are friendly to schools and churches are intimidated and preyed upon by the evil disposed; children are molested on their way to school and schools are dispersed by bands of vagabonds; but there is no redress. The accursed condition of things is an outrage upon the One Lawgiver. It is a disgrace to our land. It should make every man who sits in the national halls of legislation blush. And wish well to the Indians as we may and do for them what we will, the effect of civil agents, teachers and missionaries are like the struggle of drowning men weighted with lead, as long as by the absence of law Indian society is left without a base.

Apart from the likely alarmist exaggeration, it seemed to escape Hare's notice that the imposition of a foreign legal, educational, religious, and administrative system had led to a sorry state of affairs on many reservations. The abject poverty of reservation life was caused by the coercive and exploitive policies and presence of the dominant culture rather than caused by tribes or tribal society, but policy makers were willfully blind to their complicity. Instead of taking stock they doubled down and decided that an increased law-enforcement presence was necessary. And surely it was better to have Indian police rather than white military personnel attending to the needs of Indian communities. So the legislation of 1878 included provisions for a police force, though it wasn't fully funded until three years later. As of 1882 (again cart before the horse), there were police on reservations but no codes or laws or policies for them to follow, even as a guide, much less courts in which to try Indians accused of crimes. In 1883 a Court of Indian Offenses was created and funded by Congress. But it was clear that the agents who pushed for the bill and the legislators who drafted it had more than law and order in mind. Here was another assault on Indian cultural selfhood and autonomy.

Henry M. Teller, secretary of the interior, had been dead set against the Dawes Act, which he saw for what it was. The "real aim of this bill is to get at the Indian lands and open them up to settlement," he wrote. "The provisions for the apparent benefit of the Indian are but the pretext to get at his lands and occupy them. . . . If this were done in the name of greed, it would be bad enough; but to do it in the name of humanity, and under the cloak of an ardent desire to promote the Indian's welfare by making him like ourselves whether he will or not, is infinitely worse." Nevertheless, he was equally opposed to Indian cultural autonomy. In the preamble to the Code of Indian Offenses that could be tried in the new court, he pointed out "what I regard as a great hindrance to the civilization of the Indians, viz, the continuance of the old heathenish dances, such as the sun-dance, scalp-dance, & c.

These dances, or feasts, as they are sometimes called, ought, in my judgment, to be discontinued, and if the Indians now supported by the Government are not willing to discontinue them, the agents should be instructed to compel such discontinuance. These feasts or dances are not social gatherings for the amusement of these people, but, on the contrary, are intended and calculated to stimulate the warlike passions of the young warriors of the tribe. At such feasts the warrior recounts his deeds of daring, boasts of his inhumanity in the destruction of his enemies, and his treatment of the female captives, in language that ought to shock even a savage ear. The audience assents approvingly to his boasts of falsehood, deceit, theft, murder, and rape, and the young listener is informed that this and this only is the road to fame and renown. The result is the demoralization of the young, who are incited to emulate the wicked conduct of their elders, without a thought that in so doing they violate any law, but, on the contrary, with the conviction that in so doing they are securing for themselves an enduring and deserved fame among their people. Active measures should be taken to discourage all feasts and dances of the character I have mentioned.

The marriage relation is also one requiring the immediate attention of the agents. While the Indians remain in a state of at least semi-independence, there did not seem to be any great necessity for interference, even if such interference was practicable (which it doubtless was not). While dependent on the chase the Indian did not take many wives, and the great mass found themselves too poor to support more than one; but since the Government supports them, this objection no longer exists, and the more numerous the family the greater the number of rations allowed. I would not advise any interference with plural marriages now existing; but I would by all possible methods discourage future marriages of that character. The marriage relation, if it may be said to exist at all among the Indians, is exceedingly lax in its character, and it will be found impossible, for some time yet, to impress them with our idea of this important relation.

The marriage state, existing only by the consent of both parties, is easily and readily dissolved, the man not recognizing any obligation on his part to care for his offspring. As far as practicable, the Indian, having taken to himself a wife, should be compelled to continue that relation with her, unless dissolved by some recognized tribunal on the reservation or by the courts. Some system of marriage should be adopted, and the Indian compelled to conform to it. The Indian should also be instructed that he is under obligations to care for and support, not only his wife, but his children, and on his failure, without proper cause, to continue as the head of such family, he ought in some manner to be punished, which should be either by confinement in the guard-house or agency prison, or by a reduction of his rations.

Another great hindrance to the civilization of the Indians is the influence of the medicine men, who are always found with the anti-progressive party. The medicine men resort to various artifices and devices to keep the people under their influence, and are especially active in preventing the attendance of the children at the public schools, using their conjurers' arts to prevent the people from abandoning their heathenish rites and customs. While they profess to cure diseases by the administering of a few simple remedies, still they rely mainly on their art of conjuring. Their services are not required even for the

administration of the few simple remedies they are competent to recommend, for the Government supplies the several agencies with skill-
ful physicians, who practice among the Indians without charge to
them. Steps should be taken to compel these imposters to abandon this
deception and discontinue their practices, which are not only without
benefit to the Indians but positively injurious to them.

The value of property as an agent of civilization ought not to be
overlooked. When an Indian acquires property, with a disposition to
retain the same, free from tribal or individual interference, he has
made a step forward in the road to civilization. One great obstacle to
the acquirement of property by the Indian is the very general custom of
destroying or distributing his property on the death of a member of his
family. Frequently on the death of an important member of the family
all the property accumulated by its head is destroyed or carried off by
the "mourners," and his family left in desolation and want. While in
their independent state but little inconvenience was felt in such a case,
on account of the general community of interest and property, in their
present condition not only real inconvenience is felt, but disastrous
consequences follow. I am informed by reliable authority that frequently the head of a family, finding himself thus stripped of his property, becomes discouraged, and makes no further attempt to become a
property owner. Fear of being considered mean, and attachment to the
dead, frequently prevents [sic] the owner from interfering to save his
property while it is being destroyed in his presence and contrary to his
wishes.

The codes were clear: Indian ceremonial life was to be disrupted by
Indian police and tried in the Court of Indian Offenses, and adhering
to one's traditions was to be punished with the withholding of rations,
the threat of loss of property, and exclusion from the running of tribal
affairs. The court was governed by only nine provisions. The first three
concerned its makeup and procedures. The court would be composed of
the first three officers in rank of the police force at each agency, subject
to the approval of the commissioner of Indian affairs (although if the
local agent had reservations about their competency, he could appoint

the judges himself); the court had to meet twice a month, at a place and time designated by the agent; and the court would "hear and pass judgment upon all such questions as may be presented to it for consideration by the agent." The other provisions governed what exactly constituted an offense and what the punishment should be for different kinds of offenses:

4. The "sun-dance," the "scalp-dance," the "war-dance," and all other so-called feasts assimilating thereto, shall be considered "Indian offenses," and any Indian found guilty of being a participant in any one or more of these "offenses" shall, for the first offense committed, be punished by withholding from the person or persons so found guilty by the court his or their rations for a period not exceeding ten days; and if found guilty of any subsequent offense under this rule, shall be punished by withholding his or their rations for a period not less than fifteen days, nor more than thirty days, or by incarceration in the agency prison for a period not exceeding thirty days.

5. Any plural marriage hereafter contracted or entered into by any member of an Indian tribe under the supervision of a United States Indian agent shall be considered an "Indian offense," cognizable by the Court of Indian Offenses; and upon trial and conviction thereof by said court the offender shall pay a fine of not less than twenty dollars, or work at hard labor for a period of twenty days, or both, at the discretion of the court, the proceeds thereof to be devoted to the benefit of the tribe to which the offender may at the time belong; and so long as the Indian shall continue in this unlawful relation he shall forfeit all right to receive rations from the Government. And whenever it shall be proven to the satisfaction of the court that any member of the tribe fails, without proper cause, to support his wife and children, no rations shall be issued to him until such time as satisfactory assurance is given to the court, approved by the agent, that the offender will provide for his family to the best of his ability.

6. The usual practices of so-called "medicine-men" shall be considered "Indian offenses" cognizable by the Court of Indian Offenses, and whenever it shall be proven to the satisfaction of the court that the influence or practice of a so-called "medicine-man" operates as a hindrance to the civilization of a tribe, or that said "medicine-man" resorts to any artifice or device to keep the Indians under his influence, or shall adopt any means to prevent the attendance of children at the agency schools, or shall use any of the arts of a conjurer to prevent the Indians from abandoning their heathenish rites and customs, he shall be adjudged guilty of an Indian offense, and upon conviction of any one or more of these specified practices, or, any other, in the opinion of the court, of an equally anti-progressive nature, shall be confined in the agency prison for a term not less than ten days, or until such time as he shall produce evidence satisfactory to the court, and approved by the agent, that he will forever abandon all practices styled Indian offenses under this rule.

7. Any Indian under the charge of a United States Indian agent who shall willfully destroy, or with intent to steal or destroy, shall take and carry away any property of any value or description, being the property free from tribal interference, of any other Indian or Indians, shall, without reference to the value thereof, be deemed guilty of an "Indian offense," and, upon trial and conviction thereof by the Court of Indian Offenses, shall be compelled to return the stolen property to the proper owner, or, in case the property shall have been lost or destroyed, the estimated full value thereof, and in any event the party or parties so found guilty shall be confined in the agency prison for a term not exceeding thirty days; and it shall not be considered a sufficient or satisfactory answer to any of the offenses set forth in this rule that the party charged was at the time a "mourner," and thereby justified in taking or destroying the property in accordance with the customs or rites of the tribe.

8. Any Indian or mixed-blood who shall pay or offer to pay any money or other valuable consideration to the friends or relatives

of any Indian girl or woman, for the purpose of living or cohabiting with said girl or woman, shall be deemed guilty of an Indian offense, and upon conviction thereof shall forfeit all right to Government rations for a period at the discretion of the agent, or be imprisoned in the agency prison for a period not exceeding sixty days; and any Indian or mixed-blood who shall receive or offer to receive any consideration for the purpose herein before specified shall be punished in a similar manner as provided for the party paying or offering to pay the said consideration; and if any white man shall be found guilty of any of the offenses herein mentioned he shall be immediately removed from the reservation and not allowed to return thereto.

As with the boarding school system and allotment, the Code of Indian Offenses was designed to destroy Indian culture as a means of making Indians American, but Americans on the bottom rung of the ladder. And in each area of intrusion, coercion was written into the law, with power becoming more and more concentrated in the Office of Indian Affairs. The actions and disposition of the government that appointed itself the guardian of Indian futures seemed designed to bring about the very "disappearing Indian" that American culture so mythologized. But it was Indians themselves who made sure this didn't come to pass.

The Seeds of Tribal Resistance

Even as the Friends of the Indian and the Indian Rights Association tried to push the Dawes Act through Congress as a way of helping Indians become civilized, another organization sprang up that was opposed to such measures and committed to including Indians' points of view in policies that affected them: the National Indian Defense Association (NIDA). The organization was created in 1885 in an effort to debate and ultimately stop the policy provisions of the IRA as it pushed for allotment. NIDA, although it also took as a given the virtues of private ownership and allotment, believed in upholding some tribal rights as well. Its early members included several powerful figures: the Reverend Byron Sunderland, an abolitionist and pastor to Grover Cleveland; anthropologist James Dorsey; former chief justice of the South Carolina Supreme Court Ammiel Willard; John Oberly, the superintendent of Indian schools for the Office of Indian Affairs; Alonzo Bell, assistant commissioner of Indian affairs; and two other former commissioners, Francis Walker and George Manypenny. They were prescient in seeing that immediate severalty of communal landownership and the assumption of private parcels would retard the civilization process because without tribal governments, and given the abuses rampant in the Indian service, Indians would lack the civil structures and stability necessary to hold on to their land and make something of it—the sine qua non of making Americans of themselves. Thomas A. Bland, a founder of the organization, who had been a longtime advocate for Indian rights, published a monthly journal, *The Council Fire and Arbitrator*, that detailed the corruption and abuse in the Indian service. In the course of many trips out west, principally to Dakota Territory, he had seen firsthand what happened when land was essentially ripped out from under the feet of Indian people.

In 1868, at the end of what came to be known as Red Cloud's War, the Teton Lakota had been able to force the U.S. government to create a "Great Sioux Reservation" that encompassed all of present-day South Dakota west of the Missouri River and parts of North Dakota and Nebraska. But with the discovery of gold in the Black Hills (claims that were greatly exaggerated by the federal government), the United States had almost immediately abrogated that treaty. War boiled up again, culminating in the decimation of the Seventh Cavalry by the Lakota and their allies at the Battle of the Little Bighorn. Immediately after the battle, various Lakota leaders were induced to sign a treaty that deprived them of the Black Hills, although it was clear that the Lakota weren't aware that this was a provision of the treaty. In part because of the government's exaggeration about the gold discoveries, white people flooded into South Dakota. In 1883, Congress sought to reduce the Great Sioux Reservation by half and replace it with five smaller reservations. The remaining land was opened up to settlement and grazing. The fraud inherent in these actions was so blatant that something like a public outcry was raised, and it was loud enough to cause the government to empanel a commission (including Senator Henry Dawes) to investigate. The commission found that the federal negotiators had cajoled and coerced and threatened the Lakota so much that even by the standards of the day their actions could only be considered reprehensible. But the commission nonetheless recommended that the breakup of the reservation proceed. Bland—who counted Red Cloud among his friends, and vice versa—was outraged, and he made his outrage known to the public in *The Council Fire and Arbitrator* and among the reformers and legislators involved in the issue.

When Dawes resubmitted his legislation to Congress in December 1885, the IRA and the NIDA, which had engaged in vicious fights over its provisions, were given a chance to debate their views in front of the House Indian Committee. Bland noted that efforts to push through allotment policy might not have the Indians' best interests at heart, especially in South Dakota. He drew attention to the fact that Henry Dawes had a significant financial interest in the Chicago, Milwaukee, and St. Paul Railroad, which had obtained a right-of-way agreement with the Lakota—in fact, the bill as it had subsequently evolved differed from the 1884 version only in this regard. Bland also noted that J. C. McManima, from Pierre, was lobbying both for the passage of the allotment act and for South Dakota statehood, often in the same breath. NIDA ultimately argued that the allotment act was geared more to the benefit of the railroads than the Indians, as it gave the Indians no choice in what land they would get, and the price the government was willing to pay for the "surplus" land was criminally low. NIDA's efforts bore fruit in the final edition of the bill, which included clear language stating that tribes would have to agree to allotment beforehand. Additionally, allotment would not proceed "in severalty." Indians would have twenty-five years before the title of their allotments would revert to them as truly private property; until that time, the land would be held in trust for them by the government. These changes helped give the Indians at least some wiggle room (though not enough) in an otherwise disastrous policy.

In 1863, the Red Lake Band and Pembina Band of Ojibwe were induced by Alexander Ramsey, governor of Minnesota, to sign a treaty ceding roughly eleven million acres of prime woodlands and prairie on either side of the Red River. The Treaty of Old Crossing promised them considerable annuities and the right to hunt, fish, and travel in the ceded area in exchange for what Ramsey described as the "right of passage" for oxcarts and wagon trains headed west.

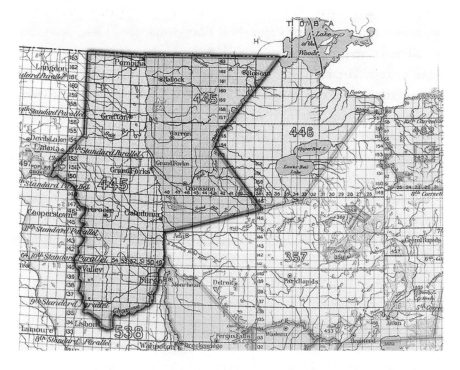

Old Crossing Treaty Map, 1863

The wording of the treaty—misrepresented by Ramsey and not adequately translated to the chiefs—was clear enough, as was the intent. The government was after nothing less than extinguishing Ojibwe claim to the whole region, as the next thirty years would prove. The chiefs who signed the treaty saw that their good faith had been misplaced, and they grew deeply suspicious of the government thereafter.

What the government didn't comprehend, perhaps, was the unique nature of leadership at Red Lake. The Red Lake and Pembina Ojibwe were the westernmost bands of Ojibwe argonauts who had, for centuries, pushed and fought and negotiated and traded their way from the Eastern Seaboard through the Great Lakes and into the headwaters of the Mississippi watershed. Ojibwe society was, in those years, very much shaped by the roles of hereditary clans. Membership in a clan—a spiritual as well as practical kind of kinship—was passed down through the father's line, and inclusion in a given clan conferred, among other things, somewhat specific social roles. The Loon Clan was a clan of leadership, civil chiefs, as were the Crane and Turtle Clans. Bear Clan people functioned as a tribal police force and warrior society and made up the great majority of the tribe at Red Lake, serving as warriors and chiefs who protected the front edge of the Ojibwe empire, where a state of nearly constant warfare with Dakota, Ho-Chunk, and Cree prevailed. These chiefs included the leaders who had been so badly betrayed by the signing of the Treaty of Old Crossing, among them Medwe-ganoonind (He Who Is Spoken To), Wemitigoozhiins (Little French Man), and Meskokonayed (Red Robed).

When government representatives returned to Red Lake in 1886, hoping to secure the approval of the tribe to relocate other Ojibwe there, and to prepare the reservation for allotment, the leaders were ready. Before they could so much as suggest terms, Red Robed stood and addressed the commission, opening with a salvo of complaints. "We have written a great many times," he noted, "but we have never received a satisfactory answer. We do not know any of our chiefs who have ceded this land; we cannot find the name of a single chief who has ever ceded this land or signed his name on paper." Commissioner Charles Larrabee was put off his game immediately. "We can see the possibility of a misunderstanding having been made at the time," he acknowledged. "But it is not in our power to rectify that mistake at the present time."

The chiefs were relentless. They rejected the commission's proposals out of hand, and indeed the right of any outsider to put a price on their land. "This property belongs to us, the Red Lake Indians. That is the conclusion we have arrived at. That is the conclusion we have all arrived at," they said. Then Red Robed and He Who Is Spoken To began a long recital of illegal timber cutting, inroads made by homesteaders, and the past false dealings of the government. After a long while, Commissioner Henry Whipple was able to read the terms the U.S. government was proposing to the Red Lake government. One of the proposals was that the rest of the Ojibwe in Minnesota be relocated to Red Lake. He Who Is Spoken To spoke again: "We wish to live alone on our premises; we do not wish any other Indians to come here." The chiefs were resolute and their response was clear: they unanimously opposed allotment. Gradually the Red Lake chiefs wore the commission down, but they were as smart as they were resolute: they could read the writing on the wall. Allotment was coming, and they would have to fight it. To that end they used as a bargaining chip another huge tract of land north of the reservation proper. The chiefs told the commission they were willing to cede much of it in exchange for opting out of allotment and as long as the Red Lake Band controlled all the land around both Upper and Lower Red Lake. He Who Is Spoken To also demanded that at the top of the treaty the commission include the sentence "It should be premised that the Red Lake Reservation has never been ceded to the United States." (In most cases, during treaties tribes relinquished title to the land and then portions of it were deeded back to them.)

The commission left dissatisfied, but they knew they'd gone as far as they could with Red Lake. After the Nelson Act was passed, however, another commission was empaneled and sent to Red Lake in the summer of 1889 to try again for allotment. The act formally known as "An Act for the relief and civilization of Chippewa Indians in Minnesota" but referred to as the Nelson Act, for its author, was at bottom a more vigorous version of previous allotment acts. It provided for the relocation of all Ojibwe people in Minnesota to the White Earth Reservation in the western part of the state. The only "relief" it would bring was the Minnesota Ojibwe's final dispossession of their land. Once again they were met in force and in consensus by Red Lake leadership. Once again the chiefs began with grievances. "We consider that the Government did not keep its agreement according to our understanding," began Chief Leading Feather. He detailed how the government's surveyors had not respected the agreed-upon boundaries. The chiefs were both specific and eloquent. Wewe (Snow Goose) said that as a result of the government's inability to control timber cutting and the ruthless practices of price-gouging traders, there "are many things which come inside the line of the reservation which can be compared to the works of the devil, and I am unable to estimate the amount of the damage done by these things. You see how tall I am. If I should be able to stand in the midst of the money, of the value of damages, what had been stolen from us, it would go over my head." One commissioner, Senator Henry Rice, wrote bitterly of the chiefs (no doubt ruing their ability to outmaneuver him diplomatically): "We found them intelligent, dignified, and courteous, but for several days indisposed to give a favorable hearing."

The commission never did get a favorable hearing on the matters it had wanted to pursue. Complaining of white encroachment on tribal land, Praying Day noted, "I can see my property going to waste; they are stealing from me on every side." A chief with the impressive name Zhaawanookamigish-kang—He Who Treads Earth from the South—told the commission, "No liquor shall ever come on this reservation. It would be the ruination of all these persons you see here should that misfortune come to them." He Who Is Spoken To piled on: "This property under discussion, called Red Lake, is my property. These persons whom you see before you are my children. They own this place the same as I own it. My friends, I ask that we reserve the whole of the lake as ours and our grandchildren's hereafter. . . . We wish to guarantee to our posterity some security; that is why we demand the reservation we have outlined on that paper." After days of tense negotiations, with Rice and the other commissioners leaning on the chiefs and the chiefs dodging all of the commission's proposals, Chief Niigaanakwad stood, as is the Ojibwe custom when speaking. "I stand before you as spokesman of the band," he said, "and to show you that my assertion is correct, I proclaim it by a rising vote." Two-thirds of the Red Lakers in attendance rose to their feet in support. "Your mission here is a failure," he told the commission. "We never wish hereafter to sign any instrument. . . . We never signed an instrument in which we did not have a voice. . . . We shall return to our respective homes." Wewe said it more simply: "I don't want to accept your propositions, I love my reservation very much; I don't want to sell it."

After six days of talks, He Who Is Spoken To rose and, speaking for all of Red Lake, told the commission, "I said that I was opposed to having allotments made to us; I do not look with favor on the allotment plan. I wish to lay out a reservation here, where we can remain with our bands forever. I mean to stand fast to my decision. . . . We wish that any land we possess should be not only for our own benefit, but for our posterity, our grandchildren hereafter. . . . We think that we should own in common everything that pertains to us; with those that are suffering in poverty, just as the same as we are." In the end the Red Lake Ojibwe ceded millions of acres of land to the north, but they were never subjected to allotment; to this day they have never opened the reservation to the sale of alcohol.

The Red Lake Chiefs didn't just survive the encounter—they learned a valuable lesson from it: they needed to maintain strong leadership that worked to create consensus among the general population of the tribe. Only by presenting a united front could they hope to stave off the U.S. government. Likewise, they noticed that on other reservations marked by dissent or populated with variously displaced and relocated bands and tribes and families, the government and its agents were very successful at playing factions off one another, empowering some people and disempowering others, until they got their way. The Red Lake leaders worked together to make sure that each and every community on the reservation was represented by hereditary chiefs. They met regularly and worked through their considerable differences. In 1918, under the leadership of Peter Graves and Paul Beaulieu, they formalized their structure of governance by creating the General Council of the Red Lake Band of Chippewa Indians. This was, arguably, the first and only tribal representative body in the United States at the time. It honored Ojibwe leadership structure and spoke to the need for a modern government to deal with modern times. When federal agents tried to work around leaders they found unsympathetic, they were met with the force of the entire general council. In 1934, when the government pushed for modern Indian government across the country, Red Lake not only was ready, but was ahead of the curve.

Red Lake Reservation also managed to withstand the assault on Ojibwe religious practices. The reservation included a number of villages along the southern edge of Lower Red Lake. Ponemah, a village at the sharp end of the spit of land that separated Lower and Upper Red Lake, was isolated and insular. Its inhabitants understood themselves to be the ones who had driven the Dakota out of Red Lake at the Battle of Battle River, and who had driven away army recruiters at gunpoint during World War I—and who for decades had prevented missionaries from getting any foothold in their homeland, even as Ojibwe villages to the south were inundated by Catholics, Episcopalians, Baptists, and Methodists. A story had it that once the Catholics had set to building a church in Ponemah, but before it could be completed, it was burned to the ground. The missionaries began rebuilding, and again the structure was burned down. The priest, frustrated, asked a Ponemah leader when he and his people were going to accept the word of God and Jesus Christ, and the man said, *"Hai, ganabaj baanimaa, baanimaa gosha"* (Oh, maybe later). Supposedly that's why the village is denoted as Ponemah on American-made maps, although the Ojibwe refer to it as Obaashing (The Place of the Clashing Winds).

Nonetheless, in 1916 the Indian agent wrote to two Ponemah chiefs— Nezhikegwaneb (Lone Feather) and Azhede-giizhig (Pelican Sky)—and threatened them with sanctions:

> *My friends it has been reported to me that you have been taking a very active part in the dances recently held on the "point" and that it was necessary . . . to direct you not to dance anymore, also that you made excuses to the effect that the government had reference to the Squaw Dances and not to the medicine dances when they requested that you discontinue your foolish abuse and over indulgence in dancing last winter. In this connection your attention is called to the law regarding the practice of Indian Medicine Men on the reservation and a further violation of this*

law will be properly punished by me. . . . It is unlawful for you to
continue in these medicine dances.

Nodin Wind, Ponemah's preeminent spiritual leader and a savvy poli-
tician, responded with a letter that he had dictated to an interpreter (he
couldn't read or write) and had signed by eighty leading members of the
Ponemah community:

We Indians in the vicinity of Ponemah, on the Red
Lake Reservation, Minnesota, protest against the ruling of the
Indian Department at Washington, D.C., prohibiting the ancient
Indian ceremony known to the white man as the "Grand
Medicine Dance." We base our protest on the following grounds.
The so called Grand Medicine Dance is not a dance in any
sense of the term. It is simply a gathering of Men, Women, and
children for the purpose of giving praise to the Great Spirit,
thanking him for the manifold blessings bestowed upon the tribe
and praying for continued health, happiness and long life.
The beating of the drum is simply an accompaniment to
the songs of praise, uttered by the congregation. As in every
church of the white man, piano or organ is found for the purpose.
There is no medicine present at this ceremony and nothing
that is supposed to be medicine: it is strictly a religious ceremony
and nothing else.
To illustrate, let us say that an Indian has been sick for some
time and eventually recovers: the members of his family and
friends will give the so called Grand Medicine Dance as a token
of respect and thanks to the Great Spirit, in other words, to God,
for his recovery. On the other hand, should he die, the same
ceremony will be performed, changed of course to deep regrets,
instead of rejoicing.
Among the whites the minister is called to administer
salvation to the sick or dying and after death the minister is called
for the same purpose.

We understand that this government gives its subjects the
freedom of worshipping as he chooses and we cannot understand
why we are deprived of this privilege.

Through dissimulation and secrecy and outright rejection of Christianity, Ponemah remained resolutely pagan. Even today there are no Christians and no churches in Ponemah. Red Lake was successful in fighting off allotment and forced conversion, if not the boarding schools. But their success in resisting meant that when their children completed school, they could return to a strong community. Other tribes were not so lucky, but they all resisted their own destruction in their own way.

THE CHICKASAW had originally been excluded from the provisions of allotment along with the other four of the Five Civilized Tribes in Oklahoma. But when they became subject to allotment and the dissolution of their tribal governments and treaty rights under the Curtis Act in 1898, they charted a different course than Red Lake. As a part of the act, the Chickasaw (along with the other four tribes) lost millions of acres and were rendered temporarily politically voiceless. But Kevin Washburn's recollection of Bill Anoatubby's approach to solving life's riddles—*If it's going to be, it's up to me*—was clearly in widespread practice in Chickasaw country long before Anoatubby came to power. Since the tribes didn't have reservations anymore, they essentially borrowed American civic structures to preserve their tribes and their tribal selves. They functioned as citizens and incorporated towns, opened businesses, bought and sold land, levied taxes, founded civic organizations, ran Indian candidates as mayors, aldermen, and city councilmen, and engaged in a frenzy of institution building.

They were so effective at this kind of work they earned the ire of the commissioner of Indian affairs. "Owing to the hostility of the governing portion of the tribe to the control of the schools by the Department [of Indian Affairs]," the commissioner reported in 1900, "the Chickasaw council has undertaken to conduct these institutions as formerly, supporting them by appropriations from their own revenues. As the coal and asphalt royalties were not to be used, the 'Regulations for education in Indian Territory' did not apply to this nation, which attempts out of its common funds to manage the scholastic interests of its people." Clearly unaware of the irony (wasn't the government interested in helping Indians become self-sufficient, resourceful, hardworking, and civilized?), he ranted on:

> Its legislature appoints a superintendent of schools, who in turn selects a local trustee for each school, which superintendent and trustees constitute the school board of the nation. The local trustees being the creatures of the national superintendent are removed by him at will. The present superintendent is a half-blood of some education, but is said to have little force of character. The trustees generally are full-bloods, the majority of whom are members of the nation's legislature. The neighborhood schools are located in isolated communities, patronized principally by full-bloods when patronized at all. The children, in many instances, and teachers also, use the Chickasaw vernacular to the almost total exclusion of English.
>
> The supervisor of schools for that nation, in his report on conditions, says that the schoolhouses are mostly small frame buildings, furnished with a few rough board benches, with rarely a desk, blackboard, or writing materials. Many of the houses are "too filthy for swine to occupy, never having been cleansed since they were built; many of the children in squalor and rags." Teachers are not chosen for merit, but by favoritism, preference being given to Chickasaws "when the local trustee does not have a noncitizen friend who wishes the appointment."

Such was the response of many among the Five Civilized Tribes to efforts at government control in this period. They learned how to adapt and engaged in a process of institution building that made them relatively strong and able to withstand much of what the government threw at them.

The Menominee, who had arguably lived in the western Great Lakes longer than any other Algonquian tribe, resisted the predations of the U.S. government in their own unique ways. Their tenure in northeastern Wisconsin and the Upper Peninsula of Michigan likely goes back to prehistoric times, unlike the Odawa and Ojibwe, who expanded west and overran them. The name "Menominee," which was given to them by the Ojibwe, means "People of the Wild Rice," which suggests that the Menominee understood the significance of the crop and harvested it extensively long before anyone else did. Slovenian Roman Catholic missionary and linguist Frederic Baraga has one of the most colorful descriptions of them (and perhaps of any tribe) in his dictionary of the Ojibwe language. He wrote that the name of the tribe was "given to some strange Indians (according to the sayings of the Otchipwes [Ojibwe]), who are rowing through the woods, and who are sometimes heard shooting, but never seen."

At the time of contact in the seventeenth century, the Menominee had consolidated their territory to an area of about ten million acres in northeastern Wisconsin. They managed to stay there, and to hold on to their land for quite some time, but in the nineteenth century, facing relocation and inroads by white settlers, they ceded land to the government in 1831, 1832, 1836, 1848, 1854, and finally in 1856. After the last cession, the Menominee were left with about three hundred thousand acres northwest of Green Bay that were almost entirely given over to forest—old-growth white and red pine. As the settlers around them cleared the land and planted crops, the Menominee watched and decided, collectively, not to follow suit. They felt about their trees much as the Red Lakers felt about their lakes: if they could protect the trees they, in turn, would be protected by them.

Oral history has it that a kind of spiritually based sustainable-yield management system was put into practice shortly after the reservation was established in 1854. According to a tribal leader, Charlie Frechette, the Menominee invoke this practice as part of many of their ceremonial proceedings: "Start with the rising sun and work toward the setting sun, but take only the mature trees, the sick trees, and the trees that have fallen. When you reach the end of the reservation, turn and cut from the setting sun to the rising sun, and the trees will last forever." The proceeds from the first trees they cut and sold went to buy flour. The tribe was in a position to use the resources it had left in order to take care of itself and to remain self-sufficient.

The government, again working in direct contradiction of its own stated ideology of "civilization" (weren't Indians supposed to learn "I" and not "we," and the value of buying and selling?), quickly put a stop to Menominee logging in 1861. They were in operation again from 1871 until 1876, when logging was halted. Again. In the government's view, land was to be cleared of trees and then planted. This was the path to civilization. It was also a path to disenfranchisement: the timber barons in Wisconsin, Michigan, and Minnesota wanted to sell the timber themselves and reap the profits. It was a cynical business. When allotment arrived in 1887, the Menominee recognized that it would forever destroy their sustainable harvest practices and fought it fiercely. In large part, they won. Menominee lands remained unallotted. And in 1890 the Menominee won a victory in Congress that allowed them to harvest twenty million board feet of their own timber. This, however, did not stop business interests with strong ties to state government from trying to take their timber as well. The aptly named Senator Sawyer from Wisconsin introduced a bill to allow private (white) companies to cut Menominee timber, but it was blocked by Senator Robert La Follette of Wisconsin.

La Follette, known as "Fighting Bob" and blessed with a great pre-Elvis pompadour, was a passionate advocate for progressive values and fought hard—as a member of the House, a senator, and the governor of Wisconsin—against railroad trusts, big business, overseas interventionism, and the League of Nations. He fought for women's suffrage, unions, and the rights of the disempowered and downtrodden. In 1908, while filibustering for more than sixteen hours straight, he asked for a turkey sandwich and a glass of milk with raw eggs in it in order to keep going. The kitchen staff, annoyed they had to work through the night, in protest dropped into the milk two eggs that had turned. Fighting Bob took one sip and noticed the mixture was off; he didn't drink the rest, but he began sweating uncontrollably and was forced to step down two hours later, having stood and talked for eighteen hours and twenty-three minutes. In 1917, while filibustering to prevent the merchant marine from arming its ships against the Germans, he yelled, "I will continue on this floor until I complete my statement unless somebody carries me off, and I should like to see the man who will do it!" In a 1982 survey of historians who were asked to name the most important senator in the history of the United States, La Follette tied with Henry Clay.

Clearly, La Follette was a great ally for the Menominee. The La Follette bill allowed the tribe to cut and process timber under the selective cutting system they favored, which harvested only fully mature trees. Appropriate specimens would be marked by forestry service specialists, and Menominee would process them under expert supervision and with the help of a sawmill, kiln, planing mill, and machine shop on the reservation at Neopit. Still, the tribe had to file suit after suit in court when the "experts" and outside interests continually ignored or violated the terms of the legislation. But because of that legislation the Menominee kept control of their forest, and eventually they won damages against businesses and the government. And after 125 years of logging and more than two billion board feet of timber harvested, they have more board feet of northern hardwoods standing on Menominee land than they started with.

IF THE FOUR HUNDRED YEARS of contact with Europeans showed anything, it wasn't merely the rapaciousness of Europeans and European colonization or the terrible effectiveness of European diseases. Rather, it showed the supreme adaptability and endurance of Indian tribes across the continent. This adaptability and toughness served Indians well in the years between 1890 and 1934, when the assaults on Indians and Indian homelands were perhaps at their most creative, if not their bloodiest. It was a new kind of Indian war, fought not by the sudden attack of cavalry or by teams of buffalo hunters. These years were more of a siege. The government's weapons were cupidity and fraud. Indians resisted. They resisted assaults on their sovereignty, assaults often made (as in the case of the Friends of the Indian and other organizations) by their own allies. But they also resisted with help offered by real allies like La Follette. What General Devers said of the French after the close of World War II is just as apt when thinking of Indian–white relationships during this period: "For many months we have fought together—often on the same side!"

Kevin Washburn, seemingly tireless on our second lap of the golf course, mused about this resilience. "One of the things the regulations regarding tribal acknowledgment required was that the tribe show continuity from 1900 to the present through public sources, such as local newspapers and county records and such. But quite a few tribes approached me and said the regulations were unfair! They told me there were no public sources. 'We went underground. We went into hiding. We hid, we went in the swamps, the mountains. . . . Remember, 1900 was only ten years after the massacre at Wounded Knee. People were really out to murder us. We weren't very visible on purpose, so don't make us show you newspaper articles, because at the time we were trying to do the opposite: we were trying to show folks that we didn't exist.'" Washburn smiled. "That made sense. So we changed the rule." Today a tribe seeking recognition from the federal government has much more flexibility in how it proves its historical existence. It is too soon to tell how tribes will use this newfound latitude, but no doubt they will be as creative as the tribes' strategies for survival have always been.

One fascinating side effect of the attempts to crush tribes and tribal solidarity was manifest in homesteading itself. The first Homestead Act, passed in 1862, was meant to pave the way for a new generation of yeoman farmers in the Jeffersonian mold. Initially it was supported by the Free Soil Party, and later by the Republican Party (it was opposed by Democrats, who feared that immigrants and poor southern whites would gobble up most of the land). The second Homestead Act was passed in 1866 and amended seemingly every few years after. In 1865, tribes in Wisconsin were allowed to claim homesteads, improve the land, file for a patent after five years, and thereby gain citizenship. Many of them did. The Cherokee and other members of the Five Civilized Tribes were given the same opportunity in the early 1900s, and they quickly realized that the government considered Indian business anything but stable, and figured they would fare better if they functioned, politically anyway, as Americans rather than Indians.

Hundreds and eventually thousands of Cherokee and Seminole and Creek and Choctaw and Chickasaw families fanned out from Oklahoma into Kansas, Nebraska, and Colorado, the first wave of a vast diaspora of Indian families into Indian homelands originally not their own. They put down roots and dug up the real roots of the prairie states and made lives for themselves as Americans. And while they might have renounced some kind of daily participation in the polity of their tribes, they brought—in their culture and their understandings of themselves and community in its most general terms—their tribes with them. The graduates of the Indian boarding schools did much the same: they brought their experiences of their tribes to school, mingled with and met other tribal people, and if they returned to their tribes, they brought all of that with them along with the academic and practical skills that would be invaluable in the conflicts ahead.

"I am a strong believer in self-determination," Washburn says, reflecting on his outlook as assistant secretary. "It's funny, but I remember something George W. Bush said. Someone asked him what qualities you needed to be the president. He said, 'You've got to have principles. People have to know what kinds of decisions you're going to make.' I remember hearing him say that. I thought, 'That's wrong!' I thought to myself, 'You just have to do justice. You just have to *be just* in each instance.' But then I became assistant secretary, faced many policy decisions each day, and I realized George Bush was right about something. Shocking. You do have to have principles. And mine are based in tribal self-determination; tribes know what's best for their tribe and they have the abilities and the experience to make their own decisions. Any issue that tribes brought to me I treated that way. Tribal self-determination was and is my principle." It was so clear—on that sunny spring day in Albuquerque—that the BIA had changed (as institutions do), but it had changed in many ways because the Indians it was supposed to serve and the Indians who were sometimes in charge of it (Ely Parker, Ada Deer, Kevin Washburn, and others) had been born into tribes and raised in tribal homelands that had survived decades of crushing control and had the outlook and skills to change it themselves. But more than that, despite the government's three-pronged assault on Indian communities and people (boarding schools, allotment, and the law), Indian tribes not only clung to the old ways but also found in them a strength that would see them through this awful middle passage. They not only clung but also strategized and fought and talked and met and thought and worked to preserve what remained, on their own terms and for themselves.

PART 3

Fighting Life:
1914–1945

I saw many things at the Northern Lights Casino on Leech Lake Reservation on March 17, 2012. I saw Josh Maudrie, fighting out of Brainerd, Minnesota, TKO Josh Alder while his coach yelled, "DO YOUR JOB! DO YOUR JOB!" Afterward Maudrie said, almost in tears, "I did it, Coach, I did it. I did my job." I saw Tim Bebeau, an Indian, TKO Keegan Osborn, while the same coach from Brainerd yelled, "DO YOUR JOB! DO YOUR JOB!" and Osborn didn't. I saw Tory Nelson defeat my cousin Tony Tibbetts after throwing a dozen illegal elbows, enough so Tony couldn't breathe after the second round. I saw a lot of Indian fighters—Tony Tibbetts and Nate Seelye and Tim Bebeau and Josh Thompson and Dave Smith. I saw some of them win and some of them lose. I saw, for the first time, Indians beating up white people in front of a sold-out crowd and I heard the crowd roar. I saw a forty-seven-year-old from the reservation town of Ball Club whose gym was called the "Den of Raging Mayhem" manage to beat my unbeatable cousin Nate Seelye. Another fighter was introduced as fighting for "Team Crazy." From the looks of him he was. As instructed, I gave a big round of applause to the King of the Cage Ring Girl and *Maxim* "Hometown Hottie" Shannon Ihrke from Walker, Minnesota. I watched my nephew tune out the fights and tune into Skrillex and my mother check her watch to see if she was missing *Law & Order.* I saw two, maybe three ex-girlfriends and my cousins Nate, Josh, Jason, Delbert, Tammie, Amber, and my uncles Jerry, Davey, and Lanny. I saw a sea of baseball caps and braids and Indians and whites and the good people of Leech Lake and Walker, Indian and white, get up and cheer along with me as we watched the fighters—many of them unprepared but willing, all of them brave in their own way—step into the cage and fight.

And as I watched the fighters and watched the crowd, it was clear we couldn't be further from the UFC. There were no sponsors and no scouts, no prepublicity or small purses, and an almost total lack of the industry of blood that has propped up boxing for the last sixty years and MMA for the last twenty. We were in the middle of the reservation in northern Minnesota and everyone had a day job or needed one. Instead of glamour we had hometown boys (and girls) who brought out the pleasure of speculation as much as of spectacle: How would I do in there? Could I do it? Could you? It was easy to feel, even if it wasn't true, that little if anything separated us from those in the cage except a willingness to be there. It was like the wrestling matches of old, where promoters mixed hometown talent with professionals and everyone had a role to play: the up-and-comer, the dandy, the rascal, the workingman, the prodigy, the returning hero, the snake, the all-American. There were all the body types, too: the farm boy, the athlete, the wrestler, the tattooed—colorful tribal tattoos, and also a lot of tattoos that suffered from what can only be called bad penmanship.

Roland Barthes might as well have been thinking about MMA on the Leech Lake Reservation when he wrote, "There are people who think that wrestling is an ignoble sport. Wrestling is not a sport, it is a spectacle, and it is no more ignoble to attend a wrestled performance of Suffering than a performance of the sorrows of Arnolphe or Andromaque." And that the "primary virtue of the spectacle, is to abolish all motives and all consequences: what matters is not what it thinks but what it sees." Maybe. But on the reservation, if not in the wrestling halls of France, there are plenty of reasons why a man might step into the cage. And there are consequences that derive from our suffering. And something, surely, other than the chain link, separates us from the combatants; something must separate us from them and also separates Indians and whites, other than our blood. Oh, I saw a lot in Walker, Minnesota, at the Northern Lights Casino on March 17, 2012. But what I didn't see was what I had largely come there to witness: my cousin Sam Cleveland was supposed to fight his last professional fight. But he didn't.

What happened to Sam? Better: What didn't? Sam is thirty-eight, on the far side of fighting age but not over it yet, not by a long shot. "I'm thirty-eight but I still got a lot of power, still got a six-pack—how many other thirty-eight-year-olds around here can you say that about?" he mused as we sat at the Bemidji State University recreation center where Sammy had gone to run and lift until he lost the final four pounds he needed to, two days before weigh-in. He was scheduled to fight the main event in the King of the Cage Winter Warriors Showdown. He had gone from 175 pounds down to 161 in three weeks of dieting and running, and his body looked hard and lean. He still had the strong square hands, the wide shoulders and powerful legs. His face showed the strain a little— that and not a few scars from years of fighting. He might have the body of a thirty-year-old, but he has the face of a fighter who has taken his share of abuse.

Sammy is my first cousin. Like me, he grew up at Leech Lake, but, as he put it, much more "in the mix." He is a favorite fighter of many around the reservation and even around the state. He was a star wrestler in high school, as his father had been. Back then he'd been a cheerful guy, all things considered. He'd grown up poor but not destitute. Had been popular in high school. Like me, he suffered a particular kind of racism as a red-haired, fair-skinned Indian on the rez. Which is to say, no one ever let him forget what he was or what he wasn't. But he weathered it well.

Sam was, by any standard, a success. He graduated from high school (Native students are almost four times more likely to drop out than whites), and so far he's avoided jail (Indian men are twice as likely to end up there). In Minnesota in 2002, Indians, who made up only 1 percent of the state population, were 6 percent of the prison population. After graduation, in 1992, he joined the army and became part of the elite Army Scouts, Second Battalion, Thirty-fifth Infantry Regiment, Third Infantry Brigade Combat Team, Twenty-fifth Infantry Division, Schofield Barracks, Hawaii. He loved it. "I really liked the army side of things. It was an elite unit, and that suited me. Always something interesting to do. But it was far from home and that was hard." Back at Leech Lake, the unemployment rate was 46 percent; the median household income was less than $20,000 a year. Yet Sam missed the reservation and the network of family and friends and the landscape of northern Minnesota, where the boreal forest meets the oak savanna and also where whites and Indians have been meeting and mixing since the early seventeenth century, often to fight but also to trade, bargain, fuck, and marry. "I was three years into my tour and I was so far away. And then Nessa [his sister Vanessa] died the last year of my tour, and it really made me miserable and I wasn't interested in reenlisting." Nessa was one of just three female cousins in a group of about twenty or thirty male first and second cousins, all of the same generation. She had a sharp kind of face, was thin and pretty, and generally, no matter where, learned early on to tear up the scenery. She grew up scrappy and lippy. She had left a party and driven through two yards and onto Highway 2 just outside Bena, where an RV hit her.

Sam called our grandfather once a week. "I took it pretty hard. Me and Nessa weren't on the best of terms; we were fighting. The weird point is that she'd stole my girlfriend from me, that's why I was so mad. I mean, who does that?" Sammy laughed—sad, rueful. Vanessa did things like that. Suddenly, all that separated Sam from everyone else (graduation, a job, a life) disappeared. It's one thing to be borne aloft on the spume of the American Dream—safety-netted by college, by working parents, by a scrim of wealth or entitlement, or even the illusion that what we do, our work, our effort, counts for something, matters in some way—and another to feel, as many Indians do, totally powerless. That's how Sam felt. He didn't reenlist. Instead, he came back to Leech Lake Reservation. "I got really angry after Nessa died. I drank a lot. I'd fought a little before that. But then after Nessa died I wanted to fight every time I went somewhere. I probably got into a couple hundred street fights. Brawls, you know."

I remember seeing Sam in those years—during holidays or around town. It seemed like every time I saw him he had one fewer teeth, or a new cast on his hand, or a new scar. Back when we were kids, he'd had a round, open, cheerful face, always ready to laugh, always laughing. But that boy's face, the face I'd known as well as my own growing up, disappeared. And in its place was the hard face of a man who liked to fight, who, not to put too fine a point on it, liked hurting people. "I couldn't change anything. Nothing I could do could change anything about Nessa, or my mom, who really fell apart. But I could fight." And that's when Sam became a lot like the rest of our tribemates: he had physical talent and he had mental talent, and none of it mattered. Or none of it felt like it mattered. None of it was of any use. Even cynicism was a luxury he couldn't afford. You need perspective to be cynical, and perspectives are sometimes a luxury purchased at a remove from the fray. He was a good street fighter, though. "There were a few guys who'd work me over when I tangled with them, but not many. I won most of those fights. I don't know if that got me into the cage or not. But I got a taste for fighting." A taste for violence, if not for fighting, runs deep in Sam's veins and throughout Indian country.

Sam was living in our ancestral village of Bena at the time. Leech Lake Reservation is a big reservation, about forty by forty miles. Within the reservation boundaries, there are a number of towns and villages tucked here and there among the swamps, rivers, lakes, and pine trees. Some of the communities are exclusively Indian, like Inger and Ball Club, some are almost all white, and some, like Bena, are mixed. Bena used to be a going concern—it was the end of the line during logging days, and all sorts of timber outfits would get the train as far as Bena and then head north to their logging camps. In the early part of the twentieth century it boasted a number of hotels, stores, and restaurants. After most of the virgin white pine and pulp was cut down in northern Minnesota, Bena managed to stay alive thanks to the growing tourist trade. As roads got better, boats sturdier, and Americans wealthier, they traveled farther and farther north in search of good fishing. Situated on the southern shore of Lake Winnibigoshish, Bena became a fishing destination. But the lake crashed eventually, and Bena—sometimes swelling to a population in the high hundreds during the summer—got smaller and smaller. Today it has a population of around 118, one gas station, a bar, and a post office. The hotels, hardware stores, restaurants, the school—all of it is gone. What have remained, however, are a few big families descended from the mix of Ojibwe Indians and Scots, English, and Irish who came to cut trees and later to take people fishing on the beautiful waters of Lake Winnie. Seelyes and

Matthewses and Lyons and Tibbettses and Dunhams and Michauds and Dormans and Drews still live there.

As much as Sam was drawn back to the reservation and to Bena out of loneliness and affection, and despite the seemingly unbreakable bonds the village exerts on those of us whose families are from there, it's a place that can encourage destruction and dysfunction. To be from Bena was in some fundamental way to be tough. If people found out they'd be fighting a Bena boy, often they'd take a pass. *Oh*, remembered my mother, *every Saturday was fight night. Bena against Federal Dam. Bena against Boy River. Bena against Ball Club. Everyone would get together and rumble and that's what they'd talk about all week.* That was back in the 1950s, but in some ways it's still true.

I didn't fit the tough mold, but Sam did. He fought at bars. He fought at house parties. He literally fought in the street. "No one could beat me, for some reason. I had a good wrestling base. I was strong. I could punch guys out and if I couldn't punch them out I just took them down to the ground."

Sam also drank a lot. His mother, my aunt Barb, who—like Sam—had done really well for a long time, began to slide after Vanessa's death. Sober for years, she began drinking and using drugs again. A host of health problems ensued. There was nothing Sam could do except fight, and that's what he did. Fighting and partying led to drugs and crime. This life went on for years. It's a wonder he didn't die. But Sam has always had stamina.

"We were involved in a little drug ring, I guess you could say," Sam recalls. A rival group, not exactly a gang, were dealing drugs around Bemidji, skinheads, and they ripped off the guys Sam was with. So Sam and his friends went to the trailer where they were staying, and he kicked down the door. "We lit them up. There were three of us against six of them. A couple of our guys brought guns, and these other guys had guns, too. But I just walked up and starting laying guys out. I turned it into a fistfight. One after another I took those guys out. I got a year for aggravated assault but ended up sitting for eight months. That was a real low point for me. I guess I fell in the wrong ruts, and I couldn't get out of them. Just for the record, it was my own choice. I could have done what my dad wanted me to do, but I didn't. I chose the wrong path, and there I was, sitting in prison." If the army had made Sam feel far from home, prison felt a lot farther.

I didn't see Sam much in the years before he got sent to prison. I missed him. I missed the old him I'd known when we were kids—cheerful, funny, ready to laugh at everyone else's jokes. But that cousin was gone. He grew angry and violent, and I wasn't sure how to tease him anymore. And then came prison.

"So when I got out, I got out on the right foot. I didn't go back to Bena." He went to live with a friend "down by the Cities. I didn't go back to Bena. I changed somehow." He was working hard, living away from the reservation, and around that time, in 2000, he heard about MMA on the radio. This was, for Sam, a kind of answer. It might, it just might, offer some structure for the fight in him, which was, by this point, as much a part of him as breathing.

OUR TRIBE, the Ojibwe, are not known for being warlike. Until the late seventeenth century we lacked any real sort of tribal identity and didn't engage in much warfare beyond small skirmishes. Loose bands, based on marriage and clan, moved seasonally between beds of wild rice, fishing grounds, and sugar bush. Hunger, more than other men, was the enemy, and battles were small and relatively rare. However, as the demand for furs increased in the East and overseas, the Ojibwe around the Great Lakes were perfectly positioned to take full advantage of it. They acted as middlemen—securing furs from the West and selling them to the East in exchange for guns and ammunition and cloth—and grew powerful in that role. Their land base grew by a factor of twenty, infant mortality went down, the standard of living went up, and the small Ojibwe bands joined together into a vast, complicated, calculating tribe that effectively controlled a major part of the fur trade.

The tribe was born out of trade, and it came of age in blood, not on horseback out on the Plains, but on foot and by canoe, in the deep woods and scattered watersheds of Wisconsin and Minnesota. In an effort to expand their territory and therefore their security, the Ojibwe began battling the Dakota, on and off. Life was war, and anyone who belonged to an enemy band was a legitimate target: men, women, children. All were killed, all were scalped. (Once, in order to show their disdain, a victorious party of Dakota refused to scalp the Ojibwe corpses; the Ojibwe, upon finding their dead untouched, flew into a rage.) In April 1850, a party of Dakota attacked an Ojibwe sugar camp near the Saint Croix River northeast of Stillwater, Minnesota. They killed and scalped fourteen Ojibwe and took a nine-year-old boy prisoner. The next day they paraded the bloody scalps and their young captive through the village of Stillwater, to the horror of the white inhabitants. The Ojibwe chief Bagone-giizhig (Hole-in-the-Day) was so incensed that during a diplomatic visit to Saint Paul the next month, he killed and scalped a Dakota man in front of his entire family in broad daylight and escaped with his entourage by canoe. He also once declared war on the Dakota and led a war party of more than two hundred against a Dakota camp of more than five hundred warriors along the Minnesota River. The night before the attack, one of the warriors said he'd had a dream it ended badly; the power of the warrior's vision persuaded the war party to turn back. Bagone-giizhig said they were cowards and continued on with just one warrior. Together they attacked the camp, killed one or two Dakota, and fled back north.

Bagone-giizhig was only one Ojibwe war chief famous for his daring if not his violence. Curly Head, Loon's Foot, Bad Boy, Flat Mouth, White Cloud—they were all fighters. But perhaps the most impressive Ojibwe warrior was Waabojiig, White Fisher. As near as anyone can figure, he was born in 1747 and showed courage and a warrior's sensibilities at a young age. During a battle with the Dakota, Waabojiig's father, Mangizid, called a cease-fire when he saw that among his opponents was his half brother, the Dakota chief Wabasha. Mangizid invited his brother into his lodge, and Waabojiig, who was only eight but had been taught from an early age that the Dakota were the enemy, hid behind the door flap and, as Wabasha stooped to enter, hit him over the head with a war club. Wabasha rubbed his head, looked down at Waabojiig, and told him, laughing, *My nephew! You're a brave one and I'm sure you'll go on to kill many of the enemy someday.* His uncle was right. By the time Waabojiig was in his early twenties, he was already a war chief, six-foot-six and with "a commanding countenance, united to ease and dignity of manners," according to an eyewitness. In one summer's campaign down the Saint Croix valley against the Dakota he killed seventy-three of the enemy, most of them with his war club.

But what to do when the fighting is over—after the Ojibwe and our enemies became friends, and after open hostilities between the U.S. government and the tribes ended at the close of the Plains Wars? What to do after the reservation period began and the martial spirit that had largely ensured our survival became an accessory to everyday life rather than its guarantor? In 1917—as tribal power and polity were being eroded by the Dawes Act, the Burke Amendment, the Curtis Act, the Court and Code of Indian Offenses; as power was being stripped from tribes and individual Indians in the 1880s and through the turn of the century; as Indian families endured assault after assault on their autonomy and collectivity; as Indian homelands were being bled of acreage and Indian families were being gutted—Indian men, in proportions far higher than any other ethnic or racial group, began signing up to serve in the Allied Expeditionary Force.

Indians had been serving in large numbers in Canada (as part of the Commonwealth) since 1914. The most decorated soldier (and certainly the most effective) in the Canadian Army was Francis Pegahmagabow. Pegahmagabow (Arrives Standing) was Ojibwe from Wasauksing First Nation on Parry Island in Lake Huron. Orphaned at an early age and raised by relatives on his reserve, he found work as a firefighter, then was drafted at the outbreak of World War I and deployed in France with the First Canadian Infantry Battalion, part of the First Canadian Division, itself the first batch of Canadian troops sent to fight in France. Within a few months, Pegahmagabow saw action at the Second Battle of Ypres in Belgium, which was the first major battle in which chemical warfare saw widespread use; the Germans relied heavily on chlorine gas. And it was arguably the first major military engagement in Europe that was won by a non-European power: it was the Canadians who saved the day and drove the Germans back. When the battle ended, there were more than 120,000 casualties on all sides.

April 24 was the worst day of fighting, with more than three thousand killed by artillery and infantry attacks along the front in the course of that single day. Pegahmagabow served throughout the entire battle, first as a scout and then as a sniper. Snipers were a relatively new addition to the apparatus of war. The term originated in British India to describe someone skilled at shooting snipe, an elusive game bird notoriously hard to shoot owing to speed and camouflage. With the addition of optic sights (scopes), sharpshooters and marksmen could more effectively kill the enemy at greater ranges and without themselves being seen. Pegahmagabow excelled at this. After Ypres, he saw action at the Somme and Passchendaele. By the time of the armistice in 1918 he had been wounded twice and was one of the most decorated Canadian soldiers in history. He was credited with 378 confirmed kills and the capture of 300 Germans.

He had a counterpart from Oklahoma, Private Joseph Oklahombi of the Choctaw Nation. In October 1918, during the Allied offensive at Saint-Étienne, Oklahombi rushed two hundred yards across open ground and captured a German machine gun position. He turned the machine gun on the Germans, killing 79 before taking another 171 captive—and holding them so for four days until reinforcements came to his aid, even while he himself was wounded in both legs and without food or water. He was awarded the Silver Star and the Croix de Guerre but was never recommended for the Medal of Honor. In comparison, twenty of the troopers who opened fire on unarmed Lakota at Wounded Knee had received the Medal of Honor for their efforts twenty-seven years earlier.

In the lead-up to 1917, when America entered the war, many Indians from northern tribes in the United States, some of which straddled the border, walked or paddled across the international boundary and enlisted in the Canadian army. The Onondaga and Oneida in upstate New York went so far as to declare war on Germany. But there has never been anything like consensus between tribes as they puzzled out how and to what extent they would work with (or against) the American government.

When the U.S. government required Indian men to register for the draft in World War I, not a few southern and western tribes bristled, as American Indians were not, generally, citizens at the time, except for some few thousand who had acquired citizenship through allotment. Yavapai activist Dr. Carlos Montezuma, who was strongly against the draft, wrote about it in his newspaper, *Wassaja*: "They are not citizens. They have fewer privileges than have foreigners. They are wards of the United States of America without their consent or the chance of protest on their part." Not a few tribes agreed. Indian men from Deep Creek Reservation in Utah and Nevada refused to register. The Indian agent ordered their incarceration. The Goshute men armed themselves and bought ammunition. Army troops were brought in, and still the tribe refused to give up the men. The army detained more than a hundred men and arrested six of them, but they were eventually freed.

In Oklahoma, Ellen Perryman, last in the line of a prominent Muscogee Creek family, planned a commemoration of the actions of "Loyal Creek" during the Civil War. It turned into an anti-draft protest that escalated into gunfire and the Creek Draft Rebellion of 1919, and Perryman was charged under the Espionage and Sedition Acts. She fled and eluded federal agents for months before she was arrested. Ultimately, her case was postponed indefinitely as long as she behaved herself—a quiet ending to an episode that had grown to involve the Oklahoma National Guard, state and local law enforcement, the Department of Justice, the U.S. Post Office, Secret Service, and the Office of Indian Affairs.

But Perryman was in the minority. The War Department estimated that more than seventeen thousand Indian men enlisted in World War I. Sixty-five hundred of those were drafted. The Office of Indian Affairs collected data, too, and they determined that around half of all the Indians who served volunteered. Some tribes sent very few of their men. Only 1 percent of Diné men served, while more than 40 percent of Osage and Quapaw from Oklahoma joined up. Meanwhile, many Choctaw Indians, also from Oklahoma, joined the American Expeditionary Forces and became the first "code talkers," as the Germans were unable to break the code of the Choctaw language. All in all, Indian participation in World

War I was as much as 30 percent of the adult male population, double the percentage of all adult American men who served.

Within months of the draft, Indians could be found in every branch of the service. Most of the Ojibwe men from Red Cliff Reservation in Wisconsin were tasked to the military police. Pablo Herrera, a Pueblo student from Carlisle Indian Industrial School, ended up commanding a balloon squadron. And five Osage men from Oklahoma served in an aero squadron as pilots. A fanciful journalist suggested that "the Aviation Corps of the Army makes an appeal to the red-skinned youth as fully as to the paleface. There is a sharp fascination to youthful imagination in learning to take to the clouds like birds of the air. And then there is a kinship with nature, too, in the religion of the genuine Indian, which makes the ability of human beings to rise and go skyward doubly alluring." As nice as this sounds, the Osage—whose lands had been allotted in 1907, with each head of household receiving 657 acres—were by 1918 fabulously wealthy because those allotments turned out to sit on top of the largest accessible oil reserves in the United States at the time. It was said that the Osage were "the richest nation, clan or social group of any race on earth, including the whites, man for man." Quite likely the Osage aviators were able to buy their commissions as readily as their wealthy eastern prep-school counterparts.

The Indian boarding schools were a rich source of Indian volunteers. Hampton Institute, Carlisle, Chilocco, Haskell, and Phoenix Indian Schools all sent hundreds and eventually thousands of students off to World War I. Even many of their underage students were encouraged to enlist. Lee Rainbow (Yuma) enlisted at age fifteen and was killed within the year. Henry Tallman (Navajo) ran away from boarding school and enlisted before finishing the eighth grade. Since most of the Indian boarding schools were organized using martial principles—uniforms, marching in formation, the use of cadets, etc.—volunteers from those schools often had an easier time adjusting to army life than their white counterparts. They were often paid more, too: their vocational training in school qualified them for positions most other draftees and volunteers couldn't fill. Graduates of the Phoenix Indian School entered the service as carpenters' mates, shipwrights, blacksmiths, electricians, and colliers. Most Indians, however, served in the infantry. Most, that is, were there to shoot and get shot at.

Whatever the cauldrons of violence on their homelands from which Indian soldiers emerged, they would have seemed small, even tame, compared with the "worldwide festival of death, [the] ugly rutting fever that inflame[d] the raining evening sky all around" that they encountered on the western front in France and Belgium. After initial clashes in eastern France, the Allied and German forces repeatedly tried to outflank each other in what became known as the "race to the sea." Beginning at the First Battle of the Marne, each force jumped north and west in an effort to maneuver around the other, but they were too evenly matched. By 1915, a mere year after the outbreak of war, the "war of movement" had devolved into an unbroken line of static trench warfare from Lorraine to the Belgian coast. The Germans, with one major exception, squatted on the territories they captured and relied on formidable defensive positions, whereas the British and French mounted offensive after offensive, launched from shallow "temporary" trenches in an effort to dislodge the Germans. The British and French suffered horribly as a result. The scale of the clashes is hard to fathom. In the ten-month Battle of Verdun the following year, the French and Germans together suffered 975,000 casualties. Farther north at the Somme, the British lost 420,000 men, the French 200,000, and the Germans 500,000 over a four-month period.

It was into this kettle of death—living belowground in muddy trenches, deprived of light and food, pestered by rats and the oozy stench of the rotting bodies of the combatants who died before them, suffering from trench foot and dysentery, subjected to mustard gas attacks, bombardment, and snipers—that Indian soldiers descended in 1918 as part of the Allied Expeditionary Force. Upon landing, the Americans were tasked with destroying German positions in France at the Amiens salient north of Paris, German positions at the Marne, and the Saint-Mihiel salient near Verdun. Indians fought in all these engagements. Among them were Sergeant Otis W. Leader, a Choctaw machine gunner in the Sixteenth Infantry Regiment. Before the war, Leader had been accused of spying for the

Germans, and in an effort to clear his name he'd joined the infantry. Leader went on to fight at Soissons, Château-Thierry, Saint-Mihiel, and in the Argonne Forest. Before he was done, he'd been wounded and gassed twice. Sergeant Thomas Rogers, Arikara, and Joe Young Hawk, Lakota, also fought at Soissons. Rogers was an incredible soldier and was cited for bravery after he captured "at night barehanded and alone, many [German] sentinels who were taken back to the American camp for questioning." During the same battle, Young Hawk was captured by the Germans while on patrol. He turned on his captors and killed three with his bare hands. During the fray he was shot through both legs but nonetheless managed to capture two more Germans and march them back to American lines.

Tales of Indian heroism abounded and fed the stereotype of the "Indian brave" who was inured to death and pain. Firsthand testimony suggests the stereotypes might have been, at least in part, true. After a young Creek officer was killed while on patrol near Château-Thierry, his company commander wrote that "Lieutenant Breeding had the distinction of being the most capable, daring, and fearless platoon leader in the division." Sergeant John Northrup, Ojibwe from Fond du Lac Reservation in Minnesota, had his leg blown off in the fighting around the Ourcq River. While he waited for evacuation he "saw another Indian soldier crawling in on his hands and knees under heavy German machine-gun fire. On the Indian's back was a badly wounded soldier. As the Native American passed by, Northrup noticed both the Indian's feet had been shot off." Major Tom Riley, the commander of the Third Battalion, 165th Infantry Division, observed, "If a battle was on, and you wanted to find the Indians, you would always find them at the front." In a particularly brutal fight during the Meuse-Argonne offensive, 476 of the 876 men in Riley's battalion were killed. He noted that the "Indians in the front ranks were thoroughly swept away. When an Indian went down, another Indian immediately stepped to the front."

These incidences of heroism may have had as much to do with army protocol as they did with any cultural or genetic predisposition to bravery. As part of the induction process, recruits were administered "intelligence" tests that included questions such as: "Bull Durham is the name of a A. chewing gum, B. aluminum ware, C. tobacco, D. clothing." "Seven-up is played with A. rackets, B. cards, C. pins, D. dice." "The most prominent industry of Minneapolis is A. flour, B. packing, C. automobiles, D. brewing." The answers to such dubious questions could determine where and in what capacity men served, and the army generally attempted to preserve "intelligence" by placing those who scored high on the test in less dangerous assignments, while those with lower scores were often assigned to infantry units. As a result, men from inner-city slums, Appalachia, the Deep South, and Indian reservations—men, that is, often without access to money, education, or social mobility—wound up in the infantry. For Indians in service, the results were disastrous: they disproportionately served as scouts and snipers and patrol leaders, "you would always find them at the front" because the army put them there, and they suffered casualty rates five times higher than the American Expeditionary Force as a whole. Yet they served in mixed regiments and battalions, a circumstance that was to ripple out in unforeseen ways through the years.

As with almost everything Indian, the question of whether to segregate Indians was attended by fierce ideological battles. Congress declared war on Germany on April 6, 1917. By the end of the month, a bill was introduced in the House of Representatives that called for the formation of "ten or more regiments of Indian cavalry as part of the military forces of the United States, to be known as the North American Indian Cavalry." One of the provisions of the bill was that Indians who served in these regiments would be granted citizenship at war's end without jeopardizing their tribal status.

The principal advocate for segregated units was Dr. Joseph Kossuth Dixon, the author of *The Vanishing Race*. Who exactly Dixon was remains somewhat shrouded in mystery. He was born in Pennsylvania, attended the Rochester Theological Seminary, and then more or less disappeared for thirty years. He resurfaced in the early part of the twentieth century as a self-appointed (and celebrated) "author, explorer, ethnologist and authority on the American Indian." He managed to team up with Rodman Wanamaker, scion of the Wanamaker department store family, who began funding expeditions into Indian country with the ostensible mission of saving the last vestiges of a "vanishing race." The first such expedition brought Dixon and a film crew to Crow Agency, where in 1908 he filmed Longfellow's *Song of Hiawatha* using Crow Indian "braves" and "maidens." What filming a New England poet's confabulation of Ojibwe and Iroquois myths had to do with actually helping Indians is unclear, but Wanamaker was happy with the film and funded a lecture circuit that had Dixon making more than three hundred appearances before more than four hundred thousand people.

Dixon returned to Montana on a second "Wanamaker Expedition." This time his mission to capture the vanishing race was more solid. He handpicked twenty-one chiefs from eleven different bands and then (ignoring the fact that more than 250,000 Indians belonging to more than three hundred different tribes then existed in the country) claimed that they represented "nearly every Indian tribe in the United States." This orchestrated "last great council of the chiefs," Dixon claimed, "had for its dominant idea the welfare of the Indian, that he should live at peace with his fellows and all men." As such, "the council became not only a place of historic record but a school for the inculcation of the highest ideals of peace" before Indians were interred in "the grave of their race."

As it happened, one of the "chiefs," Runs-the-Enemy, was a tribal policeman. Another, White Horse, was a farmer and a missionary at the Yankton Sioux Agency. And another, unnamed, had been appointed by the Indian agent to appear in the film and was anxious to get back to his fields so he could put up his hay before the fall rains. But in Dixon's thinking, the Indian and his ways were doomed to extinction. He "would not yield. He died. He would not receive his salvation by surrender; rather would he choose oblivion, unknown darkness—the melting fires of extermination." Looking back on the council, he mused sadly, "For one splendid moment they were once again real Indians." Being a "real Indian," to him at least, meant fading into the twilight of the past. *The Vanishing Race* and the accompanying photos and book were a fabulous success.

Lest he be outdone, after the second expedition, Dixon helped create a national memorial dedicated to the "Vanishing Indian"; at the inauguration, many real live Indians showed up. Then the third, most extravagant expedition was launched in 1913. Called the "Rodman Wanamaker Expedition of Citizenship," it was a mammoth undertaking. Dixon assembled a team of photographers and ethnographers and had Wanamaker outfit a special train, the Signet, to carry them on a twenty-thousand-mile odyssey through Indian America, stopping at every major reservation. At each they instructed the Indian agent to have assembled as many Indians as possible in their regalia around a temporary flagpole. Dixon would then raise the American flag as the Indians signed a pledge of fealty to the United States, symbolically ushering them into modern America from their ravaged and soon-to-die tribal past. The assembled Indians were also treated to a recorded message from President Woodrow Wilson, played back on a phonograph:

> There are some dark pages in the history of the white man's dealings with the Indian, and many parts of the record are stained with greed and avarice of those who have thought only of their own profit; but it is also true that the purposes and motives of this great Government and of our nation as a whole toward the red man have been wise, just and beneficent. . . . The Great White Father now calls you his "brothers," not his "children." Because you have shown in your education and in your settled ways of life staunch, manly, worthy qualities of sound character, the nation is about to give you distinguished recognition through the erection of a monument in honor of the Indian people, in the harbor of New York. The erection of that monument will usher in that day which Thomas Jefferson said he would rejoice to see, "when the Red Men become truly one people with us, enjoying all the rights and privileges we do, and living in peace and plenty." I rejoice to foresee the day.

The message and the narrative were clear. The story of the Indian was now the story of the death of the tribe and the continued life of the man. Assimilation was, to people like Dixon and Wanamaker—if not to the Indians themselves—the answer to the problem of continued Indian existence. But the ideology was complicated by the aesthetics that surrounded it: if Indians were to be assimilated, why parade them in regalia at the moment of their passing? If assimilation was the answer, why then elide the ways in which Indians (like the ones who posed as chiefs for Dixon at Crow Agency) were finding ways to live?

This moral and aesthetic confusion found its way into the debates surrounding citizenship and military service. Guided more by his romantic feelings about Indians than by the record of Indians in military service—which they had been a part of since well before the Civil War—Dixon lobbied forcefully for all-Indian regiments, maintaining that the "Indian spirit would be crushed if we insist that he take his stand beside the white man." Yet in the age of American triumphalism, how else to consider assimilation? And if assimilation was to be the watchword, wouldn't that be better achieved by integration into regular regiments? That's what top-ranking military officials felt, and they were backed up by Commissioner of Indian Affairs Cato Sells, who wrote that the "military segregation of the Indian is altogether objectionable. It does not afford the associational contact he needs and is unfavorable to his preparation for citizenship. . . . [The] mingling of the Indian with the white soldier ought to have, as I believe it will, a large influence in moving him away from tribal relations and toward civilization."

Tribal opinion itself was mixed. Some tribes—the Crow, Lakota, and others—wrote letters urging Congress to allow them to form all-Indian regiments. Others, like Red Cliff Reservation in Wisconsin, were glad that they were able to serve with their white neighbors. In the end, the army won that fight, and while there were some all-Indian regiments, most Indians served alongside their white counterparts. Both camps—the preservationists and the assimilationists—had the same goal and operated from the same understanding: that the old tribal ways were dead and the Indian problem would die only if tribes died.

And yet.

And yet, in the army as at boarding school, Indians did pick up skills. They became literate and learned trades. Many converted to Christianity, but many didn't. They learned how to work within (and for) organizational structures, as bookkeepers, secretaries, teamsters, cooks, drivers, and trig-germen; they built ships and baked bread and went on patrol. They did this as servicemen and as Indians. And when the war was over, they more often than not returned home. They returned changed. And they returned to a shock. Veterans arriving in White Earth Reservation in Minnesota de-scribed the land as like that of Flanders and Soissons: ravaged and bare, but not by bombs. Rather, allotments and leases had been gobbled up by tim-ber barons and the land had been clear-cut. Minneapolis had become a national center for prostheses because it had access to the straight-grained, strong, knot-free virgin white pine that was best for making them. The timber was largely cut from trees illegally (and immorally) harvested on White Earth, Leech Lake, and Red Lake Reservations.

Despite the clamoring of romantics like Dixon and others like him who sought to "help" the Indian and saw military service as a path to citizenship, at war's end fewer than half of the Indian population were citizens, and even fewer had the right to vote. Not even all the men and women who served gained citizenship. The United States, well on its way to becoming a world power, was keen to congratulate itself, and so, even as it treated its veterans shamefully and bungled its treaty obligations, it did hand out a lot of medals and flags to Indian communities around the country. Felix Renvielle, a veteran of the Argonne Forest who had wounds so critical his parents had been sent a death certificate, suffered for the rest of his life at Sisseton in South Dakota, without access to adequate medical care. Theodore D. Beaulieu, Ojibwe from White Earth Reserva-tion in Minnesota, wrote that the Ojibwe, having served in the war, never-theless were subject to an "undemocratic bureaucracy, . . . compelled to pay double taxation [and] denied the privilege of work or suggestion as to the manner of the disposition of their tribal funds" and that his people struggled "against want, hunger, and disease." Joseph Oklahombi, who returned to Oklahoma the most decorated American Indian hero of the war, remained illiterate and found work loading lumber at a mill and coal company, but that didn't last long. He turned to booze and by 1932 was surviving on his veteran's pension of twelve dollars a month. He was struck and killed by a car while walking along the road on April 13, 1960.

But not all veterans lived—or died—alone. Navajo, Eastern Cherokee in North Carolina, and Lakota on the Rosebud Reservation in South Dakota established American Legion posts. Other Indians quietly parlayed their war experience into spiritual and political leadership positions within their tribes.

The men who returned, returned having seen the world. They were the first generation of Indian people who could begin to see America from outside both the American and the Indian lens. They had been to Brest, Paris, London, Lille. And—disillusioned, war-weary, and bereft—they might have seen something policy makers and fantasists like Dixon could not. Faced with acculturation at the bottom or building a new Indian polity where they would have some say in what happened to them, the choice must have been clear. So it was not surprising that at the close of the First World War, Indian men and women began building new kinds of Indian communities and governments. And for the first time, they were armed with the tools of the modern nation-state.

A mere twenty-eight years after the massacre at Wounded Knee, American Indians had helped to perpetuate global violence and proved that they were good at it, but something else was happening, too, something that escaped notice at the time. By 1917, for the first time in more than a hundred years, American Indian births outstripped Indian deaths. Our population was on the rise.

Asked what should be done to the kaiser after the war was over (and reflecting on the service of his own people and their subsequent treatment), an elderly Lakota man responded that the German leader should be "confined to a reservation, given an allotment, and forced to farm. When the kaiser asked for help, the old man continued, the Indian agent should say to him, 'Now you lazy bad man, you farm and make your living by farming, rain or no rain; and if you do not make your own living don't come to the Agency whining when you have no food in your stomach and no money, but stay here on your farm and grow fat till you starve.'"

Still, after the end of the Indian Wars, after allotment, after boarding schools, and after World War I, history was in many ways something that happened to Indians, not something they made. Or if they made it, it was (in the words of Karl Marx) not with tools of their own choosing. The path to citizenship was no exception. While citizenship was the logical extension of assimilation, it didn't happen in any kind of uniform way. The service of Indian veterans in World War I certainly played a role in the quest for citizenship, but Indians had served with and for the United States in every single armed conflict it had fought, beginning with the Revolutionary War, not to mention against other tribes and sometimes even against their own. Despite their service, until World War I, Indians had been excluded from the citizenship clauses in the U.S. Constitution and, again, in the Fourteenth Amendment, passed in 1868.

While some Indians had gained citizenship, either through the fee-simple patenting provisions included in the Dawes and Curtis Acts, by renouncing tribal membership in order to own land outright, or by marrying U.S. citizens (this worked for women only, not men), there was a push after the war to extend citizenship to all Indians born in the United States. Once again, the push came from everyone except themselves. The Friends of the Indian and the Indian Rights Association lobbied heavily. Dixon, whose floridity never failed to eclipse the people he believed he was serving, wrote, "The Indian, though a man without a country, the Indian who has suffered a thousand wrongs considered the white man's burden and from mountains, plains and divides, the Indian threw himself into the struggle to help throttle the unthinkable tyranny of the Hun. The Indian helped to free Belgium, helped to free all the small nations, helped to give victory to the Stars and Stripes. The Indian went to France to help avenge the ravages of autocracy. Now, shall we not redeem ourselves by redeeming all the tribes?"

Dixon found a receptive audience in Congress, where reformers were increasingly disturbed by the degree of corruption and malfeasance in the Indian service. The stubbornly defended existence of Indians continued to pose the question: What kind of country, what kind of democracy, had been created and defended, and at what cost? Surely one that was capable of treating the most disenfranchised people within its borders less poorly. Citizenship for Indians, in other words, was a tool meant to curb abuses by non-Indians. It was enacted in 1924 without much fanfare. The statute read:

> Be it enacted by the Senate and house of Representatives of the United States of America in Congress assembled, That all non citizen Indians born within the territorial limits of the United States be, and they are hereby, declared to be citizens of the United States: Provided That the granting of such citizenship shall not in any manner impair or otherwise affect the right of any Indian to tribal or other property.

All of a sudden the three hundred thousand Indians alive in 1924 in the United States became American citizens. And yet they did not have to renounce their tribal citizenship as part of this quasi-magical transformation: "Provided That the granting of such citizenship shall not in any manner impair or otherwise affect the right of any Indian to tribal or other property." What this meant was profound: Indians were citizens and could vote, own property, could enjoy the "pursuit of happiness," were "equal under the law," could have wrongs redressed in court, and everything else with it. And at the same time, all the treaties not yet abrogated, all the rights to communal and tribal ownership of land, all the basic building blocks of tribal sovereignty were left in place. Indians—enjoying tribal and American citizenship—became a legally unique kind of American, both Indian and American.

Many Indians, however, didn't gain suffrage, as states often used what power they had to limit Indians' access to the ballot. These states argued that Indians shouldn't be allowed to vote because it wasn't right for them to participate in both tribal and U.S. elections, or because they didn't pay taxes on real estate, or because many of them lived on land held in federal trusteeship. Depriving Indians of the right to vote in the Southwest was a clear attempt to prevent Indian influence in local and state elections. Because there were so many Indians in that region, their participation would likely skew elections away from desired Anglo outcomes. As of 1938, seven states hadn't extended suffrage to Indians, and it wasn't until

1948—after thousands of Pueblo, Navajo, Hopi, and Apache had served in World War II—that Arizona and New Mexico (the two states with the largest proportion of Indians in the population) bent to federal pressure and allowed Indians to vote.

The Meriam Report

In 1928, four years after the Citizenship Act, the government released the Meriam Report. The massive report excoriated the government's Indian policy and was the first comprehensive assessment of Indian life in the United States since Henry Rowe Schoolcraft was asked to undertake one in 1850. The appointment of the highly practical and unsentimental Lewis Meriam as lead investigator was something of a miracle for subjects who had, so often and for so long, been written about and advocated for by sensationalists who overlaid their real lives with meanings and significance that had little to do with them.

For such a father of facts, however, precious few can be obtained about him or his views. He was born in Salem, Massachusetts, in 1883; took degrees at Harvard and George Washington universities; and received his PhD from the Brookings Institution. He worked primarily as a statistician and did serious work for the Census Bureau before he was asked to conduct a study on the lives and living conditions of Indians across the country. He assembled a team of experts from different areas—health, education, law, economics, agriculture, and "family life" among them. Once empaneled, the commission set out to see what was happening in Indian country, sometimes together and sometimes not, given the amount of ground they had to cover. Over a seven-month period they visited ninety-five locations—reservations, hospitals, schools, and agencies—in twenty-two states. It would take the team another two and a half years to organize and analyze the data they collected. When they were done they had managed to create a comprehensive, detailed, and impartial document that offered a damning assessment of how Indians had fared over the forty years the assimilation machine had been gobbling them up and churning out Americans.

The report argued with facts and details, rather than passion and hyperbole, that federal Indian policy was a disaster. Health on reservations was as poor as it was in the boarding schools. Indians made—and continued to live on—much lower incomes than white Americans. Allotment had had a horrible effect on them. The allotments often couldn't support any farmers, much less those new to the enterprise. And whatever strategies had worked for Indians in more "primitive" times had been supplanted by strategies that had been foisted on them and could not work where and how Indians actually lived. All in all, the report found that Indians were floundering on an American sea and were, as a whole, drowning.

Lost in accounts of the years between 1918 and 1956 is the knowledge that the only reason there were any Indians left at all was that they had fought. They had fought against the government, and they had fought with it. Deprived of every conceivable advantage or tool or clear-hearted advocate, they had continued to fight. Not just in the ways Dixon and people like him imagined, as warriors astride horses roaming free across the Plains, but rather as husbands and wives and fathers and mothers. As writers and thinkers. As farmers and soldiers in the Great War. But what to do when the actual fighting stops and the pressures bear down back home? What to do when you can't find the fight beyond the one for daily survival? What to do with that patrimony?

Emergence of Tribal Governments

As early as 1918, Indian tribes began to organize themselves formally despite the control exerted by the Office of Indian Affairs and the federal government more generally. At Red Lake Reservation, under the guidance of Peter Graves and the hereditary chiefs of the tribe, they

formed the Red Lake General Council, a kind of amalgam of the hereditary chieftain positions the Ojibwe had employed for centuries and newer,
representative forms of government. In 1893, at age twenty-one, Peter
Graves—by blood half white and half Ojibwe from the Leech Lake Reservation but raised at Red Lake—was recruited by the Indian agent there
to serve in the Red Lake police force. Within five years he was chief of
police. During that time, Graves—through sheer force of character—
developed a very good relationship with the agent and with all of his superiors in the Office of Indian Affairs. When a skirmish at Leech Lake
broke out in 1898 at Sugar Point and Red Lakers were eager to go down
and join the Leech Lakers in open, armed revolt against the U.S. government, Graves stood up in council and shouted down the hereditary chiefs,
saying that anyone who went down to Leech Lake would forfeit membership at Red Lake and wouldn't be allowed to return. Graves was so
persuasive—yelling, teasing, cajoling—that in the end no Red Lakers
went to Leech Lake.

He became indispensable to the Office of Indian Affairs, acting as an
unofficial diplomat between the chiefs and the government. Graves was
also—in his role as liaison and police chief—increasingly annoyed and
angered by the inroads white people were making into the sovereign territory of the Red Lake Ojibwe: timber crews, homesteaders, tourists, and
fishermen flocked to the reservation. Everything revolved around the white
people, who at times came to outnumber the Red Lakers on their own
reservation. Moreover, even though Red Lake, alone among Ojibwe tribes
in the region, had resisted the provisions of the Dawes and Nelson Acts,
the government wasn't content to let it alone. They kept trying to allot it,
and Graves knew that once they did, all of the timber and, more important, control of the lake itself would evaporate. He also knew that the
council of hereditary chiefs was not respected by the government. Something else was needed.

In 1918, Graves joined forces with the chiefs, and they drafted a constitution for the General Council of the Red Lake Band of Chippewa
Indians ("Chippewa" was the older mispronunciation of "Ojibwe" but
was in common usage among the Ojibwe). It was a unique document

203

and a bold move. Article 1 established the General Council. Article 2 recognized and codified the positions of the hereditary chiefs at Red Lake and "empowered them to be the primary political agents at Red Lake." Seven hereditary positions in all were identified in the document, and each of the seven was to appoint five representatives to the General Council. All these members were voting members. Article 3 gave the General Council the right to appoint a chairman and other officers, though none of these had voting powers. The new/old Red Lake government held its first meeting on April 13, 1918, and it became the force that governed there, gradually eroding the power and efficacy of the Indian agent just as the agent had once eroded their authority. And though it didn't happen overnight, gradually they were able to isolate and expel all of the white people living at Red Lake. But even as Red Lake took control of its destiny, wedding its ancestral modes of government to modern democratic rule, in 1934 government came to them, as it had come to Indians all across the country: from the top down, dreamed up by a few officials, and imposed uniformly in diverse communities, regardless of their needs.

John Collier and the Indian Reorganization Act

John Collier was born into a powerful political and banking family in Atlanta in 1884. Studying at Columbia, he came to believe that capitalism, if not modernity itself, was not altogether a good thing. American society, he would later say, was "physically, religiously, socially, and aesthetically shattered, dismembered, directionless." In his mind, mechanization, modern life, and the striving for money eroded community and purpose. From 1907 to 1919 he served as the secretary for the People's Institute, which taught political theory and social philosophy to workers and immigrants in New York City, focusing on ways to bolster ethnic and cultural pride through parades, lectures, and pageants. In 1920 he visited Taos, New Mexico, where he studied Pueblo life and culture. He came away changed: he was appalled by the government's efforts at forced assimilation. He understood the "Indian problem" mostly as a policy problem the government had created. Plurality, freedom of religion, the right to self-governance—basically everything that had made America what it was—had been denied to American Indians, and only restoring and strengthening Indian tribes and tribal government could help Indians emerge from the nightmare of the past fifty years.

Collier spent the next decade fighting for Indian rights, first as a part of the General Federation of Women's Clubs, where he did research for the Indian Welfare Committee. The GFWC believed, as he did, that the key barriers to Indians' well-being were the loss of land under the Dawes Act and allotment, the illegalization of Indian religion under the Office of Indian Affairs, and economic and social dependency as a result of both. He, with the GFWC and on his own, lobbied to have the Dawes Act overturned. He joined the American Indian Defense Association formed by Robert Ely in 1923 to fight the religious oppression that was part of the federal program of assimilation. He was so relentless and so effective in his quest for not just equality but plurality and fairness that he was almost single-handedly responsible for the curtailment of religious persecution and the allotment process. He was the driving force behind the research and drafting of the Meriam Report in 1928. This didn't win him many friends. A press release from the Interior Department claimed that Collier was a "fanatical Indian enthusiast with good intentions, but so charged with personal bias and the desire to get a victim every so often, that he does much more harm than good. . . . His statements cannot be depended upon to be either fair, factual or complete." Nonetheless, after Franklin Delano Roosevelt took office, Collier was appointed commissioner of Indian affairs. He served from 1933 to 1945 and made sure the New Deal was a deal that reached into and lifted up Indian communities from coast to coast. Under Collier, the New Deal came to Indian country as the Indian Reorganization Act, passed in 1934.

John Collier and Blackfeet Chiefs, circa 1934

The IRA, or Howard-Wheeler Act, was revolutionary. It put a stop to the erosion of Indian homelands through allotment, created processes by which some of the land already lost could be gotten back, and devised structures by which new lands could be incorporated. It also brought constitutions and governments to Indian communities that had suffered under the lazy (but energetically corrupt) hand of the Office of Indian Affairs. The kicker was that tribes did not have to agree to the models of government proposed in the act, or even be reorganized along the lines drawn in it. They could vote on it among themselves and decide if it worked. Article 18 read: "This Act shall not apply to any reservation wherein a majority of the adult Indians, voting at a special election duly called by the Secretary of the Interior, shall vote against its application. It shall be the duty of the Secretary of the Interior, within one year after the passage and approval of this Act, to call such an election, which election shall be held by secret ballot upon thirty days' notice."

This was a far cry from the way legislation had generally been forced down the throats of Indian communities—and land grabbed, children taken away, and rations and annuities withheld for noncompliance. And yet more subtle coercion nevertheless ensued. It was intimated that it would be difficult if not impossible to receive federal grants and assistance—for public projects, livestock and grazing, roads, hospitals, and schools—without a government in place that the U.S. federal government recognized. Moreover, the voting process was murky. Who was eligible to vote? By 1934 many non-Indians lived within the boundaries of Indian reservations as a result of allotment. Could they vote? The IRA would affect them, too. And what about absentees? Many thousands of Indians didn't live—either permanently or temporarily—in their homelands or on their reservations. It was decided that absentees counted as votes for the new government. The Navajo, in particular, were dead set against the IRA because of Collier's involvement in the Navajo Livestock Reduction Program, which forced the Navajo collectively to sell off half their livestock in an effort to curb erosion and overgrazing. Collier had the dissenters jailed and then pressed for a vote. In the end 172 tribes voted for the IRA, 73 against. To this day, many Diné regard Collier as a dictator.

If one looks through the many constitutions that came into being for tribes between 1934 and 1938, it seems clear that Collier, despite (or because of) his interest in Native life, imagined a very specific kind of government for Indian people. He had, after all, spent more of his time among Indians at Taos Pueblo than in any other place or with any other tribe. The Pueblo lived in sedentary, village-centered communities that had existed within first the Spanish, then the Mexican, and finally the American governments. No wonder the majority of the tribal constitutions adopted as a result of the Indian Reorganization Act structured tribes much in the manner of small towns across America. But Taos (and the other eighteen Pueblos) are very different from the many hundreds of other tribes and many thousands of other tribal communities around the country. Moreover, they had not been subject to the treaty process as had most other tribes, because they had not been legally defined as Indians. Pueblo tribal constitutions more closely resembled charters or ordinances for municipalities. The IRA applied the same structure to their sample constitutions. These provided for a governing body of five to nine people, a chairman, secretary, treasurer, and district representatives, election cycles, rights and responsibilities such as entering into contracts, acquiring and disposing of land, administering and collecting funds, hiring and firing, and enrollment. As a rule, Collier's suggestions and templates in the IRA did not include any kind of democratic structure like that enjoyed by the country at large: three separate independent bodies (executive, legislative, judicial), a bill of rights, or anything resembling constitutional rights. All in all, as the years began to show, IRA constitutions were grossly inadequate to the enormous job of policing large tracts of land, making education truly "local," resolving disputes not just between Indians of the same tribe but between Indians of different tribes and between Indians and their non-Indian neighbors. A Pueblo might be something like a village. But the Pine Ridge Reservation or the Blackfeet Nation or the Wind River Shoshone and Arapaho were nothing like villages at all. They were large, diverse nations, defined by treaties, had been sedentary for only fifty years, and each comprised many villages and family groups, not to mention bands. And each was still contending with the predation of outsiders who wanted a piece of what was left. Only now, in the early twenty-first century, are tribes radically rethinking their constitutions and trying to draft and redraft founding documents that fit their culture, land, history, and sense of self as a people.

Perhaps Collier felt that the combined effect of his efforts and the Meriam Report would be enough to put a stop to the depredations of the Office of Indian Affairs and that in a less aggressive mode the office was sufficient to mediate disputes, see to the health of tribal institutions, and tend the ever-evolving relationship between tribes and local, state, and federal governments. Perhaps he saw tribal sovereignty and tribal citizenship less as the defining features of Indian life and more as spices that merely flavored the tribal meal. After all, tribal sovereignty was only quasi-sovereignty: they couldn't (legally) raise armies, develop currencies, enter into treaties with foreign nations, or enter into trade relationships with, say, Germany. So, given all this, perhaps Collier thought that the constitutions that came about as a result of the IRA were adequate. They were not, and many tribes didn't like them.

The Red Lake Ojibwe, for example, having created a hybrid government twenty years before the IRA, saw no reason to change their constitution and government now. They voted against the IRA government despite immense pressure to accept it. Even the Pueblos, on whom the proposed constitutions were modeled, generally wanted no part of the switch.

"ACOMA IS CONSIDERED one of the oldest continuously inhabited settlements in North America," Brian Vallo of Acoma Pueblo says, as we visit in what is perhaps one of the most beautiful offices in America, on the campus of the School for Advanced Research in Santa Fe. Brian is quick to laugh, self-effacing, with a magical way of mixing modesty, humor, shyness, and power. At fifty, he is well-built, with black hair, a large face, and a strength and delicacy to both his words and his movements that I think of as fundamentally "Pueblo." Sitting west of Albuquerque off Interstate 40, the village was settled around 1100 CE, on a sandstone mesa that rises 350 feet from the valley floor. "One of the landmarks on the mesa top is the symbol of contact that has had significant impact on our lifeway," continues Vallo, "and that's the mission church. It's the largest earthen structure in North America. Completed in 1629. There was an obscene amount of materials, sand and stone, carried on the backs of Acoma men, women, and children to the mesa top to build the church. Not willing labor. The interesting thing about it is that it is sitting on top of a ceremonial structure that was part of the original village."

Acoma has been populated for more than a thousand years, but in the last three hundred or so, most of the community moved to Acomita, sixteen miles north of the old Pueblo. Acomita has a more reliable source of surface water and is better for crops and grazing and village life. Acoma continues to serve as the cultural and social home of close to six thousand tribal members, but only fifteen families live there year-round. By choice of the community it has no running water and no electricity. "We want to retain the integrity of the site," Vallo says. "It's occupied, but not full-time by the entire community."

He tells me about his upbringing. "I am born into my mother's clan, the Sun Clan, which is very large. My father's clan is Eagle, that's my small clan." He jokes that the only time his small clan is relevant is at birth, when his paternal aunts washed him, and again at death, when they will wash him again. And yet he was raised and influenced by his paternal grandparents. "My father was in the Air Force, so he, my mom, and I were traveling around the country. Upon our return to Acoma I spent a great amount of time in the home of my grandparents, tending to the sheep herd and farming." As a result of his upbringing, Vallo says, "I found myself listening to conversations among old people most kids my age didn't experience." Vallo's grandfather had gone to the Indian school, but after fourth grade, he ran away and came back home. He became a traditional leader who raised sheep. "It was very clear that my paternal grandfather was concerned about me being introduced into our cultural lifeways in preparation for the responsibilities I would eventually have as an Acoma man."

At the time Vallo was coming up, in the 1970s, the Bureau of Indian Affairs had a strong presence in the community, but it was a time of big change. "There was a BIA day school in Acomita, but a new elementary school was being constructed, and a new hospital. I had this fear of having to leave the day school to go to this giant new school," Vallo remembers. He spoke Acoma fluently. "It was a first language. It's all we spoke. So communicating with my peers in school was in Acoma. We joked around. It was the best way we knew how to communicate with each other. And you got home and it was all you heard. I had a hard time with English. But I eventually picked it up. I think I enjoyed my elementary school years in the old day school, where my parents had also attended school. And this transition to the new school was freaking me out! My mother's side of the family was huge and I have tons of cousins. Never a shortage of playmates." The cousins helped with the animals as much as they played together. "My grandfather had close to eight hundred sheep at the time. Raising that herd involved the entire family, other community members, and Native sheepherders. Even those of us who were children at the time."

Vallo's father eventually quit the military and came back to New Mexico, but he went to work for the BIA and was always on the road. The family remained rooted in Acoma. Brian went to the public school on the Laguna Pueblo Reservation ten miles east of Acoma. He survived the transition to a different school and a different community, but he hated high school. "I thought it was a waste of time." For Brian, as for a lot of Indian kids, there wasn't so much a split between "old ways" and "new ways." There was just . . . life. "By then we were still raising sheep. Still planting. Nothing really changed. My grandparents were getting older. The herd was reduced by half. It wasn't as much work, but it was still involved."

Both of the houses Vallo lived in growing up were constructed by his grandfathers of sandstone and mud. "My maternal grandmother's house was a four-room house. We had an outhouse, it wasn't until later we had indoor plumbing." That way of life was changing, too. "Eventually some of my classmates and their families, as a result of HUD housing, were detaching themselves from the extended family unit. Moving into their own homes." Vallo remembers looking at them and thinking how lucky they were—"their own bedrooms, a toilet." His grandparents moved into HUD housing when he was in high school. "You could get a HUD home if you were within a certain income range. Low-income housing. My father, thankfully, had a good job with the government, my mother was working for the tribe, and they exceeded the requirements for housing. So we ended up living next door to my grandmother's house in a mobile home. We thought it was so awesome! We had our own rooms. We had the avocado-green carpeting in the living room. We thought, 'This is great.'" His cousins continued to live nearby. "It was a good life. I think my parents made a lot of sacrifices and worked really hard." His father, now retired, was still living much as his own father had. "He was involved in the community. Still going out to sheep camp. Still cutting wood. Still planting. I was in awe of it even when I was in high school. He gets things done. He doesn't bullshit about anything."

The childhood Brian describes is different from that of many Indian kids I knew, including mine and Sammy's, and I can't help being a little jealous. As hard as it was, it didn't seem to bear the marks of violence or despair so familiar to so many Indians. When change did come to Acoma, the community weathered it. "There's no real ownership of land for grazing, but we have communal areas. When I was growing up in the early years my grandfather and other sheep owners were all really respectful of each other and the land resources and they would inform one another which parcels they would use, they talked about it." Over time, the community shifted from sheep to mostly cattle. There was a bigger market for beef, and the younger generation didn't know as much about shearing, butchering, and caring for sheep, or managing the land and water resources for them. "All of those things are becoming missing parts of our society, our community. Sign of the times," Vallo reflects. Still, cattle owners did "a relatively good job at maintaining the historic connection to land. So it's good there are some who are raising cattle and familiarizing themselves with the land base, know the grasses, think about erosion control, know the fence lines. There is a brain trust of people from many generations still who are familiar with the Acoma land base."

Continuity, connection. These things were possible in Acoma in ways not possible elsewhere in large part because of the continuity of their political and religious traditions. Yet Vallo, like many Pueblo people, is incredibly circumspect about the exact nature and content of their foundational myths and totally silent on the subject of ceremony. It's like the first rule of Fight Club: You don't talk about Fight Club.

"So, our creation stories and our emergence stories are where our government begins," he says cautiously. "Each Pueblo has a version of the creation, emergence, and migration stories. They aren't terribly different, but they do differ. At the time of emergence there were symbols presented to the people in a basket. There were different things in this basket. One represented leadership and protection of the people. It was foretold during this time of emergence that there would be a time, something would happen, that would cause the people to create this leadership structure. So the

212

Acoma version of this is that at Mesa Verde, somewhere in Mesa Verde, we're not sure which location, there was this event that caused the larger community to identify the hierarchy of the clan system. There was somewhat of a crisis that caused a need for this action. The story is so powerful and moving." He pauses, and I can see, in Brian's face, his mind going over the story, and then filing it away.

He continues:

"The hierarchy of the clans was established at this time at that place. The Antelope Clan, Deer, Moss clan, and Evergreen clan. These already existed, but they came together to identify leadership, hierarchy. The symbol was clear. And everyone knew what to do. So the Pueblos have what are called war chiefs and they represent these deities. The hierarchy then also accepted the responsibility to appoint the men from the larger community to serve in the capacity of war chief, their key role being providing protection for the people and guiding the migration. At that time there was a particular cycle they were following—a process of monitoring the sun and moon, the solar and lunar cycles. This process of monitoring was just evolving at that time. At the end of each cycle that core group of clans would convene to identity the next group of war chiefs. There were three war chiefs. That process continued as the migration continued. And so it was those war chiefs met with other leaders and laid out the path to make sure the migration would be safe and would be in line with what was prescribed at the time of emergence. This process of selecting leadership still exists today."

From Chaco, the groups dispersed. The Acoma and other groups continued southward, and the Acoma reached the site to which they gave their name. "When Acoma was discovered they purified the site, before people ascended the mesa top. The hierarchy met each clan group that ascended the mesa, each who offered their purpose and contribution. In other words, they had to justify their stay at Acoma. So Sun Clan leaders asked if they could stay and named their contribution, which satisfied the hierarchy, who told them they were welcome. Each clan who was welcomed was assigned an area where they would build their dwellings. This followed for each clan group." There were around thirty-two clans who settled Acoma, Vallo believes. "Today we are down to thirteen. Of the core clan groups we only have the Antelope left."

I'm fascinated by the way in which the Pueblos' own brand of political and civil government is rooted in the very real myth of their migration, just as America's founding documents are vested in the myths of its own migratory story. First contact, needless to say, complicated the Pueblo story.

"So when the Spanish arrived, and the terrible experience that came with them—the Church, Catholicism was introduced, the next thing that came with that was the demand that we needed to establish a government. And so a Spanish style of government was introduced. The king of Spain sent each of the Pueblos three silver-capped wooden canes, representing staffs of authority." These wooden staffs continue to be used today, and are similar, symbolically, to the war chiefs' canes. The Acoma people resisted Spanish rule and their paternalistic governance system, creating their own form of government that combined the indigenous and Spanish styles. Or perhaps it is more accurate to say that Spanish impositions were transformed by the Pueblos' preexisting ways.

That system required that the Pueblos appoint a governor, a lieutenant governor, and three *fiscales*, or sheriffs. "Initially, there was no relevance to the people, of course," Vallo notes. "So what it took was our community and others to really make sense of what this new form of government was going to look like. And its place within the cultural context. So at Acoma what happened was the religious leaders said, 'We have the Antelope Clan already appointing the war chiefs, let's give them the task of appointing the governor and other officials, including a twelve-member tribal council.' So that stuck at Acoma. And the Antelope Clan agreed to having that responsibility. This is how our government and officials and war chiefs are selected. Both rooted in our old ways and a response to the Spanish."

So, deeper cultural practices persisted, even while they remained hidden from the resident Franciscan friars and the Spanish—just as the canes in the Pueblos' myths and the cultural practice of appointing leaders adapted to the framework imposed upon them, and survived it. The canes lasted through Mexico's control of the Southwest, and in 1863 President Abraham Lincoln provided new canes for the Pueblos. For well over four hundred years, their political practice has remained largely the same, though different clans perform the leadership duties at different Pueblos. And in some places there are now more officials with specific roles.

"Over time, Pueblo communities have adopted constitutions—IRA government—that impacted some of the Pueblos," Vallo notes. Of the nineteen Pueblos, six now elect their officials. "They have a more democratic process. Some even select war chiefs this way. It's very controversial," says Vallo, delicately. "At Acoma we now have a governor, first lieutenant governor, second lieutenant governor, three *fiscales*, twelve-member council, tribal writer, and tribal interpreter. Appointments happen every year. Antelope Clan convenes, consults with other leaders, and appoints the new officials." The same individuals generally serve multiple terms. "I think the Antelope Clan recognizes that continuity and consistency and ability to see initiatives through are very important," says Vallo. Looked at from their perspective, the government at Acoma seems more stable and enduring than the string of colonial powers who have exerted, or tried to exert, control over the Pueblos. Brian has an answer for this. "We've been able to sustain ourselves into the twenty-first century because our process is rooted in this indigenous idea of governance and leadership. The Spanish form of government doesn't exist in the original form: it transitioned to accommodate the cultural needs. So we maintain the older ways, even the Spanish ways."

The fact that some Pueblos adopted IRA constitutions in the 1930s makes coordinating lobbying and other efforts on the federal and state level difficult. "There are some traditional Pueblo people who will say, 'Well, the government at Laguna was elected so it's not for real,'" Vallo notes. "At some point because of all the significant effects resulting from the impact of the Spanish on the pueblos, all tribes came together to establish what is known today as the All Pueblo Council of Governors." The older organization, the All Indian Pueblo Council, was established in 1598, and Vallo claims it is the oldest all-Indian multicommunity council in North America. "It's a complex thing, our way of doing things. But it's highly respected."

Vallo himself served three consecutive terms as lieutenant governor. He was twenty-two and at New Mexico State University. It was Christmas break and he had been out partying with friends in Albuquerque. The next morning at six, the phone rang. "It's my dad and he says, 'You need to come home. Where are you?'" Panicked, Vallo assumed something was wrong. And then he remembered: "Oh man, it's appointment day." Vallo's father has served in many posts—as a councilman, tribal writer, as *fiscal*, and as governor, a post he held until 2017—a total of thirty-nine years in tribal government. His maternal great-grandfather had been a key player in a big land-claims settlement and served for seventy-two years of his hundred-year life "in every position you can serve in," including war chief. "I always thought, 'My uncles served, as did my father and grandfather, they will leave me alone!'" Vallo assumed his father had been appointed again. "So I got up, told my friends I guess I got to go home. I hopped in my truck and stopped at Denny's because I thought maybe I should eat first. I went into the restaurant and I thought, 'Get your ass home, this is your dad.' So I turned around and got some coffee at McDonald's." When he arrived home, there were a lot of cars parked at his house. He got scared again. "I thought, 'Fuck! Someone passed away!'" All his relatives and clan elders were there. "I walk in and my mom starts crying. Everyone is there—grandmothers, aunts. And my mom comes up to me and says in Acoma, 'I'm so sorry, son.' I'm still trying to figure out what's going on. My uncle, the hardline uncle, tells me to sit down. And he tells me, 'You've been appointed to serve the community. So you need to go to Acoma to accept this appointment.'"

Vallo was in shock. "My response was, 'I can't do this. I have to go back to school. I don't know anything. I don't know anything about tribal government.' I was very defensive." But his uncle pulled him to his feet and said, "You will go and accept this for all the people in this room and for all our relatives." "Aren't you guys coming along with me?" Vallo asked. And the uncle said, "You'll know what to do. You'll be fine."

Vallo went to Acoma to accept the appointment, and at the end of the day he received his cane. The governor's cane was the Lincoln cane, and the old Spanish and Mexican canes were presented to the lieutenant governors. "When you take those canes home they are treated as though they are living things: they are fed, they are given water." This is a crucial role, performed by women of the household. Then Vallo contacted his roommates to tell them they'd have to find someone to replace him for a year.

He didn't go back for three years; he was reappointed twice. And the experience shifted the focus of his education. After going back to college for a year, Brian was appointed as a cultural-religious leader and realized that he needed to be able to get home quickly when he was needed. He transferred from New Mexico State in southern New Mexico to the University of New Mexico in Albuquerque. And he pursued a new major, anthropology. He continued to be deeply involved with the All Pueblo Council. His upbringing had given him an essential grounding. "The fact I was surrounded by a bunch of old men most of the time, I learned the migration and emergence and creation stories and spoke the language. Today, I'm very much a part of the maintenance of culture at home."

He's grateful for his knowledge of the traditions and for the opportunity to serve. "I think one of the things that helps us is the reflection and living by a proscribed set of core cultural values. The daily engagement we have with our natural environment—the land is so sacred and having the privilege and responsibility to care for our land is so critical. We didn't have to relocate. We didn't have to move anywhere. We stood our ground to maintain connection to our ancestral base. I think some of the elders would say this is because we had this connection to, and reciprocal protection from, the land." Indians fought the government plan after plan, policy after policy, legislative act after legislative act, and they continued to fight. And they fought using their own governments, their own sensibilities, origin stories, legends, language, and creativity. And they fought to remain Indian just as much as they fought for and in order to be Americans, but Americans on their own terms.

War and Migration

O n June 13, 1942, a representative of the Iroquois Confederacy, in full regalia, stood on the steps of the United States Capitol and read a statement to the assembled statesmen and reporters:

> We represent the oldest, though smallest, democracy in the world today. It is the unanimous sentiment among Indian people that the atrocities of the Axis nations are violently repulsive to all sense of righteousness of our people, and that this merciless slaughter of mankind can no longer be tolerated. Now we do resolve that it is the sentiment of this council that the Six Nations of Indians declare that a state of war exists between our Confederacy of Six Nations on the one part and Germany, Italy, Japan and their allies against whom the United States has declared war, on the other part.

The United States had already declared war on the Axis powers six months earlier, on December 11, 1941. Now the Iroquois Confederacy itself declared war. The member tribes of the Confederacy were fierce as enemies and even as allies: when the United States extended citizenship to all tribal people, the Iroquois Confederacy refused the gift by sending a note to the government stating that they "were not, had never been, and didn't intend to become U.S. citizens." (It should be noted that no peace had been made between Germany and the Iroquois Confederacy in 1918, and so the Confederacy was still, technically, at war with Germany and now simply added Italy and Japan to the list.)

By 1944, more than a third of the Indian adult male population had served in the war. They served in every branch of the military and fought in every theater. Many were drafted (though some, in states where they still didn't have the right to vote, resisted), and many more volunteered for service. In 1940, the median household income on reservations was $500 a year. By comparison, the median income that year for a white man (not for a household) was $956. There were few jobs, and those available to

Indians were, typically, manual labor: farming, herding, and cutting wood. Despite the efforts of people like John Collier, who thought Indians should serve in segregated units, Indians were integrated into regular units. Back home, Indian women, like many other American women, joined the workforce as factory laborers and took over the majority of the harvest. My mother's mother worked in a plant near Austin, Minnesota, turning cherries into maraschino cherries.

Some have called the exodus of Indians into the workforce and the fighting forces the first massive migration of Indians in America. It wasn't. Indians, as we have seen, had been moving and shifting, migrating, forming and re-forming as far back as the archaeological record can show. Not long before the war, during the Dust Bowl era and the Great Depression, many thousands of Indians from Oklahoma, Kansas, and New Mexico had fled to California along with others fleeing the drought and the "worst hard time." Likewise, in the 1930s, Indians in rural areas were often hired as part of Roosevelt's Civilian Conservation Corps and migrated that way.

Still, the war was transformative, and it raised Indians' visibility in the American landscape. Among the most famous group of American Indians to serve in World War II were the Navajo code talkers, though even they had analogs and antecedents. Nineteen Choctaw had transmitted messages about troop movements and dispositions, attacks and counterattacks during the waning days of World War I. They were so successful—and the Choctaw language so hard to decipher (especially with their use of euphemisms and neologisms for terms that didn't exist in their language, like "artillery" and "tank")—that between the wars Hitler sent teams of anthropologists to the United States to study American Indian languages. He didn't want Native codes to be used so effectively in what he was, rightly, sure would be the next world war.

In 1941, twenty-seven Meskwaki from Iowa joined up together and served in North Africa. The Meskwaki, often known as "Sac and Fox" in the historical record, emerged as a people on the Saint Lawrence River, where their numbers made them a force to be reckoned with in the early part of the seventeenth century. However, punishing wars with the Huron and the Iroquois Confederacy over trade routes and relations decimated the tribe, and they migrated west to present-day Wisconsin, settling in the Fox River area. They experienced a rebirth there, on the western edge of the Great Lakes. They had settled in a geographically advantageous area—the watershed of the Fox River, which connected, through tributaries and short portages, the Great Lakes with the Mississippi. And since the Fox controlled this area, they effectively controlled a large portion of the burgeoning fur trade. As a result, they fought a series of wars with the French (who, with other Indian allies, wanted the Meskwaki out of the region) that stretched over twenty years and, combined with disease, reduced the Meskwaki from more than seven thousand members to fewer than a thousand. But they remained in Wisconsin until 1830, when Andrew Jackson pushed the Indian Removal Act through Congress. Though the act was designed to remove the Five Civilized Tribes from the southeastern United States, it was also used to extinguish title and remove and relocate many tribes around the Great Lakes, including the Ho-Chunk, Meskwaki, and others.

Once again the Meskwaki were forced from their homelands, once again they were pushed farther west, this time to Kansas and Oklahoma. Some bands moved to their new homelands and made the best of it. Others stayed. In 1856, a small group of Meskwaki who had remained in Iowa got permission from the Iowa state legislature to buy land in Tama County, despite the fact that they already had title to it and had basically been usurped. In 1857 they purchased eighty acres from the government and made their settlement there. The federal government wasn't happy with this outcome and withheld annuities and other treaty obligations from the Meskwaki for a decade in order to get them to move, but they refused. They survived on a meager corn harvest, acorns, and deer. For the next thirty years they existed in a kind of policy and legislative limbo, more or less ignored by the federal government. In some ways this was good for the Meskwaki—they organized their community as they saw fit. They didn't suffer under the withered and withering hand of an Indian agent. They ran their own schools. They completely administered their own affairs. (To this day the roads and streets on the reservation and in the settlement aren't paved, for spiritual reasons. The bumpy washboard roads are a reminder that you are indeed on Indian land.)

So in 1941, when twenty-seven Meskwaki joined up to fight the Axis together, it was not the result of a long period of acculturation or even of defeat, or an attempt at mainstreaming themselves. What is staggering is that these twenty-seven constituted 16 percent of the population of Meskwaki. They all served in North Africa, and eight of them used their hard-won Meskwaki language to befuddle their enemies.

Perhaps the most famous Indian to serve in World War II was Ira Hayes. Hayes was a Pima Indian from Sacaton, Arizona. Born in 1923, he was the oldest of six children. He wasn't really known for anything other than being shy—both in grade school in Sacaton and later in high school at the Phoenix Indian School. He didn't chase girls or like being chased by them. He kept to himself. Except after the Japanese attack on Pearl Harbor in 1941, when he told a classmate that he wanted to join the Marine Corps. For some reason, he waited. He finished out the year at the Phoenix Indian School and then worked for the Civilian Conservation Corps in the spring and summer before enlisting in late August 1942.

At Camp Gillespie near San Diego, Hayes volunteered for the Marine paratrooper program and was accepted, earning his jump wings on November 30, 1942. After that he was shipped overseas; he was sent to New Caledonia and then to Vella Lavella in the Solomon Islands before he saw action at Bougainville in December 1943. He was a BAR (Browning automatic rifle) man with Company K. After that first engagement he went back to the States, was refitted and shuffled, and sent back to the Pacific with the Fifth Marine Division, tasked with dislodging the Japanese from Iwo Jima. He landed on the island on February 19, 1945, on the southern shore near Mount Suribachi. After four days of fierce fighting, Marines from Third Platoon Easy Company captured the summit of the mountain and raised a small American flag there.

The next day Sergeant Michael Strank was ordered to pick three men from his platoon and to fly a bigger flag from the summit after they had dropped off supplies there. He took Harlon Block, Franklin Sousley, and Ira Hayes. Rene Gagnon, a battalion runner, brought the larger flag, and after they scavenged a bigger flagpole, the five of them, along with Harold Schultz, raised the flag over Iwo Jima. Joe Rosenthal of the Associated Press captured the moment in what would become the most famous photo of the war.

After the flag was raised Hayes spent another month and a half fighting the Japanese who remained on the island. By the time he left with his unit at the end of March, he was one of only five remaining out of the forty-five members of his platoon: the rest had been killed. The photo made Hayes famous. In the spring of 1945 he toured the United States, raising money for war bonds. Then he rejoined his unit and was sent back to the Pacific, where he was part of the occupying force in Japan until he was honorably discharged in December.

The after-war years must have been confusing and complicated for Hayes. He was arrested fifty-two times for public drunkenness. He was unable to hold down a steady job. He once said, "I was sick. . . . I guess I was about to crack up thinking about all my good buddies. They were better men than me and they're not coming back. Much less back to the White House [for war honor ceremonies], like me." That was about as close as he came to naming his ghosts. Later, in 1954, at the dedication of the Marine Corps War Memorial, a reporter asked him how he liked all the "pomp and circumstance." All Hayes said was, "I don't." He was found dead near his home in Arizona on January 24, 1955. Cause of death: exposure and alcohol poisoning.

Just as the second flag-raising over Mount Suribachi became emblematic of the war as a whole, so, too, did Hayes's life become symbolic for many Americans of the "plight" of modern Indians. They tried to read the entire history of American Indians into it: proud peoples who had been mistreated by a government they nevertheless protected and served as warriors, only to return to reservations where they and their service were forgotten by everyone except the warriors themselves, who couldn't forget.

Who knows? Most servicemen and women fell somewhere in between the experiences of the code talkers and soldiers like Ira Hayes. My grandfather, for instance.

Eugene W. Seelye spent his entire life in the village where he grew up on the Leech Lake Reservation in northern Minnesota—with the exception of the two years and eight months he spent in the United States Army. In total he spent fifteen months overseas, in England, France, Belgium, and Germany. Growing up, I didn't know any of that. I didn't know about the war or his part in it, what he thought about it or what he felt. He was, at least to me, frightening, angry, and sharp-tongued. By the time I was born in 1970 he spent most of his time in his easy chair by the window smoking Pall Malls, nursing a kind of acidic rage. Once my uncles, knowing he had money, lined up in front of him, and the youngest, Davey, asked him for five dollars. He looked at Davey and then at his other sons and then simply said, "You think I'm fucking stupid?"

He didn't talk about the war, though hanging from some kind of knickknack shelf in the corner were ribbons on which were stitched the words "Normandy" and "France." His uniform, with the Indianhead star of the Second Infantry Division, hung in the closet behind his chair. I got up the courage to ask him about the war, once, when I was in high school. All he said was, "The worst time of my life. Wouldn't wish it on anyone." The war sat in the background, as he did, with life swirling around it and him, mute on the subject of feelings other than anger and misery.

In 1998, I went to France to promote my first novel. On my return, jet-lagged but still euphoric, I stopped in at Teal's Super Valu in Cass Lake, the seat of the reservation. I saw my grandfather standing at the deli counter ordering pork chops and potato salad. *Hey Gramps,* I said. *Hey boy,* he said in that way of his. *Where you been?* I told him I had been in France, in Paris and Saint-Malo. I explained that Saint-Malo was in Brittany, but he interrupted me to tell me he knew exactly where that was.

That was the beginning of a shift, some kind of recalibration I didn't understand. I said, *So you were in Normandy. You bet, boy,* he said. *June seventh, I imagine. Maybe later?* I asked. *June sixth, nineteen forty-four,* he said, vehemently. I said, *Maybe we should go to my mom's house, cook up those pork chops.* And, to my surprise, he agreed.

My mother sized up the situation quickly. She stood at the counter prepping dinner, standing purposely outside the conversation, as if anything she might say would end it. It was as if someone had cast a spell of volubility over her father. On he went about Belgium. The trees, the country-side. The ways the peasants (in his words) cleaned the forests of sticks and blow-downs and how the whole forest felt manicured, unlike the tangle of our northern pine and poplar forest. How he had his shoes resoled in Vielsalm. How, while bivouacked in the same village, he befriended a red-haired kid. How he carved his name in a tree near the château where they were camped. How he was wounded near Aachen, just over the border with Germany. He stayed long into the evening, even though his eyes bothered him and it was hard for him to drive after dark. He wondered, with real longing, if the tree where he carved his name was still standing. I told him I would go back to France and find my way to Belgium, find Vielsalm, find the château, find the tree. I don't think he believed me. But months later I did go back, with the map of the village he'd drawn from memory.

Vielsalm is a village on the Salm River near the German border. The Allies and the Germans traded the town back and forth a few times before the Germans were pushed back in January 1945 and then pushed farther and farther into the ruins of the Fatherland. It's not big, but the Ardennes is wild country—steep wooded ravines, small fast-flowing streams and rivers. The land is folded, crumpled in on itself. I imagined there would be one château in Vielsalm. There were at least a dozen. With the help of the man who owned the motel where I was staying, I found a likely place: the hunting retreat of Baron Vanderhaege, who, according to his grandson, fought the war in exile in England. I returned home, not sure I'd seen anything other than beautiful country. My grandfather called me the day I returned and every day after that while the pictures were being developed, and when they finally were ready he came over without even calling first. He sat at my table and paged through the photos. He pointed to one. *That's it. That's the one.* I thought maybe he was simply hoping, that there was a pleasant lie in the act of stabbing his finger into the frame. *When you face the building, there was a door on the right, in kind of a tower thing,* he said. *That's the door I used.* My heart fell. There had been no door. No tower. Nothing like that. He was wrong. Or more like: he wanted to recognize the place more than he wanted to be right. He flipped two more pictures. *See, boy. See? There's that door.* I looked, and sure enough: covered by ivy, obscured by some hedges, there was a round stone outcropping on the building, and set in the stone was a small green door.

I was almost thirty when I went to France. But it was as though I'd just become my grandfather's grandson then.

We became close. I wasn't the only one in the family curious about him, or the war, or even just his time on earth. My cousins were. His children were, too. But maybe it was just that I had walked where he fought. I had slept where he'd been sleepless. I'd seen that other place. He shared his war stories. But I was not smart enough, not a good enough listener then to be able to distinguish between a war story and a combat story. A Marine veteran of Vietnam made the distinction clear to me many years later: *Combat stories, stories about fighting, of shooting and getting shot are one thing. Those are combat stories. War stories are different. I knew a guy who was in Vietnam, and he told me nothing happened to him. He didn't fight. He wasn't in country. He said he had nothing to say about the war. I asked him what he did and he said, "I worked for Graves Registration. I got all the bodies ready before they flew them back to the States." Now that guy? He had a war story. He saw and touched and moved all those bodies. That was war.*

My grandfather shared war stories but not combat stories. He didn't talk at all about Normandy except to say that he saw guys drowning and he would rather get shot than drown. And that nothing saved him except luck. About the Ardennes he said only that they learned to hug trees because the Germans would fire tree bursts—shells aimed at treetop level, sending splinters down in all directions. The safest place to avoid those was directly under a tree. He did say that he hadn't been shot. Rather, while he was on patrol, just over the German border, one of the men in his patrol stepped on a mine. It blew off the man's legs and sent a shard of shrapnel through my grandfather's shoulder. He remarked how surprised he was to see this man, last name Van Winkle, in a hospital near Seattle after the war. He mentioned how he was attached to the 101st Airborne during the Battle of the Bulge. But mostly he talked about the land and the weather and the buildings and the forests and the people. He mentioned how the army had wanted him to be a sniper but he was too scared to be tied into a tree. How he was tasked to be a truck driver but never once got a truck to drive and so he walked and fought the whole way through France and Belgium. These were the stories he told until he shot himself in the head in 2007, just after his eighty-third birthday.

My grandmother asked me to clean up the room where he shot himself, and I did. He died without giving me the answers I thought I needed. And his death was also some kind of question rather than an answer. That day, however, I took the time to look for his discharge papers, his service record, some kind of record of his life as a soldier. As though whatever paper he kept after the war could tell me something he couldn't. I didn't find anything.

Five years after his death I petitioned the National Personnel Records Center, and after a few months, they sent me his file. It was incomplete and as haphazardly put together as he had been. He was inducted at Fort Snelling, Minnesota, on January 21, 1943, a month before his nineteenth birthday. At the time of his induction he was healthy. He stood five-foot-ten and weighed 155 pounds. He listed his race as white. He had attended eight years of grammar school and one year of high school. He received "morality and sex education training" and immunizations. He received desert training near Yuma, Arizona, and reached the rank of T/5, or corporal, before he shipped out, but by the time he embarked for the European theater he was once again a private. Most of his file is taken up with medical documents concerning his shoulder injury. But it's hard to tell when and how the injury occurred. One physician notes that according to my grandfather he hurt it throwing a rope over a truck while logging with his father in 1941. In other documents he states he hurt it while boxing in Yuma, or "roughhousing" with another soldier. Nowhere does it say he received his wound in combat. According to hospital records he was not in Normandy on June 6, 1944. He was in Indiana, where he received an operation on his shoulder on June 16.

I didn't know what to make of any of this. He left for the ETO on September 4, 1944. He was in France by September 15. He entered Belgium on October 24. By December 27, 1944, he was in England and had shoulder surgery again. He was returned to duty and entered Germany on March 6, 1945, five days after his twentieth birthday. He was awarded a good conduct ribbon, and one battle star for the campaign in Belgium, but not a Purple Heart.

After he got back to the states he went AWOL twice. They confined him to base and docked his pay. As of September 8, 1945, he was honorably discharged. There wasn't much to learn from his service record. Paper lies. So do people. And there is no way to crack open some other truth, some greater truth, as though buried there waiting to be found by me. I told my father—who served in the same war, in the Pacific—about what I found. *Look, Dave,* he said, *it's enough to know he was there. He was in it. He was a part of that.* It will remain something I don't understand. Except that the war stories he told were of the beauty of the land, the look and feel of it. That and how miserable and scared he was. How much he hated his war.

Entering the Cage

I was sitting around one night listening to the radio," says Sam. "And this advertisement came on for First Blood Ultimate Wrestling at the Lion's Den in Fridley. The ad said, 'Local fighters wanted,' and there was a number to call and so I called the number. I went down there to talk to the guy on Thursday and I fought my first fight on Saturday. I didn't know anything. I just showed up with a nut cup and a mouth guard. I was scared. I didn't know what to expect. The Lion's Den was just this little underground place and they threw a cage up in the middle of it and packed a few hundred people in there and then put two guys in the cage and let 'em go. Didn't even matter if they were matched up good or even the same size or anything. I was about a hundred and sixty-five pounds and my opponent was a hundred and ninety-five. A lot of mismatches that day. It was pretty wild."

From the start, mixed martial arts, or MMA, was about two things—

spectacle and money. It came to the United States in 1993 as the UFC (Ultimate Fighting Championship), held in Denver at the McNichols Sports Arena. There were no weight classes, and fights were one round, with no time limits, arranged tournament style—single-elimination rounds, leading up to a final. The logic of the spectacle was in part that of mismatching: Could a boxer beat a wrestler, a wrestler a kickboxer? What about kung fu and tae kwon do? What is jiujitsu and what is Brazilian jiujitsu? How would a 170-pound street fighter fare against a 400-pound sumo wrestler? It advertised itself as having one rule: There are no rules!

One way promoters and agents have of developing talent is to sacrifice new blood to the old, giving their guy a better record and more experience with little risk. The new fighters sometimes don't fall under the bus as much as they are placed there. This, in part, is what happened to Sam. He lost the first fight that Saturday in March. He took the guy down and got the full mount (straddled his opponent's chest). "I threw him down and got in some nice shots. But he was already an experienced guy and he threw me off. I didn't know anything and I got excited and lost my advantage. The other guy got me down and mounted me, softened me up with some punches and then he managed to get my back and submitted me with a rear naked choke. I didn't feel too bad about it. After that I learned you don't just walk in there. You have to train a little bit." He fought a month later but lost because the doctor stopped the fight when Sam caught an uppercut that closed his eye. "I asked him to keep going but the doctor called the fight." It wasn't until his third fight that Sam won. "I fought Jerry 'The Bomber' Lucker. I went three rounds with him. He was the first guy I fought who was actually in my weight class. He was a tough dude. That's when I felt, 'This is for me. I can beat these guys.'" Sam quit his job and moved down to Moline, where his father was living. Pat Miletich, a former UFC champion, had opened an MMA gym in Bettendorf, on the Iowa side of the Mississippi. Sam trained there for two months and learned the basics. He didn't feel like an outsider. He knew he could hang with the other guys, not a few of whom were or would be world champions. And then he got thrown under the bus when his agent put him up against Dave Menne at the Anoka County Fair. "I don't know what I was thinking. He was the best at that time. Maybe I was thinking about the $2,000 purse or something. The fight only lasted two rounds." The next day Sam went up against an Olympic-level wrestler who was already a well-trained MMA fighter. "I was a little bit out of my league right away with them two guys," he recalls. Then Sam stood up for himself. "I told my agent, 'I did you a favor with those fights. But I'm not doing any more.'"

After that, Sam's agent gave him fights with guys at his level and in his weight class and he won five fights over the next year. Everything was looking up until Sam's mother died after a suicide attempt in the summer of 2005.

When Barb died we all wondered what would happen to Sam. Would he bottom out again as he had when Nessa died? "It's funny," muses Sam. "But I was okay. It still bothers me, but I can talk about it. Not like with Vanessa. Vanessa was the first person I lost. My only sister. Since then I've lost a lot of people. But when Mom died I had a job, and a family. I was living in South Dakota by then. I had people I was responsible for, maybe that helped." He stayed in control and he kept his job and he didn't drift back into the violence that had marked his life for most of his twenties. "I couldn't change anything when Vanessa died. I couldn't do anything. Nothing I could do would bring her back. Nothing I could do would change that she was gone. Same with my mom, I guess, but by then, I had a life and a family and I was fighting. I left all my anger in the cage. When I fight, right before I step into the cage, I kind of visualize my opponent as a sickness I've got to beat—not that I am hating on the guy or anything, just that I'm not fighting him, I'm fighting some disease. Like my mom's drug addiction. Or now I think about Grandma's blindness. I visualize that, and that's what I am trying to beat. I leave all the rage and anger I've got for that."

Maybe he does. Maybe he does leave it all there. But if he does, he brings something away from the cage as well. "It feels good to win," he says. "It feels good to win at something you've worked hard at, and put your time in at, to win at something you want real bad." More than anything, that's what Sam and maybe a lot of the other Indian fighters bring to fighting in the cage: the desire to be good at something and to have a chance to win on the basis of talent and hard work. It may sound like a small thing. Or it may sound like the very idea—meritocracy—that America is built on. But it is a huge thing for an Indian man to want, a very huge and noble thing to dare to hope that hard work and talent will actually win the day. "Getting buzzed up, getting wasted or high: there's no thrill there. Not anymore. But fighting in the cage? Giving my friends and family something and someone to cheer for? There's no better feeling. It doesn't get better than that. I've got maybe a few more fights in me. I might still be competing in five years. I'll be forty-three then. But if not, that's okay." No longer does Sam dream of the UFC, of fighting under the brightest lights there are in the spectacle and sport that MMA has become. (Though some Indian fighters, like the incredibly dedicated and talented Eli Finn from Leech Lake, do nurse ambitions of the UFC, and there's no reason not to when you are that good.) "Really in a few years I'd like to open a gym. Get the tribe to sponsor an MMA team. It would be great for the kids around here, I think. It would teach them discipline. It would help them not to use drugs or whatever. You can't fight and drink and stuff at the same time. Not for long."

In the end, Sam didn't get to fight on March 17, 2012. His opponent failed to make weight at 160 and wanted to fight at 175 pounds. Sam said no. He wasn't going to sacrifice himself—not even for us, his family, his friends, his reservation. Not in that way at least. He had too much respect for himself to keep punching that wall. But earlier, in December, I had gotten to see him fight at Northern Lights Casino. He had won against a much larger opponent in the first two minutes of the first round in his trademark style—he took him down, wrapped him up, and then submitted him with strikes. He had seemed unstoppable. God, how he could hit. How could a man like him lose? How could he ever lose? It was unimaginable. Watching him then, I simply couldn't think of him doing anything other than winning. Loss wasn't the norm, it couldn't be. I didn't have the words for it then, what it felt like to watch my cousin, whom I love and whose worries are our worries and whose pain is our pain, manage to be so good at something, to triumph so completely. More than a painful life, more than a culture or a society with the practice and perfection of violence as a virtue and a necessity, more than a meanness or a willingness to sacrifice oneself, what I felt—what I saw—were Indian men and boys doing precisely what we've always been taught not to do. I was seeing them plainly, desperately, expertly wanting to be seen for their talents and their hard work, whether they lost or won.

That old feeling familiar to so many Indians—that we can't change anything; can't change Columbus or Custer, smallpox or massacres; can't change the Gatling gun or the legislative act; can't change the loss of our loved ones or the birth of new troubles; can't change a thing about the shape and texture of our lives—fell away. I think the same could be said for Sam: he might not have been able to change his sister's fate or his mother's or even, for a while, his own. But when he stepped in the cage he was doing battle with a disease. The disease was the feeling of powerlessness that takes hold of even the most powerful Indian men. That disease is more potent than most people imagine: that feeling that we've lost, that we've always lost, that we've already lost—our land, our cultures, our communities, ourselves. This disease is the story told about us and the one we so often tell about ourselves. But it's one we've managed to beat again and again—in our insistence on our own existence and our successful struggles to exist in our homelands on our own terms. For some it meant joining the U.S. Army. For others it meant accepting the responsibility to govern and lead. For others still, it meant stepping into a metal cage to beat or be beaten. For my cousin Sam, for three rounds of five minutes he gets to prove that through hard work and natural ability he can determine the outcome of a finite struggle, under the bright, artificial lights that make the firmament at the Northern Lights Casino on the Leech Lake Reservation.

PART 4

Moving On Up—Termination and Relocation: 1945–1970

In the fall of 2014, I drove from Rapid City, South Dakota, to Browning, Montana, home of the Blackfeet Nation. I wanted to know what the postwar years looked like on the Plains. The three decades from 1945 to 1975, sandwiched between World War II and the rise (and quick fall) of the American Indian Movement, have been treated as something of a blank spot on the map of Indian experience: The days of tribal warfare over. The federal assault on Indians, Indian life, and Indian homelands over, too. Reservations established as nothing more or less than basins of suffering, the time of eternal agony begun.

The first leg took me from Rapid City up to Williston. It was the right season for the drive—the crisp, dry, golden time of fall on the Plains when the aspen leaves rattle across the road with a hiss and the wheat stubble catches the light. It was, I suppose, the right season of life, too: I was getting divorced, and like most people who are ending something big, I knew no one had ever felt the way I did. There is nothing like middle age to make you feel like a teenager. The landscape helped. By god, it was some of the most beautiful land I have ever seen, shamelessly beautiful. North of Sturgis I passed Bear Butte—Mato Paha to the Lakota, Noaha-vose to the Cheyenne—where the Cheyenne leader Sweet Medicine received the spiritual gifts around which the tribe took shape. The mountain sits off by itself on the plain, the northernmost outpost of the Black Hills. After gold was discovered in the hills to the south in 1876, it was Bear Butte that served as the landmark to the hordes of speculators and miners who, with the encouragement of the United States government, broke the treaty that had created the Great Sioux Reservation. After that the land flattens out into grassy plains that roll on until they're broken by a limestone shelf near the North Dakota border.

As soon as I crossed into North Dakota I was buffeted by trucks and heavy equipment. The land—which looked much as I imagined it had before the range was closed, before cattle replaced the bison—began to show signs of wear. The roads were cracked, the fencing was gone, and great gashes in the turf opened up on both sides of the road. Sidings like those next to rail lines began to appear next to the highway. The Bakken oil fields loomed to the north. By the time I reached Williston, oil was all I saw: oil rigs, cleared and graded land, flames off-gassing the methane in the wells. All along the roads there were staging areas for heavy equipment, stacks of pipe, metal fittings, and oil rigs. Whatever trees there had been—Russian olive and willow and poplar planted as windbreaks toward the end of the Dust Bowl era—had been ripped out and burned. At a laundromat in Williston, the management had stuck a sign to the front of the large dryers: "No greasers allowed." Denny's was doing a brisk business. All of the truck stops were full of trucks. Somehow all this evidence of rapaciousness seemed more honest to me, though. At least here the land didn't lie to you like it does everywhere else in the Great Plains. At least here it's clear there is a war still being fought.

I turned west on what northerners call the Hi-Line—U.S. Highway 2, which stretches from Michigan to Seattle—toward Montana. Some say Montana is a state of mind. It is also a world unto itself. The state of Montana is a big rectangle roughly the size of Norway. It begins flat in the east and gets progressively more crumpled in the west, as though someone dropped it on the narrow end. The Hi-Line followed the old Great Northern Railway line, which was completed in the nineteenth century in order to sluice cattle from the northern Plains onto the killing floors of Chicago. As a result, Highway 2 is a straight shot into the sun, and sooner than you'd think, into the gloom of a western night. The road passed through ghost town after ghost town, small main streets that looked more like picturesque European roadside ruins. Here and there, set back from the road, the frames of farmhouses showed sky and range through their broken windows and even through their roofs. At least two of the gas stations I stopped at had gas but didn't have people. I paid with my credit card, the pump turned on, I pumped my gas, and the pump went off. Most of the towns were empty of people, too, as were the roads.

I drove through Fort Peck and then Fort Belknap; things were different. Indians walked down the road. Indian kids played in the yards. Near Wolf Point, I saw Indian kids who looked like they were floating until I saw that they were launching themselves from a trampoline over the roofline of their house. I don't remember where I stopped for the night. By nightfall the next day I made it near Browning, the capital, if you will, of the Blackfeet Nation.

I had never been to Browning and I didn't really know any Blackfeet except by reputation, but I had asked a Facebook friend, Sterling Holy-WhiteMountain, if he'd set me up with some people to talk to and show me around. When I asked where to stay, he responded, *Oh, well, you can stay with me and my sister and her husband and their kid, if that doesn't bother you.* When I got to Browning I called Sterling and asked where we should meet.

Well, he answered, *the only place to really meet is the fucking casino. We can meet there.*

Cool, I answered.

Yeah, I'll see you there in twenty minutes. I'll be there with ten of my cousins and we're gonna knock the shit out of you.

I paused, then said, *Eleven Blackfeet against one Ojibwe sounds like even odds to me.*

He laughed. *We're gonna have a great time.* And then he hung up.

The Blackfeet aren't really (or shouldn't really be called) the Blackfeet. Rather, the Blackfeet are the southernmost band of a confederation of bands—the Northern Piikuni (known as simply "Piikuni" in Canada), Southern Piikuni (the only Piikuni band in the United States and usually referred to as Blackfeet), Kainna (Many Chiefs), and Siksika (Blackfoot). According to Sterling, "Blackfeet" is a misnomer that didn't come into common usage until the Indian Reorganization Act. No one seems to know how this happened, but before that they knew themselves as "Piikuni" in their language and "Southern Piegan" to English speakers. Sterling also related that *piikuni* refers to a particular way of preparing and tanning buffalo hides. "Hard to translate in less than seven pages without three elders in attendance," also according to Sterling. The Blackfeet historical homeland stretched from the North Saskatchewan River near present-day Edmonton to the Yellowstone River in the south, and from the timbered reaches of the northern Rocky Mountains east through the foothills and the short-grass northern prairies to the South Saskatchewan River and the Cypress Hills. Primarily bison hunters, the Blackfeet weren't quite as nomadic as more Plains-centric tribes, but they cycled between different seasonal camps. They lived in small bands of eighty to two hundred people, hunting out on the Plains until winter, when they retreated to wooded river bottoms near the mountains, where there was shelter and wood and game. The Blackfeet held large ceremonial gatherings in the summer, after the chokecherries were ripe, and then they'd disperse again.

Adopting the horse, around 1730, greatly increased their range. Nascent aspects of the tribal culture began to grow, in particular the ability and desire to make war. They fought tirelessly against the Cree to the north for control of the best trapping grounds and trade relations with the French and British. They made war on the tribes to the south in order to increase their land base and their horse herds. Their enemies included the Cree, Crow, Shoshone, Cheyenne, Kootenai, Flathead, Lakota, and Assiniboine, Kalispel, Nez Perce, Plains Cree, Stoney Cree, Plains Ojibwe, and Metis—basically, everyone. They won. And became known as the "Lords of the Plains."

Although the Blackfeet had been trading with Europeans for the better part of seventy-five years, it wasn't until a small group of warriors leading a large herd of horses encountered Lewis and Clark's expedition returning from the Pacific that they met their first Americans. The explorers said they wanted peace with all Indians, and the Blackfeet and the Americans camped together for the night. In the morning, the Americans woke to find the Blackfeet trying to steal their horses and guns. They stabbed one of the Blackfeet and shot another.

Despite their capacity for making enemies and war, the Blackfeet largely stayed out of the conflicts that erupted across the Plains in the nineteenth century. They kept their peace in 1837, after the American Fur Company sent north a steamboat loaded with goods for trade with the Blackfeet, even though passengers showed signs of smallpox. The Blackfeet contracted the disease, and thousands died. Nor did they make war in 1870, after the Marias Massacre. A few hotheaded Blackfeet had attacked some settlers. The U.S. Army set forth to quell the "uprising." Encountering an unrelated and peaceful band of Blackfeet on the Marias River, they attacked anyway, killing more than two hundred women, children, and elders. But America made war against them all the same, by hiring bison hunters to eradicate the herds as a means of subduing the Lakota and other Plains tribes. Without the bison, the Blackfeet could not maintain their way of life. Weakened by disease and warfare and starvation, they had little recourse when the government illegally modified and ratified new treaties with the southern bands of the tribe, stealing millions of acres. Three of the bands settled permanently across the border in Canada, leaving only the Southern Piegan (Blackfeet) in the United States. By 1900, there were fewer than two thousand Blackfeet left, according to the report of the commissioner of Indian affairs, though tribal members put the number at half that. They were clustered around the missions and churches nearby, having adopted at least the semblance of Christianity while their children were sent to Indian boarding schools out east. And yet the embers of this proud people burned on. Over time, their numbers grew back. What remained of their culture and language was reconstituted. What remained of their land base was consolidated and protected.

Sterling showed up without his cousins in a Chrysler 300C (his father's, evidently: Sterling's Escalade gets bad mileage). Tall, thick, and affable, with short hair and an indecisive beard, he has a fondness for causing trouble and for loud, brightly patterned button-down shirts. We shook hands and he said, *Follow me,* and I pulled out behind him and we began climbing the road out of Browning into the mountains. It wasn't long before we eased into the reservation border town of East Glacier and then into Sterling's yard. The house he shares with a sister, her husband, and their kid is the one he grew up in. His mother lives across the yard in a newer house, and another sister lives across the street. The family was one of those confusing Indian families that required you to go back generations to understand just who was who and how they were related. They seemed raucous and vibrant and testy. There was always some kind of mischief brewing or opinion being contested. I am tempted to say Sterling is the black sheep of the family, but I have a suspicion that it would be easier to count the white ones.

The tribe has a reputation for being both social and fierce, friendly and unpredictable, traditional and rezzy, proud and prideful. The Lords of the Plains have a reputation these days for being at times more like lords of chaos, the reservation less a political body than a metal band tour bus. I don't know about that. Sterling settled me into his house. We ate dinner and then started talking. The talking didn't stop that night, nor the next day, or the next: the whole week was spent shifting from one talker to another. The morning after that first night, I found myself in a back room behind the convenience store/gas station owned by Sterling's father, Pat Schildt, on the outskirts of Browning. Seated across from me was a weathered old-timer, who was there to talk because Sterling and his father had asked him to.

I was pretty excited to talk to Red Hall. I like talking to old people (though we call them Elders). I like the rhythms of those conversations, so unlike conversations with people my age or younger. Red had lived through three wars, and the forgotten years from 1930 to 1960, when Indian communities emerged from the dark days after the fall of tribal government into a period of constitutional, representative Indian government. For these reasons and more I thought Red was an important person to speak with, and I'm pretty sure he'd agree.

"Red William Hall," he began. "My right name is William. People then have Indian names. But first—I want to know what you want to know. What year? I'm pretty good back to 'thirty-six. I can answer from 'thirty-six up." He spoke with a gruff sharpness. His voice was clear and crisp. He had the clipped tones of the High Plains along with a kind of "Don't fuck with me" cadence that I always think of as "elderly Indian voice." "What I'm getting at is the way I got the name Hall, that's what you want to learn, too? This guy come in here named John Hall, came in here three times, from out of Texas. Around the time of the Civil War, Hall was helping to drive cattle up from Texas, where they were so plentiful. You couldn't give a cow away. Up north you could get a better price. They brought about two thousand head to start. The grass was about like that. There was no fences here. They were getting rich that way. The train was coming in, and it could take cattle all the way from Seattle to Chicago. They started building feedlots. Every so far you had a depot and a big stockyard. We had three right here. We had Spotted Robe stockyards, Browning stockyards, we had stockyards down here at Blackfoot, unloading yards down at Carlow." Outside companies would come in and lease the reservation land to graze their stock—some sheep, but mostly cattle. To tend the cattle, "they needed good men, know what you was doing." The Indians learned from the cowboys. "After a while, the Indian caught on. They didn't know how to birth calves. How to pull them out. But they caught on." In conversation, Red is a diver: he dives straight down into whatever pool occurs to him and then, just as quickly, jumps into a different one. It took a while for me to be able to follow him.

"My grandmother was a war chief's daughter. After driving all those cattle up from Texas, Hall stayed and married her, becoming a squaw man." Interracial dating and marriage is a complicated subject, but Red has an explanation for why there was so much mixing in the old days: "Squaw men. That's why you never got inbreds out of the Indians. You laugh, but I'm telling you some facts! See—there was a reason for that. Me and my dad talked about it. You had bands, tribal bands. And once a year we had a big Sun Dance. Like a big pilgrimage. And that was wife time. So you didn't marry any of your relations, so when that tribe pulled out and pulled back you took your wife with you. That's how we did it, see? We ruled way up north to the Saskatchewan and back down to the Yellowstone. We owned this area. We kept the Crows out. Kept the Crees east. We kept 'em all out until smallpox did us in."

With the Blackfeet population so low in the late nineteenth and early twentieth centuries, and with old tribal animosities still in place, working cowboys like Red's grandfather were a viable option for marriage.

They brought their in-laws and children into the cattle business, which came to dominate the High Plains through the Dust Bowl era and past World War II. "My grandfather didn't talk much. You ask him a question and he'd say my business is my business, your business is yours." Raiding was part of the way of life. Red's wife's grandfather was a raider named White Grass. His great-grandfather took four hundred head of horses north across the border so the U.S. government wouldn't kill them. "The line [the border between the United States and Canada] didn't mean nothing to the tribe. . . . See, Indians didn't steal. They called them thieving sons of bitches. But they didn't steal. They raided. So get that straight. You raid that tribe and that tribe come raids you. Even-steven."

The Blackfeet's animosity toward other tribes persisted through the early decades of the twentieth century. "They still held that. But, you see—we fought the Germans and we fought the Japs and that healed us. Now we are all right with other tribes. We are allies now. But we weren't like that for a long time, probably up until the 1940s. That's what got them together. That and them Indian schools—Flandreau, Haskell, and Chemawa, and other schools. They'll marry a boyfriend from another tribe. And they start mixing."

Red was born in 1931, and the homeland he was born into was markedly different from the one enjoyed by his ancestors. Gone were the bison. Gone was the life built around bison and raiding. Gone was any lordship of the Plains. Instead it was as though the Blackfeet and other tribes served two lords: the United States government and the land itself. Both were uncompromising and at times inhospitable. Nonetheless, Red and his family survived on rations and cows. "I worked around stock my whole life. That's why we got so many bronc riders. World champions." Two of Red's nephews are stunt riders in the movies. He goes back to an earlier time. "But you see—they starved us to death here. Gave us smallpox, we was hanging in all the trees." The old stories don't feel old at all coming from Red: he's talking about seeing bodies "buried" in the trees according to the Blackfeet custom. As a young boy Red saw bodies in scaffolds in the trees that had been placed there during the winter of 1883–1884, when many of the tribe died of starvation, in a time known as "Starvation Winter." "They brung us all into Fort Benton. They starved us in there. All except Sits in the Middle. He went out and fought them and instead of coming in he brought his horses up to our people in Canada."

Red talked in that way particular to Indians of a certain age, where the telling isn't quite a linear narrative. Instead, what Red remembered ran and stilled and bottomed out in the lowlands of his memory, pooling there around horses and stock and fiddle playing and the railroad. These were the defining features of his landscape. He was not nostalgic in the slightest—for him, and for Indians in a lot of places, life got better as time went on, and it got a lot better with the New Deal.

Red had eleven siblings. "Eight sons. Four daughters. Three brothers of us left. I had two brothers older than me. They gone. I worked around and worked for the railroad for a long time. My older brother was in World War Two. He was in the Air Corps in Mississippi. I was in the army too. I remember when they used to give out rations here. See—Roosevelt was the guy who really helped the people. Before that it was the Dust Bowl and all that went on. We was part of it. One of the old ration houses still stands—someone lives in it now. Back then there was a jail and a post office in the front of it, and rations were given around the back. I remember first time I ever seen a grapefruit. . . . They give 'em out. People didn't know how to eat 'em. Or peel 'em. People didn't like 'em, they were too bitter. I was about seven."

Red grew up on a ranch by the river, in a log house. "Everything was log. There's one sitting up here. It was moved three times and it's still all together. They got good at it." The family weren't all in the house at the same time, as some of the children were in boarding schools. Red went to Holy Family nearby. Circumstances had changed at such schools, for the better. "They weren't mean to you." Red went to about the eighth grade. "I learned to play basketball and soccer. They weren't too mean to you there." As a kid, he'd seen people putting up teepees each year. "I got two now. I saw 'em putting up teepees for the Sun Dance. Special occasions.

More and more people are going back into their reality. College helps. That's one of the best things that helped here. The college. Before, we made fun of our language. We had to sneak and talk in schools. They might learn a little bit at school, but they get home and there is no one to talk to. You lose the language, well, that's losing your culture."

As Red tells it, in his circular way, things got better in the forties and fifties. "Roosevelt made a big change here. We had it good once he was in charge. The New Deal was a big deal here. That's when we got commodities and rations. When he come on he took the liquor back. Al Capone, you heard of him? He took it all. Roosevelt took the liquor back and that's how he fed us. The taxes off the liquor! That's when all them bigtime bootleggers went under. We were still closed, though, till 'fifty-two here. No booze on the reservation. He turned the taxes on liquor and turned them into commodities. WPA, CCC, ECW—a dollar a day. Like the work I'm doing right now. I'm still working. Ten to one, not much. Make about three hundred every two weeks besides my pension, something for me to do. But anyway, that's what it was." You can still see on the reservation the work done by the Civilian Conservation Corps. "These ditches were built. Canals. They were built by Indians. They built them with horses and plows. Ditch bank days. They'd do it all summer. Go live out there in tents. Teams. Some of them guys went all the way to Yakima, they had a boxing team, basketball team, cooks. They lived good! Baseball teams! There were guys who'd kill to earn a dollar a day. Soup lines. People were starving on the streets."

No matter how Red tells it, things had changed for the better through the 1940s and 1950s. Life on the reservation changed, and improved. The Blackfeet tribal constitution, adopted in 1935, gave them a government—flawed and inadequate, but still a government—and a process by which they could control at least some of the leases for timber and cattle. New Deal jobs programs were a boon to Indians across the region, and their numbers increased. Indian lives didn't change in spite of what was going on in the rest of America. Rather, Indian lives changed in step with the rest of the country.

Migration

When the sun rose on America after World War II, it rose on a vastly different country. The United States alone had emerged from a worldwide festival of death intact and strong. Great Britain had squandered more than 25 percent of its national wealth on the war, and the debts it incurred to the United States through the lend-lease program would hang "like a millstone around the neck of the British economy" for decades to come. Britain's "imperial century" had ended in 1914, and the empire itself, already in decline after the First World War, was finally killed off by the Second. With the country bankrupt, and the Eastern bloc growing, Britain could no longer hold on to its colonies: between 1945 and 1965 the number of people around the world who lived under British rule fell from seven hundred million to five million, with most of the remaining subjects living in Hong Kong. Continental Europe was a shell. Famine was widespread, infrastructure had been demolished. The Soviet Union, having lost upward of forty million people in the war—nine million in combat and the rest to disease, starvation, purges, forced labor, and programs of forced starvation implemented by the Nazis during their occupation of western Russia—rebuilt itself by force and made allies by coercion. It swept up satellite republics like Hungary, Poland, Estonia, Czechoslovakia, Romania, and Yugoslavia into its sphere of influence. The United States offered help under the Marshall Plan, but the Soviet Union refused that offer and instead extracted raw materials and machinery from the "annexed" countries, to their detriment. The Soviet Union made peace in the same manner it made war: with force and numbers. Under terms imposed by the Americans, Japan lost all of its colonies and possessions in China and Southeast Asia and wasn't allowed to form an army or navy; it was intentionally returned to its standard of living circa 1930.

The United States alone emerged stronger from the war. It sought to bind the struggling European republics to itself and its interests with golden handcuffs in the form of aid, loans, and protection. It invested in advantageous trade relationships, and its agricultural sector was strong. The population grew, and the standard of living rose. In 1945 a third of the country was without running water, two-fifths lacked flush toilets, and three-fifths had no central heating. More than half of those who lived on farms were without electricity. This would soon change. As more than $185.7 million in war bonds came of age, the uneducated classes were able to go to college under the GI Bill, and labor unions (despite inroads against them during the McCarthy era) ensured that working-class Americans would make high enough wages to admit them to the middle class. A new interstate highway system facilitated movement and trade across all regions of the country. A fascinating index of the system's success is the spread of the turkey vulture, which had previously been confined to the southeastern states. The interstate highways functioned as a kind of moving buffet for them; as they followed the long lines of roadkill north and west over the next two decades, they came to inhabit every part of the country.

There were other migrations during this period, too. The Great Migration brought African Americans from the South to the North, and from rural areas to urban ones, in search of better employment opportunities and to escape from racism and the constant threat of violence in the form of lynchings and beatings. In 1910, 90 percent of all African Americans in the United States lived in fourteen states, and only 20 percent of them lived in cities. By the outbreak of World War I, more than half a million African Americans had moved to the North (by 1940, a million African Americans had made the journey). Half of those lived in urban areas, and the number continued to increase over the next few decades, especially during and after World War II. By 1970, six million African Americans had migrated North; more than 50 percent of all African Americans lived in the North and more than 80 percent of African Americans lived in cities across the country.

Many reasons for this were specific to the lives and qualities of life for blacks in the South. The country had changed. How it saw itself had changed, too. In the eighteenth century Thomas Jefferson had vested the

American experiment in the flourishing of the yeoman farmer. Farmers, he thought, were "the chosen people of God, if He ever had a chosen people, whose breast He has made His peculiar deposit for substantial and genuine virtue." But it was the yeoman farmer who had ravaged the Plains and the West by tilling the soil, planting wheat, and grazing cows. When a bubble in the commodities market caused by the First World War resulted in a subsequent drop in prices, farmers tilled and planted more land, raised more cattle. The overproduction of wheat for export and overgrazing, combined with droughts in the 1920s, helped cause the "worst hard time" of the Dust Bowl. It would be foolish to consider American Indian migrations to cities in the 1940s and 1950s only in the context of federal Indian policy: American Indians moved as Americans alongside African Americans and Anglo Americans as part of large, fundamental shifts in the American demographic.

By the time World War II rolled around, America had become not only a breadbasket but a metal basket as well. American enterprise had been shifting from agriculture to manufacturing, from rural to urban, for decades. New methods of food production and mechanization changed farming as much as industrialization changed everything. Those ongoing shifts reached an apex after the war. Urban populations swelled, with not only migrating African Americans but Anglo Americans as well. America was changing, and Indian life changed with it, even where government pushed it around with its heavy hand.

The Kansas Act

The hand of the government was particularly heavy in Kansas during the 1930s. In 1885, Congress had passed the Major Crimes Act, which stipulated that "major crimes" perpetrated by an Indian against another Indian—which included murder, assault with the intent to kill, rape, larceny, and burglary—would be prosecuted in federal court. The thinking was that while states could prosecute crimes committed by

Indians against whites and whites against Indians (though such prosecutions were pretty rare), only the federal government could prosecute crimes committed by Indians against Indians, because only the federal government could regulate tribal and intertribal affairs. The Major Crimes Act itself was a response to a case that had preceded it, *Ex Parte Crow Dog*. A Lakota named Crow Dog had murdered Spotted Tail, an uncle of the Lakota war chief Crazy Horse, the latest casualty of a feud between the two men that went back to their participation in the Black Hills Wars, the Battle of the Little Bighorn, and their attempts to wrest some power for themselves after the beginning of the reservation period. The tribe tried Crow Dog, found him guilty, and punished him according to tribal law. The Supreme Court eventually ruled that the government couldn't prosecute Crow Dog. In response Congress passed the Major Crimes Act.

However, in Kansas, the federal government had abdicated its duty of prosecuting such crimes to the state by the early part of the twentieth century. In line with this precedent, in 1938 a Potawatomi Indian agency superintendent contacted federal legislators in the hopes that Kansas might be granted jurisdiction over the four tribes in Kansas: Potawatomi, Sac and Fox, Kickapoo, and Iowa. He pointed out that as a result of allotment, the majority of Indian land in Kansas had been allotted to tribal members and fell under state jurisdiction. None of the four tribes had functioning tribal courts, and without them, he claimed, the tribes faced an epidemic of so-called lawlessness. Indians who were convicted of crimes were jailed at the expense of the counties or the state of Kansas, and there was considerable expense incurred when Indians had to be transported all the way to federal courts in order to stand trial. And the Indians themselves, he said, wanted the state to take care of prosecutions. Since Kansas already prosecuted crimes that should have fallen under the Major Crimes Act, the new measure would merely confirm "a relationship which the State has willingly assumed, which the Indians have willingly accepted, and which has produced successful results." It's hard to know what pressures the superintendent or other officials brought to bear on the tribes, yet all four of them officially supported the measure. The bill was passed as a kind of trial legislation, but within a decade many other states passed similar legislation, including Iowa, North Dakota, California, and New York. The federal government was, slowly and in piecemeal fashion, getting out of the Indian business. Or at least it wanted to.

Part of the reason the federal government didn't want to deal with Indians as Indians anymore was because, by its own admission, things had gone poorly for Indians through the 1930s and 1940s. In 1943, the government conducted a new "survey of Indian conditions." Even though it was less thorough and less impartial than the 1928 Meriam Report, it managed to tell roughly the same story: Indian life was bad, it was hard. Indians were poor. Reservations were rife with disease and deplorable living conditions. Like the Meriam Report, it also had bad things to say about the Office of Indian Affairs and its successor, the Bureau of Indian Affairs: they were doing a horrible job administering to Indians and Indian communities and more often than not made things worse. Despite the similarity of the findings, however, the survey reached a radically different conclusion. The upshot of the Meriam Report had been that Indians could better administer to their own needs and affairs than the Office of Indian Affairs and that tribal governments (until then destroyed or suppressed) should be empowered in Indian communities. The report had led directly to the Indian Reorganization Act, the drafting of tribal constitutions, the creation of Indian-run courts, the strengthening of Indian police, and the like, however faulty and tardy those had been in coming. The 1943 report, however, led the government in the opposite direction.

The Indian Reorganization Act had been passed just in 1934, so it is hard to know what the surveyors and legislators and commissioners thought would be radically different in the space of only nine years of "self-determination." In any event, the Senate Committee on Indian Affairs, once again confronted with the "Indian problem" and the graft, corruption, greed, and ineptitude of the Office of Indian Affairs—and supported and emboldened by the Kansas Act and the string of other acts giving states control over Indian lives—reversed itself again. It instituted a new policy, the fifth new policy meant to "help" Indians. After enduring the policies of treaty/reservation, allotment, relocation, and assimilation, the era of termination was about to begin. And as with many previous policies, its author was something of a zealot.

Termination

A rthur Vivian Watkins was born in 1886, in Midway, Utah. The eldest of six children and a devout Mormon, he was headed nowhere but up. He attended Brigham Young Academy, then New York University, and then received a law degree from Columbia University in 1912. He moved back to Utah, practiced law, founded a newspaper, and, in 1919, began ranching, eventually owning and running a six-hundred-acre spread by the time he was in his early forties. In 1946, he won a seat in the U.S. Senate. His politics and his religion mixed early and often. As chairman of the Senate Interior Subcommittee on Indian Affairs, he did not hesitate to act on his belief that Indians were being "held back" not only by the BIA but also by laws that treated them as different from other Americans. In his opinion, Indian administration was costly, inefficient, and punitive. What was needed was "the freeing of the Indian from wardship status." In 1953, he pushed through the legislation (introduced by Henry Jackson) that became known as the Termination Act. It proposed to fix the Indian problem once and for all by making Indians—legally, culturally, and economically—no longer Indians at all. Writing to a church father in 1954, Watkins mused, "The more I go into this Indian problem the more I am convinced that we have made some terrible mistakes in the past. It seems to me that the time has come for us to correct some of these mistakes and help the Indians stand on their own two feet and become a white and delightsome people as the Book of Mormon prophesied they would become. Of course, I realize that the Gospel of Jesus Christ will be the motivating factor, but it is difficult to teach the Gospel when they don't understand the English language and have had no training in caring for themselves. The Gospel should be a great stimulus and I am longing and praying for the time when the Indians will accept it in overwhelming numbers."

Clearly Watkins's religion played a big part in his policy-making. After the necessary excesses of FDR's New Deal, the country was shifting toward smaller government. It had a staggering number of expenditures as a result of the Second World War, including a lot of money spent for the reconstruction of a Europe it had helped bomb. It was also becoming more industrial, more urban. At the same time, the newly powerful United States saw its own civil, social, and political institutions as the only effective models in the world and was deeply suspicious of manifestations of collectivity (such as tribes) because of the rising threat of communism: the citizen was king, the commune was suspect. And tribes were communal if nothing else. Nonetheless, termination (like previous policies) required some degree of participation by the tribes themselves.

The Indian Claims Commission

The Indian Claims Commission, created in 1946 under the rubric of the Indian Claims Act, is proof (if any was needed) that no good deed goes unpunished.

The commission was empowered, in large part, because of the overwhelming numbers of Indians who served in World War II and because of the overwhelmingly important nature of their service. Also—after the carnage of the war or because of it—there might have been a feeling, approaching a general feeling, that in a world that could be very cruel it might do to look in one's own backyard and fix what could be fixed there. But, as with all government initiatives, there was a self-serving component to the Indian Claims Act, too: there were so many claims against the government for wrongful taking of land through force, coercion, removal—takings in violation of not only treaty rights but human rights more generally—and there was no good process for dealing with all of them.

A century had passed since Congress had created the Court of Claims, allowing Indians to make cases against the federal government. But the Court of Claims specifically excluded tribes from bringing claims against the government because of treaty violation or abrogation. As "domestic dependent nations," with status much like that of foreign nations, each tribe had to obtain a "special jurisdictional act" from Congress to present its case to the Court of Claims. This was time-consuming and expensive, and also unfair to tribes with less clout. Often when a jurisdictional act of Congress gave a tribe the right to present a claim in the Court of Claims, the basis of the suit was so narrow that there was no real way to consider the full scope of the grievance. And such suits really worked, if they worked at all, only for monetary claims for lost land.

For instance, the Ho-Chunk (Winnebago) filed a claim in the Court of Claims in 1928. They had been removed from Wisconsin to Nebraska, and many of the Ho-Chunk had died of starvation and exposure en route or once they arrived. Rather than suffer that fate in a strange land, many walked back to Wisconsin. Others took refuge among the Omaha, where, eventually, a reservation was established for them. But the tribe was in disarray: their leaders were scattered and dead, their social and religious institutions fractured and scrambled. In 1942, fourteen years after they filed their claim, it was dismissed by the Court of Claims. The court explained that it was dismissing the case not because the Ho-Chunk hadn't experienced serious harm, but because it could not set a value on what they had lost because it could not determine comparable value between their old home and their new one. The Ho-Chunk needed a different process and a different venue if they wanted the wrongs done to them to be addressed more fully.

Moreover, by the 1940s, tribes across the country were filing more claims than ever before. Tribal citizens were getting better at understanding their rights, and tribal governments were getting better at advocating for them. By 1946, there had been more than two hundred claims filed in the United States Court of Claims, mostly for damages for unlawful land seizure or for criminally low prices paid for land taken legally, but only twenty-nine claims had been addressed by the court. The majority of the rest had been dismissed, largely on technicalities. The overwhelming numbers of Indians who served in World War II, and the important nature of their service, had resulted in some sense of obligation to Indians on the part of the government. The government needed a process by which to hear claims, but it also wanted a process that would put an end to them, once and for all. The Indian Claims Commission Act of 1947 was the result, and "finality" was its watchword.

The Indian Claims Commission expanded the grounds for a suit to include five categories of "wrongs":

(1) claims in law or equity arising under the Constitution, laws, treaties of the United States, and Executive orders of the President; (2) all other claims in law or equity, including those sounding in tort, with respect to which the claimant would have been entitled to sue in a court of the United States if the United States was subject to suit; (3) claims which would result if the treaties, contracts, and agreements between the claimant and the United States were revised on the ground of fraud, duress, unconscionable consideration, mutual or unilateral mistake, whether of law or fact, or any other ground cognizable by a court of equity; (4) claims arising from the taking by the United States, whether as the result of a treaty of cession or otherwise, of lands owned or occupied by the claimant without the payment for such lands of compensation agreed to by the claimant; and (5) claims based upon fair and honorable dealings that are not recognized by any existing rule of law or equity. No claim accruing after the date of the approval of this Act shall be considered by the Commission.

So the Claims Commission intended to address all the wrongs done to Indians by monetizing those damages, with a finish line in sight: all claims were supposed to be filed within five years of the passage of the act. As it turned out, the date would be extended by another five years as tribes— understaffed and often without their own legal teams—limped toward the finish line. The commission wouldn't finish dealing with the claims, which numbered in the hundreds, until the 1970s. The commission was extended from 1976 to 1978, after which point the claims were transferred to the U.S. Court of Claims. The last claim on the docket wasn't finalized until 2006.

While the Indian Claims Commission Act represented a "broad waiver of the United States' sovereign immunity" and was remedial in nature, it was also coercive. Cash-strapped tribes with no infrastructure and no tax base—and with crushing unemployment and chronic poverty—needed the money for sure (even if most of it would take years, if not decades, to arrive). But it was a mistake to think that the magnitude and kinds of loss could be monetized. It required a very narrow sense of reparations to think that the loss of land, which was at the heart of the Claims Commission mission, was only an economic loss and could be adequately addressed by cash payments. The loss of land had resulted in a loss of life and culture, a loss of a people's ability to be a people in the manner it understood itself. Many tribes—particularly tribes in the Southwest—had ceremonial lives that revolved around sacred sites that had irrevocably passed into private ownership. Tribes were left on small islands holding cash they couldn't use to reconstitute their cultures, their ceremonies, and their homelands.

To make matters worse, the Indian Claims Commission was used as a lever to move tribes into the next phase of federal policy. And a wind that blows one way one minute and the other way the next is not a particularly good wind for sailing. The broad demographic shifts brought about by World War II—the Great Migration, the shift from farming to manufacturing, the trend away from the broad federalism of the New Deal toward anti-collectivism and private enterprise under Truman and Eisenhower—solidified the belief in majority rule. Democracy, understood as the supremacy of the individual on one hand and market capitalism on the other, was seen as self-evidently not just the best way but the *only* way. The federal government's relationship with tribes followed this trend. As in the period from the 1890s through the 1930s, it became federal policy to try to absorb Indians into the mainstream, whether they wanted to be absorbed or not. But instead of "encouraging" Indians to become American via institutions like the boarding schools and allotments, now official thinking had it that institutions like the tribes themselves, as well as the BIA and the Indian Health Service, were blocking Indians from what would otherwise be an inevitable gravitational assimilation into the larger current of American life. It does not seem to have occurred to Watkins and others like him that the "Indian problem" was and had always been a "federal government problem."

Nevertheless, the Kansas Act of 1940 was followed by the awkwardly worded "Act to Confer Jurisdiction on the State of Iowa over Offenses Committed by or Against Indians on the Sac and Fox Indian Reservation" in 1948, the New York Acts of 1948 and 1950, and the California Act of 1949, all of them modeled on the Kansas Act. It should be noted that these acts were in direct violation of the treaties that the tribes had entered into with the federal government (not the states), which had been (and still are) the bedrock of tribal sovereignty, and that thus something beyond coercive "consultations" was surely needed to make them law. Be that as it may, the Termination Act of 1953—actually House Concurrent Resolution 108—passed concurrently with Public Law 280: a dry pair of names for exceptionally bloody acts.

The act changed the ways tribes would relate to the government to this day. Until that time—with the exception of piecemeal legislation—federally recognized Indian tribes were, or functioned as, "domestic dependent nations" and had sovereignty, or something approaching it, which meant they related to the federal government on a government-to-government basis. Public Law 280 was the first move to formally defederalize the status of the tribes in relationship to the rest of America.

Public Law 280 was ostensibly intended as a law-and-order act, spelling out how to address the wrongs committed by Indians against other Indians and giving Indians equal access to protection under the law in criminal and civil disputes. With respect to crimes other than those mentioned in the Major Crimes Act, Indians lived in a kind of legal gray area. Some crimes were prosecuted in federal court, some were tried in the Court of Indian Offenses, some were tried in tribal court. It wasn't clear. And it wasn't cheap. Public Law 280 sought to end all of that, but in so doing, it dealt a serious blow to tribal sovereignty. The law granted six states the right, ability, and responsibility to prosecute all criminal offenses and civil disputes within its borders: Minnesota (except for Red Lake Reservation), Wisconsin (except for the Menominee Reservation),

California, Washington, Oregon (except for Warm Springs Reservation), and Alaska (upon statehood). Tribes in states not covered by Public Law 280 continued to administer civil and criminal matters in tribal and federal courts. Tribes within the six states covered by the law were not offered any chance to vote on, amend, or ultimately reject the legislation. Other states had the option of adopting the provisions of the law, with some limited input from the tribes. The states that ultimately followed along and adopted some of the provisions of Public Law 280 were Nevada, South Dakota, Florida, Idaho, Montana, North Dakota, Arizona, Iowa, and Utah. Even narrowly defined and implemented, the law put most tribes under state control and state oversight, a bit as if the U.S. government had unilaterally extended Minnesota state laws to (a much smaller) Canada. And although the act had been put forward as a piece of law-and-order legislation, the states almost universally interpreted and implemented it as a regulatory directive as well. They levied taxes, administered schools, stepped into health care and licensing, and curtailed treaty rights by extending the jurisdiction of game wardens and overseeing licensing for harvesting game, edibles, and the like. This illegal overstepping would not be completely rectified by the Supreme Court until the 1980s. Tribes are still in the process of defining (and limiting) the excesses of Public Law 280.

Just as the law was transferring legal power over Indians to states across the country, House Concurrent Resolution 108—Orwellianly referred to as the "Act to Free Indians from Federal Supervision"—ended Indians' status as wards of the federal government. In legal terms, in other words, it was the death of Indians as Indians. It read in its entirety:

> Whereas it is the policy of Congress, as rapidly as possible, to make the Indians within the territorial limits of the United States subject to the same laws and entitled to the same privileges and responsibilities as are applicable to other citizens of the United States, to end their status as wards of the United States, and to grant them all of the rights and prerogatives pertaining to American citizenship; and Whereas the Indians within the territorial limits of the United States should assume their

full responsibilities as American citizens: Now, therefore, be it Resolved by the House of Representatives (the Senate concurring), That it is declared to be the sense of Congress that, at the earliest possible time, all of the Indian tribes and the individual members thereof located within the States of California, Florida, New York, and Texas, and all of the following named Indian tribes and individual members thereof, should be freed from Federal supervision and control and from all disabilities and limitations specially applicable to Indians: The Flathead Tribe of Montana, the Klamath Tribe of Oregon, the Menominee Tribe of Wisconsin, the Potowatamie Tribe of Kansas and Nebraska, and those members of the Chippewa Tribe who are on the Turtle Mountain Reservation, North Dakota. It is further declared to be the sense of Congress that, upon the release of such tribes and individual members thereof from such disabilities and limitations, all offices of the Bureau of Indian Affairs in the States of California, Florida, New York, and Texas and all other offices of the Bureau of Indian Affairs whose primary purpose was to serve any Indian tribe or individual Indian freed from Federal supervision should be abolished. It is further declared to be the sense of Congress that the Secretary of the Interior should examine all existing legislation dealing with such Indians, and treaties between the Government of the United States and each such tribe, and report to Congress at the earliest practicable date, but not later than January 1, 1954, his recommendations for such legislation as, in his judgment, may be necessary to accomplish the purposes of this resolution.

Before we look at what happened to the Menominee, it's important to know that, even by the time this cocktail of disastrous legislation was being passed, it was possible to know what might result, because there were tribes that had, in effect, lived under termination long before it became federal Indian policy. The Little Shell Band of Ojibwe provided one such cautionary tale.

The Little Shell Band was led by Esens (Little Shell), a Pembina Ojibwe leader. The Pembina generally, and Little Shell's band in particular, were unusual among the other Ojibwe bands scattered around the Great Lakes. Whereas most Ojibwe had migrated over centuries from the East Coast and by the seventeenth century had secured our homelands around the western Great Lakes, some had continued pushing farther west and wound up in the Red River valley, on the present-day Minnesota–North Dakota border. This was a buffer zone of sorts between the rest of the Ojibwe and the Dakota, whom the Ojibwe had gradually pushed into the Plains. The Ojibwe focused largely on trapping and trading to the east, and the Dakota, after acquiring the horse, expanded to the south and west. The group that became known as the Pembina had settled between them in the nineteenth century. By that time, the Dakota had more or less relinquished their claim on that area in the Treaties of Traverse des Sioux and Mendota.

The Red River valley was rich with game and waterfowl and herds of bison that wandered in from the west. But its soil is particularly well suited for farming, unlike the sandy uplands to the east and west. Between 1849 and 1850, before Minnesota statehood, Zachary Taylor resolved to open up the area to settlement. (A major accomplishment in his sixteen months as president.) Under government pressure, the Pembina and Red Lake Bands of Ojibwe signed the Treaty of Old Crossing a decade later, relinquishing their claim to the Red River valley.

Little Shell was a signatory of the Old Crossing Treaty. It was as if a gulf opened up between the Ojibwe in Minnesota and those, like Little Shell, who were on the North Dakota side of the cession. Little Shell and other Pembina Ojibwe clustered around the Turtle Mountains in the northern part of what was to become North Dakota, on the Canadian border. The Turtle Mountains were a great place to settle: almost completely forested, they provided timber, game, and shelter from the ravages of Plains weather. Wild rice grew in the rivers, creeks, and sloughs—the westernmost region in North America where it did so. From their stronghold, the Pembina Ojibwe ranged far and wide, traveling north into what was to become Saskatchewan and Alberta and as far west as central Montana in search of game and trade. The formerly woodland Ojibwe came to resemble their Plains neighbors more and more.

Even though the Old Crossing Treaty was signed in 1863, it wasn't until the 1880s that the Turtle Mountain Reservation was officially created by Congress. The Ojibwe and Dakota signed the Sweet Corn Treaty in 1858, dividing and establishing their separate territories: the Ojibwe had all the land from Minnesota through what would become North Dakota up to the Missouri River. The Dakota had the land west of there. Five years later, as part of the Old Crossing Treaty, the Ojibwe gave up all of their land in North Dakota except for the area around Turtle Mountain. It wasn't until 1882 that the boundaries of Turtle Mountain were established. (The reservation that remained covered 460,800 acres.) After 1863, Little Shell refused to sign any more treaties with the government. Every time the tribe came to the treaty table they had walked away with less.

Some Pembina thought that it might be best to negotiate from a position of strength, but Little Shell, for reasons lost to history, felt otherwise. And so the federal government did what the federal government always did. In 1884, two years after the creation of the Turtle Mountain Reservation and without consulting the Indians there, it reduced the size of the reservation, by executive order, to two relatively small townships. Their 460,800-acre reservation shrank (overnight) to a tenth its original size: a mere 46,800 acres. Little Shell was off hunting in Montana, on the western frontier of Pembina territory. During the period following the passage of the Dawes Act, in 1887, many Turtle Mountain Ojibwe (along with more easterly Ojibwe from Mille Lacs and Leech Lake) were "encouraged" to relocate to the White Earth Reservation, itself established as a kind of catchment for Ojibwe who lived in places the federal government coveted. Still, Little Shell would not negotiate and would not cede his claim to the millions of acres that rightly belonged to his tribe. So rather than contend with a leader who wouldn't negotiate at all, the federal government propped up others it arbitrarily decided to consider leaders and brought them to the treaty table. Never mind that they had no authority to sign on anyone's behalf, never mind that they didn't represent any constituency: thirty-two Pembina "chiefs" arbitrarily chosen by the federal government along with dozens of other Turtle Mountain Chippewa signed the Mc-Cumber Agreement in 1892, which formally ceded all of Little Shell's land for a pittance. When Little Shell returned to Turtle Mountain with his people, he found that not only had the other so-called leaders sold his land out from under his feet but also he had no official standing at Turtle Mountain. Overnight Little Shell and his band had gone from Indian masters of their own vast territory to landless people who, according to the treaties and founding documents of Turtle Mountain, weren't, politically and legally at least, Indian at all. They had been written out of existence by a stroke of the treaty pen.

"It was 1884, I think, Little Shell went out hunting, with a hunting party," says Sierra Frederickson. We are sitting in a brewpub in Williston, North Dakota. Sierra is Little Shell Ojibwe. "We're called the 'landless Indians of Montana,'" she tells me wryly. "You call us landless and at the same time you ask where we're from. How's that supposed to work?" Sierra is young and brilliant, a writer and a teacher at the community college here, passionately committed to advancing the cause of her band however she can.

Sierra is talking about the aftermath of the McCumber Agreement. "It was kind of a power grab by other bands around Turtle Mountain," she says. "There were only a certain amount of people who could enroll in the new rolls. A lot of Little Shell's people were métis, or half-blood, so they didn't get on the rolls and got pushed off. Some of the Little Shell people had left the reservation before the agreement was signed. They went along the Hi-Line and moved west to Le Havre, Lewiston, places like that. Others didn't go and they were rounded up and put on boxcars and brought to the Hi-Line in Montana and just dropped off." From there the Little Shell Band endured a hellish diaspora, wandering in the desert of their own former territory. They settled in small groups in Le Havre, Lewiston, and Great Falls, from there splintering into even smaller groups as they chased work. Some reservation communities—Cree at Rocky Boy, Assiniboine and Lakota at Fort Peck, Shoshone-Bannock at Fort Hall—took them in.

Sierra's own grandparents grew up on the Rocky Boy Reservation, descendants of the five or six hundred members of the Little Shell Band who left or were removed from Turtle Mountain. "My grandma's mom was born in the Sweet Grass Hills, near Browning. It's really interesting to go through, in my ancestry, to see where they were born and where they died.

It's interesting to see where everyone moved." With each split and each move, the Little Shell lost more of their sense of themselves. At stake was not merely some kind of round self-regard: without community and without place, without land, a people becomes leprous, they lose bits and pieces of themselves and the safety net that shared language, experience, lifeway, and place can provide. Sierra's life story bears some of these scars.

"I was born in Great Falls, Montana, but grew up in Bridger. My parents got divorced then. My dad was in and out of treatment a lot." The atmosphere at home was pretty violent. "We moved to get away from all of that. My mom's brother lived in Bridger. Another brother lived about thirty minutes away. So from second grade through high school I lived there. I graduated from Bridger. The population of the town is about seven hundred. It's a 'bigger small town.' We have Jim Bridger Days. They are ridiculous. There is a street dance, they block off the street but the street's not very long. It's a really small town! My parents have been there for sixteen or seventeen years. They aren't considered as being 'from Bridger.' We're probably the only Indian family in town. It's right next to the Crow reservation but . . . there aren't any Indians there.

"There wasn't a lot of racism that I noticed. Maybe more in high school and then I was more vocal about things. People would say things in class and there were no other Natives there except me, so I would say things and they would say things back. There was a little bit of that. There was an incident when someone says my dad was just an Indian and a cow thief. Things like that. But nothing really crazy. My mom is a hairdresser in Bridger, so she knows everything. My dad buys and sells cattle. A rancher, more or less. Kind of an in-between guy. Someone would call him and say, 'I want five hundred calves and I can only spend this much,' and my dad will go to the sale and buy them and get them shipped. My stepdad looks pretty Native, he's Blackfeet. My sister isn't Native, and my brother has dark blond hair and blue eyes. In my big, complicated family some of us are Native and some of us aren't, and most people in Bridger don't know we're Native or that some of us are, at least. I mean: we played Crow in basketball and you'll hear, 'The Crow are dirty. They steal, they are lazy, and they don't want to work.'"

The life Sierra's mother made with her stepfather in Bridger seems to have been a good one. The past she left behind with Sierra's biological father isn't so sweet or rosy. "I haven't talked to my father since I was a junior in undergrad, about four or five years. We had a really difficult relationship; now we don't really have a relationship at all. It's been hard since I was really little. Me in particular. My little brother was about two when they got divorced. I was five or six when they separated the first time. I actually got PTSD when I was three or four. I remember some stuff. But I've blocked a lot of stuff out. It was tumultuous. The cops came around a lot. He was in treatment two or three times for alcohol and drugs. And he would break out and come to our house in the middle of the night and he'd have his friends come over. We moved to Bridger. And we'd do visitation, once a month or so. But when I got to middle school I had a lot of questions. I asked my mom a lot. She was always good about it. She didn't want me to think bad of him. She'd say I have to accept him for who he is because I'll never get answers for some of the stuff I want answers for. My dad never came to track meets and volleyball and things like that—he said he was too far away. Four hours away in Great Falls." She pauses. "I just wanted to know why drinking was more important than us. I asked him that. Never really got an answer to that one."

It's difficult enough to pick up the pieces—of a life, of a community—if there is a place of return, some remnant of a homeland. Red Hall had a place to return to. When he ran away with his wife when they were very young, they went to Fort Belknap to stay with Red's relatives. They returned to Blackfeet country after a year. He worked in Washington and Oregon, and returned again. He served in the army and returned in the 1950s, left again to work for the railroad. Browning and the Blackfeet reservation were rooted deep within him, and he was rooted deep in the place. Red is one of those guys who not only knows where everyone is but—because his memory is so good—remembers who lived there before, when the house was built, what colors it was painted over the years, and so on. And all that back-and-forth traffic in his life that brought him from the reservation out into the world and back brought his skills and experiences on similar journeys. One result was that life got better for Red and for his reservation. In this way, the tribe reaped the benefits of the Works Progress Administration, the Civilian Conservation Corps, service in the armed forces, and the GI Bill.

But the same could not be said for their neighbors, Sierra's tribe of the "landless Indians of Montana," some of whom lived in tent encampments into the 1950s and 1960s. Without a land base, without some kind of center—no matter how corrupted or reduced it might be—there was not much the Little Shell people could do except hold on somehow. Their religion was in jeopardy, their ceremonies lost and forgotten. "I don't know what their religion was when they left Turtle Mountain. My grandma would probably know those things more. I've asked her those sorts of questions and she never really said anything about those things to me. They had dances, but it was sort of a mix. It was a mix of fiddling with Native dancing. She's told me about going to those dances. I'm away from where most of our people are. And it's not like people just hang out at the cultural center. It's not like the gas station where all the old men drink coffee. There's no real getting together and talking with other Little Shell people. We have no place to gather. But social media is how we do it. I mean—the tribe's Facebook page has been really great for us. It sounds stupid but it helps. But if there was a lot of things like ceremony going on I didn't know about them growing up."

Even though reservations have been characterized by Indians and non-Indians alike as places where hope goes to die, as a kind of final resting place for Indian lives and cultures, they are clearly much more than that. They have functioned as a home base, as a home, for Indians and have preserved—in ways both positive and negative—a kind of togetherness that has been vital to the continued existence of Native people. All of this was painfully obvious in the 1940s and 1950s, but the government did its best to unsee it. Instead, with Arthur Watkins as a passionate supporter, the federal government decided that termination was what was best for Indian people. And at the top of its list of those to terminate were the Menominee of Wisconsin.

Before the arrival of Europeans, the Menominee (who refer to themselves as Mamaceqtaw, or "The People") occupied more than ten million acres in what is now eastern Wisconsin and northwestern Michigan. They are the only Indian tribe in present-day Wisconsin who have always lived in the state. As noted in part 2, their homeland was rich beyond compare. It was covered in hardwoods and pine, studded with lakes, and fronted by Lake Michigan to the east, which produced enormous amounts of fish for the tribe. The climate of their homeland was balmy in comparison to others farther north, and the wild rice from which the name "Menominee" derives (*manoominiig* means "people of the wild rice") was plentiful. It was, as homelands go, paradise. And they had been there for a long, long time. Unlike other Algonquian people of the Great Lakes, including the Ojibwe, they were not migrants to the region. They were descended from the Old Copper and Hopewell cultures and had lived in the area for at least a thousand years before the arrival of Europeans.

The first European to meet them was the French explorer Jean Nicolet in 1634. A group of Ho-Chunk had gathered on the shore at Red Banks, near present-day Green Bay. The Indians watched the explorer approach in a canoe. As he got closer, Nicolet put on a silk Chinese robe, stood athwart the canoe, and fired two pistols in the air. After this colorful landing Nicolet traveled inland, where he met the Menominee. The explorer Pierre-François-Xavier de Charlevoix wrote about coming upon the Menominee in 1721: "After we had advanced five or six leagues, we found ourselves abreast of a little island, which lies near the western side of the bay, and which concealed from our view, the mouth of a river, on which stands the village of the Malhomines Indians. . . . The whole nation consists only of this village, and that too not very numerous. 'Tis really great pity, they being the finest and handsomest men in all Canada. They are even of a larger stature than the Poutewatamies." The Menominee were much more numerous than he gave them credit for, despite having been decimated by smallpox some years earlier. After the fur trade got into full swing and wars between Algonquians and Iroquoians of the Great Lakes—with the French and British mixed in—raged across the lakes and through the Ohio valley and eastern Wisconsin (Green Bay in particular became something of a refugee center), the Menominee clung to their homelands, and there they stayed.

It has been said that the Menominee believe that their world, our world, is a middle ground between the lower and upper worlds and forms a kind of barrier between the two. The upper world is a good world, filled with good spirits. The lower world is where evil dwells. But beginning in the nineteenth century, it probably felt to the tribe as if the middle and lower worlds had been switched. They supported the British during the War of 1812 and paid dearly afterward, when settlers began streaming into the Upper Peninsula of Michigan and Wisconsin as the timber boom got under way. As we have seen, the U.S. government did little to protect Menominee interests, much less to honor the treaties they signed with them. As they prepared for Wisconsin statehood, the federal government tried to relocate the Menominee to points much farther west, in the manner of the Cherokee and other tribes that had been removed from the American Southeast. But the Menominee would not be moved and managed to prevent it by agreeing to settle a very small reservation near the Wolf River, where they remained until the mid–twentieth century. In 1854, shortly after the reservation was established near the Wolf River, the Menominee bought a sawmill, and it was there that they developed their very successful—and sustainable—timber industry, fighting off allotment, attempts to grab their land, and efforts to impose damaging clear-cutting methods. It must have been maddening: despite their excellent self-government, their entrepreneurship, their willingness to enter into sustained trade relationships with the American economy, the blind paternalism of the government made all of that impossible. The U.S. government insisted on overseeing Menominee logging. They wouldn't let the Menominee cut their own timber and instead hired non-Native logging companies to cut on Menominee land. These contractors engaged in rampant illegal cutting (some profits of which flowed back to the Indian agent). Still, by 1871 the Menominee were harvesting and milling thousands of board feet of lumber a day. Sustainably. In 1872 they got temporary permission to continue harvesting. They purchased a shingle mill and a lathe mill. Their success, despite the efforts of the government, helped them resist allotment under the Dawes Act.

The Menominee formed their own modern tribal government six years in advance of the Indian Reorganization Act of 1934. They filed a suit against the government in 1934 for damages resulting from illegal cutting by white timber companies and damage caused by the U.S. Forest Service's decision to clear-cut the reservation after a big blowdown in 1905. It took twenty years for the suit to be settled, but the tribe was eventually awarded $8.5 million in federal court. By then, the Menominee logging operation employed several hundred predominantly Indian workers, funded a school and hospital, and paid the salaries of two doctors, eight nurses, and an orthodontist, as well as four policemen, six night watchmen, a truant officer, a game warden, and a welfare administrator. It also supported a tribal loan fund of nearly $500,000 and paid a yearly stumpage dividend to each of the twenty-nine hundred tribal members. By any measure, the Menominee were everything the government said it wanted them to be, with the exception that they did everything their own way: in common. Hence they were at the very top of the list for termination.

In 1953, shortly after the Termination Act was passed, Watkins visited the Menominee personally, since one of the stipulations of the act was that tribes had to buy into it. Watkins had come to Wisconsin to secure that agreement through coercion. He told the Menominee that if they wanted to see the $8.5 million settlement they had won in the Court of Claims, they would have to agree to termination. This was a failure of justice and of imagination. A settlement that was recompense for previous federal and private mismanagement and unlawful seizure of land and the assets on it was now recast as a reward to be granted for submission or withheld for insubordination. This failure of imagination is more pervasive and insidious than has generally been recognized, and it is shared by Indians and non-Indians alike. Such concessions made to the tribes in recognition of the horrors and tribulations of the nineteenth century, or colonialism more generally, are not pity payments or proto-welfare. Treaty rights and all of the benefits that accrue from them arise from the treaties themselves— according to the U.S. Constitution, they are the "supreme law of the land" and the tacit recognition of the inherent rights Indians possessed long before the coming of the white man. The Menominee had the right to exist, the right to government, the right to social services not because they had suffered but because some of those rights were inherent long before they were brought to the treaty table—and because others were received from the Americans in exchange for the right to settle Menominee homelands.

Had those rights been honored, the Menominee could have become the most fabulously successful tribe in the history of the world and the U.S. government would still have been obligated—by international law, by precedent, by its own founding documents, and by the treaties it signed—to honor the provisions in those agreements. Indeed, the Menominee were not uniformly or even mostly interested in termination. However, being able to control the $8.5 million settlement was crucial to their well-being, and the thinking was that it was better to agree to termination than to lose the money. They agreed to undergo termination, with a grace period of four years to get their affairs in order, a deadline that was extended for two more years. In 1961, the Menominee Reservation and the Menominee tribe, such as it was, ceased to exist. All reservation lands and tribal property were transferred to Menominee Enterprises, Inc. (MEI), a private business. Four Indians sat on the board of trustees along with three non-Indians. What had been the reservation was converted into Menominee County.

There was trouble from the start. Menominee County, since most of it was corporate-owned now, lacked a tax base. Basic services such as police, waste management, firefighting, and road construction ate up the tribe's savings. The sawmill needed renovations, and MEI couldn't afford them. The hospital funded in part by the Menominee and in part by the federal government had to close for lack of funds. Schools, utilities, and other services either closed or were cut to the bone. When Congress passed the Menominee Termination Act in 1954, the Menominee had cash assets of more than $10 million (not counting the settlement). By 1964 they had only $300,000. The tribe was so cash-strapped that the white-controlled MEI board voted to sell lake lots for summer homes (rather than log the land) in an effort to increase the tax base. Tribal members, told simply that they were voting on an "economic plan," voted for the development;

when it had been approved, MEI created a huge artificial lake and sold thousands of lake lots, diminishing what land and small amount of tribal control remained.

There was a silver lining, however. The process of termination took so long that those slated for it had the opportunity to see what a disaster it had been for the Menominee. It was, clearly, a disaster. Other tribes watched and learned and fought. And after years of struggle, the Menominee themselves were reconstituted, termination was undone, and they got their reservation back in the 1970s. But this was decades away. Termination rolled on.

Relocation

Solutions for the "Indian problem" seem only to have generated more problems for the government, not to mention for Indian people themselves. When termination became the face of federal policy, the question became: What to do with the Indians? In 1940, 56 percent of Americans lived in cities, but only 6 percent of American Indians did. In 1939, the average white worker earned twice what an Indian could expect to earn. Indians with jobs could expect to bring in, on average, twelve dollars a week. As far as Washington was concerned, the next move seemed clear: now that termination was set to take care of reservations, what was needed was an extra push to get Indians to leave their disappearing homelands and move to the city. So in the 1950s another round of legislative problem-solving erupted.

In the Southwest, the Navajo-Hopi Law funded a jobs-training program for Navajo and Hopi Indians of New Mexico and Arizona and provided money to relocate them to Denver, Salt Lake, and Los Angeles. The program was expanded by the Department of the Interior in 1951 to include other tribes and other cities in Oklahoma, Arizona, and New Mexico and expanded again in the years to come to yet more Indians and yet more cities: Cleveland, San Francisco, St. Louis, San Jose, Seattle, Tulsa, and Minneapolis. The piecemeal legislation, budget lines, and policies co-alesced into Public Law 959, passed in 1956:

> In order to help adult Indians who reside on or near Indian reserva-tions to obtain reasonable and satisfactory employment, the Secretary of the Interior is authorized to undertake a program of vocational training that provides for vocational counseling or guidance, institu-tional training in any recognized vocation or trade, apprenticeship, and on the job training, for periods that do not exceed twenty-four months, transportation to the place of training, and subsistence during the course of training. The program shall be available primarily to Indians who are not less than eighteen and not more than thirty-five years of age and who reside on or near an Indian reservation, and the program shall be conducted under such rules and regulations as the Secretary may prescribe. For the purposes of this program the Secre-tary is authorized to enter into contracts or agreements with any Fed-eral, State, or local governmental agency, or with any private school which has a recognized reputation in the field of vocational education and has successfully obtained employment for its graduates in their respective fields of training, or with any corporation or association which has an existing apprenticeship or on-the-job training program which is recognized by industry and labor as leading to skilled em-ployment.

Indian agents on reservations across the country hawked the benefits of urban living with the same fervor with which land speculators enticed city dwellers to come west and homestead a century before. Flyers and posters were made. Attractive brochures were handed out. And many In-dians signed up. One of the families whom agents reached was that of Sterling HolyWhiteMountain's uncle David Schildt, Red Hall's cousin.

"I'm from Birch Creek, Montana, on the Blackfeet Reservation," David tells me at a Starbucks in San Rafael, California. "We barely sur-vived the Birch Creek flood, my brothers Pat and Cal were with me. We missed that water by about thirty seconds. Oh shit, it was bad." He smiles but it's not a real smile. David is handsome in that way Indian men who've put on a lot of miles are handsome. He's generous and kind, and yet there is a hardness and a diffuse pain that hovers over him like a massive sustain, a sound that just won't die. "Birch Creek dam. June 8, 1964. That was when that flood broke. Swift Dam Reservoir, Birch Creek, Montana. Our neighbors who lived upstream, hell, maybe three hundred yards— three of them died. Practically everyone below us died. I don't know why we didn't."

The flood David can't get out of his mind was the worst in Montana history. Heavy snow had piled up in the mountains all winter—up to 75 percent higher than average—and with a cool spring hadn't melted much as of early summer. Daytime highs didn't reach seventy degrees until Memorial Day weekend. Snowpack alone hadn't caused serious flooding in Montana before. But in early June it began to rain. Moist air from the Gulf of Mexico collided with a western upper-level low-pressure system and freakishly high surface pressure caused by cold air sliding down the mountains. What this meant was rain: warm, heavy rain. The rain fell at a rate of one inch an hour, all of June 7 and into the early-morning hours of the eighth. By June 9 as much as sixteen inches of rain had fallen near Blackfoot, Montana. The yearly average for nearby Great Falls, Montana, was just over fourteen inches. It was too much for the earthen dam on Birch Creek above the Schildt homestead. David's grandmother told him to go down to the creek to have a look. A rock they used to jump from, normally ten feet above the water, was now so far submerged you couldn't even see it. "She's like, 'Okay, here's what I want you to do. Grab your coat and we gonna walk up to the top of the hill and sit up there for a while.'" The "hill" was more of a cut bank about 150 to 200 feet high. "It was all basically mud because of the rain at that time. We's walking toward the hill and then my uncle come running through the brush. 'Run for the hill,' he says, 'the dam broke!' . . . So we took off and we were clawing and scraping. And we got to the top and my gram got help from my grandfather and uncle. And just when we got up there the water came, and it took everything." Estimates vary, but a wall of water at least forty feet high came barreling down the creek bottom, taking everything in its path. "It was the most goddamn horrifying thing I've ever seen in my life. Like a big mass of water that went rumbling by. It chewed up everything. We saw the earth chewed up before our eyes."

David pauses. The Christmas music in Starbucks continues unabated. "I've had nightmares most of my life. Little houses along the river, mostly country folk, all of it gone. My cousin who lived before us, downstream, he lost seven kids in the flood. And his wife. He used to be the guy who watched the irrigation ditch gauge. His job was to watch that gauge to see how much water was going down that ditch." Their home destroyed, David and his brothers and sisters and other surviving relatives climbed in a truck and headed for Heart Butte—another village on the reservation but on higher ground. "We were all in the back of this truck. Neighbor kids too. We tried to get to Heart Butte. The bridge was washing out. The water was blasting over the bridge. It was usually a little creek but now it was a river. Seven of those older guys went to check the bridge. They told my grandfather that to cross it you got to get to the center and gas it. Otherwise you're not gonna make it. There were seven or eight kids hanging on the back of the truck. We made it. Barely. We went to my uncle Dave's house. There must have been twenty or thirty people stranded at his house. People crying and sobbing about people in their families that had drowned. We were cut off. No bridges anywhere. The navy flew in medical supplies and food in a helicopter. I remember the day they flew in, we hid because we was told they was giving typhoid shots, and so we went and hid under this pine tree. We wouldn't come back after they were done. But we got shots anyway."

Even before the flood, life had been hard for David and his family. Their house on Birch Creek didn't have electricity or running water. Their father—a tank commander in the Korean War and a recipient of three Bronze Stars, a United Nations Peacekeepers Medal, a National Defense Service Medal, and the Korean Service Medal—was maniacally hard on his family. David wonders if it was the war or the life or both that made his father into what he was. "Our dad brought us up hard. Treated us like we were in the military. He practically raised himself. He was kind of booted out of his house by his stepfather. Raised by his aunts since he was four. I don't think he ever got over that. I remember when he'd come home drunk, raving and ranting, hating women. We didn't understand that." His father made the children stand at attention "and listen to his war stories till he went to sleep or got laid out. Sometimes it'd be daylight. We'd have to stand at attention till he was done. We'd stand there in our old shorts. Stand at attention! My two sisters would stand there in their nightgowns. At attention! We had to listen to that shit all night long. It was crazy. It was a hard life. They call that child abuse now. We had to do that for years. We got the blunt end of that."

Whether it was the flood that took their home and their neighbors or the rage of their father that swept comfort and care away in its own torrent, life was a precarious thing. So when the opportunity came for the Schildts to move to Los Angeles as part of the relocation program, the family enrolled. Perhaps because of his war service, David's father was admitted to a vocational program that would teach him to be a diesel mechanic, even though he'd attended school only through the sixth grade. In 1968, David, his parents, and ten other siblings piled into two cars and headed down to Los Angeles.

Upon their arrival in Los Angeles, the relocation program housed them in Compton. "When we come down to L.A. it was something we couldn't even believe. You see—we never seen a black person before in our lives! So they put us in Compton in a hotel when we first got there. It had a twenty-foot wire fence around it, and it was right beside the freeway. You'd see rivers of black people coming across. And we'd run to the fence and say, 'Man! Look! Look at those people!' We couldn't believe there were so many black people in the world. They kept us there in that fenced-in motel. We didn't leave. It's Compton in 1968 and all hell is breaking loose. We were there for a month or a month and a half." Next, the relocation program found a place for the Schildts in Burbank. "The high school was the John Burroughs High School. The John Burroughs Indians! How do you like that?" It does seem rather fitting that some of the Schildts would be attending a school named after the famous naturalist. David was in junior high school and attended the Luther Burbank Middle School, named for the horticulturist Luther Burbank, famous for breeding the Shasta daisy but mostly for developing the Russet Burbank potato, a blight-resistant variety meant to revive Ireland's leading crop after the devastating Irish Potato Famine. "I didn't know a soul when I got there," David recalls. After his one-room schoolhouse back in Montana, he says, "I was in the blind, socially and academically. We had a real limited education in Los Angeles. I flunked everything. But they still let me play basketball and track and field because they probably felt sorry for me. I had to learn to adjust, learn how to interact with other people. Learn to communicate with people who couldn't understand me. I had this friend who was a soccer player. Latino. He was interested in me because we were the same skin color. Initially we communicated through sign language. Somehow I got it across to him that I was Indian. He's like, 'Oh, Indio!' He was my friend for most of that year." Another friend gave him a bike. They biked to the Hollywood Bowl and snuck into a concert featuring Bob Dylan, George Harrison, Ravi Shankar, and Janis Joplin. "We crawled clear over the top of that Griffith Park mountain. I remember how it was like to crawl through the brush and that tall grass."

They lasted a year. "My dad couldn't do nothing down there. He didn't know nothing about math. He couldn't last. The only background he had was he was a tank commander. He could kill people. That was his only skill." And so back to Browning they went. A job opened up for his mother in Columbia Falls, but David was sixteen, and he had had it by then. "My dad, drunk one time, said to me, 'You gonna be seventeen someday and you're gonna be a man and you're gonna be on your own or you'll be in the army.'" Rather than live with his father or move to yet another new place, David asked if he could go to Flandreau Indian School in Flandreau, South Dakota.

"It was the safest place I'd ever lived. Flandreau Indian boarding school. Safest place ever. Three squares a day. A roof over my head. Night matron. Day matron. School. Coaches. I had everything I needed to be secure. And I excelled. I'll tell you what: when I was down there—we had a good time down there. I was in the rodeo club. I had a great time in sports. Athlete of the year. Set records. Triple jump. Went to state in pole vault. Big handful of medals." His time there wasn't without its bumps. "Forty or so of us got some alcohol and we all got kicked out of school, the day before graduation. And they told us since we got kicked out none of our credits count. I had to go back for another half year, but I didn't mind. I liked it there." But eventually Flandreau had to come to an end: he couldn't stay there forever.

It's hard, sometimes, to understand a life, to narrate it, when it doesn't have a through line. David's life feels this way to me. It has stops and starts, changes of altitude, different scenes come in and out of focus. After Flandreau he moved back to Browning. It was the only place he really knew, even if it didn't suit him. "I went from Flandreau, being very happy, to moving back to the rez and being very, very sad. It was a different world, and I had to survive somehow. I had no one to lean on. I remember being basically on welfare. I didn't have anyone I could lean on for a job." He started to drink. "I thought, 'This isn't me. What the hell am I doing this for?' I remember once I got drunk, stayed drunk for seven days straight. Bunch of us about the same age. Seventeen to twenty-one years old. I remember that one day just shaking, I was just so . . . saturated. I went back home to Birch Creek. And I thought, 'I gotta get out of here. I've got to get out of here or I'll die.' People told me, 'Life on the rez is tough and if you live till you're thirty years old you're gonna be lucky.' I believed them. So I started trying to make plans to get out of there somehow. The only way I could see was riding bulls. Started riding bulls and bareback horses. I got into the rodeo business." Life on the rez was so unsafe that climbing on top of a one-ton bull was better than living it out at Birch Creek.

And so David left. First, he went to college in Rapid City, mostly because he could ride on the rodeo team at the National College of Business located there. Or maybe he was in Billings first and later went to Rapid City. I'm not sure. The surer thing is to say that David spent the better part of the 1970s and 1980s hanging on the backs of bulls and, later, broncos. And it's when he talks about riding that his eyes come alive and he smiles, really smiles. "I've done so many things in my life, struggling, trying to survive. The only time I ever had money: I graduated in 1987 from college. In 1988, my second time I was in school, I got this offer from

Citibank: I could either have ten K in cash or I could take ten K on a credit card. I thought, 'Shit—I'll take the cash.' I bought myself this little van, recorded my first album, and then spent the rest of it over the summer, rodeoing. Four of us were in this van. Two of us were rodeoing. One rolling party all summer long."

One of them was Lakota, Ben, their de facto manager. He didn't ride. The other non-rider was a musician, a white guy. "We had some rough wrecks that summer. I saw my buddy Byron get kicked clean out of his shirt. He was laying there in the arena. Lost his chaps. Lost his shirt. Hoofprints on his chest from getting stomped on! I asked Ben if we should call his wife, and Ben says, 'Let's wait to see if he's alive.' He walked out of there with just a cracked rib." The four of them sat around and played music a lot—David played the guitar and even got a couple of songs on the Pine Ridge radio station. They stayed at a KOA campground and lived on baloney sandwiches and small payments from a work settlement Ben had gotten for a cancer he'd developed while working with oil containers. "That's how we survived all summer. Our goal initially was we were gonna sell my tapes and live off my music, but it turned into a running drunk all summer."

Once a bull stepped on his arm, which landed him in the hospital in Browning. "I've broken so many things. Fourteen breaks in my arms. Elbows. Wrists. Elbows. Collarbones. I thought I could make a living at riding bulls. But riding for most guys lasts about fifteen years, between the ages of twenty and thirty-five. I didn't quit riding bareback horses till I was in my forties. I finally got thrown out the back door in Palm Springs in 1990. I landed on my back and neck and couldn't feel my legs. I'm fourteen hundred miles from home and I am lying in the dirt and I can't move. I could hear the clown saying, 'Are you all right?' But after a while I started to feel tingling in my arms and legs. And I'm thinking, 'This is enough. This is enough.'"

So David went back to Billings. His girlfriend was managing a horse ranch, and she let him work with the quarter horse colts and mares. He stacked hay, helped with the fencing and irrigating and basic ranch work. "When you're in a state of survival, which I've been in most of my life, it changes every day. One day you're teaching school, the next day you're digging post holes. You go from a profession to a day job. Back and forth. Teacher's aide, taught college. Ranching, rodeoing, getting into movie work. That didn't work out.

"I even tried the music business. I was in Nashville. I recorded an album down there in 1994. For some reason I still don't understand, I got to travel with Vince Gill and Patty Loveless in 1996. Friend of mine was a senior light coordinator and he called me and asked if I wanted to come out with him on a few shows. I flew down and went out on the road with them." Back in Billings, his friend called him and told him that Vince was auditioning guitarists, and David's name came up. But he didn't have the funds to get to Nashville. "I've always been one of those guys who are in the wrong place at the wrong time. I was in the wrong place at the right time. But still it didn't work out."

Another time he got a call to audition for a singing cowboy part in a film in Virginia. "I said, 'Hell, I'm trying out for a part in *Last of the Mohicans.*'" But he was bronc riding at Madison Square Garden and couldn't get there in time, so the part went to Johnny Cash instead. "That's who they got! I didn't know at the time I was up against him!" An audition for another part, a stunt job, came through a cousin. "He says, 'Here's what you're gonna do—you're gonna go in there and wait for this guy to come and pick up a tomahawk and hit him.'" David hadn't mentioned he had a broken shoulder from a rodeo injury when he got bucked. "I got hung up on the stirrups and I couldn't get away and I got pulled underneath him and he just flailed me against the ground till it broke." He could barely lift his arm. "And so the next day I was in there and the guy comes running and I go to lift the tomahawk and I couldn't." It was a year before he could ride again. "I did, though. I rode at the Cheyenne Frontier Days. I got to compete and they played my album over the PA while I was riding. It was a dream come true. And they got me interviewed and in the newspaper. And all that kind of stuff. I was forty years old and was gonna ride. I didn't think it was that big of a deal. That horse bucked me off, he threw me so high I could see both sides of the arena. That old son of a gun bucked hard. If I could of got tapped on him that would have been ninety points. He bucked me good. And I went back to Billings and I thought, 'I'm not gonna retire as a loser.' So I started bareback riding. I got back in shape again. In 'ninety-seven, I got on a real good one in Birch Creek, Montana, Father's Day rodeo. And I won it. And I thought, 'This is as good a place as any to hang it up.' And I haven't been on one since. That's where I started and that's where I ended, after traveling over the whole goddamn U.S. and Canada. I've rode a whole lot of rodeos. National Indian Finals. Rode some big rank bastards in my life. And then I've had some horses buck me off too. It all evens out. Sooner or later you gotta let it go before it kills you. . . . The horses are always young and tough. The horses stay young and you get older. The horses get younger and you are getting older and there comes a time when you shouldn't get on them. I've seen guys get killed in the arena. I've seen four guys get killed. It happens fast. When it happens it does something to your mind."

Back and forth, up and down, holding on for dear life, getting bucked off but climbing back on: riding bulls and broncs was a bit like riding life for David. But he wasn't alone. Or rather, he was alone but in good company. More and more Indians were being pulled away from their communities on reservations that disappeared from underneath them. By the time David was a teenager in Los Angeles, more than a hundred reservations—most of them in California and Oregon—had been terminated and the Indians who had belonged to them were, technically, Indians no longer. People who had been in America before America existed, whose homeland the wide country had once been, were now homeless immigrants headed to cities across the country, like the immigrants from China, Germany, Italy, Ireland, and England before them. They ran into many of the same difficulties: segregation in crowded ghettos or enclaves, lack of access to education, and lack of access to capital as redlining prevented them from joining the millions of Americans who were enjoying home-ownership and admission to the middle class.

Termination was, by the 1960s, clearly a catastrophe. The gains tribes had made under the Indian Reorganization Act were wiped away. As flawed as the IRA was and as inadequate as tribal constitutions had been as a tool for tribal governance, they had created structural changes that pointed tribes in the right direction. And the "Indian New Deal" (as some have called the IRA), along with the New Deal itself, and then the postwar boom enjoyed by most Americans had been slowly changing the circumstances of hundreds of thousands of Indians in the form of tribal employment, housing, education, and hospitals. But no more. Under termination and relocation, unemployment skyrocketed and so did the number of Indians living under the poverty line. By 1970 half of all Indians lived in urban areas, the single largest demographic and cultural shift in Indian country in a century and arguably more pervasive and transformative than the reservation system established in the mid–nineteenth century. A total of 1,365,801 acres of land were removed from trust status during this period, and twelve thousand Indians lost their tribal affiliation.

President Lyndon Johnson shifted away from a policy of termination, but it wasn't officially ended until 1970 by his successor Richard Nixon, a surprisingly good president as far as federal Indian policy was concerned. In 1970 in a special address to Congress he said:

This policy of forced termination is wrong, in my judgment, for a number of reasons. First, the premises on which it rests are wrong. . . . The second reason for rejecting forced termination is that the practical results have been clearly harmful in the few instances in which termination actually has been tried. . . . The third argument I would make against forced termination concerns the effect it has had upon the overwhelming majority of tribes which still enjoy a special relationship with the Federal government. . . . The recommendations of this Administration represent an historic step forward in Indian policy. We are proposing to break sharply with past approaches to Indian problems.

Many tribes fought long, hard legal battles to regain their federal recognition and to have their lands returned to tribal ownership. Some, like the Menominee, successfully fought to be reincorporated and have their treaty rights restored. Some are still fighting.

But still: many Indians found new life in cities. They endured the poor housing, the distance from their homelands; they learned to be diasporic. They learned to be Indians of America rather than simply Indians in America. And, as with David's extended family, relocation wasn't necessarily a one-way street: Indians moved to the city and moved back to the reservation, or their children did. And while they were in cities they mixed not only with other races but with other tribes as well. Red Hall noted that the old tribal warfare, and the intertribal bigotry that marked tribal relations in the nineteenth century, faded away as Indians from vastly different tribes found themselves living as neighbors in the city. They found they had much more in common with one another: a shared historical experience if not shared cultures, the same class values, the same struggles. Networks among tribes—forged through marriage, school, city living, and service in the armed forces—were strengthened from 1940 to 1970.

Even David found this to be true, despite all the loss he'd experienced. "I'm a relocated Indian. I see myself as a classic example of what the government wants. The government wants you separated from your family, your home, your kids, your spiritual belief system, and they got you in the city, in white America. And now . . . you're just a number. If you don't tell people you're Native, they just don't know." There were times when he didn't see anyone, he recalls. "When I was in college, when Thanksgiving would come, or Christmas . . . I was working in the kitchen, the only guy left on campus, and I didn't have any way to get home. So I'd just go downtown and drink. It was the only way to get through the misery of the holiday season. Until I realized: the holidays don't mean anything, they are just another day." These days, his girlfriend is "bringing me back around, making me human again." He now works for China Camp State Park near San Rafael, California. "It's a nice outdoors job working in that park. Worst thing that happens is the coyotes eat someone's dog." He still has most of his medals and buckles and spurs—proof of a life lived. And he has a kind of peace. "All I want to do is work, pay my bills, and go home and be happy. I don't want anything else."

And yet—behind the cowboy songs and the belt buckles and the stories of mischief—there is a kind of sorrow in him. I can feel it. Part of it may be that he still hears the floodwaters of Birch Creek. Or the stream of cars in Compton in 1968, or his father's voice telling him to stand at attention. Or it could be that David—together with many, many other Indians—still feels the effects of termination and relocation in his body and in his mind. Federal policy isn't abstract unless you're rich. If you're not, it is something that affects your life and your blood and your bones. "I don't have nothing up in Montana. I don't have any land. I don't have a job. I don't know anybody. Some relatives I get along with. Some I don't." His voice trails off and then starts up again. "I was up there in May 2005. I was in my truck near East Glacier watching the mountains and I heard this horrible screaming and then . . . nothing. I drove down to the Palomino Bar in East Glacier and there were all sorts of trucks there. I asked what was happening and they said a park ranger had gone walking and never came back. I went home and went back the next day and there was a helicopter and crime tape and I saw this woman on her knees praying and crying. I went down to the bar and asked a buddy of mine what happened. This grizzly sow and two cubs attacked that ranger and ate her. Nothing of her left but her skull and her shoes. To this day I think I hear her screaming. I hear that in my head, in my sleep I hear that. Haunts the shit out of me. I'm trying to get away from that sound. That's one of the reasons I don't go back. There's a sound of horror in someone's voice. I've never been able to get that out of my head."

PART 5

Becoming Indian:
1970–1990

W elcome to my office!" Bob Matthews shouts with a smile, his arms raised to include the white spruce towering over our heads near Rabideau Lake just off the Leech Lake Indian Reservation in northern Minnesota. That smile is many things: part prelude to something crazy, part friendly, part that of someone who's won the game you didn't know you were playing. It's late August and the pinecones are coming in. We are each carrying a five-gallon bucket, a shallow white Tupperware tray, leather gloves with the fingers cut off, and a tube of Goop. We are looking for white spruce cones. Bobby is about to say something else, but then we hear the sound of a pickup rumbling over the washboard road. Bobby squints, as if that will clarify the sound somehow. "Get in the woods! We don't want anyone to know what we're up to!" And he dives into the trees.

The northern Minnesota woods into which we dive, once virgin white pine with an understory of spruce and birch, have been logged many times since the timber boom of the late nineteenth century. In place of the lonely majesty of old growth is a wild patchwork of poplar, spruce, jack pine, birch, and Norway pine in the uplands and ironwood, sugar maple, tag alder, basswood, ash, and elm in the lowlands. The whole region is scrubby, dense, at times impenetrable, united by vast swamps and slow-draining creeks, rivers, and lakes. The land—desolate in the winter and indescribably uncomfortable and nigh impassable in the summer—is easy enough to love in the abstract and from a distance. But up close there is a texture to it, a roughness if not a majesty. The spruce grow close together and block out the sun. The forest floor is dun-colored and the roots, varicose, stick up out of the soil. I, for one, love our woods. I love the complications, the puzzle of it. Once Bobby finds cones—green,

283

gummy, crescent-shaped cones about an inch and a half long, he drops to his knees and begins picking them off the ground and putting them on his tray with astonishing speed. "Here—take a bucket, a tray, and the Goop. The Goop's so the cones won't stick to your fingers and slow you down. You ever try to pick a bushel of them sumbitches with cones stuck all over your hands? Won't happen. That tray there, that's for speed, too. That way you don't have to lift your arm so high every time you get two or three cones in your hand. Just fill up the tray and then dump it in. I'm telling you, David! It's faster that way!" Bobby picks fast. The cones rattle in his tray till it's full, and then he dumps them into his bucket. They rattle as they fall in. To me it is a pleasant sound. To Bobby it sounds like money.

In the years after the financial crisis of 2008, the nation staggered under a 10 percent unemployment rate. Housing prices dropped. Economic growth stagnated. To read the news was to feel like you stumbled onto the chronicle of some bereaved monk in Siena in the year 1348: Death. Death. Death. All the bad luck felt like proof of some greater sin, with no way to atone. As the economic crisis deepened, there was a rise in back-to-the-land narratives, in which, typically, a bobo protagonist left sterile urban life to retrieve a direct, uncorrupted relationship with the animals and plants that sustain us. In some versions the back-to-the-lander became a farmer or rancher, but in its most primal form the fantasy was (and is) of becoming a hunter-gatherer who makes sunrise treks up mountains to bag an elk—with words of thanks to the beast for the sacrifice of its life—and spends nights in an off-the-grid cabin, with larch crackling in the fireplace.

Meanwhile, at Leech Lake and on other reservations like it, there was no crisis, or rather, the crisis was ongoing. While the rest of the world tried to starve itself back into shape, Leech Lake was coasting along with at least a 30 percent unemployment rate, little to no infrastructure, few entitlements, a safety net that never was, no industry to speak of, a housing crisis that had been dire not for five years but since the reservation's founding. And the hunter-gatherer, who was supposed to have died out in North America along with the buffalo, continued to live on—just not as in the romantic Anglo fantasy. Wanting to know what that looks like, I'd come back to Leech Lake to find Bobby Matthews. You'd hear Bobby's name whispered a lot when I was growing up. Who had the best rice? Bobby Matthews. Who had the *most* rice? Bobby Matthews. Who knew where the best boughs were for picking? Bobby Matthews. Who was the damnedest trapper in northern Minnesota? Bobby Matthews. At funerals and picnics and feasts and Memorial Day services at the cemetery— wherever you went on Leech Lake Reservation and even across northern Minnesota—when talk would turn to hunting or trapping or general woodsiness, his was the name that was always the one mentioned.

Bobby is not that tall—maybe five-foot-eight—but he has the arms and shoulders of a much larger man. His hair is thinning and gray and pulled back in a ponytail. He shaves once a year, on his birthday. His eyes are powerful, deep-set, searching. His voice, calm in one moment, will rise to a shout in the next. He speaks rapidly and has the rare habit of always using your name when he speaks to you. On the phone: *Hey, it's Dave.* Response: *How's David doing?* Many of his comments begin with *So I says, "Look here . . ."* One conversation: "So Dave, so the guy says to me, 'Where'd you get all those leeches, Bob?' And Dave, I says to him, I say, 'Well, look here, goddamn it, I got 'em in the getting place, that's where.' So I says, 'Does it look like I have STUPID written across my forehead? Why would I tell you where I got my leeches?' Can you believe it, David? Can you believe it?" Bobby is excited and excitable, and he laughs a lot. There is, under all his energy and excitement, the persistent threat of violence. Not directed at me or even at any other person, necessarily. It is the deep violence of the tribe—ready to erupt if necessary but usually held in check. Whatever happens, Bobby's going to go all the way. And often he's going to do it in the third person. There is something about him that remains thoroughly undomesticated. I can't imagine him doing anything as civilized or pointless as playing golf or going to the casino. He has the aspect of the wild animals he's spent his life pursuing. But there is something else in there, too, something finer—a profound and ultimately beautiful curiosity about the environment he inhabits. He is plagued by wonder.

He has spent much of his life on the question of how nature fits together and how it can serve him. "I begin each day like this, Dave. I get up at four-thirty and I turn on the coffee and I throw one of those rice bags you get at the drugstore in the micro, and when the coffee and the rice bag are done, I sit in my chair and drink my coffee and heat up my back a little and smoke a joint and look at my books. I look at my books, Dave, going back five, ten, fifteen years. I keep notes on everything I see. The temperature. The barometric pressure. Where is the wind coming from? What little flowers—I don't even know what they're called—are in bloom and how many leaves are on the trees. I keep track of all this stuff, Dave. I keep track of all of it in my books. So I can know the patterns. So I can compare one year to the next. No one sees my books, Dave. No one. Not ever. I told Julie [his wife] that when I die all my books go with me or she can burn 'em. When I'm done smoking, I head out and get to work. I'm out the door by five-thirty."

Bobby's life follows a rigid seasonal cycle. And the cycle revolves around money: he collects, harvests, and traps, and sells what he gets for profit. In the spring and early summer, he traps leeches for bait. Late summer, he begins picking pinecones and then stops to harvest wild rice. When the wild rice harvest is done he goes back to pinecones. After cones comes hunting, trapping, and more hunting. After the ground is frozen hard, he goes out in the swamps to cut cranberry bark, which will be sold as a natural remedy for menstrual cramps. By the time that's all done, he starts leeching again. When the zombie apocalypse comes, I am certain that I want to be with Bobby. I am in awe of him.

Bobby was born in the 1940s and grew up in Bena, my family's ancestral village. Like my mother, he is an Indian baby boomer, though they and their siblings and cousins and friends did not, as a rule, enjoy the benefits of America's "imperial century" the way their mainstream peers did, especially where termination and relocation had reversed the gains of the New Deal and Collier's "Indian New Deal." Still, some of ascendant America's success trickled down. Thousands of Indians who served in World War II and Korea made use of the GI Bill. Cars became more plentiful. A by-product of the shared experience and common language instilled, however brutally, by the boarding schools was the development of an intertribal sense of identity with shared historical experiences. Members of different tribes not only met and married and befriended one another; when they returned to their own tribal communities they brought with them a social network that often extended well beyond the borders of their community or tribe or language group. The same dynamic persisted into relocation and the new era of self-government under the Indian Reorganization Act. Many Indians now had family and kinship ties across ever greater distances. When they moved to cities, they often lived in almost exclusively Indian enclaves in places like Oklahoma City, Chicago, New York City, Minneapolis, Los Angeles, Phoenix, Denver, Cincinnati, and Seattle—but those enclaves were composed of Indians of many tribes. And when they returned to the reservation they no longer experienced it as such a sequestered place. Rather than eradicate Indians as Indians and reservations as Indian places, termination allowed Indians to understand themselves as part of a much larger historical process. They pooled their knowledge and brought it with them wherever they went. It is safe to say that "the Indian" probably didn't think of him- or herself as such until after 1950.

Even the disastrous land grabs that occurred as a result of allotment had their collateral benefits. While many millions of acres passed out of Indian control and into the hands of white farmers, homesteaders, businesses, and developers, Indians learned (the hard way) how landownership worked in the context of American capitalism: fee-simple patenting, real estate taxes, land values, leases, rents, mortgages, liens. They needed this knowledge when new tribal governments were formed in the 1930s. And they needed it again when the government tried to shove termination down their throats; it helped them to fight the policy long enough that it died before their communities did. Allotment also meant that Indians suddenly had a lot of white neighbors, and many millions of Americans had Indian neighbors, too. They met and married and mingled and went to the same schools and (when there was work) worked at the same places. Contact with white people changed Indian culture, but contact with Indians and Indian cultures changed the white people who came to live among them as well.

By the time Bobby Matthews was a teenager in the 1960s, half of all Indians lived in cities and towns, and that half was in close and constant contact with the half that remained on reservations. His father, Howard, had been one of the first tribal leaders to exercise power under the IRA constitution that came to Leech Lake in the 1930s. Although Bobby was around the same age as the activists who came up in the 1960s and 1970s, he didn't have much to do with them or their movements. When I asked him if he knew Dennis Banks (the American Indian Movement leader from Leech Lake who eventually resettled on the reservation), he said, *Don't know the man. Can't say I ever met him.* Yet, at least to me, he has a similar kind of wildness, a similar intensity. And to my mind he took his own path toward the activists' goals of becoming Indian and reminding America of its promises to us—not through protest and politics, but through learning to live a life on the land, an Indian life. In the 1960s and 1970s, Indians were growing in numbers and in strength. And they were growing to be more "of America" and not merely "in America." So it should have come as no surprise that the civil rights movement that was beginning to rock the country had a counterpart that rocked Indian communities and would grow, by the 1970s, to capture the attention of the entire country.

The Rise of Red Power

Like the mass migration of Indian people from reservations to cities, the rise of Red Power, and on its heels the American Indian Movement, reflected both federal Indian policy and larger demographic shifts. After World War II, many African American veterans and ordinary citizens looked at what the fight for world freedom had given them and found America wanting: they saw a considerable gap between how America saw itself and the policies it practiced. For African Americans, segregation in housing and education, high rates of unemployment, and other forms of unequal treatment meant that they lacked the means to get ahead.

Beginning in Ohio in the 1940s and spreading to the South and East, many African Americans and their allies used the principle of direct action to bring their grievances to the forefront of American consciousness. Despite Truman's integration of the armed forces in 1948, among other measures, by the beginning of the 1950s, segregation was increasing. White people were fleeing to the new suburbs ringing American cities, helped by the government's getting into the lending industry. Guidelines issued by the National Association of Realtors to their representatives in 1950 admonished them that they "should never be instrumental in introducing to a neighborhood a character of property or occupancy, *members of any race or nationality*, or any individual whose presence will be clearly detrimental to property values in a neighborhood." While the NAACP, founded in 1909, stood true to its mission to "ensure the political, educational, social, and economic equality of rights of all persons and to eliminate racial hatred and racial discrimination" via lobbying, publicity, and lawsuits, progress was piecemeal and slow. In the spring of 1951, black students at Moton High School in Virginia protested the effects of radically unequal segregation and demanded better conditions for themselves. The NAACP joined their fight and four other cases of school segregation, efforts that culminated in *Brown v. Board of Education* in 1954. This was a key victory, but such methods were still too gradualist for many African Americans. While the NAACP and other organizations like it continued their steady work, many citizens began to take part in boycotts, sit-ins, marches, public demonstrations, and other forms of civil disobedience, often in coordination with other social justice organizations.

American Indians had been organizing similarly. In 1944, scores of delegates from fifty tribes met in Denver to form the National Congress of American Indians (NCAI). Their goal was to unite in force to stop the federal policy of termination, to work together to resist bad federal policy, and, in response to the 1934 Indian Reorganization Act, to strengthen the ties between tribal governments. The Denver congress was led largely by men who had worked in the Office of Indian Affairs, but by the time of the second congress a year later, many delegates were women, and people who worked directly for the federal government were deemed ineligible for leadership positions because of possible conflicts of interest. Yet whereas the NAACP and other African American organizations and movements had a clear common goal of equal rights under the law, as members of sovereign nations Indians had a somewhat different stance. The NCAI therefore fought for equal rights and equal protection, but it also lobbied for the restoration of treaty rights, the reclamation of land, and respect for cultural and tribal religious practices. It was, and is, a very effective organization. Among other victories, it overcame federal job discrimination against Indians, stopped a ban on reservations in the founding documents for Alaskan statehood, limited state jurisdiction over Indian civil and criminal cases, and addressed in a consistent and effective manner broad issues of health care, employment, and education. However, the NCAI had a strict policy against the kind of direct action that was proving so effective in the battles for racial equality springing up across America. Unlike the NAACP, which initially urged the students at Moton High School not to protest but then joined them, the NCAI made no such common cause with groups engaged in direct action, a resistance that earned it a reputation as being gradualist to the point of collaboration. Just as direct action for African American civil rights grew alongside more gradualist approaches initially supported by the NAACP, so, too, direct action among Indian activists and students grew up alongside the NCAI.

National Indian Youth Council and Red Power

Despite the ways in which Indian communities were growing, strengthening, and resisting, most change in the first half of the twentieth century had been imposed on Indian communities from the top down with every switch in federal Indian policy. But change was coming from within Indian communities, too. While the NCAI had attempted, through the 1950s and 1960s, to work with and from within the system, its more conservative members were purged in the 1960s, and the intellectual firebrand Vine Deloria Jr., a Sioux from Standing Rock Reservation in North Dakota, became executive director in 1964. Another organization sprang up in the 1950s, however, with a different philosophy and outlook: the National Indian Youth Council (NIYC). It was led by Clyde Warrior, a Ponca from Oklahoma who was a magnetic powwow dancer and truly a man of his people. Warrior had attended seminars and summer programs administered by the Southwest Regional Indian Youth Council meant to educate a new generation of Indian leaders on Indian history, federal policy, and the like, and he had learned from them, but he wanted more. In the late 1950s, he wrote that as the "white man tends to rate the Indian as being lazy and worthless . . . the Indian seems to make it a point to act and be exactly as he's rated." This was part of the problem. The other part of the problem was that programming meant to help Indians—national housing initiatives, health care, educational opportunities, and leadership training programs—was run by non-Indians: it came from the outside. The two parts of the problem came together in such a way as to prevent Indian people from charting their own destiny. As another young NIYC leader, Browning Pipestem, put it, Warrior wanted to take the "negative image of the Indians and shove it down people's throats."

When he ran for the presidency of the Southwest Regional Indian Youth Council in 1960, rather than prepare a speech or outline a policy position, Warrior mounted the stage, pushed back his cowboy hat, rolled up his sleeves, and exposed his brown forearms. "This is all I have to offer," he told the attendees. "The sewage of Europe does not flow through these veins." He won. His message was beginning to win, too: being Indian was good, and what culture and tradition Indians maintained were good as well, and sufficient to the task of being Indian in the twentieth century and beyond. It doesn't sound so radical in our age of identity politics, but it was radical then, especially among Indians. Hundreds of years of being missionized, colonized, reservationized, mainstreamed, marginalized, and criminalized had had a pernicious effect on Indian self-regard. How not to think of oneself as less, how not to think of oneself and one's place as at the bottom of hierarchical America after being downtrodden for a century? As leader of first the Southwest Regional Indian Youth Council and, later, the National Indian Youth Council, Warrior managed to make his philosophy felt. Instead of holding meetings in city hotels, as the NCAI did, the groups met on reservations. Every meeting concluded with drumming and singing, often led by Warrior himself. By 1966 the NIYC was involved in direct action—in the Pacific Northwest—over treaty and fishing rights. Indians from around the country participated in "fish-ins" to protest the abrogation of treaty rights in the Pacific Northwest. "It was a major source of encouragement and hope to have a Ponca from Oklahoma, a Paiute from Nevada, a Tuscarora from New York, a Flathead from Montana, a Navajo from New Mexico, a Mohawk from Michigan, and a Pottawatomie [*sic*] from Ford Motors among others offering to fight for their cause," remembered activist Hank Adams after the protest. It was doing what other organizations weren't: pursuing tribal sovereignty by engaging in direct conflict with the U.S. government in a way that embraced Indianness as the most potent weapon in Indians' arsenal, rather than settling for the weapons given to them by a government they were trying to change.

Warrior published an essay in the NIYC newspaper titled "Which One Are You? Five Types of Young Indians." The first type was the "Slob or Hood," the Indian who lived up to the worst expectations of his character; the second was the "Joker," who engaged in a kind of redface minstrelsy to prove to white society he was likable and harmless; the third was the "Redskin 'White-Noser' or 'Sell-out,'" who likewise went to great lengths to ingratiate himself; the fourth was the "Ultra 'Pseudo-Indian,'" who claimed to be Indian but had no real connection to anyone or any place; and the last was the "Angry Nationalist," who rejected the path laid out for him by American society but who needed real connection to other Indians and to Indian homelands. In Warrior's estimation, this last was the closest to the kind of Indian to be, as it was the best suited to provide the "genuine contemporary creative thinking, democratic leadership to set guidelines, cues and goals for the average Indian. The guidelines and cues have to be *based on true Indian philosophy geared to the modern times.*"

By 1970, half of all Indians lived in cities rather than on the reservation. By government design and necessity, they had become "American," but for the most part, they had become Americans at the bottom. Their life expectancy was between fifty and sixty-five years, compared with seventy and over for whites. Indian infant mortality was half again as much as that of white babies. Even as late as 1988, Indians age fifteen to twenty-five were twice as likely to die in vehicular accidents and three times as likely to commit suicide. Middle-aged Indians committed suicide twice as often as whites, had incidents of liver disease nearly six times higher, died in car wrecks three times as often, and were three times more likely to be murdered. And there were more than four times as many deaths due to diabetes among Indians aged forty-five to sixty-four as among whites of the same age. Some—like Clyde Warrior—turned their dissatisfaction into informed and passionate protest. Others, like Russell Means (later, when the American Indian Movement, or AIM, took the stage), embraced violence as an almost aesthetic calling, in their rhetoric and in fact. Others, as the statistics show, did violence to their loved ones and themselves in the form of assault, domestic abuse, rape, child abuse, drinking, drugs, and suicide. But for all the grim statistics, there were corresponding shifts in the direction of Indian lives. And the two tendencies were related.

Even as many Indians had moved to cities, they had begun looking back over their shoulders. Perhaps the most important lesson of a government that had done its best to have its way with them might be that the good old days before the coming of the white man had actually been good after all, and that to think so offered something more than the pleasure of nostalgia. Indians began looking to themselves—to their cultures and religions and lifeways—to sustain them. As unrealistic or out-of-control as some of the activist leadership may have been, the aesthetic it promoted— long hair and big belt buckles and beadwork—spoke of something deeper: a profound sense that if America wasn't going to serve Indian people, a newfound or lingering, never-quite-extinguished sense of personal and cultural dignity vested in Indian practices might. This didn't mean dismissing all the skills and opportunities their American experience had afforded them, at great cost. Indians were figuring out how to be Indian and American simultaneously. Yet they did so with growing impatience with gradual systematic change. As the 1960s drew to a close, Indian activists began to look not toward the NAACP for a model of resistance but to the Black Panthers, which had been born out of a similar dissatisfaction with gradualist approaches.

Panthers and Red Power

While the combined efforts of direct action and the steady work of the NAACP had done much to reduce the structures of racism in the South and in federal law, they had done not quite as much to address the conditions of urban blacks in the North who encountered new forms of poverty and new iterations of racism. As white flight to the suburbs increased, African Americans found themselves isolated and concentrated in decaying urban centers with few job prospects, substandard housing, failing schools, and overtly racist, nonblack police forces. For young blacks in places like Oakland, where a mere sixteen of the city's 661 police officers were black when the Black Panther Party for Self-Defense was founded in 1966, civil rights solved only part of the problem. Civil rights appeared barely able to deliver equality at the bottom of the socioeconomic ladder; how were African Americans going to achieve economic and political power? In a country that valorized the middle class, exclusion from it was just another face of imperialism. It was in response to this dilemma (and pervasive police brutality) that Huey Newton and Bobby Seale, both of whom had worked extensively in community clinics and organizations in Oakland, formed the Black Panther Party. One of the immediate catalysts was the killing of a black teen by police; the subsequent riots across the city prompted Newton and Seale to make good on their ideas to harness black urban rage and bend it toward the fight for political power. And so they set up the Panthers as a self-consciously militant force.

The Panthers' first big action was to make use of California's lax open-carry laws and have members armed with shotguns and rifles follow Oakland police around the city. They set themselves up as watchdogs on a police force notorious for its excesses. Less than a year later, more than thirty Black Panthers showed up, nineteen of them armed, at the California statehouse, where the party promoted a ten-point plan (though "wish list" might be a better description) that was later published in the Black Panthers' newspaper in November 1967. Each heading was followed by passionate and lucid argument. The headings read:

1. We want freedom. We want power to determine the destiny of our Black Community.
2. We want full employment for our people.
3. We want an end to the robbery by the white man of our Black Community.
4. We want decent housing, fit for shelter of human beings.
5. We want education for our people that exposes the true nature of this decadent American society. We want education that teaches us our true history and our role in the present-day society.
6. We want all black men to be exempt from military service.
7. We want an immediate end to **police brutality** and **murder** of black people.
8. We want freedom for all black men held in federal, state, county and city prisons and jails.
9. We want all black people when brought to trial to be tried in court by a jury of their peer group or people from their black communities, as defined by the Constitution of the United States.
10. We want land, bread, housing, education, clothing, justice and peace.

Arresting as televised images of armed black men in leather jackets outside the statehouse or in the streets were, the group also worked hard in their own communities. Beyond the violence and theatrics for which most people remember them, they had a strong community-action component to their mission. They organized citizen patrols, health clinics, day-care facilities, and schools. They disseminated information and registered voters. The party itself eventually crumbled under internal and external forces: a power-hungry leadership given to excesses of violence and prone to internecine fights and undermining by the FBI under J. Edgar Hoover, who called the organization "the greatest threat to the internal security of the country." By the 1980s, the Black Panthers had ceased to exist as a viable political force in the urban American landscape. But before it did, urban Indians in Minneapolis, San Francisco, and other American cities had been watching. And they liked what they saw.

The Rise of the
American Indian Movement

The early founders of AIM—mostly Ojibwe in Minneapolis—looked around at the South Minneapolis neighborhood along the Franklin Avenue corridor and asked themselves what the Indian Reorganization Act, the Indian Claims Commission, termination, and relocation had done for them. In 1970, the unemployment rate for Indians was ten times higher than the national average, and 40 percent of Indians, on and off the reservation, lived below the poverty level. The average life expectancy for Indians was substantially lower than the average for whites. Indians in Minneapolis also endured, as African Americans endured, racist policing, redlining of residential districts, a lack of adequate schools, and terrible housing—the worst in the state. A particular grievance, according to Dennis Banks, one of the founders of the movement, was the police's habit, on any given Friday night, of bursting into one of the Indian bars that lined Franklin Avenue and arresting everyone for drunk and disorderly conduct. They'd exploit the detainees for free labor over the weekend, then release them on Monday morning.

Banks, along with the Ojibwe brothers Clyde and Vernon Bellecourt, George Mitchell, and the Oneida Harold Powless, formed the American

Indian Movement. Like the Black Panthers, they were primarily concerned with Indians' economic independence and freedom from police brutality. And they were drawn to the militant theatrics of the Black Panthers as a way of making visible the country's most invisible minority. Their first act was to form AIM Patrols that, modeled on the Panthers, followed police around their neighborhood and documented instances of police brutality. Meanwhile other Indian militants—the National Indian Youth Council and the Red Power Movement—were planning other actions, with a view to the impact they'd make on TV.

In November 1969, students and activists in the Bay Area took over Alcatraz Island. The takeover was, initially at least, the child of Red Power and student activists, but it would become part of the mythology of AIM. The Bay Area had become one of the urban power nodes for Indians beginning in the 1950s. Some Indians had migrated there on their own from tribes across the country; others had been moved there during termination and relocation in the 1950s, and yet others had been drawn to the liberal admissions policies of the University of California system. Interest in the former prison had been brewing ever since Alcatraz was closed in 1963 because of rising maintenance costs and crumbling structures. The activists were motivated by a clause in a treaty with the Lakota saying that they had the right to occupy any abandoned federal buildings for their own use. Alcatraz was federal and, though it was far from their homeland, it was abandoned. On March 8, 1964, some forty Indians—among them two welders, a housepainter, and a Lakota navy shipyard worker named Walter Means and his twenty-six-year-old son, Russell—took boats out to the island and claimed it on behalf of America's first peoples. Allen Cottier, a descendant of Crazy Horse, read a statement in which the occupiers offered to pay the federal government forty-seven cents an acre (the going rate for unsettled one-hundred-year-old Indian land claims in California). The protesters were surprised by the degree and intensity of public support, and while the coverage eventually died out and the lawsuits fizzled, the Indians hoped that their publicity stunt would spark a movement. Five years later, it did.

Among those inspired by the Alcatraz protest was Adam Nordwall, an

Ojibwe business leader who had moved to the Bay Area from the Red Lake Reservation in the 1950s and owned a pest control company. (Later, in 1973, Nordwall would fly to Italy, don powwow regalia in the airplane bathroom, and upon landing claim the country by right of discovery.) Another was Richard Oakes, a charismatic young Mohawk steelworker who—while in the middle of a bridge contract in Rhode Island—pulled up stakes and drove to the Bay Area. "I just decided to go to California, gave up everything, and drove right across the country." Once there, he ended up working as a bartender, where he saw the worst of urban Indian life on display. "What I saw . . . was the bickering and barroom fights between the Indians, the constant drinking. Drinking seems to fill a void in the lives of many Indians. It takes the place of the singing of a song, the sharing of a song with another tribe. . . . Drinking is used as a way to *create* feelings of some kind where there aren't any. . . . I saw the end of the rainbow: the wrong end." Like Nordwall, Oakes wanted something more for Indians in the Bay Area. As the men dreamed their separate dreams, San Francisco was trying to dream up its own solution to the crumbling hulk that was Alcatraz. Lamar Hunt—Texas oilman, founder of the American Football League, owner of the Kansas City Chiefs, originator of the Super Bowl—wanted to turn the site into a complex that would include a futuristic space exploration museum, shops, restaurants, and apartments. But when the San Francisco American Indian Center burned to the ground in October 1969, Nordwall and Oakes had a place on which to pin their dreams for Indians: Alcatraz could be the site of an expanded Indian center in the mouth of San Francisco Bay.

The spirit of the concept was laudable, but the practicalities were problematic: Why build a center reachable only by boat that even the federal government couldn't afford to maintain, to serve a population so poor and so scattered that most lacked cars? As AIM chroniclers Paul Chaat Smith and Robert Allen Warrior note, "It was almost as if a collective hallucination had drifted over from the Haight." Nevertheless, plans for a takeover of Alcatraz moved quickly. Oakes met with students, Nordwall met with other leaders, and the two met each other, at a Halloween party thrown by a local reporter, and joined forces. The activist equivalent of a soft opening was announced for November 9. Boats were arranged, reporters were notified. At the appointed time, everyone gathered at the wharf—except the boats weren't there. Finally Oakes sweet-talked the owner of a three-masted schooner, the *Monte Cristo*, into bringing them across. When they neared the island, Oakes and some others stripped off their shirts and jumped into the bay to swim the last leg. They returned to the wharf an hour later, shivering, but alive with the possibility of a real takeover at some point in the future.

On November 20, Oakes and seventy-seven other Indians—mostly students—arrived on the island with plans to stay. But the occupation was fraught from the beginning. Many of the Indians hadn't brought clothing, basic supplies, warm jackets, or bedrolls. Many of them, however, brought a lot of pot. In the egalitarian and anarchic spirit of the times, the activists initially eschewed a leadership structure, but they soon had to accept that that didn't work, so they formed a leadership council. Oakes was tagged as spokesman for the occupation, but he and Nordwall quarreled from the start. (Jockeying for power and position became a recurring melody in the song of American Indian social movements beginning with Alcatraz.) At some times, the occupiers scrounged to feed themselves; at others, donated food and other supplies threatened to sink the island. On Thanksgiving the island was littered with frozen turkeys. The rock group Creedence Clearwater Revival donated a boat to the cause but failed to donate a skipper. In the news the occupation sounded great, but on the ground it was a mess.

The leaders met with representatives from the state of California, but the negotiations soured. President Nixon, notoriously uninterested in domestic affairs, nevertheless was something of a friend to "the Indian." He had been raised Quaker, and the Quakers had a long history of supporting Indian causes. His revered football coach at Whittier College, Wallace "Chief" Newman, was a full-blooded Luiseño from the La Jolla Reservation. Nixon wrote that "I think I admired him more and learned more from him than any other man aside from my father. He drilled into me a competitive spirit and the determination to come back after you have been knocked down or after you lose. He also gave me an acute understanding that what really matters is not a man's background, his color, his race, or his religion, but only his character." Nixon's vice president, Spiro Agnew, urged him to find common ground with the Indians on Alcatraz as well. Nevertheless, negotiations with the federal officials Nixon sent failed. But nothing hurt the effort more than the internecine fights between the group's leaders. They used the attention of celebrities like Creedence Clearwater Revival and Anthony Quinn and Jonathan Winters to jockey for attention. Oakes was accused of keeping donations and money for himself. In early January 1970, his twelve-year-old daughter, Yvonne, fell from a structure on the island; she died five days later. Oakes and the rest of his family left, though he continued to fight for Indian rights until he was shot to death in an altercation with a YMCA camp manager in 1972.

Conditions on the island worsened. Communication to the mainland was cut and the death of Yvonne Oakes soured many occupiers and supporters on the whole endeavor. People were living in squalor, violence spiked. Public support waxed, then waned. Cut off on the mainland, Nordwall drifted away from the occupation. With Oakes and Nordwall gone, LaNada Boyer Means (unrelated to Russell Means), John Trudell, and Stella Leach took the lead. LaNada Means (Shoshone-Bannock) was the first Native student at UC Berkeley when she entered in 1968; two years later there were only four. (She was later instrumental in establishing the Ethnic Studies Program at Berkeley: a positive and powerful postscript to a troubled moment in Indian activism.) They tried to continue negotiations to turn the island into a cultural center, but talks with Bob Robertson of the National Council on Indian Opportunity soured and died. Fires destroyed several buildings. The federal government began the process of transferring the island to the National Park Service, and on June 11, 1971, it had the remaining fifteen protesters forcibly removed. After nineteen months, the occupation was over.

In the end Alcatraz became part of the national park system. No Indian educational and/or cultural center was built there. The episode had a deep and lasting impact, however. It caught the attention (and sympathy) of the Nixon administration and was hugely influential in Nixon's decision to formally end the termination period. And it inspired AIM to bigger actions. In 1970, AIM occupied an abandoned property at a naval air station in Minneapolis in order to draw attention to Indian educational needs. In the same year, the organization took over a dam on the Lac Courte Oreilles Reservation in Wisconsin in order to secure reparations for the largely illegal flooding of much of the reservation. (The damage claims from the dams were eventually settled, though it would be a stretch to suggest that AIM's involvement led directly to the settlement.) In 1971, AIM also briefly took over BIA headquarters in Washington, D.C., in order to protest BIA policies and paternalism. Twenty-four members were arrested for trespassing. Although there were no concessions, at a BIA meeting convened after the protesters were removed, BIA commissioner Louis Bruce showed his AIM membership card.

In 1972, AIM embarked on its biggest action yet. In the summer, Robert Burnette, chairman of the Rosebud Reservation in South Dakota, gave voice to the idea of a caravan that would travel from reservation to reservation across the country in order to draw media attention to the struggles of Indians there and to the federal government's failure to address them or to meet its treaty obligations to sovereign Indian nations. He dubbed the procession the "Trail of Broken Treaties." AIM, sensing an opportunity— and eager to get back to Washington and get what it wanted, fortified with many more people and a bona fide mission—jumped on board and began organizing in cities across the country. They were emboldened by the support of tribal leadership on the reservations, including the blessing of traditional elders, and spurred on by the murder of Richard Oakes in September. George Mitchell and other leaders in Minneapolis drafted a twenty-point list of demands, and in October a caravan of cars, vans, and buses started off from the West Coast, gathering momentum as it moved east. In Minneapolis a critical mass collected, pausing for a week of meetings, civil disobedience, and car repairs before continuing on. AIM was a relatively new organization at this point and had the chance, in 1972, to learn that coalitions matter, that allies matter, that methods matter. The Trail of Broken Treaties was widely supported by Indian citizens and by a host of other organizations. Material, administrative, social, and political support for the action was offered by the Native American Rights Fund, the National Indian Youth Council, the National Indian Leadership

Training Program, the American Indian Committee on Alcohol and Drug Abuse, the National American Indian Council, the National Council on Indian Opportunity, and even the National Indian Brotherhood (an organization from Canada). But the resulting standoff with the government would be AIM's show. Never again would AIM receive that kind of broad support, especially after violence seeped into its character in the way it did.

The caravan began to arrive in Washington, D.C., a few hundred Indians strong, on November 1, 1972, a week before the presidential election. As at Alcatraz, they arrived with no food and no place to stay. The permits they had applied for, to protest near the Washington Monument, had been denied, and government officials (keenly aware of the advancing caravan) had quietly shut down any places where the Indians could protest, hold press conferences, or even stay. They found refuge in the basement of St. Stephen and the Incarnation Episcopal Church at Sixteenth and Newton in the northwest quadrant of the city, a predominantly black area. Police convened at the church and refused to leave when the pastor told them to get lost. Meanwhile, the congregation was confused, the kitchen staff was overwhelmed, and there was no space for the youth activities the church normally sponsored. Tensions escalated between the Indian activists and the black teens who wanted their space back, and soon the police stood between the two groups. Eventually the police left and tensions eased, but the situation was obviously untenable.

On November 3, the Indians headed to Lafayette Park and then, without much forethought, to the Bureau of Indian Affairs: if the White House was going to shut them out of D.C., they would go to the agency tasked with helping Indians. Late in the morning, they entered the BIA with their bedrolls and belongings and gathered in the auditorium. The leaders crowded into the offices of Harrison Loesch, assistant secretary for public land management, and John Crow of the BIA. Loesch, alarmed that the Indians intended to stay, complained that they had been let into the building only for a meeting. Everything went south from there. At an AIM press conference on the building steps, Russell Means channeled the legitimate grievances that had brought the caravan to D.C., and its frustration at the government's failure to engage with them, into what would be his characteristic tendency toward violence. He told the crowd that "without meaningful change white America will not have a happy Bicentennial celebration. You can see the frustration here, in the young people and even in the old. Our full-bloods, the chiefs of our tribes, are saying it's time to pick up guns."

Almost immediately, the government scrambled to find accommodations for the protesters—more to keep the machinery of Washington running smoothly before the election than because they were seriously worried about armed resistance. Loesch worked a minor miracle and found housing at churches, synagogues, the Salvation Army, and even at Bolling and Andrews Air Force Bases. But sensing a shift in power, the Indians not only refused to leave the BIA but also demanded a meeting with one of Nixon's representatives, preferably John Ehrlichman (who twenty months later would be convicted of conspiracy, obstruction of justice, and perjury for his part in the Watergate scandal and subsequent cover-up). Ehrlichman appointed Brad Patterson to represent the White House, and a meeting was scheduled, initially for three in the afternoon. But then the government postponed the meeting till eight that night, and in the meantime police began to mass outside the building. The occupiers got nervous, and around five p.m. they took over the building and barricaded the doors. Panic ensued. BIA workers escaped out of windows and down fire escapes. One pro-Indian lawyer was lowered to the ground out of a window by AIM leader Clyde Bellecourt.

On Friday, November 3, there were resolutions and meetings and countermeetings and then more resolutions. Security forces were ready to forcibly evict the protesters but received instructions from Nixon not to. He preferred to stall through court orders and negotiations rather than risk confrontations on the eve of the election. Some agreements were reached and the occupiers were set to leave when, suddenly distrustful, they reoccupied the building. The occupiers put out a call for help, and boxes of food and clothing were donated, and so was a teepee, which was set up out front with a sign that read "NATIVE AMERICAN EMBASSY"—just the sort of photo op AIM was keen for. Marion Barry, then on the Washington, D.C., school board, stopped by. So did LaDonna

Harris, president of Americans for Indian Opportunity, who was later instrumental in helping the Menominee regain tribal recognition and Taos Pueblo regain control of sacred Blue Lake. Late on Friday, more than a hundred protesters armed with broomsticks and makeshift clubs faced off with U.S. marshals in front of the BIA, but the marshals didn't engage them, and the situation deescalated. By Saturday the battle had moved to the courts after a judge issued an order for the arrest of the protesters, but the occupiers were still restive. Means and others painted their faces, again fanning the flames of violence. "War paint traditionally means that the Indian who is going into battle is prepared to die," he told reporters. "If federal officers are ordered to evict us, we know there will be Indian deaths." But why? And over what exactly?

The occupiers finally released the twenty-point memo they'd drafted back in Minneapolis. Its provisions included:

1. Restoration of constitutional treaty-making authority
2. Establishment of treaty commission to make new treaties
3. An address to the American people & joint sessions of Congress
4. Commission to review treaty commitments & violations
5. Resubmission of unratified treaties to the Senate
6. All Indians to be governed by treaty relations
7. Mandatory relief against treaty rights violations
8. Judicial recognition of Indian right to interpret treaties
9. Creation of congressional joint committee on reconstruction of Indian relations
10. Land reform and restoration of a 110 million-acre Native land base
11. Revision of 25 U.S.C. 163; restoration of rights to Indians terminated by enrollment and revocation of prohibitions against "dual benefits"
12. Repeal of state laws enacted under Public Law 280 (1953)
13. Resume federal protective jurisdiction for offenses against Indians
14. Abolition of the Bureau of Indian Affairs by 1976
15. Creation of an "Office of Federal Indian Relations and Community Reconstruction"

16. Priorities and purpose of the proposed new office
17. Indian commerce and tax immunities
18. Protection of Indians' religious freedom and cultural integrity
19. National referendums, local options, and forms of Indian organization
20. Health, housing, employment, economic development, and education

Many of the demands were sensible and might have been enacted with little difficulty. Framing crimes perpetrated by non-Indians against Indians as federal crimes would certainly have taken the prosecution of those crimes out of the racialized localities in which they were committed. Termination and relocation legislation was already being rolled back and could have been pushed along faster and more completely. The government might have been pressured to recommit to, and to privilege, the treaty agreements it so rarely honored. It was also not only possible but necessary to restructure or at least to restaff the BIA, given the corruption and mismanagement that had plagued the office since its inception. Other demands, however, were plainly out of the realm of possibility: giving 110 million acres back to the Indians; reopening the treaty-making process; removing the U.S. Congress from the government-to-government relationship between tribes and the federal government. The AIM leadership demanded a meeting with Nixon. Nixon refused. The "leadership," after all, had not been elected or otherwise officially appointed, so they were hardly in a position to reaffirm a government-to-government relationship between tribes and the federal government.

By Monday, whatever goodwill had existed within the government had evaporated. Election Day was twenty-four hours away. The government had in its hand a court order for the eviction and arrest of the protesters. Upon hearing this, the protesters erupted into an orgy of violence. They made a big show of ripping open cabinets, burning files and desks, and tearing out fixtures. By the time they were done, they had caused more than $2 million worth of damage. Nixon muttered that he was "through doing things to help Indians." His special consultant Leonard Garment, however, thought it was worth the effort to try for one last round of meetings.

Garment tagged Frank Carlucci to do the talking. Carlucci, a midlevel CIA agent who would later be implicated in the murder of Congolese independence leader Patrice Lumumba, would become part of the "government within the government" in the CIA and then the Department of Defense and an informal adviser under presidents Nixon, Carter, Reagan, and Bush. He seemed perfect for the job—stable, dark, sneaky, and sensitive to the place where power and desire overlapped. He immediately engaged the AIM leaders in negotiations, and by the next day, the government had agreed to give them $66,650 to help the caravan return home. The money was transferred in cash to Vernon Bellecourt in the presence of AIM leaders and officials from the NCAI, the Office of Economic Opportunity, and the White House. It is unclear what happened to it after that, but most of the caravan had to find their own way back to their communities. Rumors circulated that while a portion of the money was later used at Wounded Knee, some of it paid for AIM leadership to fly home in comfort. This was never proved. In any event, the occupation was over, with little accomplished.

AIM had begun to forge its image, however—that of the proud Plains warrior fighting the overwhelming forces of whiteness that sought to erase him. And it was a "him"—women were often forced to march in the

Meeting during the American Indian Movement takeover
of the Bureau of Indian Affairs building in Washington, D.C., 1972

Black Community Survival Conference, Oakland, California, March 30, 1972

back of a protest or asked not to march at all, as were lighter-skinned Indians. The leaders were obsessed with image and given to grandstanding.
Yet in the midst of the counterculture movement that co-opted so much
Indian aesthetic and culture, AIM was doing one thing right: it was showing Indians around the country that they were proud of being Indian, and
in the most uncomfortable ways possible for the mainstream. Indians
from reservations and cities alike were, for the first time, pushing back
against the acculturation machine that was a part of America's domestic
imperial agenda, and doing it loud and proud. My uncle Bobby Matthews
was of that generation. AIM came up when he came up, though violence
and tradition were combined differently in him.

BOBBY'S FATHER, Howard Matthews, was one of nine kids born to Izzie
Matthews in Bena, Minnesota, on the Leech Lake Reservation. She was a
full-blooded Ojibwe. Her on-again, off-again husband, Harris Matthews,
was a lumberjack, bar owner, and bootlegger, originally from Chicago.
Harris was notorious. He wore an eye patch (he'd lost the sight in his right
eye to shingles). He drove a Model A. By all accounts, he'd try anything to
make a buck. He'd rice. He'd bootleg. He trapped wearing ice skates because it was faster. Howard and his brothers and sisters grew up fending
for themselves. Most of them were sent to Tomah Indian Industrial School

in Tomah, Wisconsin, where they learned English and fought Ho-Chunks. Howard inherited his father's roving, hard-driving, not entirely legal ways of putting money in his pocket and bread on the table. He would cut pulp by hand in the woods, and when Bobby and his brother Mikey got home from school they'd put down their bags and go out to the woods and help Howard and their mother, Betty, peel and stack the logs. In the summer they all traveled to Ray, Minnesota, near the Canadian border, to pick blueberries. The owner of the general store there, Ben Huffman, paid Howard, Betty, their five children, and a handful of their cousins who came along twenty-five cents a quart to pick blueberries.

In the fall Howard took the kids out of school and they went ricing as a family. When Bobby was eleven years old, wild rice sold for thirty-five cents a pound. They sold some and they kept some for themselves. "We were raised on rice and rabbits and meat and potatoes. Some of it legal, some of it not. We'd take, oh, between five and seven deer a year. Five teenagers can eat a lot of chow. And we'd eat them deer up, from head to hoof. Howard always had something going. Rice. Cones. Trapping. Logging. He fed us off the land. And we got the benefit of that. We got to trap and fish and net and camp. We got to know the woods."

Whatever Bobby learned in the woods stayed there, at least for a while. When he was eighteen he and his cousins broke into summer cabins, mostly for the whiskey and beer. At one such cabin, Bobby grabbed an old shotgun on his way out. He got caught and got four years' probation. Then Bobby fell in with his uncle Billy. "I started in robbing banks and liquor stores and things like that." The cops knew with certainty who was knocking off the banks and stores but couldn't catch them. "We were real careful. We wore gloves and moccasins. Moccasins are quiet and they don't leave no tread." Finally, thwarted by lack of evidence, the investigator asked Bobby's parole officer to violate him. Bobby served three years, and then he went right back to what he was doing with Billy.

"I was a safecracker. I used to be able to open a safe pretty fast. There wasn't a safe I couldn't open except for those with round doors, but we'd drill them. I could open any safe with a hammer and chisel and punches. Hit the dial straight on with a sledgehammer and—*pop!*—knock it right off. That exposed the pin and then you put a big drift punch on the pin and hit it with a hammer and then the pin falls out and all the tumblers fall right back in and you open the safe. If that don't work you set up in the corner and knock a hinge off. And then start peeling back the plating. That's three-eighths-inch steel plating, but when you peel it back it exposes that fire brick. Pretty soon you get the skin off and then the fire-brick out and knock out the tumblers that way. It was exciting. An exciting life. One time we were in North Dakota. There was four of us. It was a bar. Uncle Bill was sitting at the bar drinking. He always drank Sno Shoe grog from a pint flask. I was in the back opening the safe. Bruce was supposed to be outside. Ron was supposed to be in the other side of the building watching out the door.

"Anyway, needless to say, these guys decided to look around while I was opening the safe behind the bar. So I'm getting the safe open and here comes Bruce, running up to the bar and he says, 'We're surrounded.' And I said, 'Where the hell were you?' And he said, 'I was in the back looking around.' Needless to say, I lost it. I said, 'You dumb sonofabitch.' And I walk over to the door and I looked out the shade and there were cars all over out in the street and people behind them with guns. And I thought, 'Holy fuck.' And I had a thirty-eight and Bruce had a thirty-eight revolver that sometimes would shoot and sometimes would click. And Billy says, 'What the fuck,' and he took his punch and put it in his back pocket along with his Sno Shoe grog. And I says, 'Gimme that grog,' and I took a drink. And I said to Bruce, I said, 'I tell you what, when I holler you open that door. Gimme your gun.' And when he opened the fucking door I started hollering and shooting in the air—*boom boom boom boom*—and everybody dove and I run right through the fucking cars where all the people were. People diving everywhere. My car was parked about six blocks from there. I had a beautiful yellow 'sixty-five Pontiac, brand-new. I was running like a fucker and Billy was right behind me. We got to our car and there was a cop leaning on it. Holy fuck. 'What the fuck now,

Bill?' I says. 'Wait a minute, Bobby,' he says. And he took out his Sno Shoe and took a drink and then spilled some on him and took off walking. He walked by the cop and the cop goes, 'Hey, where you going?' Billy says, 'Oh umm uh going home.' And he smelled like Sno Shoe grog! The cop walked up to him. 'Hey,' he said, 'come here a minute,' and he grabbed Billy Boy and when he did Billy Boy hit him with that punch. Down he went. 'Come on, Bobby,' he said. I run in there and fired that fucker up—*whom! whom!*—it had big pipes on the back. I headed downtown and Billy said, 'Where the fuck are you going?' And I said, 'Billy, I'm gonna go get them fucking guys.' And they heard me coming. I went around the back side of that bar and they come running out and we jumped in and we drove right straight out of town and right across the state of North Dakota with the lights off. They never did catch us. Never even got our license plates. We had them camouflaged with white hairnets, like women wear!"

Bobby's run in this line of work lasted seven and a half months. By then he'd had enough. He got work as a concrete finisher, more work as a carpenter. He quickly moved up to being a crew boss and ran crews that built some of the first housing tracts on Leech Lake Reservation. He moved to Alaska and worked as a roofer. "I hooked iron on the IDS and the Fed Reserve in Minneapolis. Worked for U.S. Steel and ran a crew of Bena boys out in North Dakota to build fences around missile silos. They jerked me around and I had words with the foreman. I had a hard time working for anyone. Got in a car crash in Alaska and came back to Minneapolis right when leeching was going big in the early 1980s. At the time I was selling weed—I'd run it from the cities up north, a trunkful of it. We'd do all sorts of things—night ricing (illegal), night trapping (illegal), and that was only the half of it. And finally, well, I turned to Julie [his wife] and I said to her, 'I think I can make more money on the straight and narrow leeching than I can doing all this other stuff.' And I quit all of it and started leeching."

After about half an hour, Bobby and I have picked a little less than a bushel of pinecones. We stand and stretch and separate to look for more.

I find the white tail feather of an eagle, a fox skull, some partridge feathers, and, finally, a scattering of cones, maybe a fifth of a bushel. We meet back at the truck. Bobby dumps all the cones in a tub. "One even bushel. That's thirty bucks, Dave. Not bad for an hour's work." I mention that, with driving time, it's more like two hours' work. "Yep. Two hours, two guys, and maybe twenty dollars in gas. We broke even. But if you really get into the cones and you pick steady all day, a guy can clear maybe fifty to eighty dollars, depending on the type of cone. Spruce are paying thirty. Norway pine and white pine a little less. Black spruce—but they won't be ready till late fall—they pay around fifty." The U.S. Forest Service had been buying acorns the previous year. "You ever try to find a bunch of acorns underneath all the leaves and brush and whatnot? It's not easy, Dave! And so I said to Julie, 'Come on, this is a waste of time,' and I drove over to the cemetery and found the caretaker and I says to him, 'Hey! Let me borrow your rake.' 'What for?' he says. 'I'm gonna rake your cemetery for you,' I tell him. You know the nice thing about cemeteries? Let me tell you: no leaves! We made between five hundred and a thousand dollars per day doing that. We made, I'd have to check my books to say exactly how much, but I think last year we made about five thousand dollars on acorns alone."

It's hard to say how many people live like Bobby Matthews does—hunting, trapping, and harvesting his way through the year—because the work is so seasonal and records are not kept for all of the activities. Late summer and early fall harvests like pinecones and wild rice give way to trapping and hunting, which stretch into winter. Once the lakes ice over and snow covers the ground, trapping continues in earnest, but that is also the easiest time to harvest cranberry bark. With spring comes maple sugaring, fishing, and, later, the bait harvest. Berries are ripe by midsummer. Then it is back to ricing and pinecones. Some of these harvests are for consumption only. It has been against the law to sell wild game since the early nineteenth century, and commercial fishing is restricted, but black markets exist for both game and fish. (One of my fondest memories from childhood is of coming home to find the hindquarter and loin of a deer being butchered on the kitchen counter by my mother, and one of my uncles driving away with beer money.) Everything else is officially for sale.

What evidence there is suggests that for most, these activities are part-time gigs done for pocket money, in periods of unemployment, or as a family activity on a sunny afternoon in the woods. There are probably no more than a few hundred who spend most of their time living off the land, and only a very proud few like Bobby Matthews who do it exclusively. The number of wild rice licenses sold decreased from about 10,000 per year in 1957, when the licenses were first required, to 1,300 in 2002, and more than half of those went to people over the age of fifty. Only 2 percent of those with licenses harvest more than two thousand pounds. Those who don't participate cite a lack of know-how and time. In Minnesota, harvesting wild rice is arguably the most efficient way to stock your larder with a supremely nutritious source of food, yet the art and practice is dying out. Less than half of the roughly ten thousand people who buy a trapping license every year reported trapping any animals, and only a few hundred reported any real profit. Only a few hundred buy bait harvest licenses, and there are no statistics on how much bait they take. The other subsistence activities of the northwoods—cutting balsam and cedar boughs for wreaths, harvesting pinecones and cranberry bark—are unregulated, so the evidence is mostly anecdotal.

Rick Baird, owner of Cass Lake Tree Seed, tells me he buys cones from around fifty different pickers each season, most of whom are Indian. "Some people come in with half a bushel. I write them a check for fifteen dollars," he tells me. "Bob Matthews is one of the best pickers. I don't write him many fifteen-dollar checks. He brings in five hundred dollars' worth of cones at a time. No one knows the woods like Bobby. No one. Maybe it's because he keeps such good notes. He could tell you where he picked twenty bushels of white pine five years ago, and they go on a five-year cycle so he knows where they'll be this year. Most people don't know things like that. And most pickers don't work as hard as he does. It's hard work. And he'll pick from dawn till dusk every day of the week." A lot of the cone pickers do it with their kids for pocket money. "Usually I get a lot of white spruce cones because they come in first. And I'll pay out fifty or sixty dollars and they tell me that's money for school clothes for their kids. One guy came in just last week with six bushels of jack pine. He told me, 'This here is brown gold.' He picked those six bushels in three hours. That's a pretty good hourly wage. Sixty dollars an hour. Though he might go out the next day, burn through a tank of gas, and come back with only one bushel." Baird buys around five hundred bushels of all species, total, for the year. He could buy more. "We have special seed stock up here. This is the only Zone 4 climate in the United States. It gets hot in the summer and cold in the winter and our seeds are especially hardy. Everyone wants them." He confirms that a skilled picker can make around five thousand dollars for the season, and there's room for more. "If a guy wanted to start picking he might get skunked in the beginning—he wouldn't know where to go, or what was in season—but after he got the hang of it he could make fifty dollars a day without working too hard."

After he pays for the cones, Baird dries them in a kiln and then spins the seeds off the cones. They are then tumbled so that the husk is removed. The seeds are sold to nurseries across the northern tier of the United States and the southern tier of Canada, and the empty cones are sold to craft supply chains like Michaels. Baird's cash outlay is around $15,000 for the cones, and he makes around $45,000 from that investment, not taking into consideration the cost and upkeep of his kiln, forklift, propane, shop, and temporary workers. "When all is said and done, I pretty much double my investment," he says.

After we're back in the truck Bobby and I go to Rabideau Landing to check on how the wild rice is coming along. The heads are nowhere near full. Bobby lights up a joint. He gets contemplative. "You know, Dave," he says, "the Creator or God or whatever you call it made the universe and all the beings in it and put this tree here and that bush there and he made the beavers and the deer and the plants that are good to eat and the ones that are good for medicine. He made all of it and it is beautiful! Abso-fucking-lutely beautiful. And I look out over that creation and sometimes I don't see it like other people do. I look out at all of it and what I see is money. And by God I am going to find a way to liberate it out of there."

AIM at Pine Ridge

In the winter of 1972, an Oglala Sioux named Raymond Yellow Thunder was murdered in Gordon, Nebraska. Yellow Thunder was a grandson of the famous Lakota war chief and progressive reformer American Horse. He had grown up near Kyle, South Dakota, on the Pine Ridge Reservation, one of seven children. His family was poor, and since they had no car he and his siblings rode their horses to school in Kyle. A great athlete and a gifted artist whom fellow students described as "rough and tumble," he dropped out of school to work as a ranch hand—fencing, breaking horses, hauling hay, mucking out stalls. He worked hard during the week and spent the weekends binge drinking in Gordon. A marriage dissolved over the drinking, but on the whole it was a life that seemed to suit him. On weekends when he didn't drink, he'd stock up on groceries and make the rounds among his siblings, distributing food along with gifts for his nephews and nieces. Often, when very drunk, he would bring himself to the police station in Gordon and ask for a cot, and the cops would oblige him. He never fought, and his manner wasn't belligerent. He was a hard worker and a hard drinker but a gentle, mellow man.

On February 12, 1972, Yellow Thunder was drinking in Gordon. At some point he crossed paths with Leslie and Melvin Hare and their friends Bernard Lutter and Robert Bayliss. According to court documents, Leslie Hare told Bayliss, who was driving, to stop the car. He got out and shoved and pushed Yellow Thunder and jumped back in the car. They had been drinking, too. Later, still joyriding around Gordon, they saw Yellow Thunder enter Borman's used-car lot. They "found him in an old pickup truck and opened the door, causing Yellow Thunder to fall to the ground." They then hit and kicked him while he was on the ground. Leslie, wearing heavy work boots, grabbed the stock rail of the pickup and jumped up and down on Yellow Thunder as he lay on the ground. The men paused and then took off Yellow Thunder's pants and shoved him in the trunk of their car and drove him around for forty-five minutes before stopping at the American Legion Club. They got Yellow Thunder out of the trunk and shoved him into the hall and allegedly told him to do some Indian dances for everyone there. Some of the patrons came to Raymond's aid, and the bartender asked if he needed any help, but Raymond waved them away. Naked from the waist down, he staggered into the frigid winter night, headed back to Borman's used-car lot. The temperature was twenty-two degrees. Later the men found him again. They picked him up and drove him back to the lot, where they retrieved his clothes for him. It's unclear whether they helped him dress. They kidnapped him again and left him at a laundromat. They threw his pants inside and then left.

The next day a Lakota boy named Ghost Dog saw him and asked him what had happened. Yellow Thunder said he'd been jumped by some white guys. That was the last time anyone saw him alive. On Sunday his boss, Harold Rucker, became alarmed when Raymond wasn't at the spot where Rucker usually picked him up on Sunday evenings; he'd always been punctual. Eight days later he was found frozen to death in the cab of the truck in the lot where his attackers had first found him. An autopsy showed he had died of a subdural hematoma caused by blunt-force trauma above his right eye. The Hares, Bayliss, and Lutter were picked up quickly: many people had seen them in the company of Yellow Thunder that night. They were charged with manslaughter and false imprisonment. As the police developed their case, rumors began to circulate that Yellow Thunder had been castrated and tortured before his death.

Yellow Thunder's nephew Severt Young Bear thought AIM could help. He took up a collection from friends to finance a drive to Omaha, where AIM was meeting. He told them about what had happened to Yellow Thunder. AIM mobilized their membership. By the end of the week, more than fourteen hundred Indians from over eighty different tribes descended on Gordon in a righteous rage. AIM organized protests and a boycott of Gordon's businesses and assembled a tribunal that it said would deliver real justice if the authorities failed to. The Pine Ridge Reservation began transferring its program monies out of Gordon banks to other holding companies. The pressure worked, after a fashion. City officials agreed to convene a human rights commission. A police officer notorious for mistreating Indians in the Gordon jail was suspended. The Nebraska state legislature instructed the state's attorney general to conduct an inquiry, and the governor sent a representative to meet with the protesters. The Hares, Bayliss, Lutter, and one other man were charged with manslaughter and released on fairly low bail. Sheridan County attorney Michael Smith characterized the incident as a "cruel practical joke" that had gotten out of hand.

Yellow Thunder's family was outraged by the insufficiency of the charges and the dismissiveness of the response, and the rumors of castration and torture that continued to circulate. A second autopsy, conducted because of AIM's interference, showed that Yellow Thunder hadn't been castrated or tortured, which reduced tensions to some degree. But the undeniable truth was that an innocent Indian man had been killed because of white drinking, white bigotry, and white violence. In the end Leslie and Melvin Hare were found guilty of manslaughter. Leslie was sentenced to six years and Melvin to two, though Leslie was paroled after two years and Melvin after nine months. Raymond Yellow Thunder died in a truck in a used-car lot at age fifty-one from a traumatic injury. One of his assailants, Bernard Lutter, died in 1991 at age seventy-seven from natural causes.

AIM's involvement in the quest for social justice in an off-reservation town known for exploiting Indians was exhilarating. Perhaps a little too exhilarating: On their way out of Gordon, a few hundred AIMsters stopped at the Wounded Knee Trading Post in the heart of Pine Ridge. The "trading post" epitomized the exploitation of Indians for outsiders' gain. A tourist attraction owned by a non-Indian, James Czywczynski, it stood on the site of the 1890 massacre at Wounded Knee Creek and sold moccasins and plastic bows and postcards showing Chief Big Foot's twisted, frozen corpse. It also lent money at supposedly punitive rates. The AIMsters trashed the place, stealing merchandise and smashing windows, and threatened and humiliated Czywczynski.

It could be argued that the physical violence that had already become part of AIM's signature style was a response to the institutionalized violence against Indians, but a tendency toward violence also permeated AIM's internal conflicts. Referring to Levi Walker Jr., an Ojibwe-Ottawa who played the Atlanta Braves' mascot Noc-a-homa, emerging from a teepee periodically during each game to perform a war dance, Means was quoted in a *Newsweek* article as saying, "It figures. All the Chippewas used to do was hang around the fort anyway." The Chippewas (Ojibwe), who had founded AIM, were not amused. Means responded dramatically, saying that he was resigning from AIM's board of directors and from the position of national coordinator: "The reasons are clear. The Whiteman has triumphed again!" His supporters rejected the resignation; after all, Means couldn't "resign from being an Indian."

A year later, AIM was back in another border town because of another murder. On January 21, 1973, Wesley Bad Heart Bull was stabbed to death in front of a liquor store in Buffalo Gap, South Dakota, just off the western border of the Pine Ridge Reservation. The two incidents were only superficially similar. Bad Heart Bull had been arrested nineteen times in the preceding two years, once for assaulting a police officer. He had been jailed for assault, disturbing the peace, and disorderly conduct. He was, to put it mildly, a little rough. There were also conflicting accounts of what had happened during the lead-up to his murder. Some said Bad Heart Bull had been picking fights at Bill's Bar in Custer, South Dakota, earlier that evening. Others said he had used an eighteen-inch log chain to beat a man named James "Mad Dog" Gleary before Gleary's friend Darld Schmitz intervened. Still others said that Schmitz had said at some point during his own drunken, violent evening that he wanted to "kill him an Indian." Whatever the cause, in front of six witnesses (four white and two Indian) Schmitz drove his knife into the chest of Bad Heart Bull, who died from blood loss on the way to the hospital.

Schmitz was arrested the same day and was set to be arraigned in Custer on January 22. In the meantime, hundreds of Indians arrived in Custer to protest the charges of second-degree manslaughter (the lowest possible for murder in South Dakota), which was typical for non-Indians who killed Indians. State troopers and law-enforcement officials gathered as well. AIM had intended to pack the courthouse with protesters, but the court said that only five of them could attend. The AIM leadership chose itself—Dennis Banks, Russell Means, Leonard Crow Dog, and Harry

David Hill. They asked the court for stiffer charges and were refused. Means left the courthouse to find Bad Heart Bull's mother, thinking that perhaps her anguish would sway the court, but state troopers barred him from reentry. Law enforcement began to draw closer, and officers grabbed Sarah Bad Heart Bull, wrestled her to the ground, and began choking her with a baton. Other Indians jumped in to help her. Law enforcement—by this time including tactical units, state troopers, sheriffs, sheriff's deputies, and FBI agents—outnumbered Indians four to one. What had begun as a protest quickly became a riot. Two police cruisers were torched. The chamber of commerce (about the size of a hotdog stand) was set ablaze. Bottles, tire irons, and cinder blocks were hurled at police and through windows. A Texaco station was smashed and set alight, as was a Standard Oil bulk station. When the riot was finally quelled, thirty Indians were charged with rioting and arson. Sarah Bad Heart Bull was convicted of starting a riot and was sentenced to one to five years in prison. She served five months. Darld Schmitz was acquitted by the all-white jury. He served one night in jail. Clearly there was little justice to be had in a white border town. And there seemed to be little justice to be had at Pine Ridge either.

While AIM had continued to grow, it lacked a solid base of support on the reservations. The movement had been born in the city, and it was essentially urban-oriented, geared to do battle with white aggression and injustice through symbolic occupations and agitprop. Despite its focus on reclaiming Indian pride by way of Indian cultures and ceremonies, and by privileging the old ways, reservation communities were not entirely sold on AIM. And where some portion of the community might be sympathetic, tribal leadership often was not. This was the case at Pine Ridge in the early 1970s.

At that time the reservation was led—some might say controlled—by Dick Wilson. Wilson had been born in the town of Pine Ridge in 1934, the same year the Indian Reorganization Act was passed, and had come to represent everything that was wrong with reservation electoral politics—a fitting symmetry. The village of Pine Ridge was the seat of the reservation. And just as Washington, D.C., is a seat of power different from, and in some ways divorced from, the rest of the country it represents, such was the relationship of such "urban centers" to their reservations. Pine Ridge held the clinic, the best schools, the municipal buildings, and the few businesses that catered to the reservation. Its residents were somewhat better off and more racially mixed than the Indians from smaller villages around the reservation. It was largely Christian, and its Episcopalian and Catholic networks were primary paths to power: traditionals and fluent Lakota speakers were often frozen out of jobs and politics. Wilson had entered politics in the late 1960s, when he ran for and won a seat as a district representative at the age of thirty-two. Almost immediately his detractors accused him of nepotism, favoritism, and mismanagement. It was said that he diverted funds for public projects into his own coffers and hired a private security force to intimidate his opponents. Nonetheless, in 1972 he was elected chairman of the reservation in a narrow contest where, again, most of his support came from village of Pine Ridge.

Wilson had had good things to say about AIM during its direct action in Gordon, Nebraska, after Raymond Yellow Thunder's murder. Wilson himself set up a housing authority on the reservation to deal with the epidemic of substandard housing, the first of its kind. But he also continued firing reservation employees and replacing them with family members. He appointed his wife as director of the tribal Head Start program and paid his brother to organize his inauguration. He stopped consulting with the large tribal council and met only with the more easily controlled four-member executive council. He awarded cheap grazing leases on tribal land to white interests and proposed opening up large portions of the reservation to mining. All of that might have been regarded as reservation politics as usual. Six previous tribal chairmen had been through impeachment proceedings, and only one had served more than one term. But Wilson went further. At the outset of his tenure, the Indian Claims Commission had been ready to award the Lakota damages for ongoing land claims dating back to the 1870s, when Custer and his Seventh Cavalry broke open the Great Sioux Reservation after the discovery of gold in the Black Hills. Claims had been filed first in the Court of Claims and again through the Indian Claims Commission. Tribal members were split over the proposed settlement, with more traditional Indians from outlying areas strongly rejecting it and progressives wanting the cash because Pine Ridge was (and still is) crushingly poor. Wilson wanted the cash. As unrest grew, so too did his reliance on his ever-growing private security force, who were aided and advised by Nixon's domestic commando force, the Special Operations Group: an illegal domestic CIA intelligence outfit. Pine Ridgers referred to them as goons, and Wilson's thugs proudly appropriated the name: they began calling themselves GOONs, Guardians of the Oglala Nation.

Until this point, AIM had not had a significant presence at Pine Ridge, but now it waded into the fray at the behest of traditional Pine Ridge residents. Russell Means was Oglala, and he called the leader of his tribe a dictator, a liar, and a drunk. Wilson said that if Means came to Pine Ridge, he'd cut off Means's braids. He said that AIM was merely a bunch of "bums trying to get their braids and mugs in the press."

In February 1973 there was enough of a backlash against Wilson to spark impeachment proceedings. Astonishingly Wilson opened the process by showing the documentary *Anarchy U.S.A.*, a film produced by the John Birch Society, an anticommunist organization that had its roots in relatively centrist conservative movements of the late 1950s and early 1960s but had veered further to the right. By this point it saw communist conspiracies everywhere, including in the American and Soviet governments, which were supposedly under the control of a "conspiratorial cabal of internationalists, greedy bankers, and corrupt politicians" who might "betray the country's sovereignty to the United Nations for a collectivist New World Order, managed by a 'one-world socialist government'" if left unexposed. Civil rights, collectivism, and liberals were the sharp point of the conspiracy, and the society had created *Anarchy U.S.A.* to prove their point. What a strange world it had become, that a Lakota-elected tribal chairman would enlist such a piece of propaganda in his own defense!

What one wouldn't give to have been in that room that day. As it turned out, Wilson was not impeached, because of technicalities. More and more AIM members came to Pine Ridge. Wilson remained in office, and the village of Pine Ridge became increasingly militarized, packed with GOONs, Special Operations Group forces, U.S. marshals, and FBI agents. Tribal headquarters were sandbagged and crowned with a .50 caliber machine gun. It was under these circumstances that Russell Means did in fact come to Pine Ridge, along with much of the rest of AIM's membership, including Dennis Banks, Carter Camp, and Vernon and Clyde Bellecourt. AIM, always marked by opportunity in ways good and bad, was already on the reservation in force to attend the funeral of Ben Black Elk, the son of renowned spiritual leader Nicholas Black Elk. Two GOONs jumped Means in a convenience store parking lot and beat him up. Undeterred, he continued to a meeting convened by traditional people in Calico to discuss what to do now that the effort to impeach Wilson had failed. Within hours, disgusted and frightened by the militarization of Pine Ridge and on the advice of spiritual leaders there, principally Frank Fools Crow, AIM caravanned from Calico to Wounded Knee. They held a ceremony at the gravesite of the victims of the 1890 massacre, and while that was going on, AIM militants attacked the village and were able to control it almost immediately. They took over the trading post and the lonely, picturesque Sacred Heart Catholic Church, along with most of the village. Again they looted the store, and one man donned a turkey-feather headdress and danced on the glass cabinets until they broke. Federal, state, and tribal law enforcement, already at Pine Ridge because of the political situations of the past year, blocked the roads and surrounded the village by the evening of February 27. The militants were surprised when it seemed clear the government was going to neither storm the village nor disappear. They were in for a siege. The protesters would remain in the village for seventy-one days.

Almost immediately they exchanged gunfire with federal and state agents. Law enforcement fired back. Backup forces and supplies arrived. Somehow the activists were able to deliver a list of demands to federal negotiators in the first days of the siege. Among the demands were that Senator William Fulbright convene the Foreign Relations Committee to hold hearings on Indian treaties; that Senator Edward Kennedy convene a subcommittee to investigate malfeasance at the Bureau of Indian Affairs; that Senator James Abourezk investigate "all Sioux reservations in South Dakota"; and that their negotiating partners be restricted to Kennedy,

Abourezk, Fulbright, Ehrlichman, their top aides, or the commissioner of the BIA or the secretary of the interior. Over the next few days the list of demands grew to include the immediate removal of Wilson from office and the appointment of Secretary of State Henry Kissinger as their negotiator.

By this point, the U.S. government had some experience dealing with Indian militants. Alcatraz was behind them, as was the takeover of the BIA; in both cases, the federal government had been careful and crafty and had managed to keep violence to a minimum while giving up relatively little. This time the occupiers were armed, however, and they held eleven hostages from the village of Wounded Knee, most of them elderly non-Native residents of the village. Russell Means, always good for a sound bite, said he wasn't afraid to die, and if he did, the hostages would die, too. The government decided to wait them out. The occupiers hadn't planned on enduring a siege. They quickly organized themselves, but they lacked food: the town's grocery store had been looted clean on the first night of the takeover. In response, Dick Wilson's GOONs set up roadblocks in every direction for fifteen miles surrounding Wounded Knee. No one was allowed through, and Wilson even required the accumulating federal agents to pass inspections at his roadblocks. The government was none too happy about this.

After ten days a cease-fire between the government and the protesters was arranged. The feds were also able to get Wilson to make his GOONs stand down and disperse. But when the roadblocks were lifted, more activists and supporters flooded into Wounded Knee, bringing with them guns and supplies. The leadership declared the Wounded Knee site the "Independent Oglala Nation" and said that as a sovereign nation it would negotiate directly only with the U.S. secretary of state. Americans across the country were shocked (and many were sympathetic) to see armored vehicles, helicopters, and federal troops on American soil. It was as if all the antiwar and countercultural protesters had been right: America had become a war zone herself.

On March 1, George McGovern and James Abourezk, South Dakota's two Democratic senators, came to Pine Ridge to see for themselves what could be done. They spoke to the eleven hostages and were surprised to learn that they were, and always had been, free to go. One of them, Wilbur Reigert, told reporters, "The fact is, we as a group of hostages decided to stay to save AIM and our own property. Had we not, those troops would have come down here and killed all of these people." The militants traded gunfire with federal agents regularly, but no serious injuries were incurred, at least at first. The militants had an odd assortment of shotguns and deer rifles, and most of their arms couldn't even reach the federal troops in their bunkers. Rumors that AIM had an M60 machine gun were untrue. The feds, however, escalated. Fifteen more APCs (armored personnel carriers) arrived along with heavy machine guns and helicopters. Despite the continued insistence of the federal government that this was a military operation, the Pentagon had a surprisingly lucid view of the situation. In a memo to the military leaders on the ground the Pentagon noted:

C. The main objective of the Indians is to draw attention to their real or imagined complaints via national media coverage to stimulate public sympathy and congressional action.

D. the Indians do not appear intent upon inflicting bodily harm upon the legitimate residents of Wounded Knee or upon the Federal law enforcement agents operating in the area, even though small arms fire has been exchanged between opposing forces.

E. Because of its isolated geographical location, the seizure and holding of Wounded Knee poses no threat to the Nation, the State of South Dakota or the Pine Ridge Indian Reservation itself. However, it is conceded that this act is a source of irritation if not embarrassment to the Administration in general and the Department of Justice in particular.

It could be axiomatic that in conflict if a weapon exists it will, ultimately, be used *because* it exists. Such was the case with the Wounded Knee siege. Despite the fact that the 1878 Posse Comitatus Act forbade using the military against American citizens, even before the siege began on February 27, General Alexander Haig authorized the use of APCs and the U.S. Air Force at Pine Ridge. The agents who manned the roadblocks were FBI agents, and U.S. marshals and military personnel wore civilian clothes rather than uniforms to disguise their presence. The military was there, illegally, and everyone knew it. Early negotiations with Ralph Erickson, assistant to the attorney general, were laughably unproductive. First he threatened force and then, abruptly, said no force would be used and disbanded the National Guard and withdrew. The government's hopes were that without a military standoff everyone would lose interest. Dennis Banks declared victory. Journalists reported that the siege was over. Instead, more protesters arrived with more weapons and more food.

On March 11, federal postal inspectors arrived at Wounded Knee to, as they claimed, investigate mail tampering. In reality they were trying to get a sense, on the ground, of what was happening in the village. With journalists observing, Means ordered the postal workers held at gunpoint and said, "If any foreign official representing any foreign power—specifically the United States—comes in here it will be treated as an act of war and dealt with accordingly." He concluded by saying spies would be "shot by a firing squad." A couple of hours later there was a gunfight between militants and federal agents. One of the agents was wounded. And the real siege was back on as APCs, tanks, and agents moved back into place.

A couple of weeks after the siege began, Harlington Wood Jr. (World War II veteran, noted legal expert, and historian of Abraham Lincoln), an assistant attorney general with the Civil Rights Division who had negotiated with Indian activists during the Alcatraz takeover, arrived to negotiate. He was the first unescorted, nonmilitary official to enter Wounded Knee. He met and talked with AIM leaders for days and brought the Indians' demands to the U.S. government. They were still fighting for the recognition of earlier treaties and for some way to deal with the corruption and violence of Dick Wilson's regime. Wood did his best but failed. Ultimately, he tried until he could no longer continue, pleading illness and exhaustion. After Wood left, one of the most intense gunfights erupted, with federal agents firing on the village with M16s and a .50 caliber heavy machine gun. One man, Rocky Madrid, was hit in the stomach but survived. This cycle—violence, demands, negotiation, breakdown, more violence—would continue.

The next negotiator was not so sympathetic or as effective as Wood had been. A month into the siege, Kent Frizzell was sent by the Department of Justice to end it. One of the first things he did was cut off power and water to the village in an attempt to starve out the protesters. Food and fuel continued to make their way in as Indians with backpacks hiked in over the hills. As the siege wore on, gunfire continued. In late March, firefights were so frequent that government agents told reporters they could no longer guarantee their safety. Many of them left. Those who remained were unable to report directly about the siege and so it began to drop from the daily coverage on TV and in newspapers. On March 25, Leo Wilcox, a Dick Wilson ally on the tribal council, was found incinerated in his car. Early reports called his death suspicious, and even though later, more extensive reports determined it was an accidental death due to a faulty fuel line, it gave Wilson all the reasons he needed to ramp up his own activities. They reestablished their own roadblocks beyond those of the government. And on March 26 a federal agent was shot in the chest and paralyzed, possibly by friendly fire, though that was never determined. After that the last news crews left and the last phone lines went down as well.

Demands, meetings, breakdown, violence, repeat. April came around, though it didn't feel like spring. The government, getting nowhere, removed the BIA and the Interior Department from the negotiations and this helped: Means and other leaders saw it as a move to more formal government-to-government relations. In early April an agreement was reached: the Oglalas would have their grievances heard by the White House, and the Justice Department would investigate criminal activity on Pine Ridge. Another stipulation was that Russell Means would turn himself in and face the charges against him. A helicopter landed to pick up Means, who was applauded and cheered by his people. Means was already accustomed to being treated as an important person: he demanded that whoever wanted him to speak on their behalf fly him first class. As Robert Warrior and Paul Chaat Smith note, dryly, that helicopter ride almost qualified as luxury travel. Before jail, however, Means was to appear in Washington, D.C., at a meeting to conclude the terms of the agreement. Misunderstandings arose immediately. The government said that Means had to order the evacuation of Wounded Knee before the meeting commenced. Means said he wouldn't do so until after. Means held a press conference and then left on a national speaking tour. He never returned to the Wounded Knee siege. On April 15, an AIM supporter and pilot from Boston dropped supplies by parachute over the village. When the militants came out to collect the supplies, government agents opened fire. On April 16, a newly arrived protester, Frank Clearwater, who had found his way to the camp with his pregnant wife, was shot in the head as he lay sleeping on a couch; he died instantly. Firefights grew in intensity and duration after that until, nine days later, Buddy Lamont was shot by a government sniper. Unlike Clearwater, Lamont was from Pine Ridge. He was a Vietnam veteran, well-liked and low-key. Everyone knew him. He wasn't a zealot. He had worked for the Pine Ridge tribal police until he was fired for criticizing Dick Wilson. After his death the Oglala who had invited AIM to come and help them, who had wanted AIM to help rid them of Dick Wilson and bring fairness and due process and clean politics to the reservation, ended the siege. They'd had enough. The AIM leaders— not from Pine Ridge—wanted to continue, but the rank and file didn't support them. A hasty agreement was drawn up and the siege ended. Banks and Means were charged with conspiracy and assault; they both got off because of a technicality.

Wounded Knee was both the high-water mark and a deeply disappointing action for AIM. The siege successfully drew national attention to many of the issues that had plagued Indian country for some time: corruption, violence, lack of due process, and the importance of treaties and sovereignty. The government, however much it had met the resistance with violence and lack of imagination, never really felt the occupation was more than a sideshow. It had been, in the words of a reporter, "war games without a war." Dick Wilson remained in office. Dissidents and Pine

Ridge tribal members continued to be killed at an astonishing rate on the reservation. Violence continued to plague AIM. Before the siege was even over, and a week after his arrival, an African American activist named Ray Robinson, an avowed pacifist who had marched on Washington with Martin Luther King Jr. in 1963, disappeared from Wounded Knee. AIM leadership claimed not to have met him or even to know who he was.

In documents acquired by Robinson's widow under the Freedom of Information Act in 2014, witnesses interviewed by the FBI said that a security team consisting of Leonard Crow Dog, Carter Camp, Dennis Banks, Frank Blackhorse, Stan Holder, Harry David Hill, and Clyde Bellecourt were with Robinson in a bunker after an altercation. When they confronted him, he grabbed a butcher knife that was lying nearby, and then "the next thing," the witness reported, "I heard a loud bang and saw Mr. Robinson's lower leg spin from the knee and rotate outward as he started to fall forward. His eyes rolled up as he went down." Another witness claimed that in the hours after his arrival Robinson was eating oatmeal when he was ordered to report to AIM leadership. He refused to get up before he finished his meal and was shot. He was then taken to the clinic, where he died. Bernie Lafferty, who claims he was present at Wounded Knee, alleges that a group perhaps including Banks, Camp, Means, Holder, and Hill were overheard discussing the murder of a black man whom they buried in the hills inside the AIM-controlled village.

Years after the siege, as federal authorities tried to solve the murder of Anna Mae Aquash (more on this later), they leaned on and got help from Darlene Nichols, Dennis Banks's onetime common-law wife. In the process of securing testimony and convictions for Anna Mae Aquash's murder, she uncovered more about Robinson. In 2001, Nichols showed up at Dennis Banks's house on the Leech Lake Reservation ostensibly to visit their daughter Tiopa; really she was there to probe Banks about Aquash's death. Nichols was nervous and failed to get Banks to talk about Aquash. But he did end up talking about Robinson's death. According to *The New York Times*, Banks said that Robinson had been shot by another AIM member during the siege. Banks recounted how he saw the corpse "shortly afterward and puzzled what to do." Banks told Nichols that eventually he found someone to "bury him where no one will know." The person tasked with disposing of Robinson's body was gone for five hours, and when he came back he told Banks that he had been buried "over by the creek." Prosecutors thought they could use this to roll up witnesses from one case (Robinson) and use them on the other (Aquash), but it went nowhere and Robinson's murder is still unsolved, his body presumably remaining somewhere along the creek. According to the Associated Press (among others), a witness told federal agents that Vernon Bellecourt knew Robinson had been murdered and that AIM "really managed to keep a tight lid on that one." Later, the murder of Anna Mae Aquash would haunt AIM as well.

Despite the destructive antics of its leadership, which hurt a great many people, Indians as well as non-Indians, and arguably accomplished little, AIM did manage to make changes in Indian country, thanks mostly to its rank and file. And the rank and file, were, perhaps, energized by the radical notions that figures like Means and Banks put forth: that Indians need not accept their position of disenfranchisement, and, even more radical, that simply "being Indian"—*choosing* to be Indian—constituted a social good. So in that sense, the leadership truly led. AIM was never very well organized. People joined and left, joined and left. You didn't need to do anything to join AIM other than say you were in. Leaving was just as easy.

In 1972, AIM members opened a new school in Saint Paul, Minnesota. Despite the empty promises of relocation, many families who had moved to the Twin Cities from their reservation homelands had stayed in the city. But if the new government policy toward Indians was "self-determination" (this was Nixon's new directive for and direction of federal Indian policy— the chance for Indian polities to decide their own direction if not their own fate), it was clear that high dropout rates and poor academic performance were two of the greatest issues. Even now, Indians drop out or don't complete high school at a rate more than three times the national average. In the 1970s, part of the problem, as community members saw it, was the ways in which education had been used against Indians for as long as anyone could remember. Boarding schools weren't far in the past. The attempts to mainstream Indians into the American educational system posed a different set of problems. The conventional curriculum, and the teachers who taught it, existed far outside Indian experience. One had to look hard to find schools that had any special programming for their Indian pupils. And what they did learn not only was far afield from their lived lives but also stood in opposition to their own self-regard. In teaching about Columbus's "discovery" of America and Thanksgiving and the "opening" of the Western frontier, Indians figured either as subaltern welcomers or impediments to progress. The Indian parents of the Twin Cities decided they wanted a school for Indians, managed and staffed by Indians, that taught the usual subjects as well as classes on American Indian culture, ceremony, and life. They wanted a school for their kids.

In 1972 the doors of the Red School House, an Indian-controlled community-based charter school, opened in Saint Paul. Other schools—the Heart of the Earth Survival School in Minneapolis and the Indian Community School—soon followed. When the government abruptly pulled grant funding from Indian schools following AIM's takeover of the BIA in 1973, members successfully lobbied to get the grants restored. By 1975 there were sixteen Indian-run schools across the United States and Canada with culturally specific curricula designed to suit the needs of their Indian students. More schools across the country would open in the decades to come.

Indians in cities sought to better their position in other ways as well. In Minneapolis, Indian community members and AIMsters worked together to launch the Little Earth housing project in 1973. Little Earth, in the center of Minneapolis's Southside, was meant to provide homes for low-income urban Indians along with on-site day care and health care and Indian-centric cultural programming. At its inception, Little Earth was the only HUD-funded Section 8 assistance-based housing project in the country that gave preference to Indians. It still is. In 1975, when the community suffered a number of financial and managerial challenges that threatened the continuance of the program, it was reorganized, and AIM—for once opting for a low-key supporting role rather than a public flameout—stepped in and became part of the governing structure of the project. Little Earth still serves the Indians of South Minneapolis.

Although AIM had a national presence, the depth of leadership and community buy-in were especially strong in Minnesota. In 1978, AIM members threw their weight behind Indian education in prison. Indian educators and spiritual leaders led classes and ceremonies at Minnesota Correctional Facility–Stillwater and in St. Cloud, a program that continues to this day. The following year, AIM created the American Indian Opportunities Industrialization Center in Minneapolis, which was meant to fulfill another empty promise that the government had made back in the 1950s. Over the past four decades it has helped train more than twenty thousand Indians for entry into clerical, construction, plumbing, and other occupations. But the growth of such opportunities through the 1970s wasn't only the product of grassroots activism. Just as the history of boarding schools and relocation had brought Indians from vastly different and scattered tribes into fruitful and sustained contact with one another, new alliances had been formed by other means as well.

War on Poverty

On January 8, 1964, with the temperature hovering around the freezing point, President Lyndon Johnson declared "war on poverty" in an impassioned State of the Union address. Speaking before a joint session of Congress, he told the assembled lawmakers:

> Unfortunately, many Americans live on the outskirts of hope—some because of their poverty, and some because of their color, and all too many because of both. Our task is to help replace their despair with opportunity. This administration today, here and now, declares unconditional war on poverty in America. I urge this Congress and all Americans to join with me in that effort. It will not be a short or easy struggle, no single weapon or strategy will suffice, but we shall not rest until that war is won. The richest Nation on earth can afford to win it. We cannot afford to lose it. One thousand dollars invested in salvaging an unemployable youth today can return $40,000 or more in his lifetime. Poverty is a national problem, requiring improved national

organization and support. But this attack, to be effective, must also be organized at the State and the local level and must be supported and directed by State and local efforts. For the war against poverty will not be won here in Washington. It must be won in the field, in every private home, in every public office, from the courthouse to the White House. The program I shall propose will emphasize this cooperative approach to help that one-fifth of all American families with incomes too small to even meet their basic needs. Our chief weapons in a more pinpointed attack will be better schools, and better health, and better homes, and better training, and better job opportunities to help more Americans, especially young Americans, escape from squalor and misery and un-employment rolls where other citizens help to carry them. Very often a lack of jobs and money is not the cause of poverty, but the symptom. The cause may lie deeper in our failure to give our fellow citizens a fair chance to develop their own capacities, in a lack of education and training, in a lack of medical care and housing, in a lack of decent communities in which to live and bring up their children. But whatever the cause, our joint Federal-local effort must pursue poverty, pursue it wherever it exists—in city slums and small towns, in sharecropper shacks or in migrant worker camps, on Indian Reservations, among whites as well as Negroes, among the young as well as the aged, in the boom towns and in the depressed areas. Our aim is not only to relieve the symptom of poverty, but to cure it and, above all, to prevent it.

Johnson's remarks were the first time that Indians had been mentioned in a State of the Union address not as belligerent enemies of the state, or a special "problem" bedeviling it, but as American citizens who deserved and needed the help of the government as much as other citizens ex-cluded from the American Dream. The shift was profound. Indians were depicted as sharing a problem with many other Americans: more than 19 percent of the population lived below poverty level. Lack of access to day care, employment, job training, adequate housing, and schools was not just an Indian problem: it was an American problem. Eight months after

Johnson's speech, the Economic Opportunity Act was signed into law. It contained eleven broad measures meant not only to alleviate poverty but also to provide structures that would help eradicate it, among them Job Corps, Youth Conservation Corps, Federal Work-Study for low-income college students, Adult Basic Education, Voluntary Assistance for Needy Children, loans to rural families, VISTA (Volunteers in Service to America), assistance to migrant workers, and small business loans. A new Office of Economic Opportunity (OEO) was tasked with implementing the legislation, and one of its directives was to bypass federal and state bureaucracies to work as closely as possible with the poor themselves, on a local level. Designed to stymie proponents of states' rights and to deal a blow to segregationist structures in the South, this directive had the perhaps unintended side effect of empowering Indian tribes to seek and secure funding without the intervention of the Bureau of Indian Affairs.

On Leech Lake Reservation in Minnesota, this meant that a young, handsome, energetic, idealistic Jewish Holocaust survivor, World War II veteran, labor union organizer, and erstwhile BIA employee could do what he did best—put power in the hands of people who, until then, didn't have any. In 1965, my father, Robert Treuer, began working as a local coordinator for a Community Action Program (CAP) administered by the OEO. At Red Lake and Leech Lake and White Earth, he met with tribal councils and district representatives and organized meetings for tribe members in small villages and larger towns. At these meetings he did what few white people had done when meeting with Indian people over the many years whites and Indians had been meeting: he asked people what they needed and what they were willing to do to get it. The lists were long: School lunches. Community centers. Job training. Elder assistance. Credit unions. An ambulance (Red Lake Reservation had none). One of his colleagues at CAP was a young Indian woman from Leech Lake, fresh out of nursing school, whom Robert had met when he was a teacher at Cass Lake High School. Now they began to date, and eventually they married. The OEO evolved an unofficial partnership with the NCAI, another marriage of sorts, and together they were able to provide real services to Indian people. Ambulance service, housing, reservation-based credit unions—these and more were the result of CAP and other government programs. Nonetheless, Nixon did his best to dismantle the OEO by installing first Donald Rumsfeld and then Frank Carlucci as director. They restructured the OEO to limit the direct involvement of the people it served, and finally, in 1981, Reagan dismantled it. But the effects of its seventeen years of existence are still being felt in Indian country and across America. The OEO was the beginning of the end of the top-down control that had been exercised on Indian people from the beginning of contact with white people.

The Indian Education Act and the Indian Religious Freedom Act

Change was coming from other directions as well, perhaps nowhere more so than in the passage of two acts that were to have far-reaching results: the Indian Education Act of 1972 and the American Indian Religious Freedom Act of 1978.

In 1967, Congress had convened a Labor and Public Welfare subcommittee chaired by Senator Edward Kennedy to look into the state of Indian education. Working through the assassination of his older brother Robert and its aftermath, Kennedy and the rest of the committee interviewed scores of Indian leaders and educators. In 1969 they delivered a report on the status of Indian education within the United States. The verdict was dismal: Indian education was a "tragedy." The result was the Indian Education Act of 1972 (IEA), which was designed to treat the pandemic of curricular missteps, low high-school graduation rates, low college attendance (and high dropout rates there as well), and high levels of unemployment. The act mandated that local educational agencies (LEAs) with more than ten Indian students (or more than 50 percent Indian enrollment) develop curricular materials and support services to meet the needs of that population. Initial funding of $18 million grew within a few years to $43.6 million. For the first time, legislation treated Indian education as an American concern, not just the purview of the BIA or tribally run schools. It also required LEAs applying for funding to "use the best available talents, including people from the Indian community," and to develop their programs "in open consultation with Indian parents, teachers, and where applicable, secondary school students." At the same time, the scope of the legislation was broad enough to deal with many issues that extended beyond cultural differences and curricular sensitivity: transportation, nutrition, providing eyeglasses and dental work, for example. It's hard to pay attention in class when you haven't eaten or your teeth hurt. For the first time, school districts, tribal governments, and parent groups could apply for grants to fund programs in public schools that facilitated Indian education. Public schools—and the vast majority of Indian students attended public schools—started to become something more than a travail. The IEA also recognized that simply completing secondary school wasn't a brass ring: it was a basic benchmark of a decent education.

By the 1980s, most high schools in Indian country, if not on Indian reservations, had Indian education programs, a dedicated staff of Indian counselors who advised students about everything from home life and drug and alcohol addiction to college (including alerting them to some scholarships specifically for Indian students). Some schools had begun to offer instruction on subjects that emerged from the lives of their students: tribal languages, customs, history, and culture. The act wasn't a panacea; Indian schooling had a long way to go, and still does. But for me, as a freshman entering the doors of Bemidji High School off the Leech Lake Reservation, it meant something to see my fellow Indians in the roles of teachers and counselors, to know that somewhere in the belly of the beast, there was an undigested kernel of, well, us.

Tribes also began to implement significant changes in Indian college education. The first tribal college in the nation, Navajo Community College, had been established on the Navajo Nation in 1968 and was accredited in 1976. Early on, it faced a dilemma: whether to emphasize "Western" curricula and adhere to the same standards and procedures as non-Indian colleges, or to tailor its offerings, even its whole approach to education, to the needs of the Diné community. The school weathered the dilemma and, now as Diné College, offers a vibrant bouquet of programs, from the technical to the artistic. In the 1980s, many other tribes, recognizing that many Indian high school students—despite the best efforts of some high school teachers and high schools—were not prepared for college, began establishing two-year accredited tribal colleges. Facing the same question the Diné had faced, most committed educators responded similarly: Why not both? By this time, research showed that culture-based bilingual programs greatly increased students' performance and competence in all subjects. So the tribal colleges set up programs that prepared some Indian students for trades like engine repair, computer technology, and construction and others for the rigors of four-year colleges and universities. All in all, in this period, Indian educational institutions, for so long part of the process of indoctrination and eradication, became places *for* Indians. In 2013, Montana became the first state to have a fully accredited tribal college attached to or administered by every reservation within its borders.

In 1999, Montana passed the Indian Education for All Act, which mandated that Indian culture and history had to be taught to all Montanans, from preschool through high school. The legislation recognized that a history of the region, if not the country as a whole, was not complete unless it seriously considered the presence of Indians and the relationships not only between tribes and the United States but among the tribes themselves as well. Such a transformation in curriculum was facilitated by the passage of the American Indian Religious Freedom Act in 1978.

Until 1978 it was, technically at least, illegal for Indians to practice their various and varied religions. The nineteenth-century laws prohibiting potlatches, giveaways, and drum dances were still on the books, even if they were seldom enforced. But if Indians weren't prosecuted for religious practice per se, they were often charged with possession of illegal objects and substances, which included eagle feathers, eagle bone whistles, and peyote. In this sense they still lacked one of the most basic of civil rights: the freedom of religion. And because for many tribes religion is tied to place, losing many sacred places to the reservation system, allotment, and subsequent private ownership made Indians also unable to practice their religion legally. Introducing the American Indian Religious Freedom Act, President Jimmy Carter wrote:

I have signed into law S.J. Res. 102, the American Indian Religious Freedom Act of 1978. This legislation sets forth the policy of the United States to protect and preserve the inherent right of American Indian, Eskimo, Aleut, and Native Hawaiian people to believe, express, and exercise their traditional religions. In addition, it calls for a year's evaluation of the Federal agencies' policies and procedures as they affect the religious rights and cultural integrity of Native Americans.

It is a fundamental right of every American, as guaranteed by the first amendment of the Constitution, to worship as he or she pleases. This act is in no way intended to alter that guarantee or override existing laws, but is designed to prevent Government actions that would violate these constitutional protections. In the past, Government agencies and departments have on occasion denied Native Americans access to particular sites and interfered with religious practices and customs where such use conflicted with Federal regulations. In many instances, the Federal officials responsible for the enforcement of these regulations were unaware of the nature of traditional native religious practices and, consequently, of the degree to which their agencies interfered with such practices. This legislation seeks to remedy this situation.

The effect of the act was profound. Ceremonies that had migrated underground and persisted only in what were, in effect, secret societies were performed in the open. Younger and urban Indians had a chance to discover and participate in traditions that had been lost to them. Within a decade, tribes in Northern California—the Yurok, Tolowa, and Karok—used the provisions of the act to file a lawsuit against the U.S. Forest Service to prevent various bridge and road construction projects from destroying sacred sites. The tribes lost the case, known as *Lyng v. Northwest Indian Cemetery Protective Association*, and other tribes lost similar lawsuits as well. But the failure of these cases established that the act was too limited to protect the geographical expression of religion.

In 1971, an old cemetery was discovered in the path of a new road being constructed near Glenwood, Iowa. Twenty-six Christian burials were found, so road construction stopped until the remains could be identified. Forensic examinations revealed that two of the skeletons belonged to an Indian woman and her child (though they, like the rest of the dead, had been buried as—and presumably were—Christians). The remains of the Anglo Christians were reburied with ceremony nearby, while those of the Indian woman and her child were boxed up and sent to a museum in Iowa. Maria Pearson, a Yankton Sioux woman living in Iowa with her family, was incensed. Why should the Indian woman and her child be treated as artifacts while the bodies of the dead white people were treated with the respect they deserved? Dressed in ceremonial regalia, Pearson waited outside the governor's office until he emerged and asked her what he could do for her. She replied that he could "give me back my people's bones" and "quit digging them up." Pearson continued to lobby against the state, museum culture, and academic mind-set that (at best) saw Indian remains as a scientific opportunity rather than as human remains. In Iowa, her work culminated in the passage of the Iowa Burials Protection Act of 1976, the first legislation in the country that sought to protect Indian remains and artifacts from exploitation. Wide-scale looting of burial mounds in Illinois and Kentucky (where skeletons were tossed aside as looters tried to secure burial objects), and subsequent protests, added visibility to the issue. Momentum built through the 1980s, and in 1990 the Native American Graves Protection and Repatriation Act was passed.

NAGPRA was, like a lot of legislation, meant to right historical wrongs and to curtail those ongoing. For instance, it initiated an official process for the return of Indian remains and funerary and non-funerary and religious objects held at state and federal institutions and in any museum or collection that received federal funds or grants. It also established procedures for the treatment of Indian remains and objects discovered during construction on state and federal land. Last, it made the trafficking of Indian remains a federal offense (though possession of remains is still legal). Although imperfect, this legislation has had a profound effect on tribes themselves and on their relationship with the federal government. To date, the remains of more than 57,847 Indian people, 1,479,923 associated funerary objects, 243,198 unassociated funerary objects, and 5,136 sacred objects have been repatriated, in what continues to be a powerful and significant homecoming for tribes across the country. Armed with such legislation, tribes can finally try to make whole, however imperfectly, what has been broken. And coupled with the growth of Indian education and the move to put more and more power in Indian hands, the legislation created a sense that centuries of hostility from the state directed at Indians were at last giving way to some restoration of Indians' ability to control and protect our cultural patrimony.

THE WAY BOBBY TALKS ABOUT IT, subsistence in practice isn't some Zen philosophy, a quiet, inward-turning wonder about how we relate to the land. The way Bobby and people like him practice it, it is the ultimate game, a mad, violent pragmatism intent on extracting calories, nutrients, and advantage. Like hunter-gatherers of yore, they know that their lives hang in the balance. In prehistoric times, the extraction was largely in service of directly feeding, clothing, and sheltering oneself and one's tribe. Today, the heirs to that way of life hunt and gather goods that are coded as money. Maybe what Bobby understands intuitively is the same thing that the German sociologist Georg Simmel posited in *The Philosophy of Money*: that scarcity, time, difficulty, and sacrifice together determine the value of an object. The Ojibwe understood this perfectly during the fur trade in the seventeenth and eighteenth centuries. Beaver had grown scarce in Europe; the few that remained were not deemed worth the sacrifice to procure. By selling furs to Europeans, the Ojibwe near the Great Lakes could make a killing in pots, cloth, weapons, and other needed goods. Anyone who bemoans the day Indians entered into such exchanges is taking for granted what were, for North American tribes, hugely beneficial technologies. Wool was light, warm, and supple. Metal pots were strong and versatile and made food preparation much more sure. A metal axe lasted for generations and saved the tremendous amounts of energy required to fabricate and use stone or bone axes. In saving time and energy, goods like these saved lives—not particular lives but the life of the tribe, ensuring its survival.

A collective view of survival is markedly different from the survivalist fantasy that, every few years or so, sends some white guy off in search of a New World version of Plato's cave: a retreat from which he engages with the natural world, often in a self-proclaimed attempt to better understand the human world he left behind. Even Bobby tried this, for his own reasons. "There was a warrant out for my arrest, so I took to the bush. I brought a gun, a fishing rod, a tent, and a knife and went to live off the land. If anyone can do it, I can. And I did. But god, it was terrible! Let me tell you what separates man from beast. Here it is: salt. That's about the only damn thing that separates us. So if you're ever in the woods, living off the land, make sure you bring salt. Why? Because everything tastes like shit without salt." Life begins to look different without the benefits of manufactured goods. How to skin without a knife? How to cut firewood without a saw? How to build without nails? Think boots, gloves, needles, thread, waterproof food storage, bullets, guns, oil, grease, kerosene, matches. Of course, people lived without these things for millennia, but they didn't live well or long.

So subsistence living is doubly plagued: you have to rely on nature to provide the leeches, cones, bark, fur, and so on. And you have to rely on a market entirely determined by humans and human wants. One could, after all, fill one's garage with pinecones or leeches. Bobby does this every year. But without a reliable network made up of people to whom one can sell them, they aren't worth a thing. So Bobby Matthews is just as careful with people as he is with his black books that detail all his "getting places." "I used to sell my leeches to some guys out of Wisconsin, but I didn't like how they did business. So, for over twenty years now, I sell to Todd Hoyhtya down south. I won't go to nobody else. He's been good to me and I've been good to him. He knows my leeches will come to him healthy. I'll never short him on my count. I always get him the leeches when I say I'm going to. Same with my cones. I put an extra tray in each bushel. So he's getting a little extra. I do the same with my leeches, I add ten percent. They never count my cones or weigh them. They never adjust the count of my leeches. They know what they're getting from me. And I tell you what: it saves me time, David! I don't have to wait around while they count out my stuff. I drop it off, they pay me, and I'm on my way, back in the bush. I don't get paid to stand around!"

Of all the things that a person can kill, collect, scavenge, trap, or snare in northern Minnesota, leeches might well be the most lucrative. More than balsam boughs, pinecones, furs, cranberry bark, or whatever else, leeches can be a job, a *real* job. For some, like Bobby, they are the mainstay. Leeches sell for eight to twelve dollars a pound wholesale. As with shrimp, the size of the leech (small, medium, large, and jumbo) determines how many leeches per pound (the "count," in leecher's jargon). The bigger the leech, the thinking goes, the bigger the fish, so the higher the price paid per pound. So if a leecher gets a hundred pounds a night, he'll take in, on average, a thousand dollars. The wholesaler takes the leeches and divides them into dozens, packed in Styrofoam containers with water, and these are sold at bait shops and convenience stores throughout the region. In 1980, the leeching industry took in $1.5 million. In 2010 in Minnesota alone, anglers spent $50 million on bait. A lot, if not the majority, of that money was spent on leeches. Minnesota is the land of ten thousand lakes. It is also the land of twenty thousand ponds and swamps where leeches abound. And as recreational fishing went through a boom in the 1980s and 1990s across the northern United States, the search for bait was fast on its heels. "Back then, leeching was like a gold rush, David. Black gold, wriggling away in the mud in all our lakes and swamps and by god I was going to get that gold out of there."

Nephelopsis obscura, the common bait leech, is a carnivorous species found in shallow lakes, ponds, and flowages in the Great Lakes region and southern Canada as far west as the Rocky Mountains. It is genetically related to the earthworm. It has a segmented body and is hermaphroditic. It does not suck human blood. Bait leeches eat dead meat: fish, turtles, other leeches, and animals that fall into the water and die. They burrow in the mud during the day and emerge at sunset and hunt. Most lakes without fish (or without many fish) support tremendous populations of leeches for the simple reason that fish eat leeches. To get the leeches out of the lakes and into your boat you must trap them. Leech traps are fairly basic. From top to bottom: a Styrofoam float with the trapper's name and license number tied to a string, from which hangs the trap (people have used tin cans and plastic buckets with holes drilled in them, perforated plastic bags, and now, more commonly, folded aluminum sheet metal), and below that a weight that keeps the trap from floating away. Traps are baited, usually with meat or, in Bobby's case, with a very specific kind of meat with other additives (he was perhaps deliberately vague on this). Traps are set at dusk and removed at dawn. It is grueling work.

As with everything else, Bobby has developed a system. "As soon as the ice goes out in April I start looking around. I've got all my lakes marked in my books. The ones that were producing the year before, my go-to lakes. And so I test them and I always try and find new territory, new lakes. I'll throw some traps out, test traps, and see what I come up with. By April eleventh of this year, I had a thousand traps out. My first yield was one hundred and eighty-two pounds. Not too good. By the twenty-third of April, I had twenty-five hundred traps in the water. I got one hundred and sixty-two pounds. That's about half of what I had two weeks before that with double the traps. What does that tell you? Tells me it's getting shittier." His days go like this: Up at four-thirty a.m., picks up his partner, hits the road, and is on the lake by five-thirty. He and his partner pick up the traps by hand, one by one from a canoe with a small trolling motor attached to the back. The traps are stowed in tubs balanced mid-thwart, and then when all two or three thousand traps are picked up, he heads back to his shop. Once there his crew of strippers remove the leeches from the traps, sort them, and drop them into stock tanks. ("I pay 'em fifteen cents per trap. Most guys can strip fifty traps an hour. That's seven fifty an hour. I've never, in over thirty years, beat a man for wages. I pay fair.") By eleven everything is out of the water, the leeches are swimming in the tanks, and the baiters have begun baiting the traps.

The traps are ready by one, and by early afternoon Bobby is back on the water setting the traps. Bobby can set about five hundred an hour. "I can set a lake in one hour. It takes me two hours to pick up all my traps. That's three hours a lake." He usually traps two or three lakes at a time and then lays off for a few days and traps different lakes. "We work hard and we work fast. We don't go to the landing and smoke cigarettes and talk about how much fun it was. A lot of leechers quit. They can't figure it out. Why is this lake producing and that one isn't? Why are these traps empty and those other ones full? The biggest thing, the most important thing, is they have to stick to it. Day in, day out. They gotta be on the water."

I am not sure exactly how much he makes a year from leeching, mostly because he won't tell me. I know that in 2012, he trapped thirty-six hundred pounds of leeches, which he sold for twelve dollars per pound—and 2012 was, by his account, a terrible year for leeches: unseasonal temperatures, sudden storms, low water. Plainly, what he makes by leeching is more than enough on which to live, and to live well. Bobby owns his home on the Leech Lake Reservation outright. His trucks and cars, too. He employs a dozen people, and he hasn't had a "day job" in years. What Bobby has is a business, but it didn't start that way.

Leeching started as a gold rush, and a certain wildness came along with it. When the market exploded in the 1980s, leeches were relatively easy to trap. Lakes close to the road were claimed first. And as they were played out—in the same manner in which veins of gold or seams of coal play out—leechers moved deeper and deeper into the swamps and woods. There is no official leeching season or leeching rights that you can buy, so lakes are taken on a first-come-first-served basis. Traps were tampered with or raided. Landings were booby-trapped. There were threats and fistfights and the occasional shot fired at the competition. Bobby took to installing motion-activated cameras at his landings. In short, the challenge of figuring out Mother Nature and the challenge posed by other humans made leeching the kind of work for which he was designed.

"So me and my partner, Ernie, have been setting this one lake off the reservation. And you know, David, I don't like to hit a lake too hard. You take all the leeches out of a lake and you kill that lake. No leeches left there to reproduce, and then what the hell am I going to do? God or whatever isn't going to plop any more leeches down there, so I usually hit a lake for a few days then lay off for a few. Mother Nature takes care of me, and I take care of her. So anyways, David, we're headed back to this one lake and there's three guys setting traps there. Everyone knows that this is Bobby Matthews's lake. So Ernie starts getting mad. He's a great big guy. Great big dark Indian guy from Red Lake. And he says, 'Well, goddammit, someone's going to get a bitch beating.' And I says, 'Hold on, Ernie, no one's going to get a bitch beating. Let's just see what happens here.' And he says to me: 'If a guy's gonna act like a bitch he's gonna get beat like a bitch.' And so I start talking to these guys and I tell them it's my lake and they say it doesn't have my name on it and why don't I go back and trap on the reservation.' And well, goddammit, David, I said, 'Go ahead, you put your traps out there and we'll see whose lake it is.' And so they had, well, I don't know, a couple of hundred traps out there. By evening I had two thousand traps to their two hundred. Some people have white floats on their traps. Some have green. Yellow. Orange. I experimented with all of them. But then I started using pink. Bright, fluorescent pink. Anyway, I turned that whole lake pink, goddammit. I didn't touch their traps. I didn't even go near them. I just stuck in ten for every one of theirs. They gave up after a week. It cost me time and it cost me money. But now everyone knows not to fuck with Bobby Matthews. Now people see pink traps and they know it's me and they drive on by. People try to talk all sorts of shit. Give me a hard time about my pink floats. But I roll pink, man! And don't care!"

But the Wild West gave way to industry, and these days, lakes are harder to come by, and there aren't as many leeches in them. In order to hit the mother lode you have to travel farther and farther away and work longer and longer hours. And as with any supply/demand market, the season has a taper to it. Fishermen want bigger leeches, because they think that bigger leeches catch bigger fish, so everyone buys those first. By the end of June, all the big leeches, the jumbos, are gone, and the lakes are producing only mediums and smalls, which take longer to strip and sort.

Instead of an 80 count or 100 count, trappers are selling 120 counts and getting bottom dollar (eight dollars per pound rather than twelve). But Bobby has solved this problem, too. "I catch all kinds—smalls, mediums, larges, jumbos. They are all different when they go in my tanks. But then, check this out, I grow them. I can turn all my leeches into larges. I got a special mix I feed them. I watch the water—temperature, hardness, clarity—real close. And by July I am the only guy around with larges. In May I sell my leeches for twelve dollars a pound. In July I sell my leeches for twelve dollars a pound. And you know how much they go for in August? Twelve dollars. No one else does this. No one else can do this. I just experiment. I read dissertations from the U of Minnesota. I call people. I study my black books. I study Mother Nature. And if someone's figured something out, I study them. I ask questions. I get curious. You gotta work hard, you gotta stick to it. But you gotta stay open, too. You gotta innovate. Sometimes, David, I think the old-fashioned way of doing things is the best way. I do. I don't think that the space age is necessarily better, but sometimes it is. And by god I love the space age. Anything that works I use it."

"You know what they say about cream rising to the top?" says Todd Hoyhtya. "Well, the cream doesn't say, 'Hey, look at me. I'm on top.'" He is talking about Bobby, naturally. Todd himself started trapping and raising bait back in the early 1980s. "We were just looking for markets. We drove around to all the bait shops and asked them what they needed and how much and then we went out and got them what they needed and how much. Pretty soon I was buying from other trappers. And when leeches hit the market we really went big." Now Todd does it all. "We raise, trap, and buy minnows, leeches, worms, maggots, angleworms, you name it." His operation supplies everyone within a two-hundred-mile radius of Mc-Grath, where he lives. They have five trucks and employ three people full-time and three part-time. They have a pecking order of trappers they buy from, determined by dependability. "If I can count on you week after week, then you're my guy. If not, not. It's a job. A hard job. You've got to eat, sleep, and shit bait to make it work."

Todd, however, sees an end to the business. "I don't see the bait business lasting another twenty years. All the suppliers, like Bobby, are aging. No youngsters want to do this. Nature won't come to you, that's part of the problem. You go to work at Walmart, they tell you what you need to know. They've got a check waiting for you. But the bait business— you have to go to it. You have to want it and try and try and try. And you might have a good day here and there. But you have to keep producing or you don't get a check." But Todd thinks the problem might be more than simply generational. "The supply is down—something has changed in the leech chain and the minnow chain. Something in the water is killing pro- duction. Urban sprawl doesn't help. All these wetlands and little lakes get filled in, and in these big subdivisions they might keep some of the wet- lands but then they dump a bunch of pan fish in there, a bunch of bull- heads so the kiddies can go down there with a cane pole—that's the fantasy, right?—and it kills all the minnows and leeches." Demand is down, too. According to Todd, there aren't as many people interested in fishing. Resorts are going out of business. Kids would rather play video games than go out on the lake. "We are the fur traders of today. Used to be, the fur trade was huge, big global business. But then fashion changed, and the supply changed, and the fur trade died. The way I see it, that's where bait is headed."

Leeching is still alive for now, though, as long as leechers have access to land. Places like Minnesota provide a lot of it. A full 10 percent of the land area is covered by water, and wetlands amount to more than ten mil- lion acres. There are more than eleven thousand lakes and six thousand rivers and streams that stretch for more than sixty-nine thousand miles across the state. And almost all lakes and navigable waters can be ac- cessed by anyone. More important, however, is land access. Twenty-five percent of Minnesota's land area is public land. The heavily farmed south- ern half of the state resembles much of the rest of the Midwest with most of the land fenced in, tilled, farmed, grazed, or otherwise used and con- trolled by farmers, private owners, and corporations. Most of that public land is in northern Minnesota, which provides a unique opportunity to live off the land. So when Bobby Matthews tells me to "step into my of- fice," he is referring to land that is owned by the public, and a relationship that is subsidized by the federal government. This runs counter to the usual mythology: The "state of nature" is paid for by the state of man. It's a uniquely American arrangement: When the colonists first came to America, the land they claimed—and what grew on it—was considered the property of the king of England. But here in northern Minnesota, for now, public land still benefits the people.

Bobby Matthews makes it all seem logical, easy somehow. Something any of us could do if we just tried hard enough. But maybe not. DM, like Bobby Matthews, has worked a lot of jobs: carpenter, logger, sawmill operator. He is Ojibwe from Michigan and has lived in Utah, Arizona, Colorado, California, and Montana, where he worked in a taco shop. When he returned to his reservation in northern Michigan, he opened a bait shop in his front yard. His house is small—more of a cabin than a house. Fiberglass insulation covered with three-mil plastic sheeting bulges from the ceiling. When I visited in the spring of 2012, the regulator on his gas range had gone out and the stove stood in the middle of the kitchen. He and his wife were cooking for their two children on a Coleman camp stove set up on the countertop. DM is tall and thin, with his hair—most of it anyway—pulled back in a ponytail. His hands are large and knobby and strong-looking. He is funny and self-deprecating and likable.

"I've been all over," DM tells me. "I used to hitchhike back in the early eighties. It was okay then. You got rides. The cops were okay. People were friendly. I was in my early twenties then. I picked up basic carpentry skills when I was twenty-one. That's what carried me through life. I could always bend a nail and hit my thumb and get paid for it." He grew up far away from his reservation, on the outskirts of Detroit. "I'd come home, but I was really tired of the cities. So I moved up north. I lived all over the North for a while. Finally I got a job at a wood mill. Everything in the U.P. is wood related. Pulp, lumber, wood fences. We were green-chaining and I stacked it. The guy with the saw would cut it to dimension and the beams came off this big conveyor chain and I'd pull it off. I'd stack it. It was hard work. And we all got laid off a week before Christmas from that mill. We hit hard times."

DM has been back on the reservation for seven years now. "If I was a flower, it's kind of like I didn't even begin to bloom till I came back here. Back here, up north, I finally felt like I could breathe. I don't want to make it sound romantic, it was really difficult. It's still really hard." He tried to get hired working for the tribe but found the process corrupt and riddled with favoritism. "How it works is that you've got to pay homage to the king around here." The same was true of getting access to tribal housing. "All the things I had to do—kiss ass, sell myself, and at the end of the day it was a no-go." Frozen out of a tribal job, and frozen out of tribal housing, DM began selling bait and working for a man up the road who had a regular job working for the tribe but dabbled in carpentry and logging on the side. He showed DM how to work with a chainsaw, how to fell a tree, to tell the difference between the trees. They cut firewood and sold that on and off the rez. DM sits back on his couch, contemplative. "Basically," he says finally, "the outlaws rescued me. You look at all these guys—these trappers and woodsmen, these hunter-gatherers: they are all outlaws. They don't live by the rules. No matter what you're doing—whether you're logging or cutting firewood or getting bait or whatever—you need start-up money. You need support. No one's supporting them, no one's giving them loans for that stuff. So all these guys gotta be outlaws. And that guy down the road, he gave me a chance and taught me stuff."

Eventually, DM's partner brought him into the bait business. They set minnow traps and leeched a couple of lakes, and DM set up the shop just down the road from his house. From May through July they sell minnows for five dollars a scoop and leeches for five dollars a dozen. When I asked him how much he made in net profits from the bait, he wasn't sure. Maybe fifty to seventy-five dollars a day for a three-week stretch in the spring. The rest of fishing season is hit or miss. Overall DM seems to be hanging by a thread. If moving back to his reservation was the defining moment of his life, there seem to be many smaller moments that have blurred that definition. The network of relationships that sustain a subsistence life— the buyers, trappers, store owners, licensing bureaus, suppliers, and clients that buttress it—is tough to break into. Without access to the people, access to the land is unfeasible, and vice versa. For every Bobby, working deep in the woods, there's someone like DM trying to find his way in, and it's grueling and depressing to be rebuffed again and again and again.

And Bobby is the rare exception in living solely off the land. "You know," says DM, getting reflective again, "all those guys who hunt and trap and collect. All those guys do a lot of other things, too. All of them sell weed. Nothing harder than that. Nothing more damaging than that. But they do it." Returnees like him aren't all that different from Bobby Matthews's grandfather, who came to the reservation from Chicago and tried to make a go of it trapping and hunting and harvesting wild rice, selling liquor on the side, until he gave the rest up and turned to bootlegging full-time. "I see the reality, the economic reality of things here. And if I were a brain surgeon, a world-class brain surgeon, they'd already have one who lived here. The people are getting left behind." From what I can tell, DM has it right. Tribes could support subsistence living through co-ops (for pinecone pickers and bait harvesters and ricers) and could create better access to markets (with trucks and warehouses to transport and store the goods). It could be a boon for historically depressed economies, but they don't seem interested in committing the resources, even though the demand is there. All of the buyers I talked to told me the same thing: that the market will bear a lot more product. There is room for more pinecone pickers and bait collectors and bough pickers. There just aren't that many people bringing it in. That may be just fine, for the most part, with the people who are already living the subsistence life and not eager for more competition, but it makes it tough for the DMs of the world who want to make the leap from marginal participants to hunting and gathering as a way of life. For them, the problem isn't Mother Nature; the problem is people. And the problems they face don't seem all that different from those that plague what we think of as the regular economy: control by the few, with success determined not only by natural ability but also by privilege, access, and connections. For hunter-gathers, as for the majority of Americans, to exist is to be a part of the service economy. Still, when all is said and done, I think I would rather share Bobby Matthews's office and DM's struggle than staff the checkout at Costco.

Jumping Bull

By the mid-1970s, AIM had been largely dismantled as a force for change. It still existed (and still does to this day), but it had been done in largely by infighting, violence, FBI meddling, and perhaps by its own insistence on "warrior affect." But it emitted one last violent gasp heard around the world in 1975, when AIMsters got in a firefight with FBI agents that left one Indian and two agents dead in a pasture near the Jumping Bull compound at the Pine Ridge Reservation.

It's hard to say how the fight started (much less what, exactly, happened). But in the summer of 1975, things at Pine Ridge were as bad as they had been before and during the occupation of Wounded Knee two years earlier, if not worse. Dick Wilson's GOONs were, in effect, terrorizing the reservation. Between 1973 and 1976 there were more than fifty homicides at Pine Ridge, many never investigated. Leo Wilcox, a tribal councilman, was found burned to death in his car under suspicious circumstances. Buddy Lamont was shot at a roadblock in 1973. John S. Moore was found with stab wounds in his neck, but his death was ruled a suicide. A young girl was raped and killed and left in a cluster of trees. A young man was found dead inside a trash barrel. No one was brought to justice, any kind of justice, for these and many other horrific crimes. It seems clear that after Wounded Knee, the FBI, working closely with the established tribal government led by Dick Wilson, wasn't as interested in solving them, or even in reducing the violence at Pine Ridge as much as it was in "law and order" of a variety that helped the security of the state.

One of the murders on the reservation that the FBI did investigate, if only cursorily, was the assassination of Jeannette Bissonnette. In March 1975, Bissonnette and a friend were parked in an empty field when someone opened fire on her car. She was struck in the back and bled to death before her friend was able to get her to the hospital. The FBI found shell casings nearby that matched a rare gun that was easy to trace to its point of sale and from there to a ranch owned by a man named Ted Lame. The ranch was not a place where GOONs were welcome, and when the FBI showed up there, they were met by a number of Indian men, AIMsters, who were in the process of digging a slit trench, as though in preparation for a standoff. The FBI left, and shortly thereafter the AIMsters left, too: they were going to attend the annual AIM conference held that year in Farmington, New Mexico. Among them was Leonard Peltier, who had been on the FBI's radar for years, and not just because he had been part of the AIM takeover of the BIA in 1972 and, subsequently, the standoff at Wounded Knee.

Peltier, métis from the Turtle Mountain Reservation in North Dakota, dropped out of high school at age fourteen and moved around out west—Portland, Oakland, Seattle—before his drifting took him into AIM's orbit. While on the West Coast, he'd met Dennis Banks, who took him on as a bodyguard and then brought him along to Washington, D.C., for protection during the takeover of the BIA. On the night of November 22, 1972—just a week or so after AIM activists had trashed the BIA headquarters in D.C.—Peltier got into a fistfight with two off-duty police officers at a bar in Milwaukee. The police said that Peltier had a gun and he drew it on them. He was arrested and charged with attempted murder.

That's where paths begin to fork in the way Peltier's story is told. Those who see him as a hero say that the officers bragged about taking him down, saying that they helped the FBI "get a big one" who had been targeted for his politics, even though in 1972 Peltier hadn't done anything much more political than accompanying Banks to Washington. Those few who don't see Peltier as a cultural hero tend to shrug as if to say that he grew up violent, engaged in violence, and was, in fact, violent, and whatever reasons the cops had for arresting him were probably very real. The only thing clear from this first full-throated encounter with the law was that Peltier was dangerous. He sat in jail for a number of months before making bail. And when he did, he skipped the state. So in addition to being wanted for attempted murder, he was now a federal fugitive. On October 21, 1973, Peltier was spotted in Pine Ridge by two BIA agents who were monitoring the funeral of Pedro Bissonnette, Jeannette's brother-in-law, from their car. Someone in another car opened fire on the agents. Unhurt, they managed to get the license plate number and determined that the car was registered to Peltier. After that, he was arrested on a weapons charge in Washington state, and he jumped bail on that, too. So by the age of thirty, Peltier was wanted in connection with three crimes—attempted murder, the attempted murder of the two BIA officers at Pine Ridge, and a weapons charge in Washington state, in addition to two federal fugitive charges for skipping out on bail.

In 1975, Peltier and his cousin Bob Robideau, who had served time for burglary and was wanted for violating parole in Oregon, along with Darrell "Dino" Butler, a prison buddy of Robideau's, set up camp at the Lame Ranch. It was unclear what they intended to do. Peltier later claimed that he and his fellow warriors were called to Pine Ridge by traditionalist Pine Ridge residents to help combat the predations of Dick Wilson's GOONs, a scourge that certainly needed to be checked. But it's hard not to wonder if men like Peltier weren't simply drawn by their own long association with violence.

On June 25, 1975, FBI agents Jack Coler and Ron Williams were driving nearby, looking for a red and white International Scout belonging to a man named Jimmy Eagle, who they wanted to question in connection with the robbery of two white ranchers near Pine Ridge. The agents had heard there was a vehicle matching that description seen near the Jumping Bull compound. As they neared the ranch, they saw three teenagers walking down the road. The kids wouldn't give the agents their names but they did say they were camped out with Indian adults at the ranch. One of the boys was carrying a rifle clip. The agents were very interested in what was going on at the Jumping Bull Ranch, not only because of Jimmy Eagle but also because of the ongoing investigation into Jeannette Bissonnette's murder. As it turned out, Jimmy Eagle and his red and white International Scout weren't at the ranch, but Leonard Peltier and his red and white Chevy van were.

If one thing had been established, it was that Peltier was not interested in going to jail and he would do almost anything to avoid it. On June 26, Agents Coler and Williams were again patrolling Highway 18 separately near the Jumping Bull Ranch when they spotted a vehicle matching the description of Jimmy Eagle's Scout. It seems to have been Peltier's van (though a Scout, built like a Jeep, is hard to confuse with a van). At 11:50, agents listening to Coler and Williams's radio communications heard them say that the van was full of Indian men with rifles. Williams radioed that the men were getting out of the car. Then: "It looks like they're going to shoot at us." After that, intense gunfire could be heard over the radio. After-action forensic reports and testimony heard at Peltier's trial suggest that the agents had followed the van onto the Jumping Bull property. They didn't make it farther than the middle of a ten-acre pasture before the Indians ahead of them took position on higher ground and fired more than 125 rounds into the agents' cars. The agents fired a total of four times with their .38 service revolvers and once with the .308 rifle. Williams was hit first, the bullet going through his left arm and entering his left side. Coler was trying to squirm around the backside of one car to get a .308 rifle from the trunk when a bullet hit the lid of the trunk and nearly severed his arm. Williams crawled back to Coler and tied a tourniquet on his arm to stanch the bleeding. The two men huddled behind the car until someone (or perhaps more than one person—this is unknown) walked down from the ridge above the pasture and executed them. Williams grabbed the barrel of the AR-15 pointed at him, and a bullet blew off three of his fingers before it entered his face from a distance of three feet. Coler was shot next, in the head and throat. Backup was too far away to help. The Indians scattered to the hills.

When the authorities combed the ranch, they found bullet casings matching the gun that had killed Jeannette Bissonnette. Peltier, Robideau, and Dino Butler separated. Butler and Robideau were apprehended and stood trial in federal court in Cedar Rapids, Iowa. They pled self-defense and were acquitted. Their defense team was very good and managed to keep from the jury photos or mention of the execution shots fired after the agents were incapacitated and helpless. Peltier fled to Canada, where he was apprehended by Canadian Mounties. After a long extradition process (during which the federal government supplied the Canadians with some very sketchy evidence) Peltier was returned to the United States. Having been in hiding and fighting extradition when the other men were charged, he stood trial separately, and his trial went differently. The prosecution proved that Peltier had motive to kill the agents, considering his previous warrants and charges. And they proved Peltier was the only one who carried and used an AR-15 assault rifle during the firefight; a casing from that gun had been found in the trunk of the agents' car, and ballistics also showed that the men had been executed with that kind of rifle. Peltier received two consecutive life sentences. He is still serving time.

Anna Mae Aquash

In 1976—long after the siege of Wounded Knee was over; not long after the final fatal shootout at the Jumping Bull compound in 1975—a rancher in South Dakota was checking on his fence line when he saw a body in the ditch. It was the battered and partly decomposed corpse of a young woman in a ski jacket and jeans. The coroner later determined she had been raped repeatedly and shot in the back of the head at close range. The body was that of Anna Mae Aquash, a young Mi'kmaq loner from Canada. Inspired by AIM, she had left her two daughters with her sister in Boston and headed west to join the militants. She wrote her sister saying, "These white people think this country belongs to them. . . . The whole country changed with only a handful of raggedy-ass pilgrims that came over here in the 1500s. And it can take a handful of raggedy-ass Indians to do the same, and I intend to be one of those raggedy-ass Indians." On her first night at Wounded Knee, Dennis Banks ordered her and some other women to perform kitchen duty. She responded that she wasn't there to do dishes: "I came here to fight." Shortly thereafter she began an affair with Banks that lasted for quite some time. Despite Aquash's fervor for the cause, sometime during and after the siege AIMsters began whispering that she was an FBI informant. The organization was paranoid about turncoats and informants. Not without cause: COINTELPRO (the counterintelligence program run by the FBI meant to disrupt and discredit domestic political organizations) had indeed infiltrated AIM and the Black Panthers and other political dissident and protest groups.

However, there was no evidence (then or later) that Aquash was anything other than what she appeared to be: a dreamy, fierce, committed Indian woman. There were also sexual politics at play: Aquash was resented by a women's faction within AIM known as the Pie Patrol: a group of Dakota women described by Mary Crow Dog as "loud-mouth city women, very media conscious, hugging the limelight." They felt that Aquash's romance with Banks could and would destabilize the movement. After the siege was over Dennis Banks went into hiding. Aquash drifted along with AIM, still wearing the "bad jacket" (the phrase used to describe someone who had been semipublicly accused of being an informant). In early June 1975, during an AIM conference in Farmington, New Mexico, Aquash was questioned by Peltier, who at the time still functioned as security for AIM. Allegedly, she was taken to a nearby mesa and was questioned by Peltier at gunpoint as to whether she was an informant for the FBI. Within weeks Peltier was wanted for the murders of the FBI agents at the Jumping Bull compound.

After the shootout with the FBI in late June 1975, AIM leadership was on the run. Banks was still in hiding—shifting from house to house in the West. Both Aquash and Darlene Nichols (with whom Banks eventually had four children) joined him at "various times," sometimes at the same time. Eventually Dennis Banks showed up at Marlon Brando's house in Los Angeles with Peltier, a fugitive wanted for the murders of the FBI agents at the Jumping Bull compound. Brando looked at Peltier and asked, "Who the hell is this?" According to Banks, "When I told Marlon, he said, 'Goddamn, you've got some nerve. But it's okay.'" They helped Brando unload his motor home (he was just back from a trip) and then he lent them the RV and gave them $10,000 in cash and they continued on their way. In November, as Banks, Peltier, Aquash, and Nichols were driving through Oregon, they were stopped by police and a gunfight ensued. Peltier bailed out of the RV and ran for the trees. He was shot in the back but got away. Banks stayed in the RV and tried to drive away, later jumping from the vehicle to elude capture. I don't know what it says that the two men fled, leaving the women behind (one of whom was the mother to not a few of Banks's children) to face charges. Nichols and Aquash were taken to jail, where they shared a cell before being split up (Nichols to Kansas and Aquash to South Dakota). Before that happened, however, the women seem to have developed some level of rapport. According to Nichols, Aquash was scared for her life: back in the RV before their capture, she said, Peltier had confessed to the women that he had killed the FBI agents at the Jumping Bull compound. He told them that one of the agents was "begging for his life, but I shot him anyway." Aquash—already suspected of being an FBI informant—was worried that she was going to be killed. Nichols didn't suffer from the same suspicion, and she had children with Banks.

After her release on bail in South Dakota, Aquash (still in love with Banks) fled the jurisdiction and failed to show up in court. Instead she went to Denver to meet Banks at a safe house occupied by Troy Lynn Yellow Wood. She waited for over a week for Banks to show up, but he never did. There were, however, many other AIMsters, principally women, drifting in and out. She wrote letters home and looked after children in the house until, after about a week, she got into a red Pinto with three other AIM members and was never seen alive again. It wasn't until years later that, with Nichols's help, Arlo Looking Cloud (a low-level AIM member) confessed to murdering Aquash with John Graham. Both men were convicted and are in prison. Prosecutors are not content with the convictions: they are certain that the two men (neither of whom had much power and neither of whom even knew Aquash) were acting on orders, but they have not been able to walk testimony up to the top. The person who ordered her murder has never been determined.

To ME, the shootout at the Jumping Bull compound and Anna Mae Aquash's murder can't be justified as an expression of AIM's (often violent) direct action, their street theater, their agitprop. It was just violence, the result of violent men who didn't want to go to jail. Many Indians muttered under their breath that "AIM" really stood for "Assholes in Moccasins." Nevertheless, a kind of cult worship, largely by white people, grew up around the AIM leadership. Also, partly as a result of Peter

Matthiessen's *In the Spirit of Crazy Horse*, Peltier was transformed into a sympathetic warrior whose only crime was defending himself against a tyrannical government. Russell Means, who was charged with domestic abuse by his Navajo wife but refused to appear in Navajo Nation court on the grounds that it didn't have jurisdiction over him (and who also allegedly beat his father-in-law), went on to write a book, *Where White Men Fear to Tread*, and to play Pocahontas's father in the Disney movie and Chingachgook in *The Last of the Mohicans*. Dennis Banks continued to work as an activist and published a memoir, *Ojibwa Warrior: Dennis Banks and the Rise of the American Indian Movement*. Shortly before his death from pneumonia at age eighty, Banks was asked by a reporter about whether he ever advocated for killing someone he "knew for certain" was a traitor to AIM. He said, "I don't know if I would participate in some sort of getting-rid-of-the-person. But I would say, 'Take care of this.' Or, 'Take the guy out, and I don't want to see him again.'" The reporter followed up and asked specifically about Ray Robinson's murder. Banks said nothing. Then the reporter asked about Aquash, someone Banks claimed to have loved and who, in turn, loved him. His response: "If there's a burning house, no one gives an order to put out the fire. Someone just goes and does it. It was people who fell into an idea."

The Jumping Bull incident was largely the end of AIM's efficacy as a prod to the nation's conscience. Strong Indians empowered by their Indianness and their unwillingness to play by the rules imposed on them was one thing; criminals who killed people because they didn't want to face the consequences for their own violent crimes was quite another. And increasingly, traditionalist Indians stood up to AIM's authority as well. In 1979, during disputes over leadership at Red Lake Reservation that devolved into gunfire, riots, and arson, villagers from Ponemah, led by Korean War veteran Eugene Stillday, built a roadblock at the Battle River Bridge and stood their ground against carloads of AIMsters drawn to the violence. "You won't get past these guys," said Stillday to one who attempted to get through by showing a pistol tucked into his waistband, prompting the Red Lake veterans to take aim with their guns. The activist got back in his car and left.

Yet much of the work that AIM rank and file had accomplished—in schools and job-training programs and housing—carried on. And somehow—despite AIM's ineffectiveness, violence, and chauvinism; despite the violence that always seemed to erupt around it—by the time the 1980s drew to a close, Indian life had become Indian again, due in no small part to the activism begun in the 1960s.

IT IS MARCH, and winter is bone-deep in the northwoods. It seems like forever ago that there was anything green and giving in this world. As brutal and bitter as the winters are in the northern reaches of the Ojibwe homelands, there is a kind of peace that falls over the land in February and March. Or if not a peace exactly, a kind of watchful waiting: April and May will erupt with their usual vernal violence soon enough. But for now the snow isn't deep at all, and the swamps and lowlands are frozen solid, so you can walk wherever you need to go. Bobby and I are driving along an abandoned railroad grade on the south edge of Leech Lake Reservation, looking for cranberry bark. "It's something new for me, David," he says. "Guys have been doing it awhile and I was against it at first. I thought it destroyed the cranberry trees, but it doesn't. They spread through their roots; they grow in clumps. If you cut it they send up new shoots. Leeching is a long way off and I go a little crazy sitting around and so I thought I'd try getting bark." Of all the things Bobby does, cutting bark feels the most relaxing. You drive around until you find a stand of highbush cranberry bushes. "Cut 'em cock thick, David." We cut with long-handled pruning shears, and we keep cutting until we have a few armfuls. These we load onto a sled and haul back to the truck. Once the truck is full to the top we head back to the house, where we have coffee to warm up. Then we go to his shop, turn on the radio, and peel the bark off the saplings with potato peelers. "See how I dull my peelers? I use a rasp and dull them up a little. If they are too sharp, they take too much wood and my quality goes down. If they are dull they take just the bark. I can tolerate about two percent wood. The rest has to be bark." I ask whether the bark actually works to alleviate menstrual cramps. "How the hell should I know? I've never had menstrual cramps, David!"

Typically, Bobby has gone all-in on this new revenue stream. "There's a guy around here who buys bark from the pickers. And he sells it to another outfit out of state. He doesn't pay much; he's keeping the price down. But what if we could do this and the pickers got a living wage?" So in addition to cutting his own bark, Bobby now buys from other pickers. "I did some research and found out who buys this stuff and I started dealing with him. I asked him how much he'd need to buy from me and he told me. And I asked him what kind of quality—how much bark and how much wood—and he told me. And I gave him exactly what he needed." Bobby dedicated the back bedroom in his house to bark processing. Racks with large wire trays run from floor to ceiling. He dumps the bark on the trays, turns on a dehumidifier and a fan, and dries the bark until it is crispy. Then he crumbles it up by hand, packs it in bags, boxes them, and ships them to North Carolina. "My guy in North Carolina will buy all sorts of stuff. Irisroot. The buds from balm of Gilead. I don't know who he sells his stuff to. Probably drug companies, places like that. We got a lot of stuff we can sell. A lot of stuff people want. And we haven't even experimented with the half of it."

Our three hours of cutting had yielded just short of ten pounds of bark. At eight dollars a pound, we had made almost forty dollars apiece. "I want people to know they can do this, David. They can do this. They can live off the land, just like I do. It beats working at Walmart or McDonald's. What could be better than spending the day in the woods, getting exercise, and getting paid for it? It's what we've done for centuries. We've always done this. And we can still do this. But we have to change our thinking. We have to work together and we got to want it. I just wish our people wanted it more."

I think the people do want it, increasingly so. Our people spent the better part of the 1960s and 1970s figuring out how to be both Americans and Indians: how to move forward into the future in such a way as to not leave the past behind; to once and forever destroy the idea that to live one kind of life meant shedding the other one; and to find some productive

balance between growth and violence, between destruction and regenera-
tion. This balance eluded the leaders of AIM. It eluded Peltier. But it did
not elude the many thousands of Indians who worked together to build
schools and clinics and jobs programs, who went to college and went to
powwows, who (like my mother) practiced the law as a way of perfecting
it while carrying herself with the kind of fierce dignity that characterizes
our tribe. As the 1970s wound down, so did the public and private violence that gave rise to, and was added to, by AIM. The effects of that
violence—done to us and caused by us—will surely be felt for years. But
we shuffled into the Reagan years with a kind of collective sigh, ready for
some peace and quiet for a change.

Months later, I called Bobby to go over some details. He had just
dropped off two pickup loads of jack pinecones. Nine hundred seventeen
dollars' worth. "I traded those cones for two rice parchers. I was thinking
of getting into the rice processing business. I've got a lot to learn. I've
never been a parcher. But if I can learn how to do it, to make rice that you
always sit down for, and I start buying rice, we might be able to drive the
price up around here so we can make a living with it. Everyone can." Before I rang off, he said, "Hey, check this out: I was out in the woods checking for cones and I saw the beavers and they'd been pulling up roots and
cutting branches, putting fresh mud on their lodges in August. Then they
stopped. They just stopped. No new feed piles. No new mud. I thought to
myself, 'Well, this is a damn strange thing! I wonder what the beavers
know that we don't?' Maybe we'll get some more warm weather before it
gets cold, David. Maybe they know what the weather is gonna do. Think
about that. Amazing, huh?"

The beavers were right. And so was Bobby. The weather was warm for
another six weeks, and Bobby was out there picking cones.

PART 6

Boom City—Tribal Capitalism in the Twenty-first Century

In February 2015, amid the cedar masks, canoe paddles, and totem poles at the Tulalip Resort Casino north of Seattle, the talk was all about pot. Indian country had been abuzz about cannabis since the previous fall, when the Justice Department had released the Wilkinson Memo, which seemed to open the way for tribal cannabis as a manifestation of tribal sovereignty. The gathering at Tulalip was technically a CLE (continuing legal education) conference, so one might have expected lawyers. A stew of lawyers in thousand-dollar suits were there, of course, but so were private equity entrepreneurs, tribal officials, and tribal potheads. One of the latter, a gangly twenty- or thirtysomething wearing Chuck Taylors, a very ripped T-shirt, and a headband that held back his lank hair, slouched low in his chair and didn't speak a word all day. His companions spoke a bit more, but with the sleepy demeanor of people who have just purchased a dime bag and smoked it all. They didn't talk business as much as they talked relationships: *We have a relationship with pot. It's a medicine from Mother Earth. Like, cannabis is tribal. It's consistent with our relationship with Mother Earth.* Wandering among them were tribal small business owners, people who ran gravel companies or sold smoked fish or espresso along the freeway. They had forked over the five hundred dollars for lunch and a name tag to explore what marijuana legalization might mean for their community—or maybe to explore where the pay dirt lay at the intersection of legalization and tribal sovereignty. The lawyers and policy people presented on state laws; the history of marijuana legalization in California, Colorado, and Washington; and the social, cultural, and political ramifications of legalization. Tribal leaders spoke about the ways in which tribal growing could be a whole new revenue stream, if not a new tribal industry. Behind these discussions were coded questions, old and new: How best to provide for a people in the absence of industry and opportunity? How to use tribal sovereignty to the best possible effect? Did tribes really want to invest in another "lifestyle economy" like tobacco shops, casinos, and tourism? No one knew what to make of the potheads.

The received notion—reinforced at every turn in editorials and investigative pieces and popular culture—is that reservations are where Indians go to suffer and die. They are seen by many Indians as well as non-Indians not as expressions of tribal survival, however twisted or flawed, but as little more than prisons or concentration camps, expressions of the perversion of American democratic ideals into greed—greed rapacious enough to take Indian land and decimate Indian populations but not quite harsh enough to annihilate us outright. But reservations are not stagnant places. Despite their staggering rates of unemployment, they are the home not only to traditional ways of living but to new tribal business as well. Pot as a tribal industry has a parent: the casino. Arguably, its arrival in Indian country had as defining an effect on the social and economic lives of Indians in the past fifty years as the mass migration of Indians to American cities. Many Indians, knowing this, refer to the time before tribal gaming as "BC"—Before Casino. So as the smell of cannabis, or at least its potential, hovers in the air, and everyone wonders what the latest "thing" will do to—or be made of—in Indian country, we can learn a lot by tracing the genetic code of tribal business back a generation.

As soon as the subject of casinos comes up with outsiders, the same questions always pop up. I present them here to dispense with them, because they get in the way of our actually understanding the effect casinos have had on Indian life.

Q: Have casinos made Indians rich?

A: Some. Of the more than 500 federally recognized Indian tribes in the United States, fewer than half (238 tribes) own and run gaming operations. For instance, in 2002, 12 percent of tribes earned more than 65 percent of all Indian gaming revenue. So some tribes do very well with gaming, others so-so, and the majority not so well at all.

Q: Do Indians get money from casinos directly?

A: Some. Some small tribes pay per capita payments to tribal members from their casino profits. The smaller the tribe and the bigger the casino, the bigger the payment. The St. Croix Chippewa Indians of Wisconsin have roughly one thousand enrolled tribal members. The tribe owns and operates three casinos. Tribal members receive per capita payments of between $5,000 and $8,000 annually. By comparison, the Pechanga Band of Luiseño Indians, who own Pechanga Resort and Casino in Temecula, California, with the same number of tribal members, distributed $290,000 annually to each of them as of 2006. Most gaming tribes, however, do not distribute per capita payments at all, and revenues, such as they are, are used in lieu of a tax base for roads, schools, eldercare, and so on.

Q: How come Indians don't have to pay taxes on any of this?

A: They do. Most Indians don't pay state tax if they work and live on their home reservations, but all pay federal income tax and property tax on land they own outright. Tribal casinos don't pay corporate taxes, but they do payroll taxes, etc., just like any other business operating in the United States. And the gaming compacts signed between tribes and states often include provisions that redirect some casino profits to states and state organizations.

Q: Have casinos destroyed Indian culture?

A: That's a stupid question. Has commerce (generally) destroyed American/Chinese/German/French culture?

Q: Why did the government give casinos to Indians?

A: The government didn't "give" us casinos. Gambling is (among many other things) a civil matter and a right we've reserved or retained. The freedom to gamble for money is a right we had long before white people showed up in the New World. Much more on this later.

Q: Isn't it sad to go into casinos and see Indians gambling? I mean, they have all sorts of other addictions to contend with.

A: Ha ha. When I walk into casinos I see way more white and Asian people gambling than Indians. The more they lose, the richer we get.

NOW THAT THAT'S OUT OF THE WAY, let's begin. Casinos, believe it or not, owe their existence to a $148 tax bill on a trailer in the village of Squaw Lake on the remote north end of Leech Lake Reservation. In the spring of 1972, Helen Bryan and her husband, Russell, were sitting at their kitchen table drinking coffee when they saw a pickup truck pull into the yard. Squaw Lake is not the kind of place one wanders into. They watched, curious, as a man got out of the truck and began measuring their trailer. Once he was done measuring, he took pictures. And then—without having knocked on the door or introduced himself or even asked the Bryans' permission to step onto their property—he got back in his truck and drove away.

As it happened, the trailer was something of a miracle for the couple. They had been able to put an $800 down payment on it in 1971 thanks to some of the GI insurance money that came to Helen's family after the death of her brother, a Vietnam vet. It was a modest two-bedroom affair, but it gave a home to Helen and Russell and their six kids—Russell and Helen slept in one bedroom, the girls in another, and the boys in the living room. They had heat, running water, and electricity at a time when having all three at once, in a home of one's own, was something of a rarity on the reservation. Helen worked at the Leech Lake Head Start for minimum wage, and Russell didn't work at all, but even on their meager income they could cover the trailer's $92/month mortgage. A few weeks after the arrival of the mysterious visitor, however, Helen received a tax bill of $29.85 for the remainder of 1971. She was confused: she hadn't thought she'd have to pay taxes on her trailer. Russell didn't care. He said they should pay it. "He wasn't mad like I was," remembers Helen. "I said it was wrong, it's got to be wrong. And how was I going to pay for taxes and feed my kids and make house payments?" She ignored the bill. But like all tax bills everywhere, it didn't go away and it was followed by others. The bill for 1972 was $118.10, bringing her total to $147.95. Helen didn't know what to do. Things were so tight for her family that the bill—small though it was—mattered a great deal. And then there's Helen's nature as well: she might be a poor young mother from a remote reservation, without access to lawyers and help, but she knew that the bill was wrong. It was just wrong. And she wasn't going to pay it.

Then Helen remembered that a legal program had been started on the reservation a few years back. The Leech Lake Reservation Legal Services Project was founded in 1967 under the auspices of the Office of Economic Opportunity, empowered by the Economic Opportunity Act of 1964. It was the first independent Indian legal-services project in the country. (It persists to this day, fighting for the legal rights of Indians under the name Anishinabe Legal Services.) Helen called them up and explained her situation to Jerry Seck, who thought she had a good case. He agreed to take it on, and he wrote down her information. Helen mailed the tax notice to the office, and over the ensuing months, lawyers from the office called occasionally. Finally, Seck phoned Helen and told her they were going ahead with her case. He promised he'd buy her a beer if they won.

The social genius of legal-services organizations is that they can take good cases and argue them in broad and interesting ways. Helen's case could have been argued narrowly: The Bryans' trailer was attached (annexed) to Indian land. As such, it was considered tribal property and exempt from state taxes in the same way that state, county, and federal lands and buildings are not taxed by states. The broader and bigger argument was that the state didn't have the authority to assess personal property tax on Indians living on Indian lands. The idealistic young attorneys at the Leech Lake Reservation Legal Services Project opted for the harder path. They lost.

The Itasca County district didn't agree with the Bryans' argument. It was a hard argument to understand, and the precedent was murky, as was the implicated legislation. But basically the reasoning was that, as the U.S. Constitution granted the federal government, not the state, power over tribes, absent express legislation or federal consent—such as the 1953 Public Law 280, which transferred some criminal and civil jurisdiction from the federal government to the states—the states had no power over the tribes. As previously discussed, PL 280 was intended to combat lawlessness and to give Indians better access to the criminal and legal systems they needed. It was not intended to do any more than that. The civil section of the law reads: "Each of the States listed . . . shall have jurisdiction over civil causes of action between Indians or to which Indians are parties which arise in the areas of Indian country listed opposite the name of the State to the same extent that such State has jurisdiction over other civil causes of action, and those civil laws of such State that are of general application to private persons or private property shall have the same force and effect within such Indian country as they have elsewhere within the State." But the states had interpreted it as a much broader transfer of civil power. The Bryans' lawyers appealed to the Minnesota State Supreme Court. They lost again. That beer, and relief from the taxes, had begun to seem very unlikely. But then the U.S. Supreme Court agreed to hear the case.

By now, many of the lawyers who had started on the case had left the legal-services team. A new lawyer stepped in. Bernie Becker, from New York, was portly, brilliant, and personable; a great ally. He argued that PL 280 had been meant as "law and order" legislation, and only that. If the government had intended PL 280 to include all civil actions (like taxation), it would have said so. And if it had been written with that intent, it would have, in effect, been "termination" legislation. Congress had passed other termination legislation and had been clear about its intent.

Part of the problem, Becker argued, was that PL 280 was vague (so vague, in fact, that it had been amended more than thirty times). He further argued that tribes had not consented to PL 280. It had been imposed on them, and if it had been imposed on them as a sneaky way to terminate them, Congress "would have 'slipped one by the Indians.'" C. H. Luther, representing Itasca County, argued that PL 280 was indeed intended as an "integration and assimilation" initiative. This argument was bullshit, just another way of saying "termination legislation," part of a host of 1950s legislation with that aim. Becker was ready for him. True, the government had wanted to terminate tribes. It had passed legislation that clearly did just that. But those laws were very clear on which rights they would no longer recognize, whereas PL 280 had no such language. And that was because it had been passed to help tribes, not demolish them. On June 14, 1976, the Supreme Court ruled unanimously for the claimants. Writing for the court, Justice Brennan noted, "The same Congress that enacted Pub.L. 280 also enacted several termination Acts—legislation which is cogent proof that Congress knew well how to express its intent directly when that intent was to subject reservation Indians to the full sweep of state laws and state taxation." In the opinion of the court, there was nothing in PL 280 "remotely resembling an intention to confer general state regulatory control over Indian reservations." Jerry Seck called Helen with the news. "I was really happy," she says. "That was $147 off my mind. And I didn't get no more tax notices." The news was picked up by Minnesota papers and by *The New York Times*, which headlined it "Justices Bar State's Taxation of Reservation Indians."

For Helen and her family, life didn't change much. She was still poor, and she remained poor. "I never got nothing from nobody," she told me in that quiet, fierce way of hers. "I never got a penny from the tribe for housing or anything like that. I supported all eight of us my whole life. But when Russell died the tribe offered to pay for his funeral and for his

369

headstone, but only if they could choose the wording for it. I said sure. So they put RUSSELL BRYAN VS. ITASCA COUNTY—VICTORY right on the headstone. That's all I got from them. The papers picked up the story and said that the ruling affected ten thousand Indians in Minnesota. I told Russell at the time if we did so much maybe if every Indian in Minnesota sent us a dollar, we'd be rich!" I think everyone should. Send your dollars to Helen (Bryan) Johnson, 60876 County Road 149, Squaw Lake, MN 56681.

Helen may not have gotten much from standing her ground, but tribes got a lot from Helen. The decision opened the door to many things the government (and most Indians) had considered closed. The power to regulate—commerce, banking, gaming, liquor, tobacco, and a host of other things—is a tremendous kind of power. Soon after the court's ruling, tribes across the country put their imaginations to work, and within a year or two, they began to test the limits of the ruling.

In 1976, the Seminole Tribe in Florida, following the lead of the Colville Tribes in Washington state, opened tax-free cigarette stores on their reservation land. This move pitted them against the sheriff of Broward County, Robert Butterworth, who felt that Indians were breaking the law. They went back and forth for some time on the issue of cigarettes, but after the Bryans won, the tribal chairman, Howard Tommie, saw an even bigger window and pushed the tribe through it. In 1979 the tribe built and planned to open a high-stakes bingo parlor. At that time, only nonprofit organizations like the Catholic Church were allowed by Florida state law to operate bingo games no more than two times a week, with jackpots no higher than a hundred dollars. The Seminole advertised that they would be open six days a week and their jackpots would be much bigger. Again, Butterworth threatened the tribe with arrest even though many local non-Indian residents were supportive of the enterprise. The day they opened for business, Sheriff Butterworth was waiting with his deputies, and they arrested people within minutes. The tribe, expecting this, promptly sued. They won in the U.S. Fifth Circuit Court of Appeals, which ruled that states have no power to abrogate or regulate treaty rights. So the Seminole didn't just reopen their bingo hall, they made it bigger.

Meanwhile, in Southern California, the Cabazon Band of Mission Indians opened a poker room and bingo hall. As in Florida, the sheriff of Riverside County immediately descended on the operation, closed the game rooms, arrested tribal members, and confiscated money and equipment. Like the Seminole, the Cabazon had expected this, and they took the matter to court as well. The state argued that the poker rooms and bingo halls violated state laws, and that under PL 280 six states, including California, had been granted criminal jurisdiction over tribes and tribal members living within those states. But this was already a losing argument. The Cabazon noted that gaming laws in California were regulatory, not criminal laws, and the courts had already ruled that states didn't necessarily have regulatory power over tribes. The court ruled in the Cabazons' favor, noting wryly that not only was some gambling legal in California, but the state actually encouraged it through the California State Lottery. Together with *Bryan v. Itasca County* and *Seminole v. Butterworth*, this ruling brought law and policy in line with sovereign treaty rights and clearly established that tribes could be into the gambling business.

California v. Cabazon Band of Mission Indians wasn't resolved until 1987, but by then, gaming enterprises were already under way across the country, with the biggest concentration of casinos in California and Oklahoma. The court might have been deliberating, but Indians—having waited in so many ways for so many years to have their sovereignty affirmed—were not. The increase in funding for tribal programs throughout the 1970s, the emphasis on improving access to education, support for the poor, funding for health care—all of this positioned Indians to move, and move fast. By the mid-1980s, elected tribal leaders had gained forty years of experience in IRA governments and forty years of experience in dealing with the Bureau of Indian Affairs and state and federal governments. They had become expert at playing with soft power, and they were prepared to make the most of the opportunity for gaming. Within a year of the Cabazon win, tribal gaming revenue was bringing in $100 million a year. The door to economic development—at least in the realm of gambling—seemed to have been flung wide open.

But not so fast: the states, a powerful lobby in their own right, were determined to have a stake in Indian gambling, or at least some measure of control. The federal government felt the same way. So in 1988, Congress passed and Reagan signed the Indian Gaming Regulatory Act. IGRA codified the process by which tribes administered gambling. It established three different classes of gambling. Class I was, more or less, traditional tribal gambling (bagese, moccasin game, hand game), social games that tribe members could continue to play without any federal meddling or oversight. Class II gambling was mostly bingo, but it also included pull-tabs, tip jars, and "non-banked" card games (like poker) where players play against one another and not the house. IGRA maintained that tribes had exclusive authority over Class II gaming so long as the state in which the tribe was located also allowed that kind of gaming, and so long as the tribe developed a gaming ordinance approved by the National Indian Gaming Commission (also established by IGRA). Tribes, ultimately, were tasked with control of Class II gaming with federal oversight.

Class III gaming was casino gaming, where the real money lay. The provisions for Class III gaming were the result of a vigorous compromise between the federal government and Indian tribes. The first provision was that whatever forms of gaming a tribe wanted to conduct in a state had to be legal in that state. (This meant that in places like Minnesota, where casino gambling was not legal, the state had the power to wrest concessions in the form of taxes in order for the tribe to secure a gaming compact with the state.) The second provision was that tribes must enter into gaming compacts with the state that entailed where and when each casino could be built, how large it could be, how much the state took, and the like. The third provision required the tribe to develop gaming ordinances to be approved by the chairman of the National Indian Gaming Commission, which would consist of a chair appointed by the president and approved by Congress and two associate or assistant chairs. Not more than two members of the commission could be from the same political party and two of the chairs had to be enrolled tribal members. Since its passing, some but not all of these positions have been held by Indians. IGRA also provided that the FBI (rather than city, county, or state law enforcement) would have jurisdiction over tribal gaming.

After the passage of IGRA, Indian gaming boomed. Revenues grew from $100 million in 1988 to more than $26 billion in 2009—more than Vegas and Atlantic City took in combined. Despite the influx of money in general, however, gaming changed little for most Indians. In 1965 the national Indian unemployment rate was 52 percent. The rate for California Indians was 53 percent. In 1993 the national unemployment rate among Indians had dropped to 37 percent. But in California, despite the rapid growth of Indian gaming, 41 percent of all Indians living there were unemployed. Between 1989 and 1995, in areas with tribal gaming, Indians living below the poverty line decreased from 17.7 to 15.5 percent. In areas without Indian gaming, Indians living below the poverty line remained static at 18 percent for those years. By 2010, when the national unemployment rate had spiked to 10 percent, the highest in thirty years, Senator Byron Dorgan, chair of the Senate Committee on Indian Affairs, noted, "There are a lot of people in a lot of areas on Indian reservations where they would welcome 10 percent unemployment." The unemployment rate for Native American communities nationwide was 50 percent in 2010, and in the northern Great Plains, it rose to 77 percent. Addressing the committee, Harvey Spoonhunter, chairman of the Northern Arapaho Business Council for the Wind River Reservation (combined Shoshone and Arapaho) in central Wyoming, noted: "The unemployment rate on the reservation exceeds 73 percent, as stated by [Senator John] Barrasso, and over 60 percent of the households live below the poverty line. With the opening of our three relatively small casinos, the marketing of our organic beef from the Arapaho Ranch to Colorado-based food stores, and our sponsorship of the tribally-chartered Wind River Health Systems, a federally supported rural health system, we have begun to provide meaningful jobs outside of tribal government for our members." Meanwhile, the Shakopee Mdewakanton Sioux Community, a tribe of only a little more than 480 members with a very large casino near Minneapolis, have boasted a 99.2 percent unemployment rate: each tribal member receives upward of $1.08 million annually.

The contrasts, while extreme, shouldn't be surprising. This is America, after all. Like all American avenues to wealth, casinos privilege the few and leave out the majority. But at Tulalip signs of a possible third way have emerged.

Two months after the "pot summit," I sat across from Eddy Pablo in the same casino. He had come armed with notes and handouts about marijuana legalization, medical uses of marijuana, and tribal dispositions about legalization and capitalization at Tulalip. Eddy is about five-foot-ten, with an absurdly strong build, dark skin, small eyes, and spiky black hair in a neat crew cut. He's thirty-one with three children and he is on the make. "I've lived here my whole life. Both my parents are from here. I'm thankful for it." He is soft-spoken but gives off that uniquely Indian sense that nothing bothers him. Yet there is plainly a kind of seething, sliding, waiting energy underneath his social self. He speaks of the business aspects of marijuana in the same tone of voice as he tells the story of how he almost died while diving. "I was diving for geoducks and the compressor ran out of gas. It feeds oxygen down to me where I was, about forty feet down. And the com went down, too. The guys on the boat thought I was dead when I was hauled up. They asked me if I was all right. And I was like, 'Fuck no, I'm not all right.' Man, I'm happy to be alive."

But to be Indian and alive is no easy thing. "My high school in Marysville was a subtle racist high school. Not so much the kids. But the teachers had no expectations for us. All of us Indian kids were underperforming. If you have low expectations, then that's all the kid will strive for. I wanted to go to college but my sophomore English grade was crappy. They put me in a special reading class." This was followed by depression and tutoring. He made it to community college but it didn't stick. He ran afoul of the law and landed in jail. After he got out, he got hooked on diving for geoduck. "You don't get to dive very much. Maybe eight days a year. But a boat can make thirteen K in three hours." Eddy becomes more animated when he talks about being on the water.

The next day he picks me up to go digging for clams on Cama Beach

Point. His car is packed with five-gallon buckets, shovels, rakes, and his son, Cruz, tucked in the backseat. As we drive, he points out the landmarks. The Tulalip Reservation—twenty-two thousand acres of Indian land—sits between Interstate 5 and Puget Sound just north of Seattle. It is indescribably beautiful. "That's where I grew up," he says, pointing at a nondescript house among a handful of other HUD homes facing a silty bay that was, until relatively recently, thick with salmon. Cedar, until recently, grew down to the shore. The winters are mild and the summers temperate. It's pretty much what the land of the Lotus-Eaters looked like in *The Odyssey*. The entire sound was filled with Indians who pulled their lives from the waters. And it's a testament to the perseverance of those Indians that there are still many of them left on the sound even though the cedar have been cut down and the salmon run is a trickle of what it once was. The reservation itself, established in the Treaty of Point Elliott in 1855, is made up of seven intermingled peoples—Duwamish, Snohomish, Snoqualmie, Skagit, Suiattle, Samish, and Stillaguamish—all considered Coast Salish. There are about 4,800 enrolled tribal members, but only about 2,500 live within the borders of the reservation. There are also about 3,000 non–tribal members who live within the boundaries of the reservation, making Tulalip like a lot of other reservations whose lands were parceled out to tribal members, with the "surplus land" being opened up for white purchase as a result of the Dawes Act and other allotment legislation in the late nineteenth century. And as on many other reservations, the nicest parcels, those right on the sound, are largely owned or leased by non–tribal members.

But unlike most tribes, people here are doing all right, economically speaking. In fact, they are doing very well. One of the poorest tribes in the country, the Oglala Sioux of the Pine Ridge Reservation in South Dakota, contains the poorest county in America, with a median household income of $30,908. The percentage of people in Pine Ridge living below the poverty level has remained much the same as it was in 1969 (54.3 percent), and grew even slightly worse in 1990 (59.5 percent). The median household income at Tulalip, by contrast, is a comfortable $68,000 per year, about $13,000 above the national average. Tribal members do get a per capita payment, though according to Eddy it's not more than $15,500 a year. The tribe, as a collective, as a *business*, is doing better as well. Every tribal building is new. The tribal office where Eddy picked up our permit is a soaring architectural treasure. The youth center. Museum. Cultural center. All of them cedar-clad and many of them LEED-certified. Where once the tribe's wealth could be measured in fish, it can now be measured in income and infrastructure.

"You see that big bluff over there?" Eddy asks as we round another curve on our way to Cama Beach. "We call that the Big Slide. Back in the 1800s that's where one of our big villages was. Right below the bluff. And the whole thing calved off and buried the village. Hundreds of people died. And the shock wave traveled across the sound there and drowned people in another village across the way." At least five people I've talked to out here have brought it up. And then they turn to the water and the fish and a brother, uncle, father, cousin who died going out on the sound.

As for Eddy, without a college degree and with three kids to support, he hustles. He dives for geoduck. Crabs. Fishes. Harvests sea cucumber. And he owns a fireworks stand. All of this together somehow makes a living. He sees marijuana as something that can be added to the mix. "We should get in the business," he says. "Not just opening dispensaries. Or growing. Our sovereignty can give us a leg up. We should grow, process, and dispense. We could control the whole chain." I wonder out loud if the tribe really wants to hitch itself to another lifestyle economy—like cigarettes and gambling.

"Look," says Eddy. "Heroin is here. Once they changed the chemical makeup of prescription drugs [like OxyContin], everyone turned back to heroin. People die from that. No one dies from pot. And the tribe wants it. The people want it. We did a survey and seventy-eight percent voted yes for bringing our code in line with the state. Fifty-three percent wanted to open it up only to medical marijuana and twenty-five percent wanted that and recreational use to be legal. It could be our niche. I mean, the way marijuana is taxed in Washington could work in our favor. The producers get taxed at twenty-five percent, the processors get taxed at twenty-five percent, and the retailers get taxed at twenty-five percent. But if we were the producers, processors, and retailers? And we're sovereign, too. So we'd have a different tax rate than a private business in Washington." As of this writing, the tribe has opened a dispensary, and brought its code in line with the State of Washington.

By now we've reached the beach. Entry is a slight hassle—the workers seem rattled by an Indian who wants to exercise his treaty rights on his ancestral land by harvesting clams—but Eddy calmly explains things to them and drives down the winding road to the beach. We unload the buckets and tools and Cruz and walk past the picnic area and down to the shingle. Here is the sound primordial: cedars and pines growing down to the edge, waves lapping and turning the silt, crawling up the gentle slope of the beach, and sliding back through the pebbles and broken clamshells with the sound of someone sucking air through their teeth. Eddy sets Cruz in a carrier facing the sea and we begin turning over shovelfuls of sand and rock. In a minute or two, Eddy says, "See, look. This is a butter clam. That one is a manila. The big ones are horse clams. They are okay. But I like the butters best." We stop talking and relax into the very old rhythm of gathering. An eagle dives over our heads, his wings making the sound of ripping cloth, to lift a fish out of the sound. We've filled two buckets of clams in an hour. We are the only ones there. "I love this," says Eddy. "I just love doing this."

We have only an hour, two at most, while the tide is out, to dig and sort. Soon the water will come back in and cover the clam beds, and they will be lost to us. So much of life at Tulalip has the same kind of rhythm. Small windows in which one can make a lot of money, slow spells when none is to be made, and then another hard push. It's not the kind of labor that breeds confidence or even certainty: no clocking in, working, clocking out, and pulling in a wage and benefits.

So how, I wonder out loud, does he make ends meet? What's his job? He gets his per cap from the tribe. He crabs a few days. He dives a few days. He goes after geoduck and sea cucumber and salmon. And in the same manner he runs his stand at Boom City in the summer. Almost everyone I talk to brings up two things: the Big Slide and Boom City. "You've got to see it," he says. "You wouldn't believe it. A fireworks bazaar. Bigger than anything. And there's a place to light them off. It's like World War Three." He seems to think this is a good thing. And in a way I suppose it is, just like his whole operation. It's not an American kind of work, but it is an Indian kind: a patchwork of opportunities that are exploited aggressively and together add up to a living. A good one. "We have a story," says Eddy as we drive away. Cruz is asleep in his car seat. "When all else fails we were instructed to dig. The clams are always there. There's food waiting there." My mind drifts back to the question of casinos. In addition to opening new avenues to wealth—and creating a wealth gap in Indian country—casinos have had another major effect: they've thrown into stark relief the vexing question of who gets to be Indian at all.

Blood Quantum and Disenrollment

America's first blood-quantum law was passed in Virginia in 1705 in order to determine who had a high enough degree of Indian blood to be classified an Indian—and whose rights could be restricted as a result. You'd think, after all these years, we'd finally manage to kick the concept. But recently, casino-rich Indian tribes in California, Michigan, Oregon, and other states have been using it themselves to disenroll those whose tribal bloodlines, they say, are not pure enough to share in the profits. As of 2017, more than fifty tribes across the country have banished or disenrolled at least eight thousand tribal members in the past two decades. Many different rationales have been used to justify it, but it's telling that 73 percent of the tribes actively kicking out tribal members have gaming operations. According to Gabe Galanda, a lawyer who has come to take on disenrollment as one of his specialties, that number is increasing and reaching epidemic proportions: more than eighty tribes in about seventeen states are disenrolling their citizens. The Picayune Rancheria of Chukchansi Indians near Coarsegold, California, disenrolled hundreds, perhaps nearly a thousand, of its tribal members in what was clearly a money grab: they wanted to keep more gaming money for themselves.

What is surprising is not that more than twenty-five hundred tribal members in California have been disenfranchised in the past decade for such reasons. It's human—and American—nature to want to concentrate wealth in as few hands as possible. What is surprising is the extent to which Indian communities have continued using a system of blood membership that was imposed upon us in a violation of our sovereignty.

In the late nineteenth and early twentieth centuries, the U.S. government entered into treaties with Indian nations that reserved tracts of land for tribal ownership and use and guaranteed annuities in the form of money, goods, or medical care. Understandably, tribes and the government needed a way to make sure this material ended up in the right hands. Blood quantum, and sometimes lineal descent, was a handy way of solving that problem. For instance, if one of your grandparents was included on the tribal rolls and you possessed a certain blood quantum—say, you were one-fourth Navajo—the government counted you as Navajo as well.

But it had another benefit, for the government at least, which believed that within a few generations intermarriage and intermixing would eliminate Indian communities, and the government would be off the hook. "As long as grass grows or water runs"—a phrase that was often used in treaties with American Indians—is a relatively permanent term for a contract. "As long as the blood flows" seemed measurably shorter.

Indians themselves knew how artificial this category of tribal membership was and used it to their own advantage. Before my tribe, the Ojibwe, established the White Earth Reservation in Minnesota in 1867, Chief Bagone-giizhig lobbied to exclude mixed-bloods from the rolls—not because they weren't Indians but because, most likely, they formed a competing trader class. Bagone-giizhig swore they would rob White Earth blind. That he was right is a bit beside the point—he probably wanted to rob it blind himself.

Something similar happened after the passage and subsequent amendment of the Dawes Act of 1887, which established a process of allotment under which vast lands held in common were divided into smaller plots for individual Indians. Although excess land could be sold off, full-blood Indians were forbidden to sell. But whites wanted the land and sent in a genetic investigator. In short order, the number of registered full-bloods at White Earth Reservation went from more than 5,000 to 408.

After Congress passed the Indian Reorganization Act in 1934, effectively ending the allotment of land, the provisions of blood quantum became ingrained in Indian communities. They determined if you could vote or run for office, where you could live, if you'd receive annuities or assistance, and, today, if you get a cut of the casino profits. Blood quantum has always been about "the stuff," and it has always been about exclusion. I know full-blooded Indians who have lived their entire lives on reservations but can't be enrolled because they have blood from many different tribes, and I know of non-Indians who have been enrolled by accident or stealth just because they'll get something out of it.

Things were different once. All tribes had their own ways of figuring out who was a member—usually based on language, residence, and culture. In the case of the Ojibwe, it was a matter of choosing a side. Especially when we were at war with the Dakota (many of whom were our blood relatives) in the early nineteenth century, who you were was largely a matter of whom you killed. Personally, I think this is a more elegant way than many to figure out where you belong. Who is and who isn't an Indian is a complicated question, but there are many ways to answer it beyond genetics alone. Tribal enrollees could be required to possess some level of fluency in their Native language or to pass a basic civics test. On my reservation, no schoolchild is asked to read the treaties that shaped our community or required to know about the branches of tribal government or the role of courts and councils. Or tribal membership could be based, in part, on residency, on some period of naturalization inside the original treaty area (some tribes do consider this). Many nations require military service—tribes don't have armies, but they could require a year of community service. Other nations take these things into account, and in doing so they reinforce something we, with our fixation on blood, have forgotten: bending to a common purpose is more important than arising from a common place.

Of course, just remaining alive and Indian for the past 150 years has been one of the hardest things imaginable. A respect for lineage is a respect for the integrity of that survival, and it should remain a metric for tribal enrollment—but not the only one. Having survived this long and come this far, we must think harder about who we want to be in the future and do something more than measure out our teaspoons of blood. Also, as Lumbee legal and political scholar David Wilkins points out, disenrollment often occurs when there is no casino money at stake. This is precisely what is happening up the road from Tulalip among the Nooksack.

The Nooksack, a Coast Salish tribe in the corner of Washington state, were, historically, much like the Tulalip and other coastal tribes in the Northwest: they lived in small villages, fished extensively, and were avid traders. They were much diminished during the nineteenth century and lost federal recognition along the way. However, they fought back and after a long road—tasked with the absurd chore of proving to the government that tried to wipe them out that they actually did exist—they won back federal recognition in 1973. At that time the tribe controlled but a single acre, but over the past forty years it has been purchasing back land, and now it has nearly twenty-five hundred acres of land in trust with the federal government. The tribe also owns and operates a small casino, but it isn't much more than a jobs program for some of the seven hundred tribal members (of more than two thousand enrolled members) who live on or near the reservation.

That story—of a small tribe that was all but destroyed or absorbed into surrounding communities but fought for its continued existence and won—might have been the whole of the Nooksacks' story. Except in 2012, the tribal chairman swerved. A tribal member named Terry St. Germain filed paperwork to have five of his children enrolled. It should have been a simple procedure. But the enrollment process stalled. When Terry's brother Rudy asked Bob Kelly, the tribal chairman, what was going on with the paperwork for his nieces and nephews, the chairman said they were missing documents, and it seemed that the St. Germain children couldn't be enrolled. Not only that: Rudy, Terry, and the rest of the St. Germains—all of whom traced their ancestry back to the same ancestor, Annie George—should be disenrolled. All in all, Bob Kelly determined that 306 living descendants of Annie George should be jettisoned. Kelly maintained that he was simply following the tribe's rules: Annie George wasn't on a 1942 federal census—United States censuses of Indians since the nineteenth century are known to be woefully inaccurate—used to determine lineal descent. And he felt it his duty to follow the rules despite the resulting social turmoil. The tribal council stopped functioning properly, meetings were canceled, tribal business was not attended to, sides were taken, a judge was fired. In a community that small, you pull one string and the tribe unravels. Kelly was passionate about the decision, not just for the rules' sake, but in order to protect Nooksack culture. "I'm in a war," he told a reporter from *The New York Times*. "This is our culture, not a game." But is it?

Culture isn't carried in the blood, and when you measure blood, in a sense you measure racial origins. Or, more accurately, you measure the social construct that race is. Culture is carried on in many ways—kinship, geography, language, religion, lifeways, habits, and even gestures—but not in blood. I think that Kelly is about as far from the truth about culture as one can be: by relying on blood to measure culture, all you are doing is showing that you don't have much culture left anyway. Blood matters. And blood is and will continue to be used as a way to determine who is in a tribe and who isn't. But it is useless to determine who is and isn't part of a culture. It should be noted that there is only one remaining fluent speaker of Nooksack—and how, for that matter, can fluency even be measured if no other speakers remain to evaluate it?

What's fascinating to me is that the whole question of culture didn't become part of the conversation about who is and who isn't Indian at all until the period AC—After Casinos. True, *being* Indian (as something one did in addition to being something one simply was) began back with the Red Power movement and was amplified by AIM. But in those early discussions and actions, being Indian was more a matter of politics and emotional affinity than a matter of culture. Even the religions claimed by AIM were antagonistic and political: AIMsters danced the Sun Dance as a way of saying "We're not you" more than as a positive assertion of religious identity. But after casinos began injecting millions and then hundreds of millions and then billions of dollars into Indian economies, culture really came to the fore of discussions of Indianness.

In part this phenomenon appears to be generational in origin. Many of the Indians who moved to cities in the 1950s, 1960s, and 1970s stayed in the cities. They put down roots, got jobs, went to school, and had families. Their urban and suburban children were raised on story after story of the rez—stories about bad cars and violent sheriffs and selling blueberries or baskets or tamales or necklaces by the roadside; about five or ten or fifteen people living in a shack; about one drunkscapade after another; about the foibles or idiosyncrasies of this or that elder. These stories became foundational myths, benchmarks of authenticity, even though they were all, in one way or another, stories of loss. Nonetheless, for many Indian kids not raised there, the reservation and the mythology around it carried the idea that there was more to being Indian than simply having a tribal ID card. The new emphasis on culture may also be a matter of class, too. By the 1980s, a recognizable Indian middle class had begun to emerge. The origins of this class can be traced back to the earliest days of the reservations—to mixed-blood Indians who set up shop as traders, foremen, loggers, miners, and the like, relying on both their Indian and their white families. Also, as destructive as the boarding school era was, it had taught many students to not only read and write but to farm, sew, and operate and fix machinery as well. And allotment had made property owners of many Indians. With that added level of security, work and capital were suddenly available to them. World War II and the social programs of the 1960s and 1970s also helped bring a few Indians into the American middle class without necessarily compromising their culture. The advent of casinos could be seen as yet another step in this progression. Gabe Galanda, the lawyer who represents the "Nooksack 306" in their battle to be reenrolled in their tribe, notes that while Indians on reservations saw their income rise 33 percent and the poverty level decrease by 7 percent after the advent of casinos, there was little evidence to suggest that the rise of income and the fall of poverty could be attributed directly to casino income.

The energy around the casinos, and the money derived from them, fed efforts to promote Indian culture, too. Casino-rich tribes—and even tribes like mine that haven't made much from gambling—began sponsoring powwows with large purses for dancers and drum groups. They built and operated museums. They continued and expanded tribal schools where students learned reading, and writing, and math but also took classes in Indian singing and drumming, crafts, and tribal languages.

All in all, by the end of the 1990s there was enough cushion for enough Indians and enough money to begin pondering, in earnest, what being Indian *meant*. Identity politics is a game usually played by people who can afford it. And by 1990, many Indians could afford it. They had enough space in their lives to want to connect to their tribes in ways that were value positive, that didn't see being Indian as a matter of being a full-blood or being enrolled or being simply "dark," as had been the case when I was growing up. Rather, being Indian became a matter of knowing your language, attending ceremony, harvesting game and wild rice or piñon or salmon. Being Indian was still to some degree a matter of blood, but it was also in the process of becoming about much more. By 2012, when tribal chairman Bob Kelly began kicking people off the rolls at Nooksack, the culture question was much larger and more nuanced than he could imagine. And for many Native people, the idea that kicking out three hundred members—or 15 percent—of your tribe was in some way protecting tribal culture was, on the face of it, ridiculous.

As Charles Wilkinson points out, by the 1970s tribes across the country had, for the first time, an "emerging litigation" capability. The legal-services organizations funded under the OEO that had helped Helen Bryan were taking root across the country. In the nonprofit sector, legal organizations like the Native American Rights Fund and the Indian Law

Resource Center also represented Indian individuals, tribes, and tribal interests in areas such as taxation, undoing the ravages of the Termination Act, and advancing Indian interests and rights internationally. This was a good time, legally speaking, to be an Indian. As the Indian legal and professional class grew, the Supreme Court kept pace, recognizing Indian rights in more than 120 decisions handed down since the 1950s that touched on tribal affairs, Indian rights, and tribal sovereignty.

The frenzy of Indian legal activity in the 1960s and 1970s—government initiatives and programs, the disposition of the Supreme Court, and non-profit organizations fighting for Indian rights—not only helped secure the idea and fact of Indian tribal sovereignty; it also "breathed life into a basic principle of American law and political science widely recognized in the early days of the Republic but dormant since the late 1800s"—namely that "there are three branches of sovereignty within the American consti-tutional system, the United States, the states (cities and counties are sub-divisions of state sovereignty), and the Indian tribes." The idea of sovereignty—until the 1980s usually explored and litigated in terms of treaty rights (usually but not always stipulated in treaties, such as the right to hunt, fish, and gather)—expanded to include gaming (the right to ad-minister to the civil concerns of the tribe).

The civil reach of sovereignty was furthered in the Southwest in the 1980s when the Jicarilla Apache were brought to court by oil and gas companies that had long-standing leases on Apache land. The Jicarilla Apache Reservation in northern New Mexico sat on top of coal, oil, and gas reserves. Those reserves had been tapped by energy companies through lucrative leases with the tribe (written and executed with the heavy hand of the BIA). In the late 1970s, the Apache were no longer content with the deals that had been struck. The tribes, unable to simply change the leases, wanted to tax the oil companies. Their constitution (revised in 1968 and approved by the secretary of the interior) gave the tribe the "authority to pass ordinances to govern the development of tribal resources," so in 1976 the tribal council adopted the Jicarilla Oil and Natural Gas Severance Tax, applicable to "any oil and natural gas severed, saved and removed from tribal lands." The oil and gas companies sued. And the case wound up in the Supreme Court in 1982. The court found for the tribe. Justice Thurgood Marshall's opinion articulated a delicious reversal of the prevailing attitude that tribes were savage, or pitiful remnants of savage people without "real" civilization. He wrote that the oil companies "avail themselves of the 'substantial privilege of carrying on business' on the reservation. . . . They benefit from the provision of police protection and other governmental services, as well as from 'the advantages of a civilized society' that are assured by the existence of tribal government. . . . Under these circumstances, there is nothing exceptional in requiring [them] to contribute through taxes to the general cost of tribal government." But there were other, less tangible shifts that emerged from the sovereignty surge in the 1980s.

My mother had been born in 1945 in the Cass Lake hospital on the Leech Lake Reservation. She grew up with her three brothers and sister and parents in a two-room cabin in Bena, a town not known for much except for spawning generations of brawlers and (eventual) convicts. My grandfather, a World War II vet, and my grandmother didn't make much. The shack had electricity but no running water, and no heat except a barrel stove. They dug a root cellar underneath the tacked-on kitchen area, and my mother had to descend a ladder into the damp depths to retrieve potatoes. Neither parent pushed education very much, and my mother was pulled from school regularly in the fall to harvest wild rice. In the summer, her uncle Howard took her along with his wife and kids near the Canadian border, on the Ash River, to pick blueberries. Her cousin, my uncle Bobby, remembers those berry-picking trips. "In the early morning we'd head out in the hills and start picking berries. You learn to pick fast and my dad was a fast picker. Sticks, twigs, green berries, he didn't care as long as he filled his baskets. We'd dump them all into packing crates but you can only carry a packing crate through the woods so far. Your arms give out! So my dad stapled some lath together, and then he cut up some inner tubes and stapled those on and bang: we had ourselves backpacks. We picked blueberries till it was really hot in the afternoon and then we'd swim over at the Ash River. At night me and Mikey would lay with our heads out of our tents and look for Sputniks. That's what we called satellites at that time." They got paid twenty-five cents a pint for blueberries.

When I ran Bobby's account by my mother, she laughed. *He said Uncle Howard took us swimming in the afternoon? That's crazy. There was no swimming. Just picking. We picked all day long. And we'd walk back to Huffman's with those damn packs on our backs and we'd be so hot we would sit down in the springs by the side of the railroad tracks—clothes, shoes, packs, and all—just to cool off. And then we'd start walking again and you'd be bone dry in five minutes. It was awful.* Harvesting rice was awful, too, in her memory. They sold most of it to buy school clothes, flour, lard, and kerosene. They got thirty-five cents a pound for wild rice in the 1950s. My mother never wanted to do any of that stuff again. So when she was a senior in high school, she decided to continue on to nursing school. When she told her father, he scoffed and sneered. Who the hell did she think she was? Nevertheless, my mother went to nursing school in Saint Cloud and graduated in three years. After that, she worked in a hospital in Moose Lake. And shortly after that, she returned to Leech Lake and got the CAP job working on health care where she met my father. They moved to Washington, D.C., in 1968.

I didn't know anything! my mother said. *There were riots all over the city. But I'd never lived in a city and I thought that's just the way the city was. I was walking down the street near Georgetown and I saw a shopping cart on the sidewalk so I figured I'd use it. I walked along with that cart window-shopping. There was trash everywhere. Windows broken. Stuff was on fire. A black lady looked at me and said, "You'd better get out of here! It's not safe!" But I didn't know!* After my older brother, Anton, and I were born, my mother wanted something more. My father asked her, *If you could do anything, what would it be?* She demurred. But he was nothing if not persistent. *Just say it, we're just talking. What would you do? No limits.* Reluctantly she said she'd like to be a lawyer because no one had stuck up for her and her family when she was a kid. No one stood up against the cops and the courts and the government.

My father cajoled her into applying to Catholic University in

Washington. She was admitted provisionally, since she didn't have a four-year degree. Three years later, juggling four kids by that time, she received her law degree. She had interned with the Native American Rights Fund in D.C. and had sat in on Supreme Court hearings for *Bryan v. Itasca County*. In 1979 we moved back to the reservation, and she and Paul Day, another young Leech Lake Indian who'd gone into law, opened their law offices in the town of Cass Lake, kitty-corner from the high school that had been of the opinion that my mother and people like her wouldn't go very far.

In the fall she made us go ricing, as she had as a girl (though without the pressure to earn). In the summer we picked berries. In the fall she took us hunting. In the early winter she taught us how to hang snares for rabbits. In the spring the family tapped maple trees and boiled the sap into syrup and finished it into sugar. My mother still hated ricing, and so did I—it was itchy and uncomfortable work—but my father loved it. She'd sit and watch us jig the rice in a shallow pit dug in the yard and lined with a tarp, separating the husks from the grains. She didn't jig much, but she offered lots of pointers from the vantage of her lawn chair. I shied away from sugaring, too—the fumes from the boiling sap gave me headaches. My parents thought I was shirking. I probably was. These weren't fun-filled moments of family togetherness, at least for me. They were tense and dank, freighted with all our problems, spoken and unspoken.

Much later I asked my mother why she'd had us do all that stuff anyway. Why bother? *I was going to make sure you did well and got into college and went on to find a good job*, she explained. *But I was also going to make sure you knew how we lived, how we lived off the land. That way, no matter what happened out there in the bigger world, you'd know how to take care of yourself back here, on the rez. You'd be able to feed yourself.* Still later, looking back, I see in my mother's actions and attitudes something I surely didn't see then—one of the less visible effects of Indian empowerment and sovereignty in the 1970s and 1980s, which came to fruition in the 1990s. Sovereignty isn't only a legal attitude or a political reality; it has a social dimension as well. The idea and practice of sovereignty carries with it a kind of dignity—a way of relating to the self, to others, to the past, and to the future that is dimensionally distinct. As such, for my mother, being Indian wasn't a condition to be cured or a past to be escaped and even improved upon. To be sure, her early struggles and the continuing struggles of Indian people across the country exist alongside, and are bound up in, what it means to be Indian. But to be Indian is not to be poor or to struggle. To believe in sovereignty, to let it inform and define not only one's political and legal existence but also one's community, to move through the world imbued with the dignity of that reality, is to resolve one of the major contradictions of modern Indian life: it is to find a way to be Indian and modern simultaneously.

THE CANNABIS INDUSTRY has started modestly at Tulalip. It is unclear what it will bring or where it will end. Some, like Eddy, think that pot shouldn't necessarily be a tribal enterprise but rather something tribal individuals can participate in, another small business arrow in the quiver of ventures and seasonal harvests that can make up an income. But how the tribe will exploit the cannabis market collectively is an open question, dependent not only on the unique politics at Tulalip but also on the way tribes do business in general.

Les Parks, the former tribal vice chairman of the Tulalip and currently the treasurer, has been at the forefront in trying to get the tribe into the business. While he was still serving as vice chairman, he put together the "pot summit." But after the summit and a subsequent election, Les stepped down, having "shot his bolt" on the whole issue, according to him, and having failed to overrule those who opposed the idea. As on most other reservations, tribal enterprise at Tulalip is controlled by a small group of people who have grown up together in a very small community. A small village council can control millions on millions of dollars, and so big decisions are often, at their core, made for very personal reasons. The Tulalip Tribes are governed by a board of directors consisting of seven members chosen through a general election who serve three-year overlapping terms, with no term limits. After each election cycle, the board votes to determine officers. This group of seven is, according to Les, in charge of seventy-two departments, from the Montessori school to a halfway house to, more significantly, the board of Quil Ceda Village—which controls the Quil Ceda Village economic zone, including the casino, an outlet mall, and a commercial district. Within that kind of political structure, governed by a tiny minority of the population, any personal conflicts are, in the old phrase, extremely political. But if the marijuana business at Tulalip is a success, it will be Les Parks, the treasurer of the tribe, who will support it.

I'm met by Les, in bolo tie, boots, and a very large, very new pickup truck. He is a busy man, and so I get in the truck and he drives me around the rez in what I can only call an effort to roll out the salmon-colored carpet. We begin at the casino—with its Four Diamond award–winning hotel, twelve stories, 370 rooms, nearly 192,000 square feet of gaming space, and seven restaurants. Then we drive the winding, oddly suburban roads of Quil Ceda Village, the only federal municipality in the United States other than Washington, D.C., and the only city with a permanent population of zero; instead it contains 131 outlet stores, a Cabela's, a Walmart, and a Home Depot. I hear from Les about George Vancouver claiming the sound for King George. Then we zig and zag past more recognizable reservation socialscapes, like the cedar-clad youth center with a $400,000 skate park under construction next to the old longhouse, and I hear about the modest origins of the reservation itself. Then past the tribal offices, a $32 million (according to Les) glass-and-cedar beauty that is the modernist administrative equivalent of the Overlook Hotel, where Les tells me about Stan Jones and other early leaders. Then past the salmon stocking ponds netted over against the birds, the Early Learning Academy for kids through age five, and the museum. Tulalip is very much like many of the other 325 (the BIA says there are "approximately" 325) reservations in America in that, instead of the cinematic desuetude that is the popular notion of rez life, it is a patchwork of business, Indian homes, non-Indian homes, trees, and land. What's different is that Tulalip seems shinier somehow, richer.

390

Les is proud of his community, and he has obviously given this tour many times. It feels both practiced and sincere. When I ask how much Quil Ceda Village makes (or the casino, or the fisheries, or anything, for that matter), he is evasive. "Oh, we do okay. It's a matter of public record we have a case in the courts that will determine if Quil Ceda Village should collect sales taxes. Right now we give it all to the city of Marysville, Snohomish County, and the State of Washington. Every year we send sixty-two million dollars in taxes to Olympia. That should give you an idea." It's understandable that a wildly successful tribe like the Tulalip don't want to say how much they're pulling in: the federal government has treaty obligations to the Tulalip to provide for housing and services, among other things, obligations that, when all is going well, the government is only too happy to let slide. So the fiscal rhetoric of reservations, if not the social rhetoric, is always one of want and need.

The tour turns personal, and so does the talk, when Les veers down a long, narrow road that ends near a creek feeding into the sound. This is where his family's original allotment was. "My great-great-grandfather must have been important because this was a good place to live, right next to the creek. It would have been full of salmon." But Les has suffered like so many Indians have suffered: he lost his mother to a drunk driver, his father wasn't around very much. The house he grew up in, long gone—rotted or burned or pulled down—was of rough-cut lumber and tar paper. He had a lot of brothers and sisters. There wasn't much to go around. Many of the people I talked to had similar stories—fathers and brothers lost to the sea, heavy drinking, absentee parents, poor living conditions. Here as elsewhere, survival was the principal challenge for Indians for well over a century. And from Les's story, like others, it's clear that a certain tolerance for conflict, pain, and uncertainty—a kind of wild and unpredictable daily drama—has been necessary to that survival. What, then, allows growth? What are the ingredients necessary for a community not only to make money but to grow real wealth? Les seemed torn as he responds.

"My sister-in-law got Parkinson's disease. It was horrible to watch. Pot helped her. It helped her pain a lot." But Les doesn't want the tribe to sell pot. Or to *only* sell it. "I want us to use our sovereignty to fast-track clinical trials for the uses of marijuana extracts. We could do it faster and better than any of the pharmaceutical companies out there. We're already talking to Bastyr University. That's where I want us to go. There are a lot of uses for extracts and there is no pharmaceutical company in North America that is looking in that direction. We could be the first." He looks off over the sound. "There's even some research that suggests cannabis extracts can be used to cure type-two diabetes. Think about that. Think about an Indian company, a tribal pharmaceutical company, that could cure the greatest threat to our health."

Fifteen percent of American Indians have diabetes, and in some communities in the Southwest, the rate is as high as 22 percent. And diabetes is only part of the problem. Along with high dropout and unemployment and poverty rates, Indians have a mortality rate from accidental death that is twice the national average. (The only thing it seems we have going for us is that we beat everyone out on the cancer scale. For some reason we don't get it as often.) Life, for many of us, is not merely bleak: it's short, poor, painful, unhealthy, and tumultuous. All of which makes Les's dream and the reality of Tulalip the more remarkable.

His own journey has been remarkable, too. Out of high school he took part in a federally funded vocational training program and studied to become an electrician. He parlayed that into a job with the tribe. From there he started his own construction company. Along the way he did what a lot of the people at Tulalip seem to do, which is to say a bit of everything: fishing, fish wholesaling, selling fireworks, buying land, and eventually running for office. There is a steady arc to his life that resembles the one that was supposed to move Americans from being poor into the middle class from the post–World War II years through the 1970s. For most Americans that arc collapsed in the 1980s, but it still seems available to at least some of the people at Tulalip. Just as Les moved from poverty to relative comfort in about thirty years, so, too, has the tribe: the original tribal offices, a small clapboard house near the marina built in 1935, could fit inside the $32 million tribal offices up on the hill many times over. That's a long way to go in a relatively short amount of time. According to the Tribal Employment Rights Organization (TERO), there are 62 registered small businesses owned and operated by Indians on the Tulalip Reservation right now, but since businesses register annually, that swells to more than 160 when there's a big project on the books. And that figure doesn't seem to include fishermen (there were by my count more than twenty boats in the fleet) or the 139 tribally owned and operated fireworks stands at Boom City, or tribal businesses in areas that are, technically at least, off the reservation. When I add all that up, I figure at least a few hundred Indians are in on the hustle—no different, in their way, from the many who sell crafts on Etsy, auction game on eBay, plow driveways, and make T-shirts on the side. There is, despite historical oppression and in contrast to the received stereotypes about Indians, an active and thriving entrepreneurial class at Tulalip.

The tribe has opened a dispensary but hasn't given up on Les's bigger vision. "Even if we can't do it, it should be done," he says. I can't help agreeing. Why shouldn't the tribe, surrounded as it is by Boeing and Microsoft and Amazon, wed tribal enterprise and wealth to technological enterprise and wealth? A pharmaceutical company could be the way to bring Tulalip's economy out from under the lifestyle economies that have marked, till now, tribal enterprise.

Tribal power is an interesting thing. With a structure like Tulalip's, power rests in the hands of a very few, and the absence of term limits makes it very easy to keep doing the same thing but very, very hard to do anything new. It takes a kind of doggedness, a kind of patience to keep putting the issue up, not investing too much political capital in doing so, election cycle after election cycle. And yet it also takes visionary leadership and stubbornness. Most tribes are caught this way, between the need for the political and economic stability on which sovereignty depends and the urgent need to change the economic and social climate. Often, doing something about the "tribal quo" means empowering people who work for the tribe but come from outside it.

One person who seems to have helped do something about it is a white corporate lawyer named Mike Taylor. Taylor represents the kind of force—the man behind the man behind the man—who has helped shape Indian country for the better part of more than forty years. If there are angels of doom and angels of mercy, surely Mike Taylor is an angel of effectiveness. He sought me out and pinned me down on my last day at Tulalip. "At Quinault, where I worked for a while," he says over breakfast, "their sole economic source of income was from the fish house. The first thing we did was to separate business from governance. If the tribe needed something from the fish house they had to ask!" He laughs. But Tulalip was far behind Quinault in the early 1970s. "You have to understand. In the bad old days there was no police here, no court. Embezzlement is what you got. The burdens of being Indian were in some way only mitigated by embezzling from the tribe. Politics was only a way to mitigate your own poverty, not a way to help other people. Tulalip was a dangerous place. There was really no one to call. Women, children, elders: they were all in danger." A few things, however, came together. The Boldt Decision in 1974, wherein a federal judge awarded 50 percent of Washington state's annual catch to tribes with treaty fishing rights, was a great boost not only to individual Indians but to a sense of tribal purpose as well. And then *California v. Cabazon* helped open up gaming in the 1980s. These court decisions have had a huge impact on tribal enterprise, at Tulalip and elsewhere. Both cases resulted from Indian civil rights cases. We forsake, if not disenroll, individual Indians today, but without them there would be no tribal fishing or gaming economies. Without their sacrifices, modern sovereignty and self-determination would look very different. Until those court decisions, "sovereignty" was mostly rhetoric.

But after the cases were won, sovereignty became real. And bankable. Those decisions affected all tribes, but not all tribes have grown in the way Tulalip has. "At Tulalip," says Mike, "you can point to the role of Stan Jones as being the important missing piece. He was on tribal council for over forty years and had a unique view of what tribes should aspire to. He had this kind of history: fishing, running his own business. He had plenty of reason to be dyspeptic with white people, because of things that had happened to him. It occasionally surfaced. Here's an example: We put out bids for the hotel. We got bids from PCL, a big company, and we were negotiating the construction contract with them. We were almost done. All that was left was the clause about dispute resolution. They wanted state court. Stan said tribal court. The president of the company came down and in the meeting he says to us, 'You have your culture and we have ours. We aren't going to use tribal court.' Stan stood up and made a speech, the essence of which was: 'Fuck you. We're not doing this.' And we went to the second bidder, who agreed to arbitrate in tribal court if necessary. They built the casino. Stan was tough but also a smooth operator. He got the Marysville Chamber of Commerce to move onto tribal land. He would do anything that would benefit Tulalip. He felt the people here deserved more than they were accustomed to. Most of the leadership we have now were schooled in the world of Stan Jones."

I think Mike had much to do with it, too. After he arrived at Tulalip, he pushed to establish a court system and tribal police. He pushed for retrocession from Public Law 280, which gave the state courts jurisdiction over civil matters but which the states often used to extend their jurisdiction well beyond its appropriate bounds. "I pushed for our own police department. Tulalip used to be a very dangerous place. It is less so now. I mean, back then, Boom City was like *Mad Max Beyond Thunderdome*. You know that people are sexually attracted to explosions? It's true! People used to come from New Jersey to buy bombs at Boom City. So the U.S. attorney came here and wanted to shut it down. And we used that! We told him, 'You support retrocession from PL 280 and we'll control Boom City.' We got the bombs out of there. We got it internally regulated. Tulalip is now a safer, more productive place. They key to growth is stability, accountability, and separation of powers. We've got all that here now."

Mike Taylor, and people like him, have shaped tribes the country over. And it's a testament to the Tulalip tribes that Mike has been allowed to do the work he has. But that work often depends on agitation from within the tribe but outside the political structure. At Tulalip that agitator is eighty-four-year-old battler Ray Sheldon.

RAY IS NOT HARD TO FIND. His home and business are located on Tulalip's main drag. All you have to look for is a large fiberglass chicken on a pole (the tribe has designated it a hazard and wants Ray to fix it) and the sign for smoked fish, with its ever-changing digs at tribal officials. (Today it says: DID THE BOARD GET A BIG PAY RAISE? and below it: BOARD SAID NO TO PAY INCREASE FOR ELDERS, WHY?) Oh, and there's also the cell tower Ray leases, which rises above the trees and can be seen for miles around. It's hard to know where on the property to find him. There is a jumble of buildings—a shop for selling the fish, a machine shop, a house, a few more outbuildings I can't quite identify, and heavy equipment and building materials stacked here and there like a kind of mortar holding the buildings together. To some it might look like a mess, but to me it looks like money. I finally locate the office, and Ray meets me at the door.

One son, Tony, is asleep on the couch after a couple hard days crabbing. His other son, Greg, busies himself with paperwork while Ray and I talk. "Try this," Ray says, handing me a package of smoked salmon. I say I will. "You got to eat that right now. Not later." So I do. He watches me and doesn't seem to relax until I'm done. "I got to get my hearing aid," he says, though I'm not sure why because he does most of the talking. He is clearly not short on opinions. There is no preamble, no getting to know each other, no feeling out. There is just drive, about as pure as it comes.

"Okay," he begins, "one thing the government did to poorer Indians, not us, but like the Navajos, poor Indians out in the sticks, they didn't put enough into Indian enterprises but they gave them Indian agents money to set up shop." Ray isn't wrong. From the beginning, reservations were staffed and administered by non-Indian agents whose degree of graft and greed was almost unparalleled in government operations. They gobbled up leases and sold them to friends and benefactors. They withheld annuity payments of cloth and food in order to get tribes—nominally sovereign—to vote the way the government wanted them to vote. Even in the best cases, the BIA exerted a paternalistic kind of care over Indian affairs. They acted as though Indians were too feeble to administer their own affairs effectively. Their tribes were too small, too big, lacked infrastructure. They had not enough education, too much dysfunction. They were unstable, emotional, unreasonable. And so on. After World War II, when many took control of their own affairs, the tribal officials who replaced the Indian agents were often as crooked and greedy as the agents they replaced. All of this was overseen by the Bureau of Indian Affairs, which earned its reputation as the most mismanaged and corrupt of federal agencies. Between 1973 and 1992 alone, audits show that the BIA stole or lost more than $2.4 billion of Indian money—from oil, gas, timber, and grazing leases. And that's for just nineteen of the roughly 150 years that the BIA has been managing Indian money.

In that kind of climate, starting any kind of tribal or private business is dicey. But it didn't deter Ray. And by the end of the day I'm not sure if anything could deter him.

"I got where I am because I worked," he says in his age-thickened voice. "I started in logging, and then fishing. Then I joined the Marines in Korea. I worked in logistics and supply because I had a year and a half of college going in. After the war I studied on the GI Bill—there were more veterans than everyone else in school. I got my BA in business! I went on to operating heavy machinery, grading, gravel, excavating. I opened my store in 1985 with a loan from the bank. I didn't get one from the tribe."

Ray has had firsthand experience of how the paternalism of the federal government and the Indian service seems to have been inherited by and live on through tribal government. He took on the general manager of Quil Ceda Village over a social issue and gave him a good old-fashioned tongue-lashing in an open meeting. Soon thereafter, Ray's son Greg was fired from his job managing the tribally owned gas station. Ray wonders if his son was railroaded by the tribe. His case went in front of tribal court, consisting of judges appointed by the very organization that had terminated him.

I spoke to Greg's lawyer about the case: "We were winning, and you know what happened next? They changed the tribal codes so that Greg couldn't bring in his own counsel. That's how they do things sometimes." For example: In 2008 a family who had fractional interest in a fifty-six-acre parcel of land they had received from their grandmother next to the outlet mall formed a corporation to develop the land. They were doing exactly what one hopes people do with their property: securing and developing it for future generations, to make the land work for them. However, the tribe blocked them. The corporation took the tribe to court, but in the meantime the tribe denied them access to sewerage and water even though it is surrounded, literally, by excellent new sewer and water systems from the outlet mall and casino. The price of the land plummeted, and the tribe was able to persuade many of the part owners to sell. Once the tribe had a majority share they sold it to themselves at a discount. Two of the original members of the corporation held out but could not sustain their opposition to the sale and eventually sold. Why would the tribe do this? "Yeah, why would they?" ponders Gabe Galanda, the attorney for the plaintiffs. "Maybe they thought they'd open up a hotel, or another retail center, and it would take business away from tribal operations. Maybe they thought it would ruin the aesthetics of the tribal operations, whatever they built would be an eyesore." Such actions are sound capitalistic logic—reduce competition, increase market share. This is good capitalism, but it's not necessarily good tribalism. "Maybe it makes sense for them to do that," muses Galanda. "But why get in the way of a frybread stand or an espresso shop? Why would you suffocate a smoked salmon business by diming them for their fiberglass chicken on a pole? I think there's a fundamental distrust on the part of tribal government of their members' ability to do it right." It's hard not to see such actions as an extension of the paternalism of the oppressors.

"I'm always on their case," says Ray Sheldon. "I don't give a goddamn what they think. What annoys me is when people in high echelon forget who they are. They say one thing one day and the next day they do the opposite." According to Ray, the contracts for building Cabela's went to a non-Indian contractor when Ray and his family had hoped to get it. Construction bills ran to $21 million. Ray wonders about insider deals. "One thing that really bothers me," he says after naming many other things that bother him, "I've been fighting for children for quite a while. One of the biggest things the tribe is being confronted with is sex abuse. Women getting sex abused. Kids getting sex abused. They aren't putting enough money or time into that program. Nothing is really being done about it." He has a way of being fiercely disgruntled about tribal matters while he clearly loves and cares very deeply for his community. It also seems to me that the tribal government at Tulalip is, overall, pretty good, pretty healthy, even though some tribal members (like Ray) feel it could be better.

Ray is, again, right—about corruption and about sexual abuse. And as different as those things seem, they are united in a way: both bespeak a malformed social and political structure, stunted, shortsighted, and inward-turning. Both have at their root the abuse of power. When people are abused, they often turn into abusers. Perhaps when whole peoples have been abused, they often do the same. And yet, despite Ray's permanent, proud disgruntlement, the Tulalip have done something to intervene in this cycle. The tribe took back power from the state over its civil matters. It managed, with Taylor's help, to separate—maybe not enough—governance from business so there is a tribal council that tends to the needs of the people and there is a business council that runs Quil Ceda Village, which generates income for the tribe. With strong leadership, the tribe flexed its muscle and bent the local economy in its own direction. Instead of having the economic zone of Quil Ceda Village annexed by Marysville, they brought the chamber of commerce to Quil Ceda. Along the way, they empowered their own citizens—in governance and law (80 percent of Tulalip's legal team is Indian) and enforcement. Now Tulalip has secured a federal highway project to rebuild an overpass and on-ramps on the north end of the reservation. The tribe is currently negotiating with the State of Washington and looks likely to be awarded a big chunk of the $16 billion earmarked for roadwork in the region. Teri Gobin, the director of the TERO program at Tulalip, makes a good point. "They're having booms in other places—like the oil fields in North Dakota—and a lot of Indians are getting in on it and doing good business. But we are trying to create stability, develop skills. The tribal vocational skills program is the only tribal accredited vocational training program in the country. It's free," says Teri. "It's free for any Natives from any community, and it's free for their spouses, too. We've even built houses for the homeless in Seattle." That's a turn-around if I've ever seen one: instead of begging HUD for funding for tribal housing (which is in very short supply around the country), they are building houses for their neighbors.

"It all comes back to the casino," says Greg from across Ray's office. "The success of the tribe centers around the casino. It brings in a lot of money. That money that comes in gets distributed in many ways. It gets distributed as projects. These projects create jobs and opportunities. The money flows everywhere. In the 1980s the tribe was, in terms of work-force, a tenth of the size it is now. The casino created high salaries, more jobs, and that's where everyone started to look for opportunity. To get into construction. Stuff like that. The casino and the per cap creates a cushion. It was like perfect timing. We got a little money in our pocket. Our government structure improved. We got more stable. . . . It all came together."

So what does it take to follow Tulalip's success story? Because, caveats aside, it *is* a success. Well: Location. Leadership. Separation. Structure. Opportunity. And hustle. It takes people like Teri Gobin and her father, Stan Jones. It takes young people who've paid their dues and want to do good, like Eddy Pablo. It takes a kind of vision like Les's and it takes an active and vocal conscience like that of Ray Sheldon. Even the thing he's most concerned about is finally beginning to be addressed: Tulalip just amended their criminal code so that there is no statute of limitations on charges of sexual abuse.

In 1994, I MOVED BACK to Leech Lake Reservation, the place I had hoped to escape when I graduated from high school in 1988. It was an important return for me. I had found graduate school both stressful and sterile. And the connection I felt to my tribe was tenuous, or felt tenuous. If any of the rest of life's efforts was going to make any sense or mean anything at all, it had to, for me, make sense in relation to my tribe and my culture. I moved home and began working for a nonprofit dedicated to strengthening Ojibwe language and culture. I wrote educational grants to fund language immersion programs with an eye toward establishing an Ojibwe language immersion school at White Earth Reservation to the west of Leech Lake.

It was hard work. When a community is whole, language grows out of the web of relationships that make that community; it is a by-product of intergenerational togetherness. However, at White Earth (and other Indian communities) it was hard to find that wholeness. There was intergenerational abuse—physical, domestic, sexual, substance. There was a pronounced lack of continuity between people and institutions. It felt like everything was a mess. My coworkers and I puzzled over the basic hurdle to our efforts to regrow and grow the Ojibwe language: it wasn't important to that many people. Young people were especially uninterested. I pondered. We had to, in some way, make language and culture cool. And if we could do that, the rest would likely fall into place. Language work felt crucial to us. Some carriers of culture are or can be extralingual, of course: kinship, politics, lifeways, traditional activities. But while culture contains these things, or is contained in them, language has a special role as a carrier of culture. More than that: our Ojibwe religion is vested in the language. It cannot be practiced in English. The death of our language would likely be the death of us, certainly the death of our ceremonial life.

We did not feel alone in our work. Even scattered on reservations and cities in six states and three Canadian provinces, and in tribes across the country, the Ojibwe displayed a marked shift in not only attitude but direction. In the 1960s and 1970s, AIM and the Red Power movements, looking outward, used occupations, armed conflict, and street theater to direct the national gaze toward the ongoing problems in Indian country. This was new and important and vital. But for them and the moment and their movements, Indian country remained a problem to be solved, a problem with which to confront America. This shifted in the 1980s and 1990s. My brother Anton, who worked with me on the language project, put it this way: "The U.S. government spent two hundred years trying to kill us, trying to take our land, language, and culture away from us. Why would we look to them to fix it? We must look to ourselves to do that." Across Indian country a new generation of activists were turning their attention and energy inward and working hard to strengthen their communities from the inside.

A number of factors precipitated this sea change. Many younger Indians now had educational opportunities long denied previous generations. They had the ability to travel and some kind of economic security that gave them the freedom to return to their culture. They also, like so many Americans of all origins, wanted something more from their lives and their country than simply the chance to get rich. They, like the rest of the new generation of Americans, wanted their lives to mean something more than could be reflected in entrepreneurial success. But for Indians, this movement was also a product of the sovereignty wars of the 1970s and 1980s: the aura of dignity conferred by seeing oneself as belonging to a sovereign people, as having rights that adhered to and derived not from the largesse of the government but from continuation of their cultures, community, and polity.

My time at Tulalip ended where modern Tulalip entrepreneurship began: at Boom City. Boom City is exactly how it sounds. For two weeks leading up to the Fourth of July, the largest fireworks bazaar west of the Mississippi rises from the gravel on a vacant lot near the casino. Plywood shanties are trucked to the site and arranged in neat rows. The awnings are opened and the sale begins. Each of the 139 stands is stuffed with fireworks. All of the stands are Native-owned, and the action is administered by a board of directors, which in turn is administered by the tribe. All of the stands are painted brightly, and many bear equally colorful names: Up in Smoke, One Night Stand, Boom Boom Long Time, Porno for Pyro, Titty Titty Bang Bang. Others bespeak proud ownership: Mikey's, Eddy's, Junior's.

It's slow when I arrive at Eddy's stand, but even so there is a lot of money changing hands. Fireworks—like gaming and, to a lesser extent, tobacco—are regulated by the state. And as sovereign nations, Indian tribes in states like Washington where fireworks are illegal enjoy a monopoly on their sale. I find Eddy deep in his stand, trying to avoid the sun. "The weather's keeping people away. Too hot." He also tells me business is slow because someone was caught earlier that day selling illegal fireworks nearby. He will be fined and unable to reopen for a day or two, but the incident has made customers skittish. "By Friday the cars will be backed up to the highway," Eddy assures me. "If you're the last man standing with a full load of fireworks on the last day you can sell it all." I wonder how much "all" means. "You can make fifteen to twenty-five thousand for the season. More if you're smart." The wholesalers set up shop on the outskirts of Boom City and circle around taking orders for the vendors. There are two espresso stands and a few food stands. Someone has lined the back of their pickup with a tarp and filled it with water, and five kids cavort and splash in it. Other kids, as young as four or five, walk through the stands chirping *Iced tea! Pop! Gatorade!* in a miniature mimic of the men and women selling fireworks, who have perfected the banter of bazaar merchants the world over: the taunting, teasing, aggressive talk designed to get people to stop and buy something. "That stops 'em, too," says Eddy, nodding at the carpet in front of his stand. "Walking around on that gravel all day hurts your feet. And then they walk on this. It's a little thing, but the little things add up to business." I can't help noticing the carpet is salmon-colored. I stop a girl no older than four wearing a sandwich board advertising iced tea and order one. She scampers back to the concession stands. A few minutes later she returns and hands over the iced tea and says, "Three dollars, please." I do the math. That's a quarter for the tea and $2.75 for the cute kid to bring it to me.

The day burns on and on. In the afternoon the sound of fireworks— many and large—can be heard nearby. There's a field on the edge of Boom City set aside for setting them off. Just as fireworks can be sold on the rez but not in the state, so, too, can they be exploded on the rez. And Boom City is happy to provide the space. It's a free-for-all. Rockets, mortars, roman candles, spinners. They all go off at once and continuously. A haze settles over the lot like the haze over a battlefield. Periodically the security guards call a halt to the explosions, but this is only to make room for even larger explosions: tribal members—and this seems to be a uniquely cultural thing—will light off upward of a thousand dollars' worth of fireworks as a "memorial" for someone in their family who has passed on. They are remembered with an exploding wall of sound.

Ideas aren't quietly laid to rest here either. Having explored the possibility of teaming up with the Lummi to start a pharmaceutical company, and having met with resistance there as well, Les has recently taken the project back. Political power, political clout waxes and wanes, and as the dynamics on the council shifted, Les, visionary and dogged, has brought the idea of a pharmaceutical company back to Tulalip. This time he has more support.

I wander back to Eddy's dazed by the fireworks and by everything else I've seen at Tulalip. This reservation—created in 1855—really seems to have been born in the past forty years. It has come alive and done exactly what federalists have always wanted: become a self-sufficient, self-supporting, entrepreneurial, relatively rich version of the American Dream—a people, a community that works hard and makes things work and gets ahead. Pretty much every reason for underperformance offered by other tribes—lack of access to education, lack of infrastructure, intergenerational sexual abuse, boarding schools, forced religious conversion, historical trauma, exploitation and loss of natural resources—has been experienced at Tulalip. And yet. What I have seen at Tulalip isn't just what a tribe could be (though there was that, too) but what America might be. If only. Tulalip is a conglomeration of separate tribes that came together (by choice, circumstance, and under pressure) to form a nation. It has suffered its own internal divisions and traumas. It has endured natural and civic disasters, gone through recession and poverty and joblessness. But it has found a way to provide free health care for all its citizens, free education for those who want it, free (excellent) childcare for working parents, a safe and comfortable retirement option for its elders, and a robust safety net woven from per capita payments that, while barely enough to support a single person and not enough to fully support a family, are enough to encourage its citizens to venture into enterprises small and large. The nation provides for its most vulnerable citizens—the young and the old. And it provides enough security for the people in between life's beginnings and ends so that they can really see what they might become.

THIS IS TULALIP. This could also be America if only the country would pay attention. It seems antithetical, even nonsensical, to consider that in order to find America you need to look at Indian communities and reservations. But it's true. The questions posed by America's founding documents and early history—What is the reach of the federal government? What should it be? How to balance the rights of the individual against those of the collective? What is, at the end of the day, the proper role of the federal government in our social structures and lives? How to balance the demands of community and modernity? How to preserve, protect, and foster the middle class?—are answered by looking at Indians, at our communities, and our history.

It's truly dark now. The moon is up but it is bloodied by the smoke of explosions over the field. The rockets arc up over where cedar once grew, and the mortars thump in a way that lodges in your chest. There is a sudden commotion. After lighting off a package of mortars, a kid runs out to check on them because he doesn't think they've all gone off. He tips the tube to look in it, and the last mortar comes out and explodes in his face. He is rushed off to the emergency room. I later learn he will be just fine: he is cut but okay.

There is no feeling of repose among the people or the tribe. You can feel it on the docks and at Boom City and in the push to make something more out of cannabis than a storefront buck. There is a seething, a yearning for more that is not quite satisfied and probably never will be. I suppose that's the other part of the American Dream—a kind of striving that might breed wealth but also just breeds more striving. The wants create a want. Eddy is calmer about it. "We've got corruption and waste and all the issues that every other tribe has. But we've got something else here. We've found a way to make it work. The thing is, we hold ourselves back from really achieving what we could achieve when we don't do things right." And that reminds me of a story Eddy told me when we were digging clams: how the people at Tulalip were created as salmon and used the power of a good mind to become human. Being human was not a natural thing; they had to work for it.

But what is left to achieve beyond what they've already got? Americans were forever trying to create Indians in their own image. And in some ways they've done it. At least they might have gotten Indians to buy into the American Dream. But it is quite possible that Indians dream differently. The American Indian Dream is as much about looking back and bringing the culture along with it as it is about looking ahead. The Tulalip are far from achieving that dream: fewer than a dozen first-language speakers of Lushootseed remain (but activists and educators are aggressively offering language classes in the area), and the old lifeways tied to the sea are as endangered as the sea itself. But they are dreaming, they are trying nonetheless.

The lights are bright between the stalls and white and black and brown people walk and talk excitedly, their eyes gleaming and taking in everything their money can buy.

Eddy watches and pauses. "Just because we are successful doesn't mean we don't have all sorts of problems. We've got a lot of money. More than most. But we still die young. We've got a bad heroin problem. We still have a lot of domestic abuse and sex abuse. Money hasn't changed that, not yet. But if we don't get a handle on those things"—he raises and opens his hands—"all our wealth could disappear." It could. But it hasn't yet. It's rising up in the sky and—boom—it goes and then the ash drifts down to settle on our upturned faces.

PART 7

Digital Indians: 1990–2018

On June 26, 1992, replicas of the *Niña*, *Pinta*, and *Santa María* docked in New York City after a three-hundred-day voyage retracing Columbus's route from Spain to the Caribbean. Created by the Spanish government to celebrate Columbus and "the friendship of the Spanish people," the boats were met by well-wishers. For five dollars you could tour the ships, and for nine dollars you could buy a reproduction of Columbus's log—presumably a highly expurgated version that made no mention of rape, torture, or slavery. The boats were also met by a handful of people protesting Columbus, colonization, genocide, and the very idea of the discovery of the New World. New York's mayor at the time, David Dinkins, brushed the protest aside, saying, "We can sometimes get so caught up with what's behind us that we fail to look ahead." The statement managed to ignore that the reality Indians faced in 1992 had been shaped by Columbus and everything he represented. The future would be shaped in the same manner.

But not only in the same manner. As much of the country celebrated the quincentenary of Columbus's discovery that fall, Indians were celebrating everything they had survived and everything they had overcome. Columbus might have discovered the New World for Europe, but in 1992, Indians were discovering themselves for themselves, and the quincentenary was a chance to take stock. It might have surprised many Americans that there were Indians left to think about that fateful first contact at all. And yet there were—more and more, in fact. In the 1990 census nearly 2 million people identified as American Indian or Alaskan Native, a 38 percent increase since 1980. Birth rates in these groups were climbing, but not that fast, and not that high: more and more people were simply identifying as Indian, because what being Indian meant had changed as dramatically as our conditions had.

The Reagan and George H. W. Bush years were drawing to a close. It was a period in which the country had tried to shrug off the ghosts of Vietnam, Watergate, the Pentagon Papers, the oil crisis, and the last vestiges of the Cold War. But ghosts are not so easily dislodged. In 1958, more than 75 percent of Americans had trusted the government to do what was right most of the time. In 1980, only 27 percent felt that way. The number climbed again through the 1980s, but it never reached the same heights. And in the 1990s, public trust eroded again with the outbreak of the First Iraq War, which entered the national consciousness, if not the national mythology, as an imperial war—a war for oil. It began to erode the resurgent sense of American exceptionalism that has been instrumental to America's self-promotion.

The beating of Rodney King at the hands of Los Angeles police, and the riots that followed the officers' acquittal, among other things, may have taken a toll on the self-regard with which Americans had long viewed themselves as well. And if the fall of the Soviet Union had at first been cast as the triumph of democracy over totalitarianism and communism (never mind that the United States had won the Cold War more on the depth of its pockets than on the strength of its convictions), these new developments at home and abroad planted a doubt: The enemy wasn't necessarily or only "out there"—there was a darkness within that must be contended with. With the Soviet Union gone, America's mixture of idealism and dirty tricks, nobility and culpability, democracy and suppression, was much easier to see. And once it was seen, the public discourse against the presumed rightness of the American way became heated. It was one thing for John Winthrop to proclaim to his congregation in 1630 that the Massachusetts Bay Colony should "consider that we shall be as a city upon a hill. The eyes of all people are upon us. So that if we shall deal falsely with our God in this work we have undertaken, and so cause Him to withdraw His present help from us, we shall be made a story and a by-word through the world." It was another to remember that the colony had made room for what is now Boston by setting the palisaded village of the Pequot

Indians on fire in 1637 and killing the men, women, and children when they tried to flee out the exits of the fort. And it is again another thing to remember that Mohegan, Narragansett, and Niantic Indians fought alongside the colonists as they extirpated the Pequot. The past might very well be a foreign country. It is also much more complicated than we would have it. So, too, the present and the future.

By the late 1980s and early 1990s, American Indian, African American, and other activists and historians and writers and students had joined forces to make America remember that its "goodness," its success, its very existence had been facilitated by the contributions of other, non-Anglo Americans and that often, despite their contributions, it continued to exist and to grow at their expense. Multiculturalism was a movement that sought to recognize these truths, which were often elided.

So 1992 was not just a time for Indians to take stock. It was a time for America to do the same. And the reflections it saw weren't entirely pleasing. African Americans, Asian Americans, Mexican Americans, Puerto Ricans, and immigrants of long standing in the United States had reason, along with Indians, to ask what, exactly, we were celebrating—and what we should be celebrating—in 1992, five hundred years since Europeans brought with them disease, religion, colonialism, and the slave trade to our shores, along with representative democracy and religious tolerance.

Christopher Columbus had always been a convenient myth for America's boosters, although he never set foot on the American mainland and didn't in fact usher in New World colonialism. Nevertheless, his story had helped focus the story of American transcendence. But by 1992, the myth began to have the opposite effect: it was a reminder, for many, of the wrongs that had been perpetrated in the New World.

The federal government had long planned a Quincentenary Jubilee to kick off 1992, to end with its own replicas of the *Niña*, *Pinta*, and *Santa María* sailing beneath the Golden Gate Bridge. But corporate sponsors retreated and the jubilee never happened. A parade and celebration in Washington, D.C., were hastily canceled when Indian activists threatened to show up in force. Parades and celebrations in Los Angeles and Denver suffered the same fate. Protesters dumped red dye in the Fox River in

411

Chicago to protest the genocide of Native Americans, and the city of Berkeley rebranded Columbus Day as Indigenous Peoples Day. In 1994, the United Nations declared August 9 as the International Day of the World's Indigenous Peoples. Times were changing. And it wasn't just the public conscious that was changing, the real lives of Indians across the country were changing, too. It was almost as if the Indian population—larger by a factor of a hundred than it was a century before—was finally waking up from a collective nightmare. Not only had Indians survived beyond all expectation. We had begun, with the generation coming of age in the 1990s, to heal the wounds inflicted upon the bodies of previous generations.

Natives and Native communities were strong enough in 1992 to do what they had been unable to do in 1492: turn the ships away. In 1492, Indians were defenseless against the ravages of disease and unprepared for extractive colonial subjugation. Moreover, we had not consistently found strength in numbers by building alliances; tribes mostly fought, and perished, alone. But by 1992, Indians were strong enough—not symbolically but really—to resist. This strength was a result of physical adaptability (no longer would disease single us out), political savvy (no longer would we fight alone), and hard-won knowledge of what we were up against. Just as the Lakota, Comanche, Nez Perce, and other Plains tribes had adopted the horse and the gun and made them their own, so, too, did modern Indians take the tools that might have spelled our end (English, technology, Western education, wage labor) and make them ours. As my cousin Scott likes to say, *Indians don't waste what we kill: we use all the parts of the computer.*

The distance and distrust between Indian communities and the educational system meant to acculturate us was being bridged. The paternalism and greed of the U.S. government was being challenged in the courts, the streets, and the classroom. The schisms in Indian families that were the result of the boarding school system were being healed. And the separation between reservation Indians and urban Indians was being eradicated. Although it would take years, local tribal knowledge and global modern life began to come together in unlikely places. One of those places is on the plates served by Sean Sherman, the Sioux Chef.

SEAN SHERMAN, the Sioux Chef, is sitting across from me at Jefe, in Minneapolis. He is not eating as I imagine a chef would eat. He does not seem to be sampling and weighing and evaluating, listening to his food the way a musician might listen to a score. Rather, he eats as though this is both his first and last meal. His eyes are a little vacant. The food goes in fast and is gone. The food (Mexican) is awesome, and so is the restaurant. (Jefe is not his restaurant, but he is friends with the chef and is a supporter.) Sean is solidly built, substantial. His hair is long and tucked back behind his ears. He has a wide face, wide jaw, widely set eyes. An Indian face. If I had not seen him in action and tasted his food, I would not be able to guess that Sean is the mastermind of the most surprising food in Minneapolis, and that his efforts at promoting indigenous cuisine are the sharpest spear being thrown into the heart of so-called authenticity across the country.

Outside the restaurant, the summer day is tailing off, dappled with sun and shade. People walk along the Mississippi, the sound of the water going over Saint Anthony Falls in the distance. The old mills along the river have been converted into condos, exposed brick and smoked glass aestheticizing the city's past. Though only some of the past is fit for commodification and so survives. For example, we are sitting steps from where, in May 1850, the Ojibwe chief Bagone-giizhig once hid from his sworn enemies. That tribal animosity between Ojibwe and Dakota has long since faded.

Earlier, Sean, his partner Dana, and I drove out to Wozupi Tribal Gardens near Prior Lake, just south of Minneapolis. Wozupi was the brainchild of a Mdewakanton tribal member who had dreamed of a "sustainable clean food source," in the words of the employee who greeted us at the farm. The tribe, which owns a very big casino, had the means to make the dream real. Wozupi was established in 2010, on five acres. Six years later, it has grown to sixteen acres, and there are plans to expand further. It produces an incredible array of heirloom, organic, and what can only be called historical indigenous varietals. Cherokee beans. Potawatomi lima. Oneida corn. Arikara yellow squash. Hidatsa shield beans. Lakota squash. Gete-okosimin (Ojibwe "old time" squash). Maple sugar and syrup. Honey. Juneberries. Chokecherries. Wild plums. Apples. Apricots. Plums. Eggs. Tomatoes. As the farm has grown, so has the tribe's vision for it. The goal now is to get their goods into all the restaurants and casinos the tribe owns, and into private homes as well. It also supplies restaurants like Jefe. Sean left with ten pints of juneberries and a box of elderberry blossoms. "These?" he responded when I asked him what they are for. "I'll make a sauce out of the berries and freeze it. Juneberries drop so fast. The blossoms I'll use to make a syrup. It's got a really unique flavor."

Sean's recipes, his whole gestalt, rest on using and combining indigenous ingredients in both old and surprising new ways. "Our philosophy and politics is: indigenous, indigenous-produced, local, organic. In that order." He isn't interested in "Indian" food per se (salmon on a cedar plank) or even in dressing up Indian comfort food (frybread or macaroni) in some new way. "I make indigenous food. I don't use pork or chicken or beef. No sugar or eggs. I try to cook only with the foods historically available to the indigenous people of the area I'm working in. So for me that means Lakota/Dakota and Ojibwe ingredients." Like? "There's so much. So much all around us," he said on the drive to Wozupi. "See that?" He pointed at a brown, sorghumesque weed in the ditch along Highway 13. "Remember what we ate on Monday? Amaranth? That's amaranth. It grows all over around here. And goosefoot. And sorrel. Not to mention berries, wild rice, squash, and corn."

Sean is Oglala Lakota and grew up on the Pine Ridge Reservation in South Dakota, but the family moved to Spearfish when he was thirteen. "I was working all the time, supporting the family," he says. As a teenager he worked in restaurants around Spearfish. Right out of high school, he worked as a field surveyor for the U.S. Forest Service in the Black Hills. His job was to go to certain coordinates and take a sample of all the plants growing within a given distance from those spots. He came to know pretty much all the plants that grew in that environment and, being curious and having worked in restaurants, he learned which ones a person could eat. In 1997, he moved to Minneapolis and got a job at California Kitchen, the "nicest" restaurant in the then relatively new Mall of America. He lasted six months. "I could not wake up and drive to work at a mall anymore," he recalled. He landed a job at Broders' Pasta Bar, a popular spot between Minneapolis and Edina. There, too, he wondered: How did this evolve? Where did it come from? What was it like a hundred years ago? Two hundred? Three? He consulted books. He moved on from Broders' to a variety of restaurants—Mexican, Asian, American. Each cuisine he mastered he followed down to its root. And now what he makes is not "artisanal" or "indigenous-inspired" but rather, archival food, in combinations that are delicious and inspiring—and for an Indian like me, something more.

The first concoction of Sean's I ever tasted was cedar tea sweetened with maple syrup. One sip, and the barstools and track lighting and tile disappeared, the space rearranged itself into a snow-covered path crowded with spruce and red pine on one side and tag alder and birch on the other. This is the trail my older brother and I walked in the winter when we were kids, an old logging track known only to us. It ran straight out of our backyard through plantation pine and on between a hill and a swamp before reaching another small hill covered in old-growth pine and a sprinkling of birch. We'd walk up the hill and look down on the Mississippi. In the summer the river wasn't much more than a rumor, but in the winter you could see it, if you looked hard, peeking out from behind the lowlands of ash and elm. We'd make a campfire and pick cedar and boil up swamp tea in an aluminum pot, while the wind scudded snow off the branches and the snow hissed at the fire's edge and a jay called in the distance to the stuttering annoyance of red squirrels around us.

The rest of the meal was equally memorable. It included smoked walleye spread with fresh blackberries and sorrel, duck pâté and maple-bruléed duck in an apple broth, a salad of foraged greens topped with tamarack blossoms—citrusy and piney and tannic—and cedar-braised bison with a flint corn cake. Dessert was a sunflower-and-hazelnut crisp with popped amaranth. Sean's skill rests less in the fusionary (though the combinations of flavors are astounding) than in something harder and more daring: he seems to trust in the flavor of the food itself, in the completeness of the ingredients in their own right.

Since debuting as the Sioux Chef eighteen months earlier, Sean has experienced a level of attention and success that most chefs only dream of, featured on radio and in magazines and at symposia. He's all over the place in Minneapolis, too, cooking for summits and special events, hosting pop-up dinners. He's helped the Little Earth housing project to establish the Tatanka food truck, developing the concept and menu and training the staff. The truck, like Sean's own brand, is adamantly, proudly, and creatively indigenous. Among a chronically malnourished and diabetes-stricken community, to serve bison and turkey and walleye pike, cedar tea, and corn is something of a revolution. And Sean's cooking has found a loyal and enthusiastic base not only among foodies and wild-food devotees but also among reservation and urban Indians, both rich and poor. To my mind, that's because the politics of Sean's food confront the private demons of pretty much every modern Indian. Whether we are urban or reservation, our story—the story of "the Indian"—has been a story of loss: loss of land, loss of culture, loss of a way of life. Yes, Indians remain—we remain across the country, as modern Americans and modern Indians. But inwardly we wonder: How much of our culture actually remains? How authentic, really, are we? At what point do we cease being Indians and become simply people descended from Indians? Sean's food, the whole conception of it, affirms us: All is not lost, it tells us. Much remains—of our cultures, our knowledge, our values. It literally rests at our feet and over our heads; all we need do is reach out and pluck it. This is a profound politics.

"You wouldn't believe how hard it has been to explain what indigenous food is," he tells me. "I've had the same conversation over and over again, over the past year and a half. I have to go back to the beginning all the time. I was in Ohio, putting on an event, and I began talking about Native American food. This woman asks, 'There's food?' Yes. 'There are Indians?' Yes. 'How'd they get here?'" He smiles and shakes his head. His

416

food is an answer to that question: it and we have always been here. And we've always been changing and adapting to climates and politics and peoples. As singular and exciting as Sean's approach to cooking is, he is part of something much larger afoot in Indian country.

For so long the Indian struggle for survival was a strategy aimed outward: to cajole, scold, remind, protest, and pester the powers that be to rule the right way in court cases, to pass the right legislation to protect tribes and tribal sovereignty, to honor treaties, and to simply remember both our past and our continued existence. But the 1990s marked an inward turn. People like Sean are engaging in a new brand of activism. Instead of, say, occupying the BIA in Washington, D.C., they occupy a cultural, social, and political space where they actively remember and promote indigenous knowledge—and not just because it serves Indians but because it serves modernity. Perhaps this is why what's happening in Indian country today is so hard to see.

Of course, every society's present is harder to see. We are forever caught up in the flow of the current moment, not just freighted with the icy inventory of the past. And recent years have not been as distinctively marked by policy shifts or judicial decisions as have the past. Whereas we can speak of the evolution of federal policy in past eras—the treaty period, allotment, assimilation, termination and relocation, self-determination—the past thirty years seem to exist largely outside the brackets of federal policy. To be sure, there have been important legislation and policy decisions that affect tribal life, just not as many. And federal Indian policy seems to have settled into the track laid down during the Nixon administration: that of self-governance, self-determination, and a government-to-government relationship between the federal government and the tribes. It is almost tempting to believe that the era-less character of our era reflects our having fallen outside the national gaze—to take it as proof of our final, fatal inconsequence. But our numbers belie this interpretation, as do our actions. Tribes—affirmed and reaffirmed as sovereign nations—still do battle with the government. Activism is a permanent necessity. But our focus is different now: we've turned inward.

In the 1960s and 1970s, to be a "woke" Indian might have meant joining the Trail of Broken Treaties and caravanning to Washington to occupy the BIA. Now it just as likely means sitting in a classroom at a state university and learning a tribal language. Although Native American languages have been on the decline since 1492, and only twenty of them out of many hundreds are expected to remain viable into the twenty-second century, programs teaching these vanishing languages are on the rise. These programs are intent on bringing the Indian past into the present, and they are also intent on bringing the present into Indian lives. Manuelito Wheeler, a Diné language activist, recruited Diné voice actors from across the Southwest (there remain more than one hundred thousand Diné speakers in the United States) and dubbed *Star Wars*, and later *Finding Nemo*, into that tongue. Speakers of Ojibwe and Choctaw and a host of other Native languages are using Facebook and YouTube and Twitter to speak and promote and communicate in the languages of the First People. And increasingly, Indians are founding, controlling, and populating tribal and community colleges on reservations—more than forty of them across thirteen states at last count—to study Native languages alongside computer science, math, English, history, and business administration. Transforming education into something that we do for ourselves, rather than something that is done to us, goes a long way toward healing the long rift between Indians and the educational system.

In its misguided efforts to solve the "Indian problem," the United States government in a sense created Indians over and over and over again. For decades, our political and social reality was determined—usually for the worse—by the government's approach to our existence. Allotment exacerbated reservation poverty, boarding schools disrupted family and culture; to be "Indian" was to be defined by those problems, the definition always shifting in such a way as to produce Indians with problems. But Indians like the Sioux Chef have found a way to exist outside those definitions. For him and for many like him there is no contradiction between indigenous knowledge and modern life. This, too, contributes to the invisibility of Indians in the present tense. These days, Indians aren't out in the world only or merely "being Indian"—but they're not, as outsiders might assume, "passing" or acculturating. The census tells a different story:

more and more people are claiming Indianness than ever before. There is no longer any reason not to. I remember, back in 1991, as I and others were trying to start an American Indian studies program at Princeton, an administrator said out loud, during a meeting, that one couldn't be both a professor and a medicine man. I had no idea what he was talking about. I couldn't see any contradiction there. *Who says?* I responded angrily. *You? Who are you?*

Similar forces are driving one of the areas that Indians are just now beginning to address: personal and community health. The government, in doing its best to exterminate the bison, gave us flour and lard as replacements. Poor diet did damage to our culture and our health. Obesity, diabetes, heart disease, cancer—these are the products of oppression. Sarah Agaton Howes is one of those fighting not just against a system but for her community.

WE ARE IN A BOUGIE COFFEE SHOP—actually, the only coffee shop of its kind—in Cloquet, a former logging town just off the Fond du Lac Reservation in northern Minnesota. Sarah is cheerful and funny and pretty, a mother of three and proprietor of House of Howes, a contemporary Ojibwe design, art, and lifestyle store. She is also a passionate runner who is, she says, known as "the Run Stalker" of the reservation. She pretty much lives in activewear.

"I grew up in my grandma's house on Reservation Road, just out here," she recalls. She lived in Cloquet for most of high school, and then in Duluth. I had first met Sarah at Ojibwe ceremonies in Wisconsin and had always thought of her as Ojibwe, but she corrects me. "My grandma's dad built that house after the Cloquet fire in 1918. He was Creek. I'm Ojibwe and Creek." Sarah's dad was a cop—"The only Native cop in the whole county. He had a full-time job. That was rare for men around here back then." Her mother is from California, of Norwegian descent. "My mom was traveling the country, she wanted to live off the land. My dad was like, 'My grandparents' house is out there, no plumbing, no nothing. I don't know any woman who'd want to live there.' And she's like, 'I do!'

and that was that. They met when he was an AIMster and they went to big drum ceremony. But as I grew up they got into this really weird church, so I didn't grow up going to ceremony." Her father's job influenced the family, too. "That kind of job makes you see people in a certain way, one way. And so we got more and more isolated. He knew all the bad things that were happening in the community and I think that kinda pulled us away from what was going on in the community. We still lived there, but it created an isolation." So the family kept to themselves in their two-story house. Sarah did spend a lot of time with her cousins, but her Ojibwe life withered. Surprisingly, it was their diet—or the consequences of it—that changed things. When Sarah was eleven, her father had a heart attack. The event shook him. "He completely changed his life. Again. He went back to ceremonies, he went back to our roots. Everything shifted at that point." Her parents divorced, and Sarah stayed with her mother. Her father was secretive about his newfound ceremonial life, so she didn't know much about it, and she never got the chance to find out much. Her father had developed diabetes, and like his own father, he died at forty-nine, when Sarah was twenty. "Average for an Indian in those days," she says. "Unhealthy eating, too sedentary, genetics, and stress." Now she has brothers who are into their forties, and she worries about them, too.

Despite her father's secretiveness, his late-life connection with traditional ways "planted a seed," as she put it. "He created the possibility of other directions for me. So in my twenties it was me trying to find that life, basically. Trying to find my way back to it." After high school and college, she married and got pregnant. "I was five days overdue. I was having contractions. They did a stress test. They told me everything looks fine. They sent me home. I had contractions all night. I went back in the next day and everyone makes this face: We need to go to the hospital." Her baby had no heartbeat. "This is a time in your life when the whole page turns. I remember thinking, no, no. Well . . . wake her up! Do SOME-THING. This is the 2000s. This doesn't happen. I hadn't known anybody who lost a baby." Her baby was stillborn. "We don't know why. I had to make peace with that, with not knowing. Then I had a miscarriage. It was rough. I was on this desperate mission to have a baby." Finally she gave birth to a son. "It was both wonderful and horrible. Scary as hell. I used to stare at him breathing. I didn't sleep. I would wake myself up because I thought it was my job to keep him there." The experience had changed her. "I'm not the same person, I'm different in every way."

Sarah was desperate to get pregnant again. It was all she thought about. During a checkup, a doctor tried to talk to her about her weight. "I was really heavy then. I weighed about two hundred eleven." The doctor told her she was likely to develop diabetes within ten years if she didn't change something. "She was a tribal doctor and she was being nice. She didn't want to discourage me." Her son, Rizal, had started eating real food, and Sarah was careful about his diet. "I'm feeding him organic squash and stuff like that. And me? I'm eating potato chips and grilled cheese!" Sarah came from a place where everyone was significantly overweight, and she could see that "eventually these two worlds were gonna merge. Eventually he was going to start eating chips and cheese and not eat squash and I'm gonna have diabetes. I didn't want him to watch me take shots, or watch me in the hospital."

That was when she started going back to ceremony. After her daughter died, people had suggested it, but she had demurred. "I thought those big ceremonies were for when you were really, really sick. Not for being sad." But then she met someone who told her she was going to ceremony and invited her along. The friend told her what to bring, what to do. "I had no idea of even what was going to happen. But it was like . . . I had to get to a better place. A good place physically, spiritually, mentally. Even with my kid, I had anxiety and fear: that someone was going to take him away from me." For Sarah it was as if she was waking up into her ceremonial life and life before was something that she didn't understand: she had been a person she didn't recognize.

Choosing to deal with her grief through ceremony was one of the first big healthy choices she'd made in her life. She began to see how her physical health was connected to her spiritual and mental health. But she didn't know many physically healthy Indians. One woman from her reservation, who also attended ceremony, had run a half marathon in Duluth. "I'd never even run a five K! And she's like, 'Us Native people should be out there!' Externally, I blew her off. I was like: No way. But internally, she must have planted a seed in me." Sarah did the 5K. "It took me forever. It took me so long the police car had to drive behind me at the end, like I was the president!" She laughs, and it's a great laugh. "I remember getting to the finish line and people were cheering for me. It was a major moment." When her daughter died in utero, "I felt I died, a little," but this was embracing life, saying, "I want to live. I want to be alive. I want my son to see me be a fully vibrant person. I want to, I want to . . . run. I want to move. I want my body to work. I wanted to know what it would feel like not to be a prisoner in my own body. To be overweight like I was for so long there was so much I never even tried to do. So much I never attempted. So much of my life was wasted that way."

Sarah started out with small, realistic goals. She wanted to lose the eleven pounds she thought of as her "grief weight" and get back to her "regular" weight of two hundred pounds—though even then she recognized on some level that there was nothing "regular" about standing five-foot-five and weighing two hundred pounds. After she ran that first 5K, she joined a Weight Watchers group on the reservation. She didn't know anything about cooking or nutrition, but she followed the program, cutting out fat and junk food and eating nothing but chicken breasts and broccoli for a month. Her husband did it with her. Soon they added other foods to their diet, trying a new healthy recipe every week. She had never been so disciplined, but she had decided to go through ceremonies in June and to have another baby, and she knew where she wanted to be for that to happen. She lost eighty pounds in six months, got pregnant, and had a healthy daughter. Then she set about losing the weight she'd gained in pregnancy. "I thought, 'I've been through this, I can do it.' And I knew how to do it." She lost sixty pounds. "People asked, 'Are you on meth? Are you eating?' I had to *show* people I was eating and was being healthy. Those models weren't out there."

Sarah began running with other Indian women. "There was this one girl I started running with. She lost over a hundred pounds. Diet and exercise. And together we are like: We can do this. We have to show other people." She met a serious runner who encouraged her to run a half marathon. "At that point I'd run two miles, maybe three, up and down my road in my sweats. No gear. No nothing. And I was like, 'You think?'" Her friend paid for her registration and trained with her. "The first time I ran on a trail with a group of Indian women I was like, 'What is happening right now? I'm out here running in the woods with a bunch of Anishinaabekwe. All these Indian women running through the woods? It hasn't happened in a hundred years around here!' And it was one of those clear moments in life. One of those moments you *know*: This is *exactly* what I'm supposed to be doing right now. This is exactly perfect."

From there, Sarah started organizing the group—"like herding cats a little bit"—but at least three and as many as seven of them have run together, long runs of ten miles or so, at least once a week, kids and jobs notwithstanding. She started a private group on Facebook called Kwe Pack. She'd rope in any woman who had ever even thought of running through the sheer power of her enthusiasm. "I became *that* person. I was like, 'Hey, if you can run three you can run six. If you can run six you can run twelve. I am the Run Stalker.'" She does it without formal tribal support or grant money or program funds—"Nothing but the will for Indian women to gather and run through the woods towards better health, towards strength and camaraderie." She keeps it exclusive to women. "We need our own spaces, it's important we learn how to support each other as Anishinaabekwe." She does it because it's important, that's all. "And I like it like that. I like that it's just us in the woods—no grants, no supervisors, no paid employees. It's so important for these women to support each other, to do this together." It might seem like a small thing Sarah is doing, gathering a dozen or so women to run in the woods, but in Indian country, perhaps the most radical mode of resistance is to choose to be healthy.

Not content with her weekly runs and short races, Sarah has begun training for and running ultra-distance races. Marathons. Ultramarathons. Trail races. "We're trying to change it back: we're trying to make it *normal* to be healthy." When she first moved back to the reservation, passing cars would slow down to get a look at her, wondering if she'd escaped from the nearby treatment center. "Or they'd ask me if I got a DWI, because I wasn't driving. It was so abnormal to see Indians out running." Now, everyone knows who they are. "'That's them girls that run,' they say. Everybody knows us. I try to run in the community so people see us. And we're making a difference. It's becoming normal. I feel that shift." It amuses me to imagine that while the archaeological record from five thousand years ago in Florida and coastal California consists of large shell middens, five thousand years from now, on Sarah's reservation, the record will likely consist of running shoes, earbuds, computer parts, and vegetables.

CHELSEY LUGER IS ALSO PART of the force that's creating the shift toward health. We met in Grand Forks, North Dakota, at Urban Stampede Coffee. Chelsey is short, lean, and muscular. Her mother is Ojibwe from the Turtle Mountain Reservation in North Dakota, and her father is Lakota from Standing Rock Reservation, also in North Dakota. Being Indian in Grand Forks meant having white friends. She was a hockey and basketball cheerleader, but also "always the girl in class that they couldn't joke around with. They couldn't joke about Native people or black people or gay people. I'd speak up." Her friends would say, "Yeah but you're different, your parents have good jobs." It was true that Chelsey's upbringing defied the stereotypes about Indians and Indian life. Her parents not only had college degrees and solid achievements but also were deeply invested in their children's education. Working on her undergraduate degree, her mother had taken her to class as an infant (her mother went on to earn her master's and her doctorate). "I took my first Indian studies course when I was six months old! I just cannot imagine at my age the responsibilities she had when she was my age." But, as Chelsey did not hesitate to point out to her classmates, many Indians' lives defy the stereotypes.

Despite being viewed as an exception, Chelsey didn't have it easy. Racism and exclusion run deep in places like Grand Forks. "By the time I was in high school I was really a spitfire. I was just pissed off all the time. I was so angry." She got in physical fights, verbal fights, both in Grand Forks and on the rez. "On the rez I was White Girl, and here in Grand Forks I was that Indian girl. It was constant. I felt like I couldn't win. I'm grateful for it now. It turned me into a chameleon. I can go anywhere. I can do anything." Where she wanted to go was out. Two cousins had gone to Brown University. One "put the bug in my head to aim high." He helped her study for the ACT, and she got into Dartmouth. The college was home to the oldest program serving Indian students in the country and had made recruiting them something of a mission, resulting in the largest and most robust Native student organization of any elite college in the country. Chelsey took advantage of the school's Native fly-in program to get an introduction. But even at Dartmouth, prejudice followed her. "When I first got in, people always asked, 'How did you get into that school?' They thought I got in because I was Native. I mean, I had great ACTs and straight A's. How the hell do you *think* I got in? And I wrote a really good essay and I have experiences and I have something to contribute."

Despite its efforts toward Indians, Dartmouth had a tradition-bound, conservative, privileged student body. It also had a heavy binge-drinking culture. As in high school, Chelsey was accepted, but she'd never partied as she did at Dartmouth. And she was still angry. Yes, she was with people from all around the world, but she couldn't find her niche. "I couldn't find a Lakota/Ojibwe/German/French girl there at all! Just me." She laughs. "I used to get into a lot of verbal altercations." Once in the dining hall she confronted a fellow student wearing a T-shirt with an Indian head on it. "I'm like, 'Hey what's up with that? You know there's some controversy about that, right?' He says, 'Yeah.' I said, 'You know I'm Indian, right?' He says, 'Yeah, now I do.' We get into that whole discussion. He's getting really uncomfortable. And he's squirming and I am so *happy* because he's so uncomfortable." He paid for his food and took his tray. "I was behind him. And I'm like, 'Hey, I'm not done talking to you yet.' And then I said, 'You want to say it?' There's this stupid chant or cheer: *Wahoo, wahoo wa, wahoo wa.* I said, 'You want to say it now? *Wahoo WA*, mother-fucker!' I said it right when he got to his table full of all his frat brothers. His buddies were laughing at him." Eventually she realized that her anger was driving her. "I hit rock bottom," she recalls. "I realized my temper wasn't doing me any good. I saw that I wasn't getting through to people that way." She recognized that she wanted "to carry myself with a certain sense of dignity. And I didn't want to allow people to make me angry. I realized that anger was a weakness." Now she thinks that it's "good to be passionate but not so good to be angry. It's not productive."

Her sophomore year, she got involved with the Native community. She had no intention of majoring in Native American studies. "I go to ceremonies. I know my culture. Why would I study it?" she thought. But then an older student told her to take a course with a particular professor and, she says, "My eyes were opened." She took another course, and another. "Eventually I learned there was all this stuff I never knew I needed to learn but I really needed to learn it." She became deeply involved in Native American studies, stopped partying, and did well in her classes.

After Chelsey graduated from Dartmouth, she moved to New York and began working in the sex crimes unit of the DA's office. She had always wanted to be a lawyer, but her work in the sex crimes unit cured her of that. The work felt right, but life didn't so much. "I was disconnected from home. My head wasn't there. I was avoiding it, I think. I didn't go to ceremonies for years." Her parents flew her home for a visit every few months, "but if you're only there for a week you're not really *there*. I didn't realize it, but I was becoming very unwell. I was so wrapped up in my life in New York." She was becoming increasingly materialistic and fixated on finding a way to make money and become powerful and make a name for herself. "I was lost. So, so lost. I gained weight. I wasn't looking like myself."

She started working out again, harder than ever before, and started serious weight training for the first time. "I'd done a lot of sports but I'd never done that. And I loved it. I got really into it. I started eating better. But still: fitness was about image. About looking a certain way. Get a certain outfit. Get dressed up. Go to the club." Still, she recognized she didn't want to be a lawyer, so she decided to go to journalism school. "I was a broadcast concentrator. I didn't want to be a writer yet. I was, 'I'm gonna be on TV!'" But exposure to network executives made her realize that "they don't care about diversity of opinion. They already have their opinions. They liked me because I had that ethnically ambiguous face. Those were terms they used! They wanted me because I could represent Asians and Mexicans and other ethnicities."

Other changes occurred, too. She stopped drinking entirely. "I woke up one morning and said, 'I just don't want to do this anymore.' I was feeling like: 'Damn, it's time to realize, it's time to *know* this substance has a spirit. It's dangerous. It's out to get me. It's out to get my people. And it's doing its job. I'm going to reject this.' It didn't matter that I wasn't an alcoholic. What mattered was that my history, my genetics, my ancestry, is not in line with that substance. My body does not like alcohol. It was a blessing I got that sign before it could really control me. Ever since then, I've not drunk. No drinks. Goodbye."

Bit by bit, Chelsey got control over her life. Like Sarah, she realized that her poor health and poor choices were related to her distance from her culture, religion, and ancestral self. But then, over social media, she met Thosh, a photographer who worked for the Native Wellness Institute. On the way to a photo shoot with him, Chelsey got a call. "Something with my dad was going down in North Dakota and it broke my heart. I started crying." When she apologized for her outburst, Thosh told her a similar story from his own family. It helped. "And since then, we've been close. He was born and raised on the rez, Pima from Salt River, Arizona. We really connected. And the photos turned out great! If you look at those photos, no one would guess I was bawling my eyes out just before. But *that* was the day: the day we started talking about indigenous fitness. About warrior strength."

Becoming healthy physically and mentally, Chelsey found, enabled her to relate differently to other Native people, too. "I could better address those I disagree with if I approached them with compassion. I had to swallow my pride and say, 'I don't always have to be this angry Native girl. I can channel that anger into productivity.' It takes a lot to condition yourself, to tell yourself that's not who you necessarily have to be. To drop that mentality was really challenging. But I still work on it all the time." Returning to culture, to her Indian self, to an Indian self separate from all the hurt her people have felt, changed her. "All of it instilled in me an incredible sense of pride. I was better able to articulate my thoughts and feelings and better able to understand why my people were in the condition they were in. When you're able to defend yourself with thought, when you have those tools, you become less angry. Anger is one of the lower entries on the emotional scale. Anger is easy. Jealousy is easy. It's more difficult to feel compassion. It's easier to yell at someone than it is to sit across from them and tell them you're upset. It became easier for me to talk to people."

As with Sarah, it was social media—being a digital Indian—that enabled Chelsey to extend her reach: out to other Native people and back to the very best parts of being Native. "I realized I had allies across Indian country. It's crazy I found that through social media because it can be such an unhealthy resource." Eventually Thosh and Chelsey put their heads together and formed Well for Culture (WFC), an organization that put into practice what they and others had been feeling. WFC is a hybrid beast: part indigenous knowledge clearinghouse, part lifestyle and fitness resource, part political exhortation for Indians to think about their health, and part a platform for Thosh and Chelsey to work with tribes and schools on issues affecting Indian youth. "We'd been chatting back and forth. Maybe make a website. Or do something. We weren't really doing anything together. Thosh was a photographer. We had common interests, but that was it. We communicated and talked about wellness and fitness." Thosh was already into the indigenous perspective on it—ancestral diet, Mother Earth gym. Chelsey was still "doing fitness out of insecurity. I wasn't in a place where I was feeling very confident. Two years later I'm learning more and more about indigenous fitness, ancestral diet."

But while there are a lot of people around Indian country working on these things, Chelsey knew from experience that there wasn't a distinct movement, a particular place where people could connect it all. "So I said to Thosh, 'We should do this: form a website, gather resources for us and for other people.'" They weren't just focused on weight loss; they were about claiming an indigenous life, bringing ancestral knowledge to bear on health and fitness. "Our people have been healthy for centuries, and it's only a short while we've been unhealthy."

When they work with kids, they make fitness look cool—by showing how it makes people appear strong and fierce and dignified. "I tell the kids I work with, 'I used to have all those pictures—holding up drinks, partying.' But I tell them, 'You could look like this. And I show them what Thosh and I do. I show them pics of Native people doing cool things.'"

They talk to Natives of all ages about how being well for themselves and their families is also a way of being well for the culture. "Because without wellness we can't have our culture. You can't go to a ceremony if you're drunk. You can't do that stuff if your body doesn't function properly. You can't hear stories and get teachings from elders if you're not well. You can't sustain your family or teach your children. So if you're not well, there goes your culture. And it goes the other way, too. I was fit but we weren't doing well. And it was my culture that brought me to real fitness. And that sense of pride I was able to feel from finally associating all those things back to my heritage, and being able to look at the fitness and wellness movement as ancestral knowledge—that made me so proud and so excited. That's my culture." With colonization had come barriers between what had been elements of a holistic culture. "Health over here, education over there. It's not natural for us. Our Native economies were nonexistent. You couldn't have an economy without a spirituality. You couldn't have a harvest without physical health. Everything was intertwined. What we're trying to do is to re-indigenize fitness. We acknowledge that we can't turn back the clock. We have jobs. Some of us work nine to five. We are not 'traditionalists.' We don't think we're going to go back to the way we were before. Our people have always evolved and adapted, and WFC is continuing that path." Ancestral knowledge, they believe, is a way to move forward, not back.

Fitness can be re-indigenized. Go for a run. Work out outside when you can—Mother Earth gym. "At my dad's, for example," says Chelsey, "we are on a ranch and there's this big yard behind a hayfield full of broken-down cars and tractors and we flip tires and jump on hay bales and pick up a pipe and do squats with that. In Navajo country, you're not going to drive two hours to the gym but you could hunt or fish—that's a path to fitness, too." So is incorporating ancestral foods into one's diet.

Chelsey is quick to remind me that she and WFC are part of a movement. "We're not the leaders. We're not the authorities. We're not gurus. We're not the authors of this. We're just facilitating this digital space, we are bringing people together." They see themselves as ambassadors rather than purveyors. "We always tell the kids we talk to, 'I grew up eating Pop-Tarts and frozen pizzas. I didn't start eating veggies until college. My mom didn't make me eat vegetables. My mom was incredible but she didn't have the time or energy to force me to eat things I didn't want to eat.'" They counsel people that it takes a little time for the body to adjust to new foods, but all of a sudden "these sweets and plastic foods don't taste good." They don't pressure or guilt-trip, but they do encourage people to change. "These Native kids pay attention. They hear things and they pick up on it and take pride in that. They have answers and they take pride in knowing." When the kids bring up frybread, they explain that it's not actually a traditional indigenous food, it's something Natives had to make do with. "Sometimes people get defensive, but we are able to make the conversation positive. We say we grew up with it and like it and we say frybread is not power. We say frybread kills our people. It's that serious. It causes diabetes and heart disease. We have to look at those colonial foods as a kind of enemy." There are other ways for people to claim their heritage. And they see that new sense of direction manifesting in the next generation. "These new kids, something is changing, something is shifting, you can feel it."

Changes could be felt legislatively as well. In the 1990s and 2000s, a slew of laws affirmed (legally and in terms of policy) the kind of shift in Indian life that had occurred in the lives of Sean, Sarah, Chelsey, and many thousands like them. In 1990, Congress passed the Native American Languages Act, the Indian Arts and Crafts Act, and the Native American Graves and Repatriation Act. The Native American Languages Act (NALA) put money behind efforts to undo the damages done by residential boarding schools, where, as we have seen, the government tried to eradicate our languages over the course of educating three generations. The Indian Arts and Crafts Act served to protect Indian artists by making the sale and distribution of "Indian" art made by non-Indians and advertised as "authentic" a crime. In 2013, the Violence Against Women Act (VAWA) that had been passed in 1994 was reauthorized and significantly revised. Among the new provisions was the empowerment of tribal courts to charge and prosecute non-Natives who raped or assaulted Native women on Native land. This was important legislation for Indian communities. More than two-thirds of Indian women are assaulted in their lifetime, and more than a third are raped. The majority of Native women are married or partnered to non-Natives, and the majority of rapes and assaults take place in or near their homes. Yet for decades, those who attacked Indian women were able to escape prosecution through jurisdictional loopholes or simply because local authorities were reluctant to prosecute. The revised VAWA is a potent weapon for the defense of Indian women.

In 2007, Senator Sam Brownback of Kansas introduced "a joint resolution to acknowledge a long history of official depredations and ill-conceived policies by the federal government regarding Indian tribes and offer an apology to all Native Peoples on behalf of the United States." The resolution was eventually passed and signed by President Obama as a rider on a defense appropriations spending bill, appropriately enough, albeit in a form like iced tea left too long in the glass. Rather than a full-throated apology from the United States, Obama apologized "on behalf of the people of the United States to all Native peoples for the many instances of violence, maltreatment, and neglect inflicted on Native peoples by citizens of the United States." So it was an apology made on behalf of a constituency in semi-private, accompanied by no public ceremony, and without any teeth whatsoever: the resolution included a disclaimer making it clear that the "apology" did not authorize or support "any legal claims against the United States, and the resolution does not settle any claims."

Still, a half-felt apology to Indians is better than fully formed policy inimical to our existence. All in all, the period 1990–2015 had a pointillist feel to it: one can see points of light—disparate, separate—beginning to come together into a picture of Indian survival, resilience, adaptability, pride, and place in modern life. Many of these points came together in

North Dakota on and near the Standing Rock Reservation during the pipeline protest that erupted there in 2016.

THE TEN-MONTH PROTEST on the edge of the Standing Rock Reservation against the continued construction of the Dakota Access Pipeline (DAPL) began in early 2016 and was shut down in February 2017, soon after Donald Trump took office. The pipeline, which became operational on May 14, 2017, now carries more than 400,000 barrels of oil a day from the Bakken oil fields in northern North Dakota to Patoka, Illinois, over 1,172 miles, across four states, and under the Missouri and Mississippi Rivers. The original route took the pipeline past Bismarck, North Dakota, but that route was rejected because it was too close to the municipal water supply. The alternative route put the pipeline across the Missouri just upstream of the Standing Rock Sioux Reservation. And this is where the pipeline became an Indian problem. The project was fast-tracked, meaning that the permitting process was streamlined; meaning that DAPL (along with its parent company, Energy Transfer Partners) was not subject to the usual permitting process for large interstate projects except where the pipeline was to cross major bodies of water and where it might affect ceded, historically important, religiously significant tribal lands; meaning that DAPL had to conduct cultural and environmental impact surveys in liaison with the state (North Dakota) and with tribes whose homelands the pipeline crosses (even if the pipeline doesn't actually cross through the reservation). DAPL was legally obligated to consult the Standing Rock Sioux, among other tribes. Which it did. Kind of. While the pipeline route was being planned, Energy Transfer Partners engaged in extensive surveying. According to documents filed in federal court: "Where this surveying revealed previously unidentified historic or cultural resources that might be affected, the company mostly chose to reroute. In North Dakota, for example, the cultural surveys found 149 potentially eligible sites, 91 of which had stone features. The pipeline workspace and route [were] modified to avoid all 91 of these stone features and all but 9 of the other potentially eligible sites. By the time the company finally settled on a construction path, then, the pipeline route had been modified 140 times in North Dakota alone to avoid potential cultural resources. Plans had also been put in place to mitigate any effects on the other 9 sites through coordination with the North Dakota SHPO [State Historic Preservation Officer]. All told, the company surveyed nearly twice as many miles in North Dakota as the 357 miles that would eventually be used for the pipeline." Three other tribes in North Dakota met and conferred with DAPL planners, and the pipeline was moved accordingly. And then the company tried to meet with a representative of the tribal version of the SHPO, the tribal historic preservation officer, Waste'Win Young. The DAPL liaison spoke to Young on the phone a few times after the pipeline plan went public, but then, according to court documents, it seems the company had trouble reaching her. The Army Corps of Engineers was also duty-bound to make sure the pipeline worked with the state and with tribes. Accordingly, Joel Ames (retired Navy chief, Osage Indian, and tribal liaison with the Army Corps of Engineers) also tried to reach out to Young, but to no avail. He recorded five attempts to meet and confer with her but was unsuccessful.

On October 2, other Corps personnel also sought to hold an arranged meeting with the Tribal Council and Dakota Access on the Standing Rock Reservation. But when the Corps timely arrived for the meeting, Tribal Chairman David Archambault told them that the conclave had started earlier than planned and had already ended. Ames nevertheless continued to reach out to Young to try to schedule another meeting throughout the month of October. When the new meeting was finally held at the reservation on November 6, though, DAPL was taken off the agenda because Young did not attend.

As a first cut, the Corps reviewed extensive existing cultural surveys both within and outside the Lake Oahe project area to determine whether the work might affect cultural resources. Then, on October 24, the Corps sent out a letter to tribes, including the Standing Rock Sioux, with information about the proposed work and maps documenting the known cultural sites that the Corps had already identified. These included sites that the Corps considered to be outside the projected area of effect. In addition, the letter requested that any party interested in consulting on the matter reply within thirty days. No response was received from the Tribe. The Corps did receive responses from other tribes and the North Dakota SHPO, which it considered. After granting an extra three weeks for additional responses, on December 18 the Corps made an initial determination of "No Historic Properties Affected" for the soil-bore testing. The Corps mailed out this decision in a Determination of Effect letter to the North Dakota SHPO and all affected tribes on the same day. The letter explained that the Corps had concluded that no historic properties would be affected by the tests and clarified that a previous "not eligible" determination had already been made for a nearby site that would also not be affected by the work. The Corps also emailed Young again the next day to seek possible dates for a January 2015 meeting with the Tribe to discuss DAPL. No response is in the record.

I don't know why Young and tribal chairman David Archambault II didn't meet or consult with DAPL when the window to consult was open. On the day the Army Corps of Engineers green-lit the project publicly Young registered a complaint. This was in December 2014. Deadlines were once again extended. Meetings were once again scheduled. Meetings were once again canceled. Again more deadlines passed, and passed again. A year passed like this. But finally, in the spring of 2016, the tribe and the Corps and DAPL representatives met no less than seven times. As a result the tribe had a chance to bring its own experts to bear on the question of cultural impacts. Meetings were held on and off the reservation, trips to the actual sites in question were taken by officials from all three groups, together. As a direct result DAPL reopened consultations with tribes in the spring of 2016. Three tribes—including the Osage and Upper Sioux— identified previously overlooked sites and the pipeline was adjusted accordingly. Standing Rock, however, declined to participate in these surveys because of "their limited scope" and instead "urged the Corps to refine the area of potential effect to include the entire pipeline." This wasn't going to happen. And without input from the tribe (because the tribe refused), construction began.

Not pleased, the tribe set up a protest camp even as it filed an injunction against the proposed crossing. The camp quickly grew to include Indians from more than three hundred different tribes, professional activists, and foreign rights organizations. While it lasted, it was the largest gathering of Indians in the United States since the same tribes (Lakota, Cheyenne, and Arapaho) formed the tribal armies that defeated the U.S. Cavalry at the Little Bighorn, not far from the #NODAPL protest camp. Whatever crooked path led from planning to execution, and whatever the possible missteps of the tribe, the protest was organized and peaceful and humane. While the tribe argued in court that the pipeline would destroy sacred sites, the Mni Wiconi protest (*mni wiconi* means "water is sacred" in the Lakota language) was primarily about fighting the danger to drinking water posed by the pipeline. The latter argument is bigger, because it hinges on tribal sovereignty and the protection of natural resources. However, the tribe and the protesters were working together, and this in itself was novel. Other tribes joined the protest, some from far away. Tribal authorities from all over the country sent food, firewood, and supplies. Tribes from Mexico sent dancers. The Maori sent hakas via Facebook. By October more than a million people had checked in via Facebook.

Things got violent fast. The protesters were determinedly anti-violence and pro–peaceful direct action; the private security teams, not so much. They loosed attack dogs on protesters. The activists were pepper-sprayed, arrested, hosed down with water cannons, and shot with rubber bullets. All along government officials and security forces and company representatives decried how the Indians were trespassing on private property, as though this was the greatest crime one can engage in in a society so shaped by ownership. Maybe it is.

As the tribe was setting up the protest camp and activists from around the country were arriving, in court the tribe officially objected to the pipeline on the grounds that it violated the National Historic Preservation Act. This is important. As much as the tribe (as a sovereign Indian nation) talked about water and tribal lands, their objections were rather narrow. They did not file motions under the Clean Water Act or the Rivers and Harbors Act. I don't know why the tribe limited their claims to cultural/

historical ones. The protest, however, was more wide-ranging. The protesters made a broad call about the need to protect sacred sites and clean water and to push the country to think harder about clean (or at least cleaner) energy. The "story" of the protest, however, is largely a story we've heard before: that the government has always undervalued the rights of indigenous people and continues to do so, that indigenous people are the stewards of the land, that Indians continue to get shafted by the government. But to rest on that story would be to miss the bigger and more fundamental one.

The story of the pipeline is not another iteration of the "Indian problem": that Indians, sadly, lost, and with them having lost, it's hard to know what to do with them, especially when they are in the way. The chairman of the Standing Rock Sioux Tribe, David Archambault II, wrote in *The New York Times* that justice looks different in Indian country. He pointed out the irony that on the day the white militants who had occupied the Malheur National Wildlife Refuge in Oregon were acquitted in federal court, federal and state forces descended on unarmed "water protectors" at Standing Rock with pepper spray, armored vehicles, and rubber bullets. This is seen as evidence that Indians are treated differently under the law than non-Indians; that Indian concerns are somehow less vital than those of other American citizens; that the white militants have a government problem but Indians have an Indian problem.

To be sure: Indian reservations and Indian communities have been chronically underserved by the justice system and, given the remote location of many reservations, have over the past 150 years been disproportionately affected by large "public" works and extractive industries, largely out of sight and mind of the rest of the country. The construction of the dam at the confluence of the Cannonball and Missouri Rivers that created Lake Oahe in 1962 completely submerged historical Mandan and Hidatsa sites, for example. Uranium and coal mining on Navajo lands has had crushing environmental impacts in the Southwest. Northern Minnesota reservations were completely deforested in the early 1900s to feed the needs of growing urban centers like Minneapolis and Chicago. But it would be a mistake to think of all of this as an "Indian problem." Rather, the Indian problem has always been a government problem. And how the government does business affects us all. The Malheur militants were acquitted largely because their takeover occurred on federal land. The water protectors were arrested because they trespassed on private land (made private by historical theft of the Great Sioux Reservation). DAPL to a large degree escaped federal oversight in the first place because almost all of it passes through private, not public, lands. Where the pipeline does cross public land and waters, the Army Corps of Engineers relied on "Permit 12" processing, which allowed the company to avoid the cumbersome process of pulling upward of thirty discrete permits for different aspects of the project and running those through nearly as many different government branches and commissions; instead, DAPL and Energy Transfer Partners pulled one permit and, once the Army Corps of Engineers approved it, they themselves became responsible for making sure they are in compliance with most of the permitting requirements, with the Army Corps checking in once every five years. In other words, the company basically polices itself.

The most important part of this whole sordid process to note and notice is not what the government is willing to do to Indians, or what the government is willing to allow to happen to the land and the water. It is that *we created a government that is doing this to us*. It is the government we empowered that created a Supreme Court that ruled in favor of Citizens United; that privileges private ownership over the common good; that fast-tracks enormous projects at great environmental cost in order to assure us of cheap energy to fuel our out-of-control consumption. We have, with our votes and our energy, opted for smaller government (and for government agencies like the EPA and the Army Corps of Engineers that seem to exist to safeguard business interests rather than the public interest) that is unable and unwilling to do the job of detailed overseeing, thus creating the opportunity for enormous environmental and social crimes by corporations.

Every protest contains a contradiction: people or groups of people set aside the way business is usually done, stand up to the state, and through protest urge the state to change. That is, they break the "rules" (violently sometimes, and at others with nonviolent direct action) in order to convince the rule makers that they need to change the rules, which is itself a kind of state-sanctioned process. However, at Standing Rock, Indians from all over North America protested, in (some) never-before-seen ways. And in this they, too, were living the changes Chelsey and Sarah talked about so passionately regarding their own growth.

The people of Standing Rock and the protesters who gathered there didn't just object to where the pipeline crossed: they objected to the pipeline in its entirety. And here is where the court case and the protest diverged: the protesters protested the existence of the pipeline, while the Standing Rock Sioux Tribe sought an injunction only on the basis of federal laws protecting the tribe's interest in preserving sacred sites.

What made this Indian protest different from others were its manner and its reach. The protesters referred to themselves not as protesters but as water protectors. Theirs was a nonviolent protest that spoke broadly to environmental and policy concerns in a way non-Indians could see affected them, too. There was no "leader," no titular head. For the first time, activists, individuals, tribal government, and the tribal governments of other Indian nations all banded together in common cause. Away from camp at least, the protest didn't have a face or a personality as much as it had faces and personalities. Many of the water protectors had day jobs—as lawyers, environmental activists, filmmakers, and even drone pilots. Many of them were close to nodes of power. And an overwhelming number of the leaders were women, a novelty in Indian protest. The protesters were making a stand on behalf of all Americans for better processes, better decisions, and better laws for our energy future, to protect all of us.

A friend asked me recently with some frustration, "Where is our Martin Luther King? What do we want exactly?" I thought about this and I remarked that we don't have a Martin Luther King. Coming from a household where my father had made us listen to King's speeches on records, I had always considered this a loss, a gap, a hole. But maybe it's not. Maybe we don't have one because we both don't need and can't have a King. We Indians are a plurality. We have always been a plurality. There are more than five hundred different tribes in the United States, and we all have different cultures, histories, landscapes, and ways of organizing politically. And we are not only "still here"—we are here and are working to undo the violence of the ages. We are united by the legacy (and current practices) of colonialism to be sure. But we are and have always been more than what the government has done to us or tried to do to us and failed: mainstream us. And while, like African Americans, we have fought for and won some (but not all) of our civil rights and equal protection, we have always fought for something quite different from that, too: that we are American and Indian, and as Indians we belong to sovereign nations and have treaty rights—pared down though they may be—that have always been our rights, rights we had long before the United States existed. Nor do we have, as does the African American civil rights movement, a single institution like slavery to define our struggle and a hard date for when that was to have ended.

But the protest at Standing Rock does have something King possessed that confers dignity in the face of dire opposition. We have the same kind of spiritual calling, a sense of a collective mission beyond worldly things, not only to ennoble ourselves through protest but also to ennoble the democratic republic that seeks to diminish us.

David Archambault II wrote that the conflict was proof that this is the same old story of cowboys versus Indians, proof that the government, once again, is against us. But to say that the story of DAPL is another expression of cowboys versus Indians is to repeat the mistakes of past protests and movements: when we situate ourselves in a position of powerlessness, we make ourselves subaltern. Not only that: we absolve ourselves of our complicity in how the world of power around us has been shaped. It absolves our tribal leaders of their reluctance to show up for meetings and to fight intelligently, diligently, and thanklessly in the trenches of numb process. It also absolves all of us—Indians and all other Americans—of the greatest sin of all: that we made the government that is doing this to us. And that's where the civil rights movement and Dr. Martin Luther King Jr. become more relevant: we have to show up to get up. Cynicism isn't a politics. Neither is irony. We have to participate, at cost and peril, in shaping our government and thereby shape its processes—including how, where, and why pipelines are approved, permitted, planned, and built. The hard work of the civil rights movement wasn't engaged to change city busing in Montgomery; those protesters meant to change the laws and heart of the country for themselves and future generations. The water protectors were aiming just as high by appealing to tribal sovereignty, working with tribal governments, forging international alliances, being gender inclusive, and striving for parity. But the success of the civil rights movement was vested in the degree to which activists voluntarily endured injustice and injury by marching in the street and by encouraging others to march into classrooms, and county boardrooms, and colleges and law schools, and the voting booth. In that way this protest is the same.

It might appear as though all that work, all that spirit, was wasted: within days of taking office Trump canceled Obama's executive order, pipeline construction continued and was completed, and the camp was forcefully dismantled by the government. It was a huge loss, but that loss wasn't for nothing. As on my own reservation, other tribal governments contemplating granting easements to pipelines across their ancestral lands now have to contend with a newly awakened tribal population that has been educated about pipelines and their consequences. Other rural communities—farmers, municipalities, and the like—have also become involved. What might have been seen as nothing more than an instance of an Indian problem is seen as an American problem. The protest made the difference. And the next time it won't be so easy.

At a dinner recently in Albuquerque, while we were looking up at Sandia Peak, a man who worked for the Indian Health Service told me something of the work he's doing. He mentioned that for many Indians in the Southwest, especially the elderly, access to health care, especially for mental health, is extremely difficult. Who, he wondered, would drive two hours to Navajo Medical Center in Shiprock, for instance, to talk to a therapist? Assuming they even have a car, or a license. He also told me—and this was something I couldn't verify—that Indians possess and use smartphones at a rate that far exceeds the national average. *Think about it,* he said. *So many Indians are transient: they move from here to there, they sleep on a cousin's couch. They don't have homes and so don't have computers. For many Indians out there, their smartphones are their laptops and desktops, their only computers.* And so his staff thought they could make use of that and began offering mental health services via Skype and FaceTime for Indian veterans and others too sick or too remote to come in. I wondered out loud if he could use the same thinking to develop apps where Indians—who suffer from diabetes at staggering rates—could check their blood and enter it into a program that would then feed into their health records at IHS. It would make monitoring and treating diabetes so much easier and could emphasize preventive care in ways not yet explored. And maybe do something else as well.

In 1891 the superintendent of the centennial census, Robert Porter, wrote in his findings that "there can hardly be said to be a frontier line." That sentiment was taken up again by Frederick Jackson Turner in 1893. For modern Indians, however, the "new frontier" has shifted; it brings the past into contact with the future. Sean and Sarah and Chelsey are each in their own way doing this through cuisine and health. Others are doing it through language revitalization and education.

It's happening in politics, too. More than eighty Indians ran for public office across the country, at every level, in 2018. Peggy Flanagan (Ojibwe), who served on the Minneapolis school board before landing a seat in the Minnesota legislature in 2015, won the race for lieutenant governor of the state. Voters elected Deb Haaland (Laguna Pueblo) and Sharice Davids (Ho-Chunk) to the House of Representatives for New Mexico and Kansas, respectively—the first Native women elected to Congress. (Both Democrats, they will join Representatives Tom Cole, Chickasaw, and Markwayne Mullin, Cherokee, both Republicans from Oklahoma.) In Idaho, however, Paulette Jordan (Coeur d'Alene) lost her bid to become the first American Indian governor in U.S. history. Not only did record numbers of Indians run for public office, record numbers of them were women. Thirty-one women campaigned for seats in state legislatures, three in gubernatorial races, and four for Congress.

This is impressive not just in terms of numbers. As with the Standing Rock protest, the influx of Native women into positions of leadership, or poised for leadership, is shaping Indian communities in new ways. In 2018, candidates of both parties ran on platforms that privileged health, education, and family; taken together, they are breathing new life into our democracy precisely at a time when our democracy seems to be in crisis. As dismal as the outcome of the Standing Rock protests might seem, it's important to remember this: There were Indians everywhere in the picture. Indians were working for the oil companies and for the Army Corps of Engineers, to regulate the construction of the pipeline, at the same time that Indians were fighting it, as politicians and activists. The old western frontier might have been closed in 1890, but the modern Indian frontier doesn't face that direction anyway.

I remember being a lonely Indian kid on the margins of Leech Lake, certain only that there was no one else out there like me, stuck in a kind of radical subjectivity. Surely my sense of my own isolation was hardly unique: many teens, and many teen Indians, feel this way. For so long we were undone by our solitude and by the differences within our communities, which loomed as great as the differences and distances between us and the dominant culture. This began to change during the boarding school era, when Indians from different tribes were shoved together at school. That isolation was further eroded during and after World War II, when Indians served together and with a wide variety of other Americans. The digital Indians of the next generation are more and more quickly closing the gaps that separate us. In past eras, it might have been enough for Indians merely to survive; the biggest shift I can see in my own lifetime is a kind of collective determination to do much more than that.

Our identity politics reflects this sea change. When I was a kid on the reservation, who was or wasn't authentically Indian was determined largely in those endless clashes over how dark you were, whether you were enrolled, whether you came up hard, how much damage you could do to yourself and others and still keep on living. This is no longer true. To be Indian today seems to be more a matter of action. I hear it all around me— at powwows and ceremony and online. *Do you speak your language? Gidojibwem ina? You hunt? Did you go ricing this year? You headed to the drum dance? Did you go to Standing Rock?* Less and less do we define ourselves by what we have lost, what we have suffered, what we've endured.

We have grown diverse in Indian country. The numbers tell part of the story. Not only have those who identify on the census as Indian risen from about 200,000 in 1900 to over 2 million by 2010; another 3 million identify as Native and something else. Of this ever-increasing population, in 2010 more than 70 percent lived in urban areas, continuing the trend begun in the years after World War II. Indians are young, too: 32 percent are under age eighteen, compared with 24 percent of the overall population. On reservations, the median age is twenty-six, compared with thirty-seven for the nation at large. And these many young millions are doing things. Between 1990 and 2000, the income of American Indians grew by 33 percent, and the poverty rate dropped by 7 percent. There was no marked difference in income between Indians from casino-rich tribes and those from poorer tribes without casinos. Between 1990 and 1997 the number of Indian-owned businesses grew by 84 percent. And the number of Native kids enrolled in college has doubled in the past thirty years. All of these demographic changes—rapidly increasing population, better education, more opportunities for business and work, a burgeoning urban population and a youthful reservation population—have begun to erase many of the old hurdles and divides. The city is not necessarily the place to which one escapes from a reservation, but it is a community, a homeland, in its own right. Reservation people go to the city and bring the reservation with them, and city Indians go back to the reservation and bring the city with them.

The net effect of all this diversity is a sense that we are surging, but in a more constellatory than uniform fashion. No longer does being Indian mean being helplessly characterized as savage throwbacks living in squalor on the margins of society, suffering the abuses of a careless, unfeeling government. We seem to be everywhere, and doing everything. Social media helps connect us. Chelsey and Sarah and the water protectors and powwow Indians and corporate types and college kids and Indian soccer moms and everyone else are in increasingly close contact, and I can't help feeling we are using modernity in the best possible way: to work together and to heal what was broken.

Epilogue

In 1863, Hehaka Sapa (Black Elk) was born near the banks of the Powder River in what would later become Wyoming. His family was an important one: his father was a respected medicine man, and they were closely related to the famous war chief Crazy Horse. In his own words: "I am a Lakota of the Oglala band. My father's name was Black Elk, and his father before him bore the name, and the father of his father, so that I am the fourth to bear it. He was a medicine man and so were several of his brothers. Also, he and the great Crazy Horse's father were cousins, having the same grandfather. My mother's name was White Cow Sees; her father was called Refuse-to-Go, and her mother, Plenty Eagle Feathers. I can remember my mother's mother and her father. My father's father was killed by the Pawnees when I was too little to know, and his mother, Red Eagle Woman, died soon after."

The world of Black Elk's youth was an Indian world. Of course his people, the Lakota, had been dealing with—meeting with, trading with, fighting with—white people for centuries. And even the fact that Black Elk was born on the Powder River and not on the Mississippi or the Minnesota or the Red River was the result of centuries of growth and migration and displacement. In 1862, one year before Black Elk's birth, the Dakota in Minnesota had revolted and risen up against encroaching white settlers and corrupt Indian agents in what became known as the Dakota War of 1862. After the rebellion was quelled, thirty-eight Dakota were hanged in Mankato, Minnesota, in the largest mass execution in U.S. history. The world hadn't held still before his birth, and it would not hold still after. But his world, such as it was, was still a Lakota world, and he and his tribe were its authors.

Black Elk learned to ride and to shoot. He was much like any other

Lakota boy at that time. But at age four he began to have visions—uncommonly detailed spiritual visions that came to him at night but also during the day. They scared him, and he spoke of them to no one. Then, when he was nine, as his family was breaking camp, heading west to hunt near the Rocky Mountains, he fell ill. At first, while eating in the teepee in the village his legs were suddenly laced with pain. The next day he was out riding with his friends, and when he jumped off his horse his legs buckled and he fell to the ground. His friends helped him onto his horse and brought him back to the village. His legs and arms were swollen and puffy. He was delirious and feverish. No one knew what to do and it seemed likely that he would die. A medicine man was sent for, and Black Elk slipped in and out of consciousness. It is impossible to know for sure, but it seems likely that he was laid low by viral or bacterial meningitis, an infection of the brain and spine that strikes suddenly and brings acute painful swelling of the legs.

As his body failed him and he began slipping away, he was granted a vision. It was long, ornate, and powerful: the kind of vision most people will never have. In it, Black Elk was shown—by degrees—all of creation and his place in it. He was able to see the past and the future of his own people and also the ways in which Indian lives would meet and mix with the American future. Near the end of his vision he stood on a tall mountain and looked down at the world at his feet: "And as I stood there I saw more than I can tell and I understood more than I saw; for I was seeing in a sacred manner the shapes of all things in the spirit, and the shape of all shapes as they must live together like one being. And I saw that the sacred hoop of my people was one of many hoops that made one circle, wide as daylight and as starlight, and in the center grew one mighty flowering tree to shelter all the children of one mother and one father. And I saw that it was holy." And as quickly as his sickness and vision came to him, they began to leave: "When the singing stopped, I was feeling lost and very lonely. Then a Voice above me said: 'Look back!' It was a spotted eagle that was hovering over me and spoke. I looked, and where the flaming rainbow tepee, built and roofed with cloud, had been, I saw only the tall rock mountain at the center of the world. I was all alone on a broad plain now with my feet upon the earth, alone but for the spotted eagle guarding me. I could see my people's village far ahead, and I walked very fast, for I was homesick now. Then I saw my own tepee, and inside I saw my mother and my father bending over a sick boy that was myself. And as I entered the tepee, some one was saying: 'The boy is coming to; you had better give him some water.'

"Then I was sitting up; and I was sad because my mother and my father didn't seem to know I had been so far away."

Black Elk would travel farther. First he would travel down the path of violence with the rest of his tribe when—harassed—they finally lured Custer and the Seventh Cavalry in for the final conflict at the Little Bighorn. As the battle raged through gulches and over the hills, the central violence always seemed to retreat in front of him. He rode on and on until he was finally in the thick of the main battle, enveloped in a dust cloud filled with the voices of dying men, the screaming of horses, the thudding of hooves and bodies. In the aftermath, "Black Elk picked his way farther up the gulch, followed by the younger boys. By the time they reached the top, most of the gray horse troops were dead. But not all. The boys surrounded those retaining the slightest spark of life, shot them full of arrows, pushed those already in their bodies farther in. Black Elk continued on. He noticed a dying soldier with an engraved gold watch hanging from his belt; he took the watch and shot the dying man. He ascended the hill to where greater numbers of soldiers lay in clumps and guessed this was where the fight had ended. One of the boys ran up and asked him to scalp a soldier; Black Elk handed over the scalp and the boy ran off to show his mother. Another man writhed before him, flapping his arms and groaning in pain. Black Elk shot a blunt arrow into the soldier's forehead and the man toppled backward. His limbs quivered and stopped. Black Elk kept climbing. He'd made three or four kills this day, but now each kill was like the other. He later told John Neihardt [his biographer] that he took no pleasure in them."

Black Elk's vision had been one of peace and healing, a vision of a world that was one "hoop" made up of smaller hoops, as he put it. How remarkably similar this is to the dreams dreamed by the founding fathers:

of a nation conceived in liberty and devoted to peace. And like the founding fathers, Black Elk and his people would engage in unspeakable violence. They would have to kill and be killed on their way to a more perfect peace promised to them by their better selves. Between the Battle of the Little Bighorn and Wounded Knee, more violence was to come. Rather than engage the Cheyenne, Arapaho, Lakota, and other tribes on the battlefield (though this did happen as well), the government chased and harried the tribes and burned their food and lodges whenever they were found.

Buffalo hunters continued exterminating the buffalo. The first transcontinental telegraph line was completed in 1861. In 1865 the United States was once again united. In 1869 the transcontinental railroad spanned the continent. After the Little Bighorn in 1876, Plains tribes, so long resistant to reservation life, began trickling and then streaming into agencies and reservations. In 1882 six hundred Lakota and Yanktonai found a big herd of bison west of Standing Rock Reservation. They killed more than five thousand bison. This was the last large hunt of bison by an American Indian tribe. By the 1890s only a few hundred bison remained. The old life was gone. A new life was beginning.

Black Elk decided to do what many men—including famous chiefs and warriors—did once open hostilities were over: he joined Buffalo Bill's Wild West show. He toured all over the United States and Europe acting out in front of astonished audiences the very battles (like Custer's Last Stand) in which he had participated. How surreal it must have been: to act in the myth machine while the real life for which he'd fought so hard was passing beyond his reach. He eventually returned and was living with his mother near Wounded Knee on that cold, clear December 29 in 1890 when the government surrounded Spotted Elk's band of Miniconjou and Hunkpapa at Wounded Knee Creek. Black Elk was not in the initial assault at Wounded Knee. He arrived with reinforcements—after the band was surrounded and disarmed, after Black Coyote's rifle went off, after the soldiers opened up with their Hotchkiss guns, after the soldiers trained their cannons and guns from the high ground down onto the men, women, and children running for their lives, down the gully and onto the plain. Armed only with a bow for which he had no arrows, Black Elk charged the soldiers repeatedly. When they scattered, he helped what Indians he could to safety. But Black Elk and the others fighting with him weren't able to dislodge the soldiers completely, and singly and in small groups they began to melt away, back to Pine Ridge Agency.

Black Elk was shaken by what he'd seen, "Men and women and children were heaped and scattered all over the flat at the bottom of the little hill where the soldiers had their wagon-guns, and westward up the dry gulch all the way to the high ridge, the dead women and children and babies were scattered. When I saw this I wished that I had died too, but I was not sorry for the women and children. It was better for them to be happy in the other world, and I wanted to be there too. But before I went there I wanted to have revenge. I thought there might be a day, and we should have revenge . . ." Before he could get his revenge, however, Black Elk had "one last obligation" to fulfill. "He plucked up the orphaned baby he'd stowed in a place of safety. He saw now it was a girl. He held her close and kept his buckskin at an easy gait so the girl would not be jostled. He rode back to the Agency and hunted for the family. In time, she would be adopted by the father of his future wife and named Blue Whirlwind. Other infants would be plucked up by warriors and taken home that day. Many would be adopted by the families of their saviors."

The next day, while riding up White Clay Creek toward another spasm of the fighting that was rippling across the area, Black Elk was shot. "All this time the bullets were buzzing around me and I was not touched. I was not even afraid. It was like being in a dream about shooting. But just as I had reached the very top of the hill, suddenly it was like waking up, and I was afraid. I dropped my arms and quit making the goose cry. Just as I did this, I felt something strike my belt as though some one had hit me there with the back of an ax. I nearly fell out of my saddle, but I managed to hold on, and rode over the hill. An old man by the name of Protector was there, and he ran up and held me, for now I was falling off my horse. I will show you where the bullet struck me sidewise across the belly here (showing a long deep scar on the abdomen). My insides were coming out. Protector tore up a blanket in strips and bound it around me so that my insides would stay in. By now I was crazy to kill, and I said to Protector: 'Help me on my horse! Let me go over there. It is a good day to die, so I will go over there!' But Protector said: 'No, young nephew! You must not die to-day. That would be foolish. Your people need you. There may be a better day to die.' He lifted me into my saddle and led my horse away down hill. Then I began to feel very sick." Soon after, African American regiments (Buffalo Soldiers) showed up and reinforced the Seventh Cavalry, and the fighting was over.

Though the fighting was over, life was not. Black Elk married and had a family. He converted to Catholicism and became a catechist at the Catholic church in Pine Ridge. Many Indians prefer not to think about Black Elk's later years and consider his conversion as a kind of surrender, a confirmation that the old ways were in fact dead. Maybe, maybe not. Black Elk was determined to live and to adapt. That doesn't make him less of an Indian, as I see it; it makes him more of one.

THERE WERE A FEW SKIRMISHES after Wounded Knee, in South Dakota, Utah, Nevada, Arizona, New Mexico, and Minnesota. But most of the most famous chiefs—Sitting Bull, Crazy Horse, Geronimo, Chief Joseph, Red Cloud, Bagone-giizhig, Tecumseh, Black Hawk, Cochise, Quanah Parker—were either dead, imprisoned, or in retirement. At the time of first contact, around 1500 CE, Indian populations in North America had been, according to sober estimates, around five million. There were more than five hundred distinct tribes spread over the entire continent—from the Florida Keys to the Aleutian Islands. The deserts of the American Southwest hosted some of the most advanced social groups, who built cities that still stand today. At the confluence of the Missouri and the Mississippi, where St. Louis now stands, was a city of more than twenty thousand. Along the resource-rich Eastern Seaboard, the coast was populated, without break, from Florida to Newfoundland. But four hundred years of warfare, disease, and starvation had taken its toll. According to the U.S. Census, there were only 237,000 Indians in the United States in 1900.

The story of the land parallels that of the population. The United States comprises 2.4 billion acres. By 1900, Indians "controlled" only 78 million acres, or about 3 percent. As we've seen, this outcome wasn't the result of a single regime or episode or factor, and it didn't happen overnight. But Wounded Knee came to stand in for all of it: the final blow, a full stop to a long sentence of pain and dispossession.

Wounded Knee has been seen not only as the end of Indian life but also as the end of a kind of American life. The frontier, Frederick Jackson Turner posited, had made America what it was. But the frontier was closed, and its memory was already being turned into myth in dime novels, westerns, and Wild West shows. Indians were on the way out, moving from a life in the world to a kind of museum existence. The guns were cleaned and put away, and the dirty work of death by administration and display begun. What would happen to American innovation? To the perfection of democracy? To the American Dream itself?

But not so fast.

As I've tried to show in the preceding pages, Indians lived on, as more than ghosts, as more than the relics of a once happy people. We lived on increasingly invested in and changed by—and in turn doing our best to change—the American character.

It pains me to think about Wounded Knee. It also pains me, for different reasons, to read about it in books like Dee Brown's. What hurts is not just that 150 people were cruelly and viciously killed. It is that their sense of life—and our sense of their lives—died with them. We know next to nothing about them. Who among them was funny? Who kicked his dog? Were they unfaithful, or vain, or fond of sweets? The tiny, fretful, intricate details are what make us who we are. And they are lost again and again when we paint over them with the tragedy of "the Indian." In this sense, the victims of Wounded Knee died twice—once at the end of a gun, and again at the end of a pen.

We die, too, in our own minds. And this is perhaps the saddest death of all. We are so used to telling the stories of our lives, and those of our tribes, as a tragedy, as a necessarily diminishing line—once we were great, once we ruled everything, and now we rule nothing, now we are merely ghosts that haunt the American mind—that we deprive ourselves of the very life we yearn for. I cannot shake the belief that the ways in which we tell the story of our reality shapes that reality: the manner of telling makes the world. And I worry that if we tell the story of the past as a tragedy, we consign ourselves to a tragic future. If we insist on raging against our dependency on the United States and modernity itself, we miss something vital: as much as our past was shaped by the whims and violence of an evolving America, America, in turn, has been shaped by us.

The violence itself was certainly influenced by the shifting frontier of conflict between tribes and settlers. As America emerged from its adolescence in the early 1800s, the question of how the federal government would work with and against the states it united was thrown into doubt by the Indian removals from the Southeast. The modern Supreme Court was shaped by the questions of community and obligation between the government and sovereign Indian nations throughout the 1970s, 1980s, and 1990s. At Standing Rock, the water protectors have reminded us of pressing modern questions that are fundamental not only to Indian struggles but also to our national identity: What, and who, is most important? To what degree does and to what degree should the government privilege private property and corporate interests over the public good? And what, after all, is the public? In order to answer these questions, I think we have to find a new way to think. Black Elk mourned that a dream died in the snow at Wounded Knee. It is up to us to do the next thing: to dream a new one.

Walter Benjamin, the German critic and thinker, wrote:

To articulate the past historically does not mean to recognize it 'the way it really was.' . . . It means to seize hold of a memory as it flashes up at a moment of danger. . . . In every era the attempt must be made anew to wrest tradition away from a conformism that is about to overpower it. . . . Only that historian will have the gift of fanning the spark of hope in the past who is firmly convinced that *even the dead* will not be safe from the enemy if he wins. And this enemy has not ceased to be victorious.

452

Today is that "moment of danger." This book is an attempt to rescue the dead from the enemy by looking beyond Wounded Knee. It is not about the heart that was buried in the cold ground of South Dakota but rather about the heart that beats on—among the Dakota, to be sure, but also among the Diné, Comanche, Ojibwe, Seminole, Miwok, Blackfeet, and the other tribes around the country. And while Wounded Knee was the last major armed conflict between Indian tribes and the U.S. government, there have been many battles since 1890: battles fought by Indian parents to keep their children, and by the children far away at boarding schools to remember and keep their families and, by extension, their tribes, close to their hearts; battles of Indian leaders to defeat allotment and other destructive legislation; battles of activists to make good on the promises their leaders couldn't or wouldn't honor; battles of millions of present-day Indians to be Indian and modern at the same time. We are, in a sense, the children and grandchildren and great-grandchildren of those hundreds who survived Wounded Knee and who did what was necessary to survive, at first, and then—bit by bit—to thrive.

The *how* of the telling shapes the *what*. How we see the people, their lives, their actions, and the meanings that obtain from those lives and actions shapes the present and the possible future. This book is meant to tell the story of Indian lives, and Indian histories, in such a way as to render those histories and those lives as something much more, much greater and grander, than a catalog of pain. I have tried to catch us not in the act of dying but, rather, in the radical act of living. Because at the heart of the political convulsions that now grip the "lovely, trustful, dreamy, enormous country" we love lies a human question. A simple one.

What kind of country do we want to be? Is this government of ours one that should merely get out of the way so that America can once again be, in Ronald Reagan's words, a place "in which people can still get rich"? Or is our government meant to be the angel (avenging or otherwise) of our better nature? It has always bothered me that the very idea of paying attention to or knowing Indian history is tinged with the soft compassion of the do-gooder, as a kind of voluntary public service, like volunteering at an after-school program. But if we treat Indian stories this way, we do more than relegate Indians themselves to history—as mattering only in relation to America's deep and sometimes dark past. We also miss the full measure of the country itself. If you want to know America—if you want to see it for what it was and what it is—you need to look at Indian history and at the Indian present. If you do, if we all do, we will see that all the issues posed at the founding of the country have persisted. How do the rights of the many relate to the rights of the few? What is or should be the furthest extent of federal power? How has the relationship between the government and the individual evolved? What are the limits of the executive to execute policy, and to what extent does that matter to us as we go about our daily lives? How do we reconcile the stated ideals of America as a country given to violent acts against communities and individuals? To what degree do we privilege enterprise over people? To what extent does the judiciary shape our understanding of our place as citizens in this country? To what extent should it? What are the limits to the state's power over the people living within its borders? To ignore the history of Indians in America is to miss how power itself works.

John Adams, writing to Thomas Jefferson in 1816, urged him to remember that "Power always thinks it has a great Soul, and vast Views, beyond the Comprehension of the Weak." If anything, the lives of Indians—our struggles to and success in surviving—remind us that our souls have great power. We need to recall the mute agony of the Indian woman, her name lost to history, who was abducted by Columbus, given to Michele da Cuneo, sold, traded, raped, and likely consigned to the sea. We need to remember the strength and dignity of the Otoe chief Medicine Horse, who responded to the federal commissioner trying to take his land in 1873 by saying, "We are not children. We are men. I never thought I would be treated so when I made the Treaty." We need to remember the anguish of the Indian father who received news of his daughter's death at Flandreau Indian School in 1906: "Those that were with her say she did not suffer, but passed away as one asleep. Lizzie was one of our best girls. . . . I am very sorry that you could not have seen your daughter alive, for she had grown quite a little and improved much since you let her come here with me." To remember these stories and all the others is to remain humble in power, and to be called to tend to the troubled soul of the country; it is to remember that our very lives exist at the far side of policy. It is to remember the good and the bad, the personal and the social, the large and the small. It is not to capture Indians, per se, but to capture the details of our lives. We are, for better or worse, the body of our republic. And we need to listen to it, to hear—beyond the pain and anger and fear, beyond the decrees and policies and the eddying of public sentiments and resentments, beyond the bombast and rhetoric—the sound (faint at times, stronger at others) of a heartbeat going on.

Acknowledgments

I began writing this book the week my father died in the winter of 2016. Not an easy time. I have felt both the loss of him and his presence every day since. And in the ultimate balance of things his presence is felt more keenly. But it was the living who made all the difference as I wrote and it is they I would like to thank. It is, of course, largely impossible to thank everyone who needs to be thanked here. This book sat in my mind for years before I sat down to write it. And when I did finally begin, that, too, took years. I owe a great debt to everyone at Riverhead Books and to my editor, Becky Saletan, in particular. You were patient, and brilliant, and when you said you wanted my best work, not my fastest, I took you at your word. I would also like to thank my agent extraordinaire, Adam Eaglin, for seeing the book inside the idea and for making everything possible. The School for Advanced Research in Santa Fe housed me for five months. The writing began there and wouldn't have been possible otherwise. The peace and quiet coupled with the energy of brilliant colleagues was indispensable. I would also like to thank my students and colleagues at the University of Southern California. You kept me company through the long birth of the book and supported me intellectually and materially. Being a teacher keeps me awake, it keeps me alive and engaged. I owe you all. Most of all, I am indebted to my fellow Indians across the country. Bobby Matthews, Santee Frazier, Sterling HolyWhiteMountain, Red Hall, Pat Schildt, Dave Schildt, Sierra Fredrickson, Eddy Pablo, Gabe Galanda, Ray Sheldon, Sarah "Southside" Agaton Howes, Chelsey Luger, and more (many more) opened their homes and lives and hearts to me. If I didn't have space to mention you here, or if your stories didn't end up in the book: you are not forgotten. Thank you. I like to think each of you in your own way did it not for me but to have a chance to come together to talk out our past with the idea that it will help create a better future for our people. I would also like to thank my family. My father and mother—Robert Treuer and Margaret Seelye Treuer—have always inspired me. I was not an easy child, and I apologize. I am not an easy man, and for that I also ask your forgiveness. My children endured long separations from me when I was on the road. I love you. More than anyone else, this book is for you. You are cheerful and smart and funny and interesting, curious, and kind: everything I hope to be someday. Also thanks to my inspiration and my love: Abi Levis. I couldn't do this without you.

A Note on Sources

This book contains no composite characters or pseudonyms. All dialogue in quotation marks was recorded digitally. Reconstructed dialogue appears in italics. In the words of the inimitable Barbara Tuchman, "I have tried to avoid spontaneous attribution or the 'he must have' style of historical writing: 'As he watched the coastline of France disappear, Napoleon must have thought back over the long . . .' All conditions of weather, thoughts or feelings, and states of mind public or private in the following pages have documentary support." I have tried my best to frame opinion as opinion and fact as fact, if for no other reason than that Indian lives and Indian history have long been given the fancy treatment of poetic and loose interpretation. If we are going to imagine our past and reimagine our future, we are going to have to do it with curiosity and care. This book is, obviously, a mélange of history, reportage, and memoir. It is also my take on things, my read of our shared Indian past, present, and future. Errors of fact are mine. Errors of perspective are mine as well. I have no doubt that had the writers and thinkers and Indian citizens on whom I've relied faced the same task, they would have written different books. For better or worse, this is mine.

Notes

Prologue

3 **It is estimated that by the late 1870s:** "Time Line of the American Bison," National Bison Range Wildlife Refuge Complex, U.S. Fish & Wildlife Service, https://www.fws.gov/bisonrange/timeline.htm.

5 **"The coming of the troops has frightened the Indians":** Quoted in H. W. Brands, *The Reckless Decade: America in the 1890s* (Chicago: University of Chicago Press, 1995), 18.

6 **"there was a woman with an infant in her arms":** American Horse, quoted in "Documents Relating to the Wounded Knee Massacre" (personal accounts of Wounded Knee, from interviews by Eli S. Ricker; *Black Elk Speaks*; reports and testimony relating to the Army investigation of the Battle of Wounded Knee and the Sioux Campaign of 1890–1891) (ID 1101), *Digital History*, http://www.digitalhistory.uh.edu/disp_textbook.cfm?smtID=3&psid=1101.

6 **"Helpless children and women with babes in their arms":** John A. Haymond, *The American Soldier, 1866–1916: The Enlisted Man and the Transformation of the United States Army* (Jefferson, NC: McFarland, 2018), 237.

8 **"they can go about getting it":** Kevin Abourezk, "From Red Fears to Red Power: The Story of the Newspaper Coverage of Wounded Knee 1890 and Wounded Knee 1973" (master's thesis, University of Nebraska, Lincoln, 2012), 39, https://digitalcommons.unl.edu/cgi/viewcontent.cgi?referer=https://www.google.com/&httpsredir=1&article=1029&context=journalismdiss.

8 **General Nelson Miles relieved Colonel James Forsyth:** Peter R. DeMontravel, *A Hero to His Fighting Men: Nelson A. Miles, 1839–1925* (Kent, OH: Kent State University Press, 1998), 204–7.

8 **"Why should we spare even a semblance":** Ibid., 207.

8 **"the miserable wretches" . . . "The *Pioneer* has before declared":** Quoted in Ned Halley, afterword to L. Frank Baum, *The Wizard of Oz [sic]* (London: Collector's Library, 2009), 177.

8 **"The United States lies like a huge page":** Frederick Jackson Turner, "The Frontier in American History" (1893), in *The Frontier in American History* (New York: Henry Holt, 1921), 12.

9 "We shall never be happy here any more": Simon Pokagon, *The Red Man's Rebuke* (Hartford, MI: C. H. Engle, 1893), 12–13.

10 "What is life?": Quoted in post to *Native History Magazine*, February 18, 2013, http://www.nativehistorymagazine.com/2013/02/chief-crowfoot-on-life-and-death.html.

10 "greatest concentration of recorded experience and observation": Dee Brown, *Bury My Heart at Wounded Knee* (1970; New York: Henry Holt, 1970, 2000), xxiii.

11 "If the readers of this book": Ibid., xxv.

17 "Men make their own history": Karl Marx, *The Eighteenth Brumaire of Louis Bonaparte* (CreateSpace, 2013), 7 (trans. Saul K. Padover, from 1869 German edition).

Part 1. Narrating the Apocalypse: 10,000 BCE–1890

22 The Spanish crown in particular had depleted its resources: Simon Newman, "Merchants in the Middle Ages," The Finer Times, http://www.thefinertimes.com/Middle-Ages/merchants-in-the-middle-ages.html; and Allen Pikerman, "The Iberian Golden Age: European Expansion: Exploration and Colonization, 1400–1650," 2002, International World History Project, http://history-world.org/iberian_golden_age.htm.

22 The effects were dramatic: Newman, "Merchants in the Middle Ages."

23 "While I was in the boat, I captured a very beautiful Carib woman": Klaus Brinkbäumer and Clemens Höges, *The Voyage of the Vizcaína: The Mystery of Christopher Columbus's Last Ship*, trans. Annette Streck (New York: Harcourt, 2006), 156. Also found at Katie Halper, "Five Scary Christopher Columbus Quotes That Let You Celebrate the Holiday the Right Way," *Raw Story*, October 13, 2014, https://www.rawstory.com/2014/10/five-scary-christopher-columbus-quotes-that-let-you-celebrate-the-holiday-the-right-way/.

23 "'enemies of the Catholic church'": Andrés Reséndez, *The Other Slavery: The Uncovered Story of Indian Enslavement in America* (Boston: Houghton Mifflin Harcourt, 2016), 26.

24 "Who is this Columbus who dares give out my vassals as slaves?": Ibid., 28.

24 "would have sent many Indians": Quoted ibid. (emphasis in original).

24 All had the same tale to tell: "Columbus Controversy," History, https://www.history.com/topics/exploration/columbus-controversy.

27 dated to as many as nineteen thousand years ago: Ann Gibbons, "Oldest Stone Tools in the Americas Claimed in Chile," November 18, 2015, *Science*, http://www.sciencemag.org/news/2015/11/oldest-stone-tools-americas-claimed-chile.

30 Archaeological evidence: John E. Clark and Dennis Gosser, "Reinventing Mesoamerica's First Pottery," in *The Emergence of Pottery: Technology and Innovation in Ancient Societies*, ed. William K. Barnett and John W. Hoopes

(Washington, DC: Smithsonian Institution Press, 2015), 209–19, retrieved at http://users.clas.ufl.edu/dcgrove/mexarchreadings/reinventing.pdf.

32 **"to encourage them to abandon hunting"**: "Jefferson's Secret Message to Congress," January 18, 1803, *Rivers, Edens, Empires: Lewis & Clark and the Revealing of America*, Library of Congress, http://www.loc.gov/exhibits /lewisandclark/transcript56.html.

33 **"I think our governments will remain virtuous"**: Thomas Jefferson to James Madison, December 20, 1787, Jefferson Quotes & Family Letters, http://tjrs.monticello.org/letter/1300.

33 **"To promote this disposition to exchange lands"**: Thomas Jefferson to William Henry Harrison, February 27, 1803, Founders Online, National Archives, https://founders.archives.gov/documents/Jefferson/01-39-02-0500.

34 **"wheresoever they may be found"**: *Laws of the Colonial and State Governments from 1633 to 1831 Inclusive* (Washington, DC: Thompson and Romans, 1832), 186.

35 **"Neither superior technology"**: Roxanne Dunbar-Ortiz, *An Indigenous Peoples' History of the United States* (Boston: Beacon Press, 2014), 96.

36 **When it concluded, the United States secured**: Charles Flowers, Peter B. Gallagher, and Patricia Wickman, Seminole Timeline, Seminole Tribe of Florida, History, http://www.semtribe.com/History/TimelineText.aspx.

36 **"Am I a negro, a slave?"**: Quoted in "Billy Bowlegs in New Orleans," *Harper's Weekly*, June 12, 1858, 376, https://archive.org/stream/harpersweek100bonn# page/376.

36 **As was typical, American losses were framed**: Michael Warren, "Dade's Massacre Reenacts Start of Second Seminole War," http://floridatraveler.com /dades-massacre-recalls-seminole history/.

37 **"The government is in the wrong"**: Adam Wasserman, *A People's History of Florida 1513–1876: How Africans, Seminoles, Women, and Lower Class Whites Shaped the Sunshine State* (Self-Published, 2009), 303.

37 **The total cost to fight the Seminole**: "The Causes and Effects of the Seminole Wars," Florida Memory, State Library & Archives of Florida, https:// www.floridamemory.com/onlineclassroom/seminoles/lessonplans/4thgrade /4th-causes.php.

38 **Life seems to have been particularly good**: Alice B. Kehoe, *North American Indians: A Comprehensive Account*, 3rd ed. (New York: Routledge, 2005), 209.

38 **"After around 3000 BCE"**: Ibid., 32.

38 **One archaeological site in southern Maine**: Ibid.

38 **Elaborate burial practices disappeared**: Ibid.

40 **Bison were habituated**: Nancy Blumenstalk Mingus, "Origin of the Name 'Buffalo,'" from *Buffalo: Good Neighbors, Great Architecture* (Arcadia, 2003), http://www.buffaloah.com/h/bflo/origin.html.

41 **Portuguese explorer Gaspar Corte-Real:** Pietro Pasqualigo, ambassador to
    Portugal from Venice, to his brothers in Venice, October 19, 1501, http://
    nationalhumanitiescenter.org/pds/amerbegin/contact/text1/gcreal.pdf.

41 **In 1580 an English crew who had landed in Maine:** James Axtell, *After
    Columbus: Essays in the Ethnohistory of Colonial North America* (New
    York: Oxford University Press, 1988), 177.

41 **French explorers brought Indians back to France:** Kehoe, *North American
    Indians,* 225.

41 **In 1592, well before the Seneca had direct:** Mary Ellen Snodgrass, *World
    Epidemics: A Cultural Chronology of Disease from Prehistory to the Era of
    Zika* (Jefferson, NC: McFarland, 2017), 56.

42 **"laughed his Enemies and the Enemies of his People":** Alfred A. Cave,
    The Pequot War (Amherst: University of Massachusetts Press, 1996), 151.

43 **In the various climates found in this vast and fecund area:** Michael Perry,
    "Woodland Period," 1996, Office of the State Archaeologist, University of
    Iowa, http://archaeology.uiowa.edu/woodland-period-0.

44 **In Ohio some mounds were found to contain:** Alice Kehoe, *North
    America Before the European Invasions,* 2nd ed. (New York: Routledge,
    2016), 85.

44 **One burial mound at the Mound City:** "Hopewell (1–400 A.D.)," Heil-
    brunn Timeline of Art History, The Metropolitan Museum of Art, http://
    www.metmuseum.org/toah/hd/hope/hd_hope.htm.

44 **Large villages replaced small seasonal camps:** "Mississippian Period AD
    1100–1541," Fort Smith National Historic Site (Arkansas), National Park Ser-
    vice, https://www.nps.gov/fosm/learn/historyculture/mississippiperiod.htm.

44 **One burial site there contained twenty thousand shell beads:** Jack Page, *In
    the Hands of the Great Spirit: The 20,000-Year History of American Indians*
    (New York: The Free Press, 2003), 70–71.

45 **"made frequent signs to us to come on shore":** "The Great Lakes Fur Trade:
    All Because of a Beaver," North West Company Fur Post, Minnesota Histori-
    cal Society, http://sites.mnhs.org/sites/sites.mnhs.org.historic-sites/files/docs
    _pdfs/The_Great_Lakes_Fur_Trade.pdf.

46 **With the exception of the Huron:** James F. Pendergast, "The Confusing Iden-
    tities Attributed to Stadacona and Hochelaga," *Journal of Canadian Studies*
    32, no. 4 (Winter 1998), 149–67, https://utpjournals.press/doi/10.3138/
    jcs.32.4.149.

47 **The hope at Quebec was to catch furs:** Michael McDonnell, *Masters of
    Empire: Great Lakes Indians and the Making of America* (New York: Hill
    and Wang, 2016), 29.

50 **"not permit any Nation to establish posts there":** Ibid., 152.

50 **"stabbed him to death":** Ibid., 154.

50 **"killed, boiled, and ate Memeskia":** Ibid.

52 **These were people who knew what they were doing:** Page, *In the Hands of the Great Spirit*, 72.

52 **Contrary to the myth of the desert:** "Sonoran Desert Network Ecosystems," Sonoran Desert Inventory & Monitoring Network, National Park Service, https://www.nps.gov/im/sodn/ecosystems.htm.

54 **"one of the cleverest bits of passive solar architecture":** Page, *In the Hands of the Great Spirit*, 81.

57 **The Zuni seem to have been waiting for them:** Ibid., 138–40.

57 **After three days they emerged:** Ibid.

61 **Nevertheless, the U.S. government prevailed:** Peter M. Whiteley, *Deliberate Acts* (Tucson: University of Arizona Press, 1988), 14–86.

61 **When the Americans arrived:** Kehoe, *North American Indians*, 144.

61 **In 1863 the military launched:** Ojibwa, "The Navajo Long Walk," May 2, 2010, Native American Netroots, http://nativeamericannetroots.net/diary/487.

64 **It was a place apart:** Robert Petersen, "California, Calafia, Khalif: The Origin of the Name 'California,'" December 15, 2015, KCET, https://www.kcet .org/shows/departures/california-calafia-khalif-the-origin-of-the-name -california.

66 **It is estimated that in 1770:** A. L. Kroeber, *Handbook of the Indians of California*, Smithsonian Institution Bureau of American Ethnology Bulletin 78 (Washington, DC: Government Printing Office, 1925), 880–91.

66 **In 1832 the number was 14,000:** Dorothy Krell, ed., *The California Missions: A Pictorial History* (Menlo Park, CA: Sunset Publishing, 1979), 316.

67 **"must be expected" that "a war":** Brendan C. Lindsay, *Murder State: California's Native American Genocide, 1846–1873* (Lincoln: University of Nebraska Press, 2015), 231.

69 **Farther inland, evidence is emerging:** Loren G. Davis, "New Support for a Late-Pleistocene Coastal Occupation at the Indian Sands Site, Oregon," *Current Research in the Pleistocene* 25 (2008), 74–76, retrieved at http://wpg .forestry.oregonstate.edu/sites/wpg/files/seminars/2008_DavisCRP.pdf. See also "Paisley Caves," *Archaeology*, August 11, 2014, https://www.archaeology .org/issues/145-1409/features/2370-peopling-the-americas-paisley-caves; and "Paisley Caves," *The Oregon Encyclopedia*, https://oregonencyclopedia.org /articles/paisley_caves/#.Ww3jM6kh2i4.

69 **Skeletal remains of (mostly) young men:** Kehoe, *North America Before the European Invasions*, 106.

72 **Coastal populations that were around two hundred thousand:** Robert Boyd, *The Coming of the Spirit of Pestilence: Introduced Infectious Diseases and Population Decline Among Northwest Coast Indians, 1774–1874* (Vancouver: University of British Columbia Press, 1999).

73 **At last, disease, exhaustion, and starvation:** Native Voices (Native Peoples' Concepts of Health and Illness), Timeline, U.S. National Library of Medicine,

National Institutes of Health, https://www.nlm.nih.gov/nativevoices/time line/308.html.

73 **One of the men, Kimasumpkin, protested:** "Whitman Massacre Trial," Highlights of the Oregon State Archives, http://sos.oregon.gov/archives /exhibits/highlights/Pages/whitman.aspx.

73 **"I was not present at the murder":** Quoted in William Parsons and W. S. Shiach, *An Illustrated History of Umatilla County and of Morrow County* ([San Francisco?]: W. H. Lever, 1902), 62.

76 **They adopted the bow and arrow around 500 BCE:** Page, *In the Hands of the Great Spirit*, 47–49.

80 **They plied the lowlands of south and central Texas:** "Coahuiltecan Indians," *Handbook of Texas Online*, https://tshaonline.org/handbook/online /articles/bmcah.

82 **By that time their population had dropped:** S. C. Gwynne, *Empire of the Summer Moon: Quanah Parker and the Rise and Fall of the Comanches, the Most Powerful Indian Tribe in American History* (New York: Scribner, 2011), 274.

84 **"the tallest race of men in North America":** George Catlin, letter no. 30, *Illustrations of the Manners, Customs, and Condition of the North American Indians . . .* (London: Henry G. Bohn, 1845), vol. 2, 40.

85 **When the ice sheet retreated:** Alan J. Osborn, "Paleo-Indians," *Encyclopedia of the Great Plains*, http://plainshumanities.unl.edu/encyclopedia /doc/egp.na.080.

87 **It wasn't long, however, before the former:** Francis Haines, "The Northward Spread of Horses Among the Plains Indians," *American Anthropologist* 40, no. 3 (1938), 429–51.

88 **"There is something deeply ironic":** James Wilson, *The Earth Shall Weep: A History of Native America* (New York: Grove Press, 1998), 248.

91 **Between ten thousand and fifteen thousand Blackfeet:** Michael J. Ables, "Smallpox: The American Fur Company Pox Outbreak of 1837–1838," Electronic Journals Hosted by University Libraries, Wichita State University, http://journals.wichita.edu/index.php/ff/article/viewFile/128/135.

92 **So it was not merely the Indians' lack of immunity:** Ibid.

93 **William Mayo:** Helen Clapesattle, *The Doctors Mayo*, 2nd ed. (Rochester, MN: Mayo Clinic, 1969). Found also in James V. Fenelon, *Redskins? Sports Mascots, Indian Nations and White Racism* (New York: Routledge, 2017), 59–60; and in "Dakota War of 1862," Alchetron, https://alchetron.com /Dakota-War-of-1862.

93 **"saw one squaw lying on the bank":** Quoted in Helen Hunt Jackson, *A Century of Dishonor* (New York: Dover Books, 2003), 344; see also "The Sand Creek Massacre," Native American Nations, http://www.nanations.com /dishonor/sand-creek-massacre.htm.

93 **"one little child":** Jackson, *A Century of Dishonor*, 344.

Part 2. Purgatory: 1891–1934

101 **Kevin Washburn slips off his cowboy boots:** Author interview with Kevin Washburn, March 11, 2016. All quotations of Washburn are from interviews with the author.

104 **"In case any agent of the ministry":** "July 1, 1775: Congress Resolves to Forge Indian Alliances," This Day in History, History, http://www.history .com/this-day-in-history/congress-resolves-to-forge-indian-alliances.

104 **"I would recommend that some post in the center":** George Washington to Major General John Sullivan, May 31, 1779, Founders Online, National Ar- chives, https://founders.archives.gov/documents/Washington/03-20-02-0661.

105 **The Oneida, despite being a member:** "The Revolutionary War, Oneida's Legacy to Freedom," Oneida Indian Nation, http://www.oneidaindiannation .com/revolutionarywar/.

105 **Polly Cooper, an Oneida woman with the entourage:** Alejandra Smith, "Oneida," George Washington's Mount Vernon Digital Encyclopedia, http:// www.mountvernon.org/digital-encyclopedia/article/oneida/.

105 **"The United States acknowledges the lands reserved to the Oneida":** "The Revolutionary War, Oneida's Legacy to Freedom."

105 **The Oneida contributions to American victory:** Joseph T. Glatthaar and James Kirby Martin, *Forgotten Allies: The Oneida Indians and the American Revolution* (New York: Hill and Wang, 2010), 5.

107 **"The President is willing to grant them peace":** Donald L. Fixico, *Bureau of Indian Affairs: Landmarks of the American Mosaic* (Santa Barbara, CA: Greenwood Press, 2012), 32.

107 **The commission also forced the Seminoles to sell:** Ibid.

107 **"It does not seem a great task":** Ibid., 33.

107 **A Seneca, he was born and raised:** "Ely Parker 1770–1844: Parker Family Tree," *A Warrior in Two Worlds: The Life of Ely Parker*, PBS, http://www .pbs.org/warrior/content/timeline/crisis/parents.html.

108 **"'to sound the war whoop and seize'":** C. Joseph Genetin-Pilawa, *Crooked Paths to Allotment: The Fight over Federal Indian Policy After the Civil War* (Chapel Hill: University of North Carolina Press, 2014), 39.

108 **The Parker home became a meeting place:** Ibid., 45.

109 **"We are all Americans":** Arthur C. Parker, *The Life of General Ely S. Parker: Last Grand Sachem of the Iroquois and General Grant's Military Secretary* (Buffalo, NY: Buffalo Historical Society, 1919), 133, retrieved at https:// babel.hathitrust.org/cgi/pt?id=hvd.32044014840516.

109 **"what should be the legal status":** "Instructions to the Board of Indian Commissioners," in Francis Paul Prucha, ed., *Documents of United States Indian Policy*, 3rd ed. (Lincoln: University of Nebraska Press, 2000), 126.

110 **"the first aggressions have been made by the white man":** Parker, *The Life of General Ely S. Parker*, 139.

110 **In 1871, Ely Parker resigned:** Ibid., 156.

110 **"No Indian nation or tribe within the territory":** U.S. Title Code 25, Section 71, "Future Treaties with Indian Tribes," Legal Information Institute, Cornell Law School, https://www.law.cornell.edu/uscode/text/25/71.

112 **"the Indian agent had, in effect":** Sharon O'Brien, *American Indian Tribal Governments* (Norman: University of Oklahoma Press, 1993), 272.

112 **"There are bluffs and bunches of timber":** Richard Harding Davis, "The West from a Car Window," *Harper's Weekly*, May 14, 1892, 461, https://babel .hathitrust.org/cgi/pt?id=mdp.39015014126026;view=1up;seq=439; and *The West from a Car-Window* (New York: Harper & Brothers, 1892), 158, 160.

112 **"Their supplies had been limited":** Clark Wissler, *Red Man Reservations* (New York: Collier Books, 1971), 64, quoted in Fixico, *Bureau of Indian Affairs*, 61.

113 **"It has become the settled policy":** Thomas Jefferson Morgan, in *Fifty-ninth Annual Report of the Commissioner of Indian Affairs to the Secretary of the Interior* (Washington, DC: Government Printing Office, 1890), vi.

113 **"wear civilized clothes":** Henry Dawes, quoted in Gerald E. Shenk, *"Work or Fight!" Race, Gender, and the Draft in World War One* (New York: Palgrave Macmillan, 2005), 54.

113 **Grant and Ely Parker hoped:** Cathleen D. Cahill, *Federal Fathers and Mothers: A Social History of the United States Indian Service, 1869–1933* (Chapel Hill: University of North Carolina Press, 2011), 19.

115 **"My friends, I have been asked to show you my heart":** In-mut-too-yah-lat-lat [Chief Joseph], speech at Lincoln Hall, Washington, D.C., 1879, published in *North American Review* 128, no. 269 (April 1879), 412–34. Courtesy Cornell University's Making of America, http://psi.mheducation.com/current /media/prints/pr_105.html. "Clarke" in the online document has been edited to "Clark" here.

124 **"It was late in the afternoon":** "Standing Bear's Speech," from *The Indian Journal*, Timeless Truths, http://library.timelesstruths.org/texts/Stories_Worth _Rereading/Standing_Bears_Speech/.

126 **"I wanted to go on my own land":** U.S. Courts Library, Eighth Circuit, "Chief Standing Bear: A Person Under the Law," 5, http://www.lb8.uscourts .gov/pubsandservices/histsociety/neb-chiefstandingbear-booklet.pdf.

126 **"During the fifteen years"** . . . **"On the one side"** . . . **"Every 'person' who comes"** . . . **"1. That an Indian is":** *Standing Bear v. Crook* (1879), in Francis Paul Prucha, ed., *Documents of United States Indian Policy*, 3rd ed. (Lincoln: University of Nebraska Press, 2000), 150–52.

129 **Yet even as people:** Gretchen Cassel Eick, "U.S. Indian Policy, 1865–1890 as Illuminated Through the Lives of Charles A. Eastman and Elaine Goodale Eastman," *Great Plains Quarterly* 28 (Winter 2008), 27–47, http://digital commons.unl.edu/cgi/viewcontent.cgi?article=2396&context=greatplains quarterly.

130 **"Look Upon Your Hands!":** Helen Hunt Jackson, *A Century of Dishonor* (Norman: University of Oklahoma Press, 1995), xiii.

130 **"If I could write a story":** "Helen Hunt Jackson Tries to Write Her Uncle Tom's Cabin," New England Historical Society, http://www.newengland historicalsociety.com/helen-hunt-jackson-tries-write-uncle-toms-cabin/.

131 **"We could not fit the negro for freedom":** Quoted in Cahill, *Federal Fathers and Mothers*, 27.

131 **"every man is born into the world with the right":** Ibid.

131 **"The reservation shuts off the Indians":** Ibid., 29.

131 **"keeps the Indian more dependent"** . . . **"fatal to the Indian":** Ibid.

131 **"Treating the black man as chattel":** Ibid.

133 **"A great general has said":** *Proceedings of the National Conference of Charities and Corrections* (Denver, June 23–29, 1892), ed. Isabel C. Barrows, (Boston: Geo. H. Ellis, 1892), 58–59.

134 **"The 'civilizing' process":** Luther Standing Bear, recollections of 1879 experiences at Carlisle school, 1933, quoted at http://faculty.whatcom.ctc.edu /mhaberma/hist209/luthsb.htm.

136 **"I want to tell you something":** Quoted in Barbara Landis, "Carlisle Indian Industrial School History," *Carlisle Indian Industrial School (1879–1918)*, http://home.epix.net/~landis/histry.html.

137 **"It was deemed necessary to establish":** Arthur Grabowski, Superintendent, Haskell Institute, in *Annual Report of the Commissioner of Indian Affairs to the Secretary of the Interior for the Year 1886*, quoted in Charla Bear, "American Indian Boarding Schools Haunt Many," *Morning Edition*, May 12, 2008, NPR, http://www.npr.org/templates/story/story.php?storyId=165 16865.

137 **"[Grace] was at the office yesterday":** Brenda J. Child, *Boarding School Seasons: American Indian Families, 1900–1940* (Lincoln: University of Nebraska Press, 1998), 48–49.

138 **"I understand you will let me know":** Ibid., 49.

138 **"the parents of these Indian children":** John S. Ward, United States Indian Agent, Mission Agency, California, in *Annual Report of the Commissioner of Indian Affairs to the Secretary of the Interior for the Year 1886*, quoted in Bear, "American Indian Boarding Schools Haunt Many."

138 **"Compulsion through the police":** John P. Williamson, Dakota Agency, in *Annual Report of the Commissioner of Indian Affairs to the Secretary of the Interior for the Year 1886*, quoted in Bear, "American Indian Boarding Schools Haunt Many." The word "metered" in Bear's version has been corrected to "meted," as appears in older editions of the report.

139 **"We would cower from the abusive disciplinary practices":** Margaret L. Archuleta, Brenda J. Child, and K. Tsianina Lomawaima, eds., *Away from Home: American Indian Boarding School Experiences* (Phoenix: Heard Museum Publications, 2000), 42.

139 **"When the school is on the reserve":** Prime Minister John A. Macdonald, in *Official Report of the Debates of the House of Commons of the Dominion of Canada*, May 9, 1883, 1107–08, quoted in "Residential Schools in Canada: Education Guide," 2, http://education.historicacanada.ca/files/32 /Residential Schools_English.pdf.

140 **Annie Dickson . . . Andrew Big Snake:** List compiled from Child, *Boarding School Seasons*, appendix 4, 112–13.

140 **According to the Meriam Report:** Institute for Government Research, Studies in Administration, *The Problem of Indian Administration* (Meriam Report) (Baltimore: Johns Hopkins Press, 1928), https://files.eric.ed.gov/fulltext/ ED087573.pdf; also found in "The Challenges and Limitations of Assimilation: Indian Boarding Schools," *The Brown Quarterly* 4, no. 3 (Fall 2001), 4.

141 **"if the labor of the boarding school" . . . "there are numbers of young children":** *The Problem of Indian Administration* (Meriam Report), 375.

141 **"is in no sense educational":** Ibid.

141 **"there is no individuality":** Ibid., 386.

142 **"maintain a pathetic degree of quietness":** Ibid., 329.

142 **"The generally routinized nature of the institutional life":** Ibid., 393.

143 **"At present the rich Indians" . . . "Congress and the Executive of the United States are the supreme guardians":** *Annual Report of the Commissioner of Indian Affairs to the Secretary of the Interior for the Year 1886* (Washington, DC: Government Printing Office, 1886), vi, xi–xii, retrieved at http://images .library.wisc.edu/History/EFacs/CommRep/AnnRep86/reference/history .annrep86.i0004.pdf.

144 **"must be imbued":** John Oberly, Bureau of Indian Affairs, *Annual Report of the Commissioner of Indian Affairs, for the Year 1888* (Washington, DC: U.S. Department of the Interior, 1888), lxxxix.

144 **"We must make the Indian":** Merrill E. Gates, "The Indian of Romance," address to 14th Lake Mohonk Indian Conference, 1896, *Proceedings of the 14th Annual Meeting of the Lake Mohonk Conference of Friends of the Indian* (Lake Mohonk, New York, October 14–16, 1896), ed. Isabel C. Barrows (Lake Mohonk Conference, 1897).

145 **"Be it enacted by the Senate and House of Representatives":** An Act to Provide for the Allotment of Lands in Severalty to Indians on the Various Reservations . . . , 49th Congress, 2nd session, Our Documents, https://www .ourdocuments.gov/print_friendly.php?flash=true&page=transcript&doc =50&title.

149 **"It is still the conviction of this office":** Department of the Interior, "Annual Report of the Pine Ridge Agency," South Dakota, August 1, 1913.

150 **For the purposes of determining:** Melissa L. Meyer, *The White Earth Tragedy: Ethnicity and Dispossession at a Minnesota Anishinaabe Reservation* (Lincoln: University of Nebraska Press, 1999).

150 **"I have lost my wife and left me with six children"**: Child, *Boarding School Seasons*, 15.

151 **"was first sent away to boarding school"**: Ibid.

152 **"Civilization has loosened"**: Bureau of Indian Affairs, *Annual Report of the Commissioner of Indian Affairs, for the Year 1877* (Washington, DC: Government Printing Office, 1877), 2.

153 **"real aim of this bill is to get at the Indian lands"**: Frank Pommersheim, *Broken Landscape: Indians, Indian Tribes, and the Constitution* (New York: Oxford University Press, 2009), 128.

153 **"what I regard as a great hindrance . . . These dances, or feasts, as they are sometimes called"**: Code of Indian Offences (1883), https://en.wikisource .org/wiki/Code_of_Indian_Offenses. See also "Courts of Indian Offenses" (November 1, 1883), in Francis Paul Prucha, ed., *Documents of United States Indian Policy*, 3rd ed. (Lincoln: University of Nebraska Press, 2000), 159.

156 **"hear and pass judgment upon all such questions"**: Ibid.

156 **"4. The 'sun-dance,' the 'scalp-dance,' the 'war-dance'"**: Ibid.

160 **He drew attention to the fact**: Jo Lea Wetherilt Behrens, "In Defense of 'Poor Lo': National Indian Defense Association and Council Fire's Advocacy for Sioux Land Rights," *South Dakota History* 24 (Fall/Winter 1994), 161, retrievable at https://www.sdhspress.com/journal/south-dakota-history-24-3 /in-defense-of-poor-lo-national-indian-defense-association-and-council -fires-advocacy-for-sioux-land-rights/vol-24-no-3-and-no-4-in-defense-of-poor -lo.pdf.

161 **The wording of the treaty**: "The Old Crossing Chippewa Treaty and Its Sequel," Internet Archive, https://archive.org/stream/pdfy-fa00v1iDcvybuUVD /The%20Old%20Crossing%20Treaty_djvu.txt.

162 **"We have written a great many times"**: Anton Treuer, *Warrior Nation: A History of the Red Lake Ojibwe* (Saint Paul: Minnesota Historical Society Press, 2015), 81.

162 **"We can see the possibility of a misunderstanding"**: Ibid.

163 **"This property belongs to us"**: Ibid.

166 **"My friends it has been reported to me"**: Ibid., 153.

167 **"We Indians in the vicinity of Ponemah"**: Ibid., 154.

169 **"Its legislature appoints a superintendent of schools"**: *Annual Reports of the Department of the Interior of Indian Affairs for the Fiscal Year ended June 30, 1900: Report of the Commissioner of Indian Affairs* (Washington, DC: Government Printing Office, 1900), 110–11.

170 **"given to some strange Indians"**: Frederic Baraga, *A Dictionary of the Otchipwe Language, Explained in English* (Cincinnati: Jos. A. Hemann, 1853), 243.

170 **"Start with the rising sun"**: Ronald L. Trosper, "Indigenous Influence on Forest Management on the Menominee Indian Reservation," *Forest Ecology*

and Management 249 (2007), 134–35, http://courses.washington.edu/dtsclass
/TEK-Menominee.pdf.

172 **"I will continue on this floor"**: Stacy Conradt, "5 Famous Filibusters," Mental Floss, http://mentalfloss.com/article/49360/5-famous-filibusters.

173 **"For many months we have fought together"**: Phillip B. Davidson, *Vietnam at War: The History 1946–1975* (Oxford: Oxford University Press, 1988), 100.

Part 3. Fighting Life: 1914–1945

180 **"There are people who think that wrestling"**: Roland Barthes, *A Barthes Reader*, ed. Susan Sontag (New York: Hill and Wang, 1982), 18.

180 **"primary virtue of the spectacle"**: Ibid.

181 **He graduated from high school**: Statistics are drawn from Patrick Stark, Amber M. Noel, and Joel McFarland, *Trends in High School Dropout and Completion Rates in the United States: 1972–2012*, Compendium Report, U.S. Department of Education, National Center of Education Statistics, NCES 2015-015, https://nces.ed.gov/pubs2015/2015015.pdf, and Christopher Hartney and Linh Vuong, *Created Equal: Racial and Ethnic Disparities in the US Criminal Justice System*, National Council on Crime and Delinquency, 2009, http://www.nccdglobal.org/sites/default/files/publication_pdf/created-equal.pdf.

181 **In Minnesota in 2002**: Andy Mannix, "Minnesota Sends Minorities to Prison at Far Higher Rates than Whites," Minneapolis *Star Tribune*, April 14, 2016, http://www.startribune.com/minnesota-sends-minorities-to-prison-at-far-higher-rates-than-whites/374543811/.

187 *My nephew!:* As related by Anton Treuer.

188 **The Onondaga and Oneida**: "Onondagas to Declare War on Germany," Leadville, Colorado, *Herald Democrat*, August 1, 1918, 2, https://www.coloradohistoricnewspapers.org/cgi-bin/colorado?a=d&d=THD19180801-01.2.18.

189 **"They are not citizens"**: Quoted in Ojibwa, "World War I and American Indians," July 6, 2010, Native American Netroots, http://nativeamericannetroots.net/diary/573.

189 **The army detained more than a hundred men**: Ibid.

189 **Ultimately, her case was postponed**: Ibid.

189 **All in all, Indian participation**: Russel Lawrence Barsh, "American Indians in the Great War," *Ethnohistory* 38, no. 3 (Summer 1991), 277.

190 **"the Aviation Corps of the Army"**: Ibid.

190 **"the richest nation, clan or social group"**: Margo Jefferson, "Books of the Times: Digging Up a Tale of Terror Among the Osages," *The New York Times*, August 31, 1994.

190 **Lee Rainbow . . . Henry Tallman**: Barsh, "American Indians in the Great War," 279.

190 **Graduates of the Phoenix Indian School:** Thomas A. Britten, "American Indians in World War I: Military Service as Catalyst for Reform" (Ph.D. diss., Texas Tech University, 1994), 111, https://www.google.com/url?q=https:// ttu-ir.tdl.org/ttu-ir/bitstream/handle/2346/16718/31295008461237.pdf ?sequence%3D1&sa=D&ust=1520875284596000&usg=AFQjCNHd0 ujOF61QMmbzUs0XolKALyndPQ.

191 **"worldwide festival of death":** Thomas Mann, *The Magic Mountain*, trans. John Woods (New York: Alfred A. Knopf, 1995), 706.

191 **Farther north at the Somme:** C. N. Trueman, "First World War Casualties," History Learning Site, April 17, 2015, http://www.historylearningsite.co.uk /world-war-one/world-war-one-and-casualties/first-world-war-casualties/.

192 **"at night barehanded and alone":** "An Indian Gets a Move on Himself: A Match for Twenty Huns," *Word Carrier* 46 (October–December 1918), 20, quoted in Thomas A. Britten, *American Indians in World War I at Home and at War* (Albuquerque: University of New Mexico Press, 1997), 77.

192 **During the fray he was shot:** Britten, *American Indians in World War I at Home and at War*, 77.

192 **"Lieutenant Breeding had the distinction":** Ibid.

192 **"saw another Indian soldier crawling":** Ibid.

192 **"Indians in the front ranks":** Herman Viola, *Warriors in Uniform: The Legacy of American Indian Heroism* (Washington, DC: National Geographic Press, 2008), 68.

193 **"Bull Durham is the name":** "IQ Tests Go to War—Measuring Intelligence in the Army," History Matters: The U.S. Survey Course on the Web, http:// historymatters.gmu.edu/d/5293. See also Richard Conniff, "God and White Men at Yale," *Yale Alumni Magazine*, May/June 2012, https://yalealumni magazine.com/articles/3456-god-and-white-men-at-yale?page=3.

193 **they disproportionately served as scouts and snipers:** Barsh, "American Indians in the Great War."

193 **"ten or more regiments of Indian cavalry":** Joseph Kossuth Dixon, *North American Indian Cavalry*, Argument before the Committeee on Military Affairs, House of Representatives, 65th Congress, H.R. 3970, July 25, 1917, retrieved at https://babel.hathitrust.org/cgi/pt?id=inu.32000009944994;view= 1up;seq=7.

193 **"author, explorer, ethnologist and authority":** Russel Lawrence Barsh, "An American Heart of Darkness: The 1913 Expedition for American Indian Citizenship," *Great Plains Quarterly* 13 (Spring 1993), 92, http://digitalcommons .unl.edu/cgi/viewcontent.cgi?article=1750&context=greatplainsquarterly.

194 **"nearly every Indian tribe" . . . "the grave of their race":** Joseph Kossuth Dixon, *The Vanishing Race, the Last Great Indian Council; a Record in Picture and Story of the Last Great Indian Council, Participated in by Eminent Indian Chiefs from Nearly Every Indian Reservation in the United States,*

Together with the Story of Their Lives As Told by Themselves—Their Speeches and Folklore Tales—Their Solemn Farewell and the Indians' Story of the Custer Fight (New York: Doubleday, Page, 1913), 9, 200–13.

194 **"would not yield":** Ibid., 4.

194 **"For one splendid moment":** Ibid., 214.

195 **"There are some dark pages":** *The Indian's Friend: The Organ of the National Indian Association* 23–29 (July 1913), 2.

196 **"Indian spirit would be crushed":** Britten, *American Indians in World War I at Home and at War*, 40.

196 **"military segregation of the Indian":** Ibid., 43.

197 **Not even all the men and women:** Ibid., 160.

197 **"undemocratic bureaucracy":** Theodore D. Beaulieu, *The American Indian* (Washington, DC: Society of American Indians, 1920), 141.

198 **American Indian births outstripped Indian deaths:** Nancy Shoemaker, *American Indian Population Recovery in the Twentieth Century* (Albuquerque: University of New Mexico Press, 1999), 75.

198 **responded that the German leader:** Britten, *American Indians in World War I at Home and at War*, 185–86.

199 **"The Indian, though a man without a country":** Quoted in "Native American Citizenship: 1924 Indian Citizenship Act," Nebraska Studies 1900–1924, http://www.nebraskastudies.org/0700/frameset_reset.html?http://www.nebraskastudies.org/0700/stories/0701_0146.html.

200 **"Be it enacted by the Senate":** Ibid.

204 **"empowered them to be the primary":** Anton Treuer, *Warrior Nation: A History of the Red Lake Ojibwe* (Saint Paul: Minnesota Historical Society Press, 2015), 196.

204 **"physically, religiously, socially":** John Collier, "Does the Government Welcome the Indian Arts?" *The American Magazine of Art. Anniversary Supplement* 27, no. 9, part 2 (1934), 10–13.

205 **"fanatical Indian enthusiast with good intentions":** Laurence M. Hauptman, *The Iroquois and the New Deal* (Syracuse, NY: Syracuse University Press, 1981), 28.

206 **"This Act shall not apply":** Wheeler-Howard Act (Indian Reorganization Act, June 18, 1934), Article 18, Sovereign Amonsoquath Band of Cherokee, http://www.amonsoquathbandofcherokee.org/ira1934_wheeler_howard_act.html.

209 **"Acoma is considered one of the oldest":** All quotations from Brian Vallo were recorded in May 2016.

218 **"We represent the oldest":** Jim Windle, "Six Nations Confederacy on the National Stage," *Two Row Times*, September 21, 2016, https://tworowtimes.com/news/local/six-nations-confederacy-on-the-global-stage-in-1942/.

218 **"were not, had never been":** Todd Shaw, Louis DeSipio, Dianne Pinderhughes, and Toni-Michelle C. Travis, *Uneven Roads: An Introduction to U.S. Racial and Ethnic Politics* (Thousand Oaks, CA: CQ Press, 2015), 66.

218 **By comparison, the median income that year:** Linton Weeks, "The 1940 Census: 72-Year-Old Secrets Revealed," NPR, https://www.npr.org/2012/04/02/149575704/the-1940-census-72-year-old-secrets-revealed.

220 **In 1856, a small group:** Johnathan L. Buffalo, "Meskwaki: A Brief History," Meskwaki Nation, https://www.meskwaki.org/about-us/history/.

221 **After that he was shipped overseas:** "Ira Hamilton Hayes, Corporal, United States Marine Corps," Arlington National Cemetery, http://www.arlington cemetery.net/irahayes.htm.

222 **"I was sick":** Viola, "Fighting the Metal Hats: World War II," *Warriors in Uniform*, 93–94.

222 **"pomp and circumstance":** H. Paul Jeffers, *The 100 Greatest Heroes: Inspiring Profiles of One Hundred Men and Women Who Changed the World* (New York: Citadel Press, 2003), 135.

225 *Combat stories, stories about fighting:* Author conversation with Rick Berg, 2014.

Part 4. Moving On Up—Termination and Relocation: 1945–1970

239 **By 1900, there were fewer than two thousand:** *Annual Reports of the Department of the Interior of Indian Affairs for the Fiscal Year ended June 30, 1900: Report of the Commissioner of Indian Affairs* (Washington, DC: Government Printing Office, 1900), 1.

240 **"Red William Hall," he began:** All quotations from Red Hall are from author interviews with him in October 2014.

245 **"like a millstone":** Dorothy Crisp, *The Dominance of England* (London: Holborn, 1960), 22–26.

246 **More than half of those who lived on farms:** S. Mintz and S. McNeil (2016), "Overview of the Post-War Era" (ID 2923), *Digital History*, http://www.digitalhistory.uh.edu/era.cfm?eraid=16&smtid=1.

246 **By 1970, six million African Americans:** "World War I and the Great Migration," History, Art & Archives, U.S. House of Representatives, http://history.house.gov/Exhibitions-and-Publications/BAIC/Historical-Essays/Temporary-Farewell/World-War-I-And-Great-Migration/; and "The Second Great Migration," *In Motion: The African-American Migration Experience*, Schomburg Center for Research in Black Culture, New York, http://www.inmotionaame.org/print.cfm;jsessionid=f830444661458729315793?migration=9&bhcp=1.

247 **"the chosen people of God":** Thomas Jefferson, *The Jeffersonian Cyclopedia: A Comprehensive Collection of the Views of Thomas Jefferson Classified and Arranged in Alphabetical Order Under Nine Thousand Titles*

Relating to Government, Politics, Law, Education, Political Economy, Finance, Science, Art, Literature, Religious Freedom, Morals, etc., ed. John P. Foley (New York: Funk & Wagnalls, 1900), 323.

248 **"a relationship which the State":** 507 U.S. 99 (1993), 107, retrieved from *Negonsott v. Samuels*, Justia, US Supreme Court, https://supreme.justia.com /cases/federal/us/507/99/case.html.

250 **"the freeing of the Indian":** Renée Ann Cramer, *Cash, Color, and Colonialism: The Politics of Tribal Acknowledgment* (Norman: University of Oklahoma Press, 2005), 20.

250 **"The more I go into this Indian problem":** Carolyn Grattan-Aiello, "Senator Arthur V. Watkins and the Termination of Utah's Southern Paiute Indians," *Utah Historical Quarterly* 63, no. 3 (1995), 281.

252 **Often when a jurisdictional act:** Nancy Oestreich Lurie, "The Indian Claims Commission Act," *The Annals of the American Academy of Political and Social Science* 311, no. 1 (May 1, 1957), 56–70, https://deepblue.lib .umich.edu/bitstream/handle/2027.42/66718/10.1177_000271625731100 108.pdf?sequence=2.

253 **"(1) claims in law or equity arising":** Indian Claims Commission Act of 1947, in Charles Joseph Kappler, ed., *Kappler's Indian Affairs: Laws and Treaties: Compiled Federal Regulations Relating to Indians*, vol. 6 (Washington, DC: Government Printing Office, 1971, http://digital.library.okstate.edu/kappler/vol6/html_ files/v6p0323b.html#mn3. Also available on the Library of Congress website: 79th Congress, section 2, chap. 959, https://www.loc.gov/law/help/statutes-at -large/79th-congress/session-2/c79s2ch959.pdf.

253 **The last claim on the docket:** "Lead Up to the Indian Claims Commission Act of 1946," US Department of Justice, https://www.justice.gov/enrd/lead -indian-claims-commission-act-1946.

254 **"broad waiver of the United States' sovereign immunity":** Ibid.

256 **Tribes in states not covered:** Ada Pecos Melton and Jerry Gardner, "Public Law 280: Issues and Concerns for Victims of Crime in Indian Country," American Indian Development Associates, http://www.aidainc.net/publica tions/pl280.htm.

256 **"Whereas it is the policy of Congress":** House Concurrent Resolution 108, 67 Statute B122, August 1, 1953, Native Media Center, University of North Dakota, https://arts-sciences.und.edu/native-media-center/_files/docs/1950-1970 /1953hcr108.pdf.

259 **Never mind that they had no authority:** "The McCumber Agreement," North Dakota Studies, https://www.ndstudies.gov/content/%E2%80%9C -mccumber-agreement%E2%80%9D.

264 **They are the only Indian tribe:** "Menominee Culture," Indian Country Wisconsin, http://www.mpm.edu/content/wirp/ICW-54.html.

264 **"After we had advanced five or six leagues":** Pierre-François-Xavier de Charlevoix, *Journal of a Voyage to North America*, ed. Louise Phelps

Kellogg (Chicago: Caxton Club, 1923), retrieved at https://archive.org/stream /journalofvoyaget02char/journalofvoyaget02char_djvu.tx.

266 **The Menominee formed their own modern tribal government:** "Menominee Culture."

267 **Four Indians sat on the board:** Menominee Indian Tribe of Wisconsin report, 2010/2018, http://witribes.wi.gov/docview.asp?docid=19079&locid=57.

268 **Indians with jobs could expect to bring in:** Nancy Shoemaker, *American Indian Population Recovery in the Twentieth Century* (Albuquerque: University of New Mexico Press, 1999), 80. The 1939 wages are adjusted for inflation using the U.S. Department of Labor/Bureau of Labor Statistics inflation calculator found at https://www.bls.gov/data/inflation_calculator.htm.

269 **"In order to help adult Indians":** Public Law 959, in Kappler, *Kappler's Indian Affairs: Laws and Treaties: Compiled Federal Regulations Relating to Indians*, retrieved at https://dc.library.okstate.edu/digital/collection/kapplers. Also available on the Government Printing Office website, https://www.gpo .gov/fdsys/pkg/STATUTE-70/pdf/STATUTE-70-Pg986.pdf.

270 **Daytime highs didn't reach seventy degrees:** Butch Larcombe, "The Flood of 1964," *Montana Quarterly*, retrieved at https://www.scribd.com /document/212124250/The-Flood-of-1964.

278 **Under termination and relocation:** Patricia K. Ourada, *The Menominee Indians: A History* (Norman: University of Oklahoma Press, 1979).

278 **A total of 1,365,801 acres:** "Land Tenure Issues," Indian Land Tenure Foundation, https://iltf.org/land-issues/issues/.

278 **"This policy of forced termination is wrong":** President Richard Nixon, Special Message to the Congress on Indian Affairs, July 8, 1970, retrieved from Gerhard Peters and John T. Woolley, *The American Presidency Project*, http://www.presidency.ucsb.edu/ws/?pid=2573.

Part 5. Becoming Indian: 1970–1990

283 **"Welcome to my office!":** All quotations from Bobby Matthews are from author interviews with him, 2014–2015. Sections of this chapter first appeared in "Off the Land: What Subsistence Really Looks Like," *Harper's Magazine*, November 2014, https://harpers.org/archive/2014/11/off-the-land/.

289 **"should never be instrumental":** Luigi Laurenti, *Property Values and Race: Studies in Seven Cities* (Berkeley: University of California Press, 1960), 17 (emphasis in Laurenti).

289 **"ensure the political, educational, social, and economic equality":** Mission statement, NAACP, Washington, DC, Branch, http://naacpdc.org/dc branch.htm.

291 **"white man tends to rate the Indian":** Paul Chaat Smith and Robert Warrior, *Like a Hurricane: The Indian Movement from Alcatraz to Wounded Knee* (New York: New Press, 1996), 41.

291 **"negative image of the Indians"**: Ibid., 70.

291 **"This is all I have to offer"**: Mark Hamilton Lytle, *America's Uncivil Wars: The Sixties Era from Elvis to the Fall of Richard Nixon* (New York: Oxford University Press, 2006), 308.

292 **"It was a major source of encouragement"**: Bradley G. Shreve, *Red Power Rising: The National Indian Youth Council and the Origins of Native Activism* (Norman: University of Oklahoma Press, 2011), 120.

292 **"genuine contemporary creative thinking"**: Quoted in Lisa Brooks, "Intellectual History," in *The Oxford Handbook of American Indian History*, ed. Frederick E. Hoxie (New York and Oxford: Oxford University Press, 2016), 529 (emphasis added).

293 **Their life expectancy was between fifty**: S. Ryan Johansson, "The Demographic History of the Native Peoples of North America: A Selective Bibliography," in *Yearbook of Physical Anthropology* 25 (1982), 145.

293 **And there were more than four times**: C. Matthew Snipp, "The Size and Distribution of the American Indian Population: Fertility, Mortality, Migration, and Residence," in *Changing Numbers, Changing Needs: American Indian Demography and Public Health* (Washington, DC: National Academies Press [US], 1996), https://www.ncbi.nlm.nih.gov/books/NBK233098/.

294 **For young blacks in places like Oakland**: Jessica McElrath, "The Black Panthers," retrieved at https://web.archive.org/web/20070407155740/http://afroamhistory.about.com/od/blackpanthers/a/blackpanthers.htm.

295 **"1. We want freedom"**: "History of the Black Panther Party: Black Panther Party Platform and Program" ("What We Want, What We Believe," citing *The Black Panther*, November 23, 1967, 3), The Black Panther Party Research Project, https://web.stanford.edu/group/blackpanthers/history.shtml.

296 **"the greatest threat to the internal security"**: Quoted in "Hoover and the F.B.I.," *A Huey P. Newton Story*, PBS, http://www.pbs.org/hueypnewton/people/people_hoover.html.

296 **Indians in Minneapolis also endured**: S. Mintz and S. McNeil (2016), "The Native American Power Movement" (ID 3348), *Digital History*, http://www.digitalhistory.uh.edu/disp_textbook.cfm?smtid=2&psid=3348.

298 **Later, in 1973, Nordwall would fly**: "The Discovery of Italy," *Miami News*, September 23, 1973, retrieved at http://astro1.panet.utoledo.edu/~ljc/disc_italy.html.

298 **"I just decided to go"**: Smith and Warrior, *Like a Hurricane*, 5.

298 **"What I saw"**: Ibid.

298 **"It was almost as if a collective hallucination"**: Ibid., 12.

299 **"I think I admired him more":** Quoted in Dean Chavers, "Richard Nixon's Indian Mentor," *Indian Country Today*, April 10, 2016, https://indiancountry medianetwork.com/history/events/richard-nixons-indian-mentor/.

300 **She was later instrumental in establishing:** Dean Chavers, "How Alcatraz Helped Native American Students," *Indian Country Today*, July 26, 2017, https://indiancountrymedianetwork.com/education/native-american-students/alcatraz-helped-native-american-students/.

303 **"without meaningful change white America":** Robert Treuer, "Seven Days in November," *The Washingtonian*, May 1978, 109.

303 **Loesch worked a minor miracle:** Ibid.

303 **One pro-Indian lawyer was lowered:** Ibid.

304 **"War paint traditionally means":** Ibid., 106.

304 **"1. Restoration of constitutional treaty-making authority":** Congressional Record of April 2, 1973, https://www.gpo.gov/fdsys/granule/GPO-CRECB-1973-pt8/GPO-CRECB-1973-pt8-5-1; see also "Trail of Broken Treaties: 20-Point Position Memo," American Indian Movement, October 1972, www.aimovement.org/ggc/trailofbrokentreaties.html.

306 **The money was transferred in cash to Vernon Bellecourt:** Treuer, "Seven Days in November," 99.

312 **The number of wild rice licenses:** "Inventory & Management," Minnesota Department of Natural Resources, http://www.dnr.state.mn.us/wildlife/shallowlakes/wildrice.html.

312 **Only 2 percent of those with licenses:** Ray Norrgard, Gary Drotts, Annette Drewes, and Nancy Dietz, *Minnesota Natural Wild Rice Harvester Survey: A Study of Harvesters' Activities and Opinions* (St. Paul: Minnesota Department of Natural Resources, Division of Fish and Wildlife, 2007), retrieved at http://files.dnr.state.mn.us/fish_wildlife/wildlife/shallowlakes/wild-rice-harvester-survey-2007.pdf.

312 **Less than half of the roughly:** Margaret Dexter, "2007 Trapper Harvest Survey," in "Trapping Harvest Statistics," Minnesota Department of Natural Resources, Division of Fish and Wildlife, retrieved at http://files.dnr.state.mn.us/publications/wildlife/populationstatus2008/7_trapping_harvest.pdf; and Margaret Dexter, "2014 Trapper Harvest Survey," in "Trapping Harvest Statistics," Minnesota Department of Natural Resources, Division of Fish and Wildlife, retrieved at http://files.dnr.state.mn.us/publications/wildlife/population2015/6-trapping-harvest.pdf.

314 **"rough and tumble":** Stew Magnuson, "Remember Raymond Yellow Thunder's Life," *Native Sun News*, posted at Indianz.com, February 13, 2012, http://www.indianz.com/News/2012/004568.asp.

314 **He was a hard worker:** Smith and Warrior, *Like a Hurricane*, 112–13.

314 **Later, still joyriding around Gordon:** *State v. Hare* (*State of Nebraska v. Leslie D. Hare, State of Nebraska v. Melvin P. Hare*), 208 N.W.2d 264 (1973)

190 Neb. 339, June 8, 1973, Justia, US Supreme Court, https://law.justia.com /cases/nebraska/supreme-court/1973/38761-1.html.

314 **"found him in an old pickup truck":** Ibid.

314 **The men paused and then took off:** Ibid.

315 **By the end of the week:** Smith and Warrior, *Like a Hurricane*, 115.

316 **Leslie was sentenced to six years:** Russell Means, *Where White Men Fear to Tread: The Autobiography of Russell Means* (New York: St. Martin's Press, 1995), 215.

317 **"It figures. All the Chippewas used to do":** *Newsweek*, January 31, 1972, quoted in Smith and Warrior, *Like a Hurricane*, 136.

317 **"The reasons are clear":** Russell Means to AIM chapters, January 31, 1972, quoted in Smith and Warrior, *Like a Hurricane*, 136–37.

317 **couldn't "resign from being an Indian":** Smith and Warrior, *Like a Hurricane*, 137.

317 **Whatever the cause:** Terry Devine, "Death of Bad Heart Bull Sets Off Riot," Washington, Pennsylvania, *Observer-Reporter*, February 12, 1972, A12, https://news.google.com/newspapers?nid=2519&dat=19730212&id=IMt dAAAAIBAJ&sjid=fl4NAAAAIBAJ&pg=972,2012037&hl=en.

317 **Schmitz was arrested:** Means, *Where White Men Fear to Tread*, 151.

317 **In the meantime, hundreds of Indians:** *State v. Bad Heart Bull* (*State of South Dakota v. Sarah Bad Heart Bull and Robert High Eagle*), Supreme Court of South Dakota, 257 N.W.2d 715 (1977), September 16, 1977, Justia, US Supreme Court, https://law.justia.com/cases/south-dakota/supreme-court /1977/11531-1.html; and Devine, "Death of Bad Heart Bull Sets Off Riot."

319 **He appointed his wife as director:** Smith and Warrior, *Like a Hurricane*, 196.

319 **Six previous tribal chairmen:** Ibid., 195.

320 **"bums trying to get their braids":** Terri Schultz, "Bamboozle Me Not at Wounded Knee," *Harper's Magazine*, June 1973, https://harpers.org/archive /1973/06/bamboozle-me-not-at-wounded-knee.

320 **"conspiratorial cabal of internationalists":** Chip Berlet and Matthew N. Lyons, *Right-Wing Populism in America: Too Close for Comfort* (New York: Guilford Press, 2000), 177.

323 **"The fact is, we as a group":** Smith and Warrior, *Like a Hurricane*, 208.

323 **"C. The main objective of the Indians":** Ibid., 213.

324 **"If any foreign official":** Ibid., 218.

326 **He had worked for the Pine Ridge tribal police:** Ibid., 259.

326 **"war games without a war":** Ibid., 234.

327 **"the next thing," the witness reported:** Associated Press, "FBI Confirms Civil Rights Activist Was Killed in 1973 Wounded Knee Protest," *New York Post*, February 19, 2014, https://nypost.com/2014/02/19/fbi-confirms-civil-rights -activist-was-killed-in-1973-wounded-knee-protest/.

327 **Bernie Lafferty, who claims:** "FBI Confirms Black Activist Was Killed During 1973 Occupation of Wounded Knee," CBS News, February 20, 2014,

https://www.cbsnews.com/news/fbi-confirms-activist-ray-robinson-was
-killed-during-1973-occupation-of-wounded-knee/. See also "Bernie Lafferty
Speaks About Ray Robinson's Killing Inside Wounded Knee 1973," *News
from Indian Country*, July 17, 2007, http://www.indiancountrynews.com
/index.php/investigations/ray-robinson/889-bernie-lafferty-speaks-about-ray
-robinsons-killing-inside-wounded-knee-1973.

328 **"shortly afterward and puzzled what to do"**: Eric Konigsberg, "Who Killed
Anna Mae?" *The New York Times*, April 25, 2014, https://www.nytimes
.com/2014/04/27/magazine/who-killed-anna-mae.html.

328 **"really managed to keep a tight lid on that one"**: "FBI Confirms Black Activist Was Killed During 1973 Occupation of Wounded Knee."

328 **Even now, Indians drop out:** "High School Dropout Rates: Indicators on
Children and Youth," Child Trends, DataBank, November 2015, https://
www.childtrends.org/wp-content/uploads/2014/10/01_Dropout_Rates.pdf;
also see Patrick Stark, Amber M. Noel, and Joel McFarland, *Trends in High
School Dropout and Completion Rates in the United States: 1972–2012*, Compendium Report, U.S. Department of Education, National Center of Education Statistics, NCES 2015-015, https://nces.ed.gov/pubs2015/2015015.pdf.

330 **"Unfortunately, many Americans live on the outskirts"**: Lyndon B. Johnson, Annual Message to Congress on the State of the Union, January 8, 1968,
retrieved from Gerhard Peters and John T. Woolley, *The American Presidency
Project*, http://www.presidency.ucsb.edu/ws/?pid=26787.

334 **"use the best available talents"**: *The Indian Education Act of 1972—A Brief
History, Analysis, Issues and Outlook* (Washington, DC: Department of
Health, Education, and Welfare, Office of Education, 1973), 14–15, http://
files.eric.ed.gov/fulltext/ED111553.pdf.

334 **For the first time, school districts:** Ibid., 18.

335 **In 1999, Montana passed the Indian Education for All Act:** "Indian Education for All, MCA 20-1-501," MontanaTribes, http://www.montanatribes
.org/files/iefa-law.pdf.

336 **"I have signed into law S.J. Res. 102"**: Jimmy Carter, American Indian Religious Freedom Statement on Signing S.J. Res. 102 Into Law, August 12, 1978,
retrieved from Gerhard Peters and John T. Woolley, *The American Presidency
Project*, http://www.presidency.ucsb.edu/ws/index.php?pid=31173.

337 **The remains of the Anglo Christians:** Thomaira Babbit, "NAGPRA as a
Paradigm: The Historical Context and Meaning of the Native American
Graves Protection and Repatriation Act in 2011," *Proceedings of the Native
American Symposium*, November 2011, 61–70, http://www.se.edu/nas/files
/2013/03/NAS-2011-Proceedings-Babbit.pdf.

337 **"give me back my people's bones"**: David M. Gradwohl, Joe B. Thomson,
and Michael J. Perry, "Still Running: A Tribute to Maria Pearson, Yankton
Sioux," *Journal of the Iowa Archeological Society* 52 (2005).

338 **To date, the remains of more than 57,847:** National NAGPRA [Native American Graves Protection and Repatriation Act], Frequently Asked Questions, National Park Service, U.S. Department of the Interior, https://www.nps.gov/nagpra/FAQ/INDEX.HTM.

349 **Between 1973 and 1976:** Timothy Williams, "Tribe Seeks Reopening of Inquiries in '70s Deaths," *The New York Times*, June 15, 2012, http://www.nytimes.com/2012/06/15/us/sioux-group-asks-officials-to-reopen-70s-cases.html.

349 **The FBI found shell casings nearby:** Scott Anderson, "The Martyrdom of Leonard Peltier," *Outside*, July 2, 1995, https://www.outsideonline.com/1835141/martyrdom-leonard-peltier.

350 **Those who see him as a hero:** "Post-Trial Actions, Criminal," International Leonard Peltier Defense Committee website, http://www.whoisleonardpeltier.info/LEGAL/CRIMINAL.htm.

351 **On June 26, Agents Coler and Williams:** Douglas O. Linder, "Testimony of FBI Special Agent Gary Adams in the Leonard Peltier Trial" (March 17–18, 1977), *Famous Trials*, http://www.famous-trials.com/leonardpeltier/762-adamstestimony.

353 **"These white people think this country":** Quoted in Konigsberg, "Who Killed Anna Mae?"

353 **"I came here to fight":** Ibid.

354 **"loud-mouth city women":** Mary Crow Dog, *Lakota Woman* (New York: Grove Press, 2011), 138.

354 **They felt that Aquash's romance:** Konigsberg, "Who Killed Anna Mae?"

354 **In early June 1975:** "Anna Mae [Aquash] Timeline I—Wounded Knee," *News from Indian Country*, January 1997 and ongoing, http://www.indiancountrynews.com/index.php/investigations/286-aquash-peltier-timeline-1975-2010/2101-annie-mae-timeline-i-wounded-knee; and Chris Summers, "Native American Prisoner to Fight On," BBC News, April 24, 2004, http://news.bbc.co.uk/2/hi/americas/3654785.stm.

354 **Both Aquash and Darlene Nichols:** Konigsberg, "Who Killed Anna Mae?"

354 **"When I told Marlon":** Dennis Banks, *Ojibwa Warrior: Dennis Banks and the Rise of the American Indian Movement* (Norman: University of Oklahoma Press, 2004), 301–2.

354 **he lent them the RV and gave them $10,000 in cash:** Konigsberg, "Who Killed Anna Mae?"

355 **"begging for his life, but I shot him anyway":** Ibid.

356 **"I don't know if I would participate":** Ibid.

356 **"If there's a burning house":** Ibid.

356 **"You won't get past these guys":** Treuer, *Warrior Nation*, 296.

Part 6. Boom City—Tribal Capitalism in the Twenty-first Century

363 *We have a relationship with pot:* All previously unpublished quotations from Gabriel Galanda were recorded in June–July 2015.

365 **For instance, in 2002, 12 percent:** "National Indian Gaming Commission Tribal Gaming Revenues [1998–2002]," National Indian Gaming Commission, https://www.nigc.gov/images/uploads/reports/gamingrevenues 2002to1998.pdf.

365 **By comparison, the Pechanga Band:** Vince Beiser, "A Paper Trail of Tears: How Casino-Rich Tribes Are Dealing Members Out," *Harper's Magazine,* August 2006, https://harpers.org/archive/2006/08/a-paper-trail-of-tears/, retrieved at http://faculty.humanities.uci.edu/tcthorne/Hist15/disenrollment atpechanga2000.htm.

365 **And the gaming compacts signed between tribes and states:** "California Tribal Casinos: Questions and Answers," California Legislative Analyst's Office, February 2007, http://www.lao.ca.gov/2007/tribal_casinos/tribal_casinos _020207.aspx.

367 **"He wasn't mad like I was":** Quoted in David Treuer, *Rez Life* (New York: Grove Press, 2012), 228–29.

367 **Helen called them up:** Ibid.

368 **"Each of the States listed . . . shall have jurisdiction":** 28 U.S. Title Code, Section 1360, "State Civil Jurisdiction in Actions to Which Indians Are Parties," Legal Information Institute, Cornell Law School, https://www.law .cornell.edu/uscode/text/28/1360.

369 **"would have 'slipped one by the Indians'":** Treuer, *Rez Life,* 234.

369 **"The same Congress that enacted Pub.L. 280" . . . "remotely resembling":** *Bryan v. Itasca County,* 426 U.S. 373 (1976), Justia, US Supreme Court, https://supreme.justia.com/cases/federal/us/426/373/case.html.

369 **"That was $147 off my mind":** Treuer, *Rez Life,* 236.

369 **"I never got nothing from nobody":** Ibid., 237.

370 **Again, Butterworth threatened the tribe:** Matthew L. M. Fletcher, "The Seminole Tribe and the Origins of Indian Gaming," *FIU Law Review* 9 (2014), 255–75, esp. 265, retrieved at https://digitalcommons.law.msu.edu /cgi/viewcontent.cgi?article=1543&context=facpubs.

370 **The day they opened for business, Sheriff Butterworth was waiting:** "Native American Casino," *World Heritage Encyclopedia,* WHEBN0015712084, http://www.gutenberg.us/articles/eng/native_american_casino.

371 **Within a year of the Cabazon win:** Charles Wilkinson, *Blood Struggle: The Rise of Modern Indian Nations* (New York: W. W. Norton, 2005), 335–36.

372 **The first provision was that whatever forms of gaming:** Indian Gaming Regulatory Act, National Indian Gaming Commission, https://www.nigc.gov /general-counsel/indian-gaming-regulatory-act.

373 **But in California, despite the rapid growth:** "Socio-Economic Inequities Suffered by California Indians," UCLA American Indian Studies Center, https://www.aisc.ucla.edu/ca/Tribes12.htm.

373 **In areas without Indian gaming:** "Casinos Not Paying Off for Indians," ABC News, August 31 (no year noted; after 1997), http://abcnews.go.com /US/story?id=95944&page=1.

373 **"There are a lot of people":** "Unemployment on Indian Reservations at 50 Percent: The Urgent Need to Create Jobs in Indian Country," 111th Congress, 2nd session, January 28, 2010, 1, https://www.indian.senate.gov/sites/default /files/upload/files/January2820102.pdf.

373 **The unemployment rate for Native American communities:** Ibid.

373 **"The unemployment rate on the reservation exceeds 73 percent":** Ibid., 59–60.

373 **Meanwhile, the Shakopee Mdewakanton Sioux Community:** Timothy Williams, "$1 Million Each Year for All, As Long As Tribe's Luck Holds," *The New York Times*, August 9, 2012, http://www.nytimes.com/2012/08/09 /us/more-casinos-and-internet-gambling-threaten-shakopee-tribe.html?_r=1.

375 **One of the poorest tribes in the country:** "Pine Ridge Indian Reservation— Demographics & Population," Black Hills Knowledge Network, https://www .blackhillsknowledgenetwork.org/community-profiles/pine-ridge/pine-ridge -indian-reservation-demographics-population.html#.WrFEioJG3Jx.

375 **The percentage of people in Pine Ridge:** Ronald L. Trosper, "American Indian Poverty on Reservations, 1969–1989," in *Changing Numbers, Changing Needs: American Indian Demography and Public Health* (Washington, DC: National Academies Press [US], 1996), https://www.ncbi.nlm.nih.gov /books/NBK233100/.

375 **The median household income at Tulalip:** Tulalip Reservation, Washington Economy Data, TownCharts, http://www.towncharts.com/Washington /Economy/Tulalip-Reservation-CCD-WA-Economy-data.html.

378 **Blood Quantum and Disenrollment:** This section on disenrollment includes the majority of my op-ed "How Do You Prove You're an Indian?," published in *The New York Times* on December 20, 2011, http://www.nytimes.com /2011/12/21/opinion/for-indian-tribes-blood-shouldnt-be-everything.html.

378 **As of 2017, more than fifty tribes:** David E. Wilkins and Shelly Hulse Wilkins, *Dismembered: Native Disenrollment and the Battle for Human Rights* (Seattle: University of Washington Press, 2017), 67.

378 **Many different rationales have been used to justify it:** Ibid., 67–78.

378 **According to Gabe Galanda:** Gabriel S. Galanda and Ryan D. Dreveskracht, "Curing the Tribal Disenrollment Epidemic: In Search of a Remedy," *Arizona Law Review* 57, no. 2 (Summer 2015), 383–474, http://arizonalawreview.org /pdf/57-2/57arizlrev383.pdf.

378 **The Picayune Rancheria:** James Dao, "In California, Indian Tribes with Casino Money Cast Off Members," *The New York Times*, December 12, 2011, http://www.nytimes.com/2011/12/13/us/california-indian-tribes-eject -thousands-of-members.html?scp=2&sq=tribal&st=cse.

380 **In short order, the number of registered full-bloods:** Melissa L. Meyer, *The White Earth Tragedy: Ethnicity and Dispossession at a Minnesota Anishinaabe Reservation* (Lincoln: University of Nebraska Press, 1994), 170.

381 **disenrollment often occurs:** Dao, "In California, Indian Tribes with Casino Money Cast Off Members."

382 **All in all, Bob Kelly determined that 306:** Brooke Jarvis, "Who Decides Who Counts as Native American?" *The New York Times Magazine*, January 18, 2017, https://www.nytimes.com/2017/01/18/magazine/who-decides-who-counts-as-native-american.html?_r=0.

382 **"I'm in a war":** Quoted ibid.

383 **Gabe Galanda, the lawyer who represents:** Gabriel S. Galanda, "Attack on the Tribal Middle Class, Part II," *Indian Country Today*, November 3, 2011, https://indiancountrymedianetwork.com/news/opinions/attack-on-the-tribal-middle-class-part-ii/.

384 **As Charles Wilkinson points out:** Wilkinson, *Blood Struggle*, 242.

385 **As the Indian legal and professional class grew:** Ibid., 241.

385 **"breathed life into a basic principle of American law":** Ibid., 249.

385 **"there are three branches of sovereignty":** Ibid.

385 **"authority to pass ordinances" . . . "any oil and natural gas":** 18 Land & Water L. Rev. 539 (1983), Indian Law—Tribal Authority to Levy a Mineral Severance Tax on Non-Indian Lessees—*Merrion v. Jicarilla Apache Tribe*, HeinOnline, http://heinonline.org/HOL/LandingPage?handle=hein.journals/lawlr18&div=25&id=&page=.

386 **"avail themselves of the 'substantial privilege'":** *Merrion v. Jicarilla Apache Tribe*, 455 U.S. 130ff (1982), *Merrion v. Jicarilla Apache Tribe*, No. 80-11, Argued March 30, 1981, Reargued November 4, 1981, Decided January 25, 1982, Justia, US Supreme Court, https://supreme.justia.com/cases/federal/us/455/130/case.html.

386 **"In the early morning we'd head out in the hills":** Author interview with Bobby Matthews, March 2014.

390 **Then we zig and zag past more recognizable:** Kari Bray, "'Worth the Wait': Lake Stevens Skate Park Could Open by August," Everett, Washington, *HeraldNet*, December 9, 2016, http://www.heraldnet.com/news/plans-for-skate-park-in-lake-stevens-finalized/.

392 **Fifteen percent of American Indians have diabetes:** "National Diabetes Statistics Report, 2017: Estimates of Diabetes and Its Burden in the United States" National Center for Chronic Disease Prevention and Health Promotion, Division of Diabetes Translation, Centers for Disease Control and Prevention, https://www.cdc.gov/diabetes/pdfs/data/statistics/national-diabetes-statistics-report.pdf.

392 **For some reason we don't get it as often:** Steven Parker, "Native Americans: The Facts," HealthGuidance for Better Health, http://www.healthguidance.org/entry/6323/1/Native-Americans-The-Facts.html.

397 **All of this was overseen by the Bureau of Indian Affairs:** *Arizona Republic* staff, "BIA Cannot Account for $2.4 Billion Audit Documents Tribes' Fears That Bureau Severely Mismanaged Trust Funds from 1973–1992," Spokane, Washington, *Spokesman-Review*, April 14, 1996, http://www.spokesman .com/stories/1996/apr/14/bia-cannot-account-for-24-billion-audit -documents/.

398 **In 2008 a family who had fractional interest:** Manuel Valdes, "Family, Tulalip Tribe Feuding over Lucrative Land," KOMO News (Seattle), February 12, 2012, http://www.komonews.com/news/local/Family-Tulalip -tribe-feuding-over-lucrative-land-139191534.html.

399 **The tribe is currently negotiating:** "Recent Transportation Revenue Packages," *Transportation Resource Manual*, Washington State Legislature, 2017, 27, http://leg.wa.gov/JTC/trm/Documents/TRM%202017%20Update /5%20-%20Recent%20Revenue%20Package%20-%20%20Final.pdf.

399 **"They're having booms in other places":** Author interview with Terri Goban, May 2015.

401 **"The U.S. government spent two hundred years trying to kill us":** Author interview with Anton Treuer, 2015.

Part 7. Digital Indians: 1990–2018

409 **"We can sometimes get so caught up":** "In 1992, America Discovers Columbus," *The New York Times*, June 28, 1992, https://www.nytimes.com/1992 /06/28/nyregion/in-1992-america-discovers-columbus.html.

409 **In the 1990 census:** Edna L. Paisano et al., "We the . . . First Americans," U.S. Department of Commerce, Economics and Statistics Administration, Bureau of the Census, September 1993, https://www.census.gov/prod/cen 1990/wepeople/we-5.pdf.

410 **In 1958, more than 75 percent of Americans:** "Public Trust in Government: 1958–2017," Pew Research Center, U.S. Politics & Policy, http://www.people -press.org/2017/12/14/public-trust-in-government-1958-2017/.

410 **"consider that we shall be as a city upon a hill":** John Winthrop, "A Model of Christian Charity" (1630), "John Winthrop Dreams of City on a Hill, 1630," *The American Yawp Reader*, http://www.american yawp.com/reader /colliding-cultures/john-winthrop-dreams-of-a-city-on-a-hill-1630/.

418 **Manuelito Wheeler, a Diné language activist:** Matt Hansen, "The Future of America's Endangered Languages," *The Week*, June 29, 2015, http://theweek. com/articles/563549/future-americas-endangeredlanguages.

431 **In 2013, the Violence Against Women Act:** Jennifer Bendery, "At Last, Violence Against Women Act Lets Tribes Prosecute Non-Native Domestic Abusers," *The Huffington Post*, March 6, 2015, https://www.huffingtonpost .com/2015/03/06/vawa-native-americans_n_6819526.html.

431 **Rather than a full-throated apology:** Rob Capriccioso, "A Sorry Saga: Obama Signs Native American Apology Resolution; Fails to Draw Attention to It," *Indian Country Today*, January 13, 2010, http://indianlaw.org/node/529.

431 **So it was an apology made on behalf:** Ibid.

432 **over 1,172 miles, across four states, and under the Missouri and Mississippi Rivers:** Gregor Aisch and K. K. Rebecca Lai, "The Conflicts Along 1,172 Miles of the Dakota Access Pipeline," *The New York Times*, last updated March 20, 2017, https://www.nytimes.com/interactive/2016/11/23/us/dakota-access-pipeline-protest-map.html.

432 **"Where this surveying revealed previously unidentified historic":** United States District Court, District of Columbia, *Standing Rock Sioux Tribe, et al., Plaintiffs, v. U.S. Army Corps of Engineers, et al., Defendants*, Civil Action No. 16-1534 (JEB), signed, September 9, 2016, retrieved from National Indian Law Library, https://www.narf.org/nill/bulletins/federal/documents/standing _rock_v_army_corps.html.

433 **"On October 2, other Corps personnel also sought":** Ibid.

434 **"their limited scope":** Ibid.

441 **In 1891 the superintendent of the centennial census:** Steven Otfinoski, *A Primary Source History of Westward Expansion* (Mankato, MN: Capstone Press, 2015), 29.

441 **Thirty-one women campaigned:** Julie Turkewitz, "Native American Women Running for Office, Including a Seat in Congress" (from *The New York Times*), *The Seattle Times*, March 19, 2018, https://www.seattletimes.com/ nation-world/nation/theres-never-been-a-native-american -congresswoman-that-could-change-in-2018/.

442 **The numbers tell part of the story:** "About Tribes: Demographics," National Congress of American Indians, http://www.ncai.org/about-tribes/demograph ics; and "U.S. Census Marks Increase in Urban American Indian and Alaska Natives," Urban Indian Health Institute, February 28, 2013, http://www.uihi .org/wp-content/uploads/2013/09/Broadcast_Census-Number_FINAL _v2.pdf.

Epilogue

445 **"I am a Lakota of the Oglala band":** [Nicholas Black Elk], *Black Elk Speaks: Being the Life Story of a Holy Man of the Oglala Sioux*, ed. John G. Neihardt (Albany: State University of New York Press, 2008), 7–8.

446 **it seems likely that he was laid low:** Joe Jackson, *Black Elk: The Life of an American Visionary* (New York: Farrar, Straus and Giroux, 2016), 57.

446 **"And as I stood there I saw more than I can tell":** Black Elk, *Black Elk Speaks*, 33.

446 **"When the singing stopped":** Ibid., 36–37.

447 **"Black Elk picked his way farther":** Jackson, *Black Elk*, 119–20.

449 **"Men and women and children were heaped"**: Nicholas Black Elk, *Black Elk Speaks: The Complete Edition* (Lincoln: University of Nebraska Press, 2014), 163.

449 **"one last obligation"**: Jackson, *Black Elk*, 332.

449 **"All this time the bullets were buzzing around me"**: Black Elk, *Back Elk Speaks: The Complete Edition*, 167.

452 **"To articulate the past historically"**: Walter Benjamin, "Theses on the Philosophy of History" (VI), in *Illuminations*, ed. Hannah Arendt, trans. Harry Zohn (New York: Schocken Books, 1968), 255 (emphasis in original).

453 **"lovely, trustful, dreamy, enormous country"**: Vladimir Nabokov, *Lolita* (New York: Knopf Everyman's Library, 1992), 186.

453 **"in which people can still get rich"**: Ronald Reagan, Remarks at the Republican Congressional "Salute to President Ronald Reagan Dinner," May 4, 1982, retrieved from Gerhard Peters and John T. Woolley, *The American Presidency Project*, http://www.presidency.ucsb.edu/ws/index.php?pid=42478.

454 **"Power always thinks it has a great Soul"**: John Adams to Thomas Jefferson, February 2, 1816, Founders Online, National Archives, https://founders.archives.gov/documents/Jefferson/03-09-02-0285.

454 **"We are not children"**: Peter Nabokov, *Native American Testimony* (New York: Penguin Books, 1999), 137.

454 **"those that were with her say she did not suffer"**: Brenda J. Child, *Boarding School Seasons: American Indian Families, 1900–1940* (Lincoln: University of Nebraska Press, 1998), 65–66.

Index

Page numbers in italics refer to illustrations.